A GUIDE TO EDUCATIONAL RESEARCH

Edited by

PETER GORDON

University of London Institute of Education

THE WOBURN PRESS
LONDON • PORTLAND, OR.

First published in 1996 in Great Britain by
THE WOBURN PRESS
Newbury House, 900 Eastern Avenue, London IG2 7HH

and in the United States of America by
THE WOBURN PRESS
c/o ISBS,
5804 N.E. Hassalo Street, Portland, Oregon 97213–3644

British Library Cataloguing in Publication data

A guide to educational research. – (The Woburn education series)
   1. Education – Research
   I. Gordon, Peter
   370.7'8

Library of Congress Cataloging in Publication data
A guide to educational research / edited by Peter Gordon.
   p. cm. – (The Woburn education series)
   Includes index.
   ISBN 0–7130–0192–5. – ISBN 0–7130–4024–6 (pbk.)
   1. Education–Great Britain–Research. 2. Education–Research.
3. Research–Great Britain–Vocational guidance. 4. Research–
Vocational guidance. 5. Education–Great Britain–Curricula.
6. Education–Curricula. I. Gordon, Peter, 1927–   . II. Series.
LB1028.25.G7G85   1996
370'.78'0941–dc20
                                       96–7845
                                           CIP

ISBN 0–7130–0192–5 (cloth)
ISBN 0–7130–4024–6 (paper)

Printed and bound in Great Britain by
Bookcraft (Bath) Ltd., Midsomer Norton, Somerset

A GUIDE TO EDUCATIONAL RESEARCH

THE WOBURN EDUCATION SERIES
General Series Editor: Professor Peter Gordon

CONTENTS

INTRODUCTION

Peter Gordon

The purpose of this book is twofold: to present a clear account of recent developments in educational research in a number of subjects and fields; and to suggest possible areas of research which might profitably be pursued by students in colleges and higher education institutions.

Each chapter, which draws on international as well as British research, is written by a leading practitioner, and there are extensive bibliographies to help the reader. The topics chosen are necessarily a selection from what is on offer in educational research, but we believe that they represent a substantial starting-point for those wishing to become engaged in this field. As many of the contributors have stated, the Education Reform Act of 1988 (ERA) has had a major effect on the content of the curriculum and the process of educational assesment. The nine 'subjects' examined in this book represent a fair proportion of those that comprise the National Curriculum. In addition, it was considered essential to scrutinise other areas with an important bearing on the nature and execution of educational practice, such as education policy, gender, children's learning and curriculum study. These are dealt with in the last six chapters.

Bill Marsden, in his chapter on geography, sets out a research agenda which takes into account a consideration of a balanced and interactive approach between the variables of subject content, the needs of the child and the needs of society, structuring material under key concepts or key ideas. This is contrasted with the content-overloaded and assessment-led National Curriculum model. Marsden highlights the neglect of the international dimension in present-day geographical research; other areas which could with profit be investigated include ideologies of geographical education, and systematic historical studies and comparative research in aspects of geographical education.

As Martin Booth points out, the Schools Council History 13–16 Project, with its stimulating and innovative approach to teaching the new history, gave rise to much research. A good example is the Concepts of History and Teaching Approaches (CHATA) project, which examined students' ideas about what is involved in understanding the past and in creating historical discourse; and second order concepts, such as evidence and explanation, which produce the keys to progression. Booth, in examining United States history research findings, favours more detailed ethnographic analyses of classroom practice, and the need to address the issues of assessment, recording and feedback in the subjects.

Tony Burgess, in his chapter on English, demonstrates that one consequence of the ending of the Schools Council for Curriculum and Examinations by the government in 1982 was a reduction in support for curriculum research which created fundamental perspectives. Instead, funded projects in development work, such as oracy and writing, took their place. Reading standards are close to the centre of the national education debate and there are many interesting studies in progress, including links with language and literature. Burgess describes well the influence of recent work in cultural, literary and media theory, linguistics and social semiotics on accepted presuppositions in language, thinking and learning processes.

The low status of music in schools, borne out in the 1960s by the *Newsom Report* (1963) and *Enquiry 1. Young School Leavers* (1968), was largely due to the passive nature of the enterprise, often consisting of 'music appreciation', and a distinction between the classical and vernacular. Piers Spencer outlines the subsequent radical departure from these approaches, with students actively involved as performers and composers, greatly helped by the development of new technologies. For a number of structural reasons listed by the author, music is once more the Cinderella of the curriculum. Spencer suggests fruitful areas for research, including how music is rationalised by those who teach it and how it is experienced by those who learn; between specialist and generalist notions of music education; and between what is learnt in the classroom and what is publicly exhibited as musical achievement.

Since 1944, religious education has been the only compulsory subject in the curriculum. Leslie Francis describes the impressive tradition of research from the 1940s, which received new impetus in the 1960s through seven key figures whose impact is reflected in current research in the subject. This continuity is seen, for example, in studies on religious thinking. Some newer research aspects are faith development, religious judgement, complementarity, measuring and locating attitudes, religious experience, life questions, prayer and school worship, and the religious distinctiveness and effectiveness of the different denominational schools. Francis concludes with a future research agenda which could lead to greater conceptual clarity and improved techniques of assessment.

If, as Jon Ogborn shows, the greater part of research effort in science education from the 1970s was directed towards the investigation of knowledge and learning in individuals, in the past decade it has shifted to a much wider social and cultural context. This pays greater attention to the public understanding of science, to informal sources of scientific understanding and to language and imagery. Ogborn regrets the absence of technology in the science curriculum or an examination of the close relationship between the two subjects. Attitudes to science represent a difficult area to investigate, though girls' achievement or underachievement in the subject continues to attract attention. Similarly, the fundamental problems of assessment in science education as a diagnostic tool requires further investigation.

Richard Kimbell, like Ogborn, advances several reasons for a higher profile for technology, a comparatively recent subject, but since 1990 a compulsory study for all five to 16-year-olds in the National Curriculum. Kimbell highlights technology's ability to develop pupils' understanding of the need for change and to suggest new ideas and models. As the only National Curriculum subject to be defined exclusively in process terms, current research is involved in descriptions and presciptions of the process, the extent to which it is possible for an abstracted model of problem-solving to accommodate the teaching and learning of conceptual knowledge as a resource, and in establishing a basis for progression, by building a coherent model of progression towards capability.

It is surprising that, given hitherto strong government support for economic literacy, neither economics nor business studies featured as core and foundation subjects in the National Curriculum. Although popular in schools at both GCSE and A level, much of the research in economics and business studies has originated in the United States rather than in the United Kingdom. Nevertheless, as David Whitehead shows, the scope of research undertaken is impressive: it includes the relative effectiveness of alternative pedagogical practices; cognitive gain; economic literacy; the understanding of economic concepts; school-industry links; gender and race; and assessment and examinations.

Colin Wringe traces the evolution of the now universally accepted paradigm in modern foreign language teaching of so-called communicative competence, which has replaced the behavioural notions of repetition and reinforcement typified by the language laboratory. Much of the theoretical work in language learning is located in departments of applied linguistics, though their findings, unfortunately, owing to the demands of the National Curriculum, are regarded as of marginal importance to language teachers. Nevertheless, many valuable research projects are listed, such as the potential for a policy of first language diversification, the implementation of the National Curriculum in Modern Foreign Languages, and ethnographic approaches, involving investigating the attitudes and degree of ethno-centrism of older primary and younger secondary school pupils and the way language textbooks and the work of foreign language teachers may influence them. Systematic surveys of language learning in higher education and the language needs of industry and commerce have also been undertaken.

* * * *

A theme that recurs throughout the papers in the first part of this book is the changing nature of educational research since the late 1980s and the extent to which it is policy-driven. The first chapter in the second section by Stewart Ranson examines education policy, focusing particularly on its theorising nature. This analysis, which is concerned with the role of the state in education policy and its reform, draws upon political theory as well as political sociology. Ranson explains the changing traditions of education policy analysis in the last 20 years and postulates three areas that need attention in order to develop an adequate theoretical framework of the role of policy in the public domain: conceptualising policy, theorising public policy and seeking a philosophy of public purpose. In conclusion, Ranson states the need for a *practical* theory in order to understand the values, purposes, conditions and practice of public policy in a democracy.

The study of the curriculum as an academic discipline in the United Kingdom has developed over the last three decades. It has provided many useful insights into the nature of curriculum change, evaluation and assessment, development and research and aspects of educational policy. John Elliott identifies three traditions of curriculum research: first, technical-rational, which advocates a curriculum planned in the light of pre-specified learning objectives; second, critical social research, which involves implementation studies in the curriculum field that aim to translate national policy objectives into practice; and third, experimental innovation, assuming a process model of curriculum design and development, with the notion of 'teachers as researchers'. This last partnership model contrasts with the more instrumental approach adopted by the 'school effectiveness' movement, which tends to focus on surface features of schools as organisations rather than innovative curriculum experiments and learning systems.

A complementary study to Elliott's is provided by Kathy Sylva, who describes some psychological underpinnings of children's learning in order to evaluate recent changes in primary education in the light of new research into psychological development. Drawing on a significant number of studies, Sylva demonstrates the different ways by which children follow successful or unsuccessful careers: when schools change pupils' self-concepts, goals about success and social responsibility, they exert powerful influence not only on subsequent education but also on adult employment and community participation. The social processes of learning deserve greater investigation.

Seamus Hegarty deals with a specific aspect of this problem in his chapter on special education. Since both the Warnock Report (1978) and the 1981 Education Act identified special educational needs in terms of learning difficulty which called for special education provision, the concept of handicap has been replaced by a concern with appropriate effective learning and educational settings. Hegarty sets out a full agenda for research in special education, which includes more attention to the refining and extension of existing theories of learning. Some examples of research areas under investigation are: studies of integration programmes and their efficacy in relation to segregated ones; the nature of specific learning difficulties; and a more intensive study of further education, which encompasses a good deal of special needs provision.

Until the 1970s, gender issues in education were either frequently ignored or all-male samples were the norm. As Sara Delamont explains in her chapter, the rise of the feminist movement produced educational researchers who wished to investigate sex differences in the outcomes of school and higher education, such as examination results; to explore how females experienced learning; and to conduct active research to try to change both the experiences and the outcomes. The area of gender studies includes both males and females, as can be seen from the research cited in this chapter. Delamont notes that, compared with England and to some extent Scotland, there is a lack of data on gender and schooling in Wales and Northern Ireland. Even so, there are few English studies on girls' and boys' experiences in denominational schools and public schools, and few comparisons of the lives of pupils in mixed and single-sex schools, and there is a scarcity of investigations of gender issues within ethnic and linguistic minority communities. At the macro level, there is a need for an historical investigation of changing education policy since 1944 and its impact on gender.

The final chapter, by Keith Watson, deals with the field of comparative education. Formerly, it had largely described education systems within specific national contexts; at the present time, it focuses on educational phenomena – students, teachers, curriculum, finance, teacher education and on specific educational outcomes. During the late 1980s and the 1990s, the growing commitment of aid agencies to improve the efficiency and effectiveness of education systems is reflected in the research areas outlined by Watson: privatisation and the financing of education, decentralisation of power, the impact of reform in less developed countries, community education, the changing role of aid agencies in shaping the educational agenda of sovereign nation states and problems of administration and planning in small states. The scope for new research here is almost endless, and would be of assistance to both policy makers and planners.

Several of the authors who have contributed to this book have expressed concern that, given the official climate of opinion which places priority on policy-related research and evaluation reports, the traditional long-term research projects, which may raise matters of fundamental importance, may cease to exist. It is hoped that the map of educational research, as set out in the following pages, will persuade the reader that there is a place and a need for both policy-related and fundamental research in education as the twenty-first century draws near.

March 1996

1

GEOGRAPHY

Bill Marsden

The last three decades have been a period of continuing change in geography: in geographical research, geographical education and geography teaching. In 1972, the Geographical Association published two sources of reference about research and publication in geographical education, respectively by Graves and Lukehurst[1] and by Naish.[2] These both drew attention, among other things, to work in the history of geographical education; in the relationship between school geography and developments at the research frontiers; in the purposes and justification of geography in the school curriculum; in the development of children's thinking and geographical education; in methods of teaching geography; in geography's cross-curricular links; and in its contribution to international understanding. These all remain significant issues. The interlocking facets of frontiers' geographical research, the mediation of geographical educationists, and aspects of teaching geography in school will be explored chronologically, starting with the dramatic changes in geography and education in the 1960s. The criteria of evaluation of each phase of change will be focused on the following key variables:

(a) Geographical distinctiveness

(b) Educational value

(c) Social relevance.

There will be, finally, in the light of the consideration of each phase in the changing 'state of the art', an appraisal of research in geographical education and suggestions for a possible agenda for development in the politicised climate of the 1990s. In support of the discussion overall, there will be reference to what must be inevitably a selective review of contributions to the literature in what has always been a complex and contested curriculum debate.

THE CHANGING 'STATE OF THE ART'

1 The 1960s: Conceptual Revolutions

(a) The 'New Geography'

Criticisms of the old regional geography paradigm gained momentum in the universities of Britain during the 1950s and 1960s, and culminated in an academic revolution. As is well known, the focus of geography was as a result shifted from the study of unique places to the investigation of more general patterns in space, and from the traditional methodology of an areal synthesis to statistical and other analytical methods imported from mathematics and the physical and social sciences. This was the 'new geography', the product of the 'quantitative revolution'.

Likewise in schools, rigid and outmoded regional studies remained dominant in the early 1960s.[3] True, a more 'enlightened traditionalism'[4] had gained some ground, based on fieldwork at home and on case-studies of detailed localities further afield. These benefited from improvements in technology which made possible more vivid presentation of distant places in the classroom. In the world of the 'new geography', as it spread into the more prestigious secondary schools, even this approach was dismissed as idiographic and therefore suspect.

One of the advantageous features of the 'new geography' was the stimulus it gave to communication between teachers in universities, colleges, and independent and state schools. University geographers assisted dissemination in schools in a way that had not been witnessed in half a century. Joint conferences of schoolteachers and academic geographers were arranged.[5] The January 1969 edition of the journal *Geography* was devoted to these new developments, and included contributions by academics such as Chorley and Gregory, and also from teachers and college lecturers who were important influences in disseminating the new geography into schools. They included Everson, Fitzgerald and Walford. Another important influence was the American High School Geography Project, led by a notable American geographer, Helburn,[6] whose materials demonstrated ways of translating the ideas drawn from the academic frontiers fairly directly into school practice. Many school texts devoted to the new geography appeared during the 1970s, from Everson and Fitzgerald,[7] Bradford and Kent,[8] Briggs[9] and others. There was even a pioneering primary series, *New Ways in Geography*, by Cole and Beynon, which is still in print.[10]

This is not to say there were no opposing currents in the waves of enthusiasm for quantification and discovering patterns in space. They included the die-hard traditionalists, whose preoccupation had been with writing massive regional texts. But they also included those who, like Alice Garnett,[11] foresaw a fragmentation of the discipline and a loss of distinctiveness, through the increasing and 'well-blinkered' specialisation she discerned among younger academics.

(b) Curriculum Theory

While geographical educationists of the 1960s were discovering names such as Chorley and Haggett, they were also becoming acquainted with some equally influential educationists, well-known in the United States, but new to us in Britain, including Bloom,[12] Gagne,[13] Tyler,[14] Taba,[15] Bruner[16] and Phenix.[17] They offered models of rational curriculum planning, based on specification of objectives related to a psychology of teaching and learning. Their frameworks demanded not only a consideration of the fundamental aims of education, but also the translation of these aims into more detailed operational objectives. These in turn were to be linked with a selection of content (drawn from 'areas of experience' or 'disciplines of knowledge'), and a selection of learning experiences (based on an evaluation of the capabilities and interests of pupils). The resulting programmes of study were to be evaluated for diagnostic purposes, and fed back into the system as evidence for making changes. As we shall see, the objectives model, though much criticised by 'educational progressives', was to have a crucial impact on geographical education and the curriculum in general in the 1970s and 1980s.

In terms of our three criteria, the shift from traditional regional to quantitative geography, to an extent, represented:

(i) *A retreat from distinctiveness*, in that the heart of the subject, that is the synthesis of physical and human elements of geography through place, was lost in the rush to highly specialised systematic studies.

(ii) *An enhancement in educational rigour*, though with an inbuilt element of élitism. Given the priority of the desire to improve the intellectual standing of the subject, it was predictable that the quantitative revolution in schools should be widely regarded as being more appropriate to more able than less able pupils.

(iii) *A detachment from social relevance*, in the emphasis on abstract patterns and aggregation of evidence. To many, the human face of geography, as well as its traditional distinctiveness, was at risk.

2 The 1970s and early 1980s: Convergence and Divergence

(a) The Work of Geographical Educationists

During the 1960s, the culmination of the 'enlightened traditionalism' previously cited was perhaps best represented by Long and Roberson's methodological text, *Teaching Geography* (1966).[18] This laid stress on fieldwork and sample studies. During the 1970s, a shift of emphasis can be identified between Bailey's methodological text, similarly entitled *Teaching Geography*,[19] which stressed the geographical dimension in geographical education, including the 'new geography'; and those of Graves, who was one of the first to draw together the positive aspects of 'enlightened traditionalism', the 'new geography' and, above all, curriculum theory, in methodological texts with titles subtly different from those of Long and Roberson, and Bailey, such as *Geography in Education*,[20] and *Curriculum Planning in Geography*.[21]

A similar approach was offered in Marsden's *Evaluating the Geography Curriculum*.[22] Its structure was based on current models of curriculum planning, stressing the importance of curriculum theory as well as geographical content. Like Graves's *Geography in Education*, it explored historical as well as contemporary contexts. It also paid more attention than hitherto to the importance of good assessment practice, another educational issue of moment in the 1970s. Hall, in *Geography and the Geography Teacher*,[23] covered many similar elements of curriculum study as applied to geography, and also appraised the examination system and the ongoing Schools Council projects in the subject.

Geographical educationists were also involved during the 1970s in editing a growing series of texts which brought together a range of issues relating to geography and education, as seen through the eyes of different writers. Examples of such texts were the collections by Bale, Graves and Walford,[24] Graves[25] and Williams.[26] Papers of the first Charney Manor Conference, which brought together academics, geographical educationists and teachers, were published in Walford's *New Directions in Geography Teaching*.[27]

In terms of our criteria, these works in general gave considerable priority to the educational dimension, stressing the importance of rational curriculum planning, of taking account of the needs of the child, of promoting meaningful learning, and of enhancing teacher skills. They offered, in general, cautious support for the 'new geography', but were equally concerned to maintain the benefits of 'enlightened traditionalism'. They contained more than a hint of the importance to come of new trends towards social and environmental relevance.

(b) Schools Council Projects
These methodological texts hardly had the direct impact on geography in schools as the government-funded Schools Council projects of the 1970s. Geography was a particular beneficiary of Schools Council sponsorship, with no fewer than four development projects:

(i)   *Geography for the Young School Leaver* (GYSL), from 1970 at Avery Hill College of Education, London, directed by Rex Beddis, designed to meet the needs of less able children.

(ii) *Geography 14–18*, from 1970 at the University of Bristol Department of Education, directed by Gladys Hickman.[28]

(iii) *History, Geography and Social Science 8–13*, from 1971 at the University of Liverpool Department of Education, directed by Alan Blyth.[29]

(iv) *Geography 16–19*, from 1976 at the University of London Institute of Education, directed by Michael Naish, the Bristol project having in the event concentrated on the 14–16 age range.[30]

The most influential of all was probably the Avery Hill project.[31] It learned from the mistakes of earlier 'top-down' Schools Council projects and was very successful in diffusing its ideas, sensitively connecting up with local and regional networks. It was in a seller's market, too, for there was precious little quality material for less able children at a time when the school leaving age had recently been raised to 16. Avery Hill materials were lavishly presented, and were based on themes of a high degree of social relevance, designed to win the interest of less able children. Significantly, the project saw early the need to engage with the public external examination system at 16+, if it was to be influential. As a result, a special Avery Hill Geography Examination Syllabus, based on the project's ideas and materials, was introduced by different public examining boards.

(c) Issues-based Geography
While on the one hand there was a convergence of thinking between the conceptual revolutions in curriculum theory and the 'new geography', the latter, as Alice Garnett had predicted, provoked fragmentation. One reason was that it was diffused by some of its disciples in universities and schools with almost religious zeal as the 'one best system'. This provoked confrontation. It is significant that at about the same time the progressive principles of the 1967 Plowden Report, the perceived more permissive approaches associated with the decline of the grammar schools and rise of comprehensive schools, and student unrest in the universities, were also exciting public interest and criticism. The combination of progressive trends at primary, secondary and tertiary levels, was too much for far-right opinion to stomach. Strong political reaction ensued.

Among some geographers, there was concurrently a revulsion against the abstraction, dehumanisation and retreat from social relevance that the positivism of the quantitative revolution was seen to represent. In turn, new and overlapping foci emerged, namely:

*	behavioural geography	*	environmental geography
*	welfare geography	*	radical geography

The first of these was rather different from the other three, but was important in identifying human agency and individual perceptions as geographical factors, and in opposing both environmental and social determinism. The other paradigms advocated not only social and environmental content, but also the encouragement of a commitment to do something about the issues: in other words to engage in political action. In school terms, the developing environmental concern of the 1960s was reflected in a shift of emphasis from environmental study (the environment for education) to environmental education (education for the environment).[32] Pioneering attempts at the geography of social concern, as represented in the GYSL materials, could similarly be regarded as social concerns for education rather than education for social concerns – in that studies of decaying urban environments, leisure activities, and the like, were seen first and foremost as a means of catching the interest of less able children, and therefore of being especially relevant to the needs of inner-city schools.

The distinction between social concerns for education and education for social concerns was evident in the varying commitment to coverage of controversial social and environmental issues in geography. Different degrees of intensity of issues-pervasion into the curriculum were identifiable, from

* *issues-permeated* geography, to

* *issues-based* geography, to

* *issues-dominated* geography.

Proponents of welfare geography were clearly oriented towards the latter two levels. One of the problems of such an orientation is that issues-based or issues-dominated work is virtually by definition multi-disciplinary. For if the prime focus is on the issue, then disciplines like geography, but never geography alone, must permeate and illuminate the themes, which is the basis, for example, of the world studies courses so effectively delineated in Fisher and Hicks.[33] This seems to me an entirely legitimate way to proceed. But it is not a distinctively geographical way. Fisher and Hicks accepted the necessity of geographical permeation into world studies arrangements, rather than the alternative of issues-permeated work, as a built-in component of a subject-based geographical framework.

An important element of curriculum theory in the 1960s was the distinction between cognitive and affective dimensions of education. Attitudes of children were increasingly regarded as worthy of equal consideration as learning abilities. One obvious argument was that positive attitudes promoted academic achievement. There was, in addition, convergence between this notion and the developing thinking of geographical educationists in the 1970s in the aftermath of the quantitative revolution. As part of the welfare orientation of geography, more attention was given to the promotion in children of more positive attitudes to the environment and to other peoples.

One of the justified criticisms of the old geography, based on the major natural regions of the world, was its association with environmental determinism and political jingoism. Conveniently for imperial instruction, in all of the major natural regions a part of the British Empire was there to be taught. Similarly, implicit determinism was to be found in some of the detailed sample studies of other parts of the world, which continued to concentrate on 'primitive' peoples in 'hostile' environments. Indeed, one excellent primary series from the pedagogic point of view, written by Archer and Thomas,[34] was less sure-footed in the social dimension, stereotyping other peoples by presenting them as simple though pleasant, their children as always happy, but at the same time as exotic and having few needs. On the basis of the such materials – and many were far worse – there was indeed some cause to be suspicious of the worthwhileness of studying distant places in the primary school during the 1950s and early 1960s. In the event, the amount of distant place geography taught in primary schools declined during this period. The consequence was that schools effectively cocooned their children in the parochialism of local studies. Much of the geographical entitlement was lost, at a time when research by Jahoda[35] and Carnie[36] was suggesting that children must be caught young if favourable attitudes to other peoples were to be developed. Articles at the time by Marsden,[37] Wright[38] and Hicks[39] showed negative stereotyping as continuing, whether explicitly or implicitly.

Interest in economically developing countries, their exploitation and the quality of life of their people, was predictably not confined to geographical education, for indeed the issues are multi-disciplinary. It was argued that a balanced picture of problem issues could better be achieved through integrated studies than through pursuing separate subjects. Additionally, the comprehensivisation of secondary schools in the 1960s and 1970s had also led to calls for a shift from a subject-centred to an integrated structure in the secondary curriculum, one seen as more conducive to motivating less-able pupils. Thus, many schools switched in the lower secondary levels from separate courses in history and geography to integrated humanities or social studies. Various forms of integration emerged, including variants strongly related to geography, such as environmental education, European studies, world studies, global education and peace studies. Some excellent teaching ideas emerged, for example, in books co-authored by Hicks and Steiner,[40] and from Selby and Pike.[41] An important methodological source which predated these publications was Huckle's *Geographical Education: Reflection and Action*.[42] This work was supplemented by vivid first-hand materials produced by world aid and other agencies, including the Centre for World Development Education in London and the Development Education Centre in Birmingham. Children from primary level upwards were rightly encouraged to show active as well as merely abstract interest by engaging in school links[43] and fund-raising exercises.

Few in the field would have questioned the social and educational importance of these trends, which were intended to shift children from an early age away from their domestic concerns, as Dewey long before had intended subjects like geography to accomplish.[44] In terms of our criteria, however, queries arose over what had become, in some cases, issues-dominated work. The social concern element arguably became top-heavy and tended to produce bias, overwhelming other educational criteria. In many instances the geographical distinctiveness of the work was lost – cartoons replaced cartography in textbooks, and speech-bubble type artwork, often of crude quality, replaced photographs of real places, infiltrating a new form of stereotyping, even worse, of caricaturing human beings.[45] The careful textual build-up of a balanced selection of evidence was overridden by slogan-type and for/against generalisations. Whereas the materials of, for example, the Geography 16–19 project, were packed with potential evidence as support for enquiry-based learning,[46] the so-called enquiry promoted in texts for younger and often less able children was in some cases little more than an incitement glibly to offer an opinion. In educational terms, far from generating meaningful learning and reflective thinking, which are surely key criteria of educational worthwhileness, texts and internally produced work-sheets fostered simplistic responses to profound and intractable world problems, as Michael Storm[47] discerned: '...we are asking them to build generalisations and to analyse complex relationships on the basis of a very slender stock of basic information.' A number of geographical educationists, including Fien and Slater,[48] Huckle[49] and Lambert,[50] have sought to inject a more rigorous basis for the accommodation of the values and attitudes dimension within a radical framework aimed at infusing social and political concerns into school work in geography,

Subjects such as geography and history and various types of integrated studies have undoubtedly been used in the past for the promotion of what were accepted at the time as undeniably good causes, whether of religion, imperialism, eugenic approaches to health education, or capitalism. Justified as promoting the essential and often agreed social and political exigencies of the time, educational values in any progressive sense were overridden by recourse to instruction through inculcation (the pedagogy) and indoctrination (the associated content – the doctrine or belief system being inculcated).

Subjects, or cross-curricular components (not called such at the time) served essentially a means to the greater ends of, in Britain, in the first place, religion and, later, of nationalism and imperialism.[51] Similar jingoism and negative stereotyping of other nations was endemic in the educational syllabuses of colonising countries, and became even more so in this century in Fascist and Communist states.

3 The late 1980s and early 1990s: Polarisation and Politicisation

(a) The Influence of the Inspectorate

The attack on the 'education industry' from the political right had, in fact, begun in the 1970s. Civil servants and politicians demanded an increasing influence in the school curriculum, which had hitherto been regarded as a 'secret garden', tended by educationists. In a speech in 1976, the then Labour Prime Minister, James Callaghan, made it clear that henceforth the 'garden' would have to become more open to public scrutiny.[52] When the Conservative government of Margaret Thatcher began its long term in office in 1979, the stage was set for what has been called 'the tightening of the ratchet'.The early stages of this process were exemplified in an increasing number of official papers produced by Her Majesty's Inspectorate. The 1978 *The Teaching of Ideas in Geography*[53] and comparable pamphlets in other subject areas appeared in the early stages of this new trend. The concurrent critique in *Primary Education in England* was also the work of HM Inspectorate and the Department of Education and Science.[54] It was censorious about many aspects of primary schooling, not least the teaching of geography. So, too, was Alexander in the early 1980s.[55]

One important contribution to the debate was HMI's *Geography from 5 to 16: Curriculum Matters 7* of 1986,[56] which, while no doubt not going far enough to appeal to more radical voices in the field, none the less was progressive in urging attention to controversial issues and social and environmental concerns in geography. In a well-balanced summary, it stressed also the need to provide an entitlement for all pupils which reflected good geography and good educational practice. It manifestly was influenced by the curriculum thinking of the 1960s and early 1970s. There was emphasis on principles of match and progression. It was to be seen as a more balanced and expansive view of curriculum renewal than later HMI statements such as *The Teaching and Learning of History and Geography* of 1989.[57] The ratchet was by then well and truly being tightened.

(b) The Influence of the Geographical Association

For over 100 years the Geographical Association, founded in 1892, has played a key role in support of geographical education and geography teaching in schools. It is the organisation that brings together geographers as academics and geographers as teachers. During the last two decades the Association has been very active in publishing guidance for teachers. Apart from its main journal, *Geography* (which in its early years was called *The Geographical Teacher*), it also produces *Teaching Geography*, mainly for secondary schoolteachers and, more recently, *Primary Geographer*, geared to generalist primary schoolteachers. In addition, it has produced practical handbooks, including one for the secondary phase edited by Boardman,[58] and one for the primary phase, edited by Mills.[59] It has also offered a wide range of advice on, for example, fieldwork, information technology, teaching slow learners, and on cross-curricular links, not least those between geography and technical and vocational education, and geography, schools and industry.

Its main achievement in the last decade, however, has been its politically timely and sophisticated intervention to secure for the subject a place in the National Curriculum. In the Department of Education's pamphlet on *The School Curriculum* of 1981,[60] geography was not identified as a separate subject in the school timetable, though a geographical contribution to integrated studies was envisaged.[61] By 1985 the case for the subject was still not officially accepted. So the Geographical Association invited the then Secretary of State for Education, Sir Keith Joseph, to address the Association.[62] He asked geographers in turn to answer seven key questions in order to justify the place of their subject in the Curriculum. This the Association did in its *A Case for Geography*.[63] The publication arrived on the desk of Kenneth Baker (the next Secretary of State) about the time he was deciding on the foundation subjects in the National Curriculum. He recognised that the geographical lobby had got its act together and accepted the case. Various accounts have been offered of the success of this campaign, by Bailey[64] and Walford,[65] and also of the work of the National Curriculum Geography Working Group, by Rawling[66] and Morgan.[67] What is clear is that part of the reason for the success of subjects like geography and history in gaining a place in the National Curriculum was that in the social subjects area they were seen as politically safer bets than the social sciences as such and associated cross-curricular areas such as peace studies. Arguably, the right choice was made for the wrong reasons. What were left out were the distinctly lower-caste cross-curricular themes such as Education for Economic and Industrial Understanding, and Education for Citizenship, much suspected by Ministers of State.[68]

(c) The National Curriculum in Geography: a Return to Place
In the calculus of advantage and disadvantage, many geographers would claim that, for all its faults, the National Curriculum has strengthened the

position of geography in schools. It has made explicit geography's

(i) position *as of right* in the National Curriculum for all pupils from 5 to 16, representing a major advance, at primary level in particular;

(ii) *distinctiveness*, in returning *place* to the centre of the stage, focusing on detailed localities and other scales of place, and on spatial studies into which geographical themes and skills must be permeated, thus linking physical and human aspects of the subject through places in an authentically geographical way; and highlighting the importance of skills of *graphicacy* and *fieldwork* techniques;

(iii) dependence on *enquiry-based* learning; though perhaps more strongly in the preamble than in the implementation;

(iv) capacity to function as a *bridging subject* in the curriculum, connecting the humanities and the sciences;[69]

(v) special contribution to *environmental awareness* and the development of *world knowledge* and *global understanding*.

There were, however, fundamental flaws in the pre-Dearing National Curriculum for geography:

(i) The programme was *overloaded with content*, particularly at upper primary level (Key Stage 2).

(ii) The curriculum was *assessment-led*, which has caused many to suspect that teachers would concentrate on meeting National Curriculum requirements by cramming in content rather than developing understandings and skills: that is, they would 'teach to the test'.

(iii) This problem was made worse by the absence of an explicit *theory of learning* behind the orders for geography, which again might lead teachers to build up programmes of study not by means of carefully thought out conceptual frameworks, but through an accumulation of content.

(iv) Worst of all, the statements of attainment were *tied to content*. Thus arbitrary and unsustainable judgements were made, for example, that volcanic eruptions should be taught at Level 4, and the distribution of earthquakes and volcanoes in relation to tectonic plates at Level 5, and so on. There seems to have been no concept of a *spiral curriculum* in which it is seen as desirable to enable the progressive coverage of volcanoes at different stages, with increasingly refined and complex levels of understanding.

(v) The curriculum was and is still being subject to *political interference* in its evolution, as a result of which, in particular, controversial issues and international understanding, while not ignored, have been downgraded in importance.

In terms of our initial criteria, those who have sought a distinctive geographical contribution to the curriculum for all age groups, can in this sense be reasonably satisfied. The National Curriculum does demand distinctive geography. Whether or not it is associated with educational worthwhileness will depend on whether teachers can avoid the negative influences of an assessment-led curriculum. It is to an extent to the advantage of geography that the government does not take its assessment too seriously. On the other hand, teachers taking a narrow view might also wish not to take the subject too seriously either, if it is seen as of low priority in a core-subject dominated curriculum, as some schools will conceivably feel obliged to give precedence to those elements that are publicly measured. An additional need is the input of large resources into INSET work to develop teacher skills and confidence in delivering an genuinely geographical input, and also the associated pedagogic insights to be able to generate meaningful, enquiry-based learning. As far as social relevance is concerned, much of the curriculum content makes it relatively easy to build in this dimension, if teachers so wish. But they can also choose to marginalise it, a procedure which would no doubt be supported by secretaries of state.

4 Towards an International Dimension

As geography is arguably one of the subjects most fitted to promote international awareness, the revival of nationalism must be a major cause for concern. It is salutary to compare the Statutory Orders for Geography in England and Wales with the International Geographical Union's International Charter for Geographical Education. In fact, on the face-value basis of much of their content, the National Curriculum and the International Charter are not incompatible. Each regard geography as an entitlement for all primary and secondary school pupils. Where there is a significant difference is predictably in relation to the priority given in the Charter to the international dimension. Thus, in its guidance on principles relevant to the selection of regional studies, the Charter indicates that these should be designed to provide a balance in terms of scale, location in the world, diversity of type, and relevance. The same sense of global priorities failed to emerge from the Statutory Orders of the National Curriculum in geography. It is a pity that a government which subscribes to the principles of international and European declarations on human rights and education is not willing to give a practical lead to teachers in these areas.

A RESEARCH AGENDA FOR GEOGRAPHICAL EDUCATION

1 An Aspect of Neglect: Fundamental Research

Since the surveys of Graves/Lukehurst and Naish in the early 1970s, there have been periodic reviews of the state of research in geographical education, both at national and international levels. Over the period, there has been a general perception that certainly fundamental research in this area has been of limited quality and impact. Thus Wolforth in 1980[70] asserted that of all the branches of geography, geographical education had the most weakly defined research dimension. Schrettenbrunner[71] has consistently been critical of methodological deficiencies in relation to empirical research in geography. More recently, Knight[72] has found that of 239 articles on geographical education in the period 1986–91 in the *British Education Index*, only about 10 per cent could be categorised as research-based.

What is clear is that there is a large amount of publication in geographical education. What is also clear is that apart from the majority of it not being truly research-based, it is also highly fragmented. Nothing approaching a coherent research tradition can readily be discerned. There was perhaps an element of an emerging, if narrow, coherence in the 1976 International Geographical Union's *International Research in Geographical Education*,[73] in the two sections of the publication focusing on spatial stages development in children, and on classroom teaching styles in geography, and also in its focus on the historical perspective four years later.[74] A 1984 IGU collection, *Research and Research Methods in Geographical Education*,[75] did not have the same coherence as the 1976 publication, taking the form of a collection of disparate articles from ten different countries, useful though these were as comparative information. The same could be said of the IGU 1988 *Skills in Geographical Education*,[76] and 1992 *International Perspectives on Geographical Education*[77] collections, in which, once again, priority was given to the dissemination of information about the development of geographical education in many different countries – a thoroughly justifiable endeavour, but not one fostering the cause of a coherent and rigorous research agenda. The current research and development projects of the Geographical Education Commission of the IGU[78] are also wide-ranging but appear to give priority to action research and development rather than to fundamental research. Another problem is that IGU publications are not widely disseminated. However, a recent Australian publication sponsored by the Commission, *International Research in Geographical and Environmental Education*, offers a fresh outlet for research papers. A new publication edited by Williams, *Understanding Geographical and Environmental Education: the Role of Research*,[79] will also offer a more accessible summary of 'the state of the art' of research in geographical education.

The rest of this chapter will concentrate on fundamental rather than action-based research, not because the latter is seen as unimportant, but because it is arguable that in the last decade the swing has been heavily in this direction and a balancing process is needed. While much has been made of the fact that fundamental research has had little effect on classrooms, from a number of points of view this stance is difficult to defend. The impact of fundamental research in the philosophy and other sub-fields of education was, for example, translated into the curriculum theory which had an enormous impact on the Schools Council projects of the 1970s. Similarly, the influence of basic work on spatial cognition and mental mapping is evident in many later teaching schemes. So has the work on multi-culturalism, gender and social welfare, drawn from the frontiers of research, crept into the thinking of teachers in the classroom. Of course, the impact is often indirect and gradual. There are few quick fixes available.

In the British context, a number of reasons can be advanced for the relative lack of fundamental research in geographical education:

(a) Geographical educationists enter the research environment late. They have had experience of teaching but are not necessarily rapidly socialised into the values of fundamental research. They are torn between the pressures of publication at the university end and the feeling that they wish their work to have some tangible value for the classroom.[80] Many would claim, too, that while they have time to produce small-scale articles for teacher journals, they are constrained by heavy teaching loads from taking on long-term fundamental research projects.

(b) Unlike, for example, scientists, geographical educationists, at least in the older universities, are usually working alone or with a single colleague, often a part-timer. Few institutions are large enough to generate a critical research mass in a specific area like geographical education.

(c) Similarly, in the 1970s there were strong influences to make research in educational areas classroom-based. Action research became the watchword, as distinguished academics, such as Stenhouse,[81] Elliott,[82] and others, persuasively presented views of the 'teacher as researcher', and of the need to root research in the tangible problems faced by classroom teachers, in reaction to the image of research as esoteric and detached from reality. Hebden and Fyfe[83] and Fien,[84] among other geographical educationists, have all firmly nailed their colours to this mast.

(d) The major research and development projects of the Schools Council in the 1970s in geography were also primarily curriculum development rather than research projects, though there was a research spin-off as well. They generated, apart from materials, many articles designed to disseminate their work and the purposes behind it, which encouraged ideas of the 'new professional' teacher, that is, the idea of classroom-based action research.

(e) As Graves has suggested,[85] a characteristic of the 1980s has been the pressure to undertake policy-related research, particularly in those areas prioritised and funded by the government. Again, the thrust of the exercise has been to concentrate on work that can be seen as immediately useful: 'quick and dirty' is a cynical label attached to such projects, implying that the research groups have to come up with the right answers within an unrealistic time span. There is a strong wave of official opinion in support of funding research teams to produce evaluation reports rather than research monographs. The shift is away from fundamental long-term research.

(f) Finally, the whole spirit of the time has over the last ten years been one of instability and relentless and bruising change, which makes it difficult to get any long-term research projects off the ground. So the prevailing official climate of opinion, which denigrates research that is not merely useful, is also a discouragement.

There is arguably, therefore, a case in principle for urging a return to the values and rigours of fundamental research. It is not that there has been an absence of such work in geographical education: but that there has not been enough of it, and it is doubtful whether the field is now taken seriously enough. It is acknowledged that it is difficult to draw a clear line between fundamental and action-based research. The very term 'fundamental' would no doubt be contested by those converted to action-research. Let us consider the problems, therefore, under the headings of traditional research in education: that is as related to the history of education; the philosophy of education; the psychology of education; the sociology of education; and curriculum theory. This is not a plea for going back to esoteric armchair reflection, but for avoiding the simplistic dichotomy which postulates that research, to be justified, has to relate to what is seen at the time to be rapidly applicable to schools and classrooms. One advantage workers had in the late 1960s and 1970s was an impressive body of basic educational research in these traditional areas which cried out for application to geography and other areas of the curriculum. It is arguable whether so wide-ranging a resource is available today.

2 The Fundamental Research Fields of Education

The Psychology of Education

The general area of the psychology of education is one from which important findings for geographical education have continued to be forthcoming. There have now been two decades of work which have suggested that Piaget and Inhelder's[86] interpretations of the development of children's spatial abilities were too narrow, and have led to under-expectations of primary age children, so far as the development of mapping skills was concerned. Research into early children's work suggested that through the use, for example, of surrogate toys, children could be authentic map-makers at the age of three.[87] Investigations of the development of early mapping skills, both empirical and classroom-based, have been undertaken by a whole range of researchers including Boardman,[88] Catling,[89] Gerber,[90] Blades and Spencer,[91] Matthews[92] and Watkin.[93] Links have been established between mapping skills, navigational skills and orienteering.[94]

Associated with the development of spatial cognition is the perceptual dimension. A large amount of work on how children perceive their environments was triggered in the 1970s by Gould and White's *Mental Maps*.[95] Questions of experience, image, and how it affects personal behaviour, are interestingly linked with the development of spatial cognition and have formed a fruitful line of research by, among others, Downs and Stea,[96] Hart,[97] Moore,[98] Spencer *et al.*,[99] and Ward.[100] Based on Bronfenbrenner, Matthews[101] has suggested an ecological framework for the exploring the environmental systems of childhood: beginning with the *microsystem* of family relationships; going on to the *mesosystem* of community structures; then the *exosystem* of social structures; and finally the *macrosystem* of global structures. In methodological texts for primary teachers, Bale[102] and Wiegand[103] have highlighted the importance of making practical use of children's early extra-mural experiences.

Another important development, reinforced by the greater interest subject specialists have tended to show in other subject areas since the onset of the National Curriculum, has been the search for links between the development of children's mapping skills and children's drawing skills. In the world of art education there is similar interest in these phenomena, as in work by Brittain[104] and Joicey.[105] There are obvious overlaps with fieldwork, as well represented in the earlier work of the Schools Council's *Art and the Built Environment* project.[106]

The Sociology of Education

Sociology is a very broad area of the social sciences covering, among other things, social theories and social structures as related to the family, social stratification, gender, ethnicity, the economy and so on. It is not least preoccupied with questions about the generation and transmission of beliefs and ideologies. Here it is necessary to cut a long and complex story of potential relationships with geographical education short, and concentrate on a particular area of great significance over the last two decades, namely the interest in what might broadly be termed welfare geography,[107] which clearly has a sociological undercarriage. As we have seen, welfare geography has been a persistent thread in teaching and research in the subject over the last twenty years, and stemmed in part from revulsion against what were seen as the dehumanising forces of quantitative geography. Such approaches were based on the idea that geography was not just an academic study, nor one that merely sought to change attitudes. What was necessary was the use of the subject to make a better world. Thus an activist approach was promulgated.

The political spectrum associated with these developments ranged from what might be called the liberal-humanist to the radical-Marxist. Another influential work of this time was Peet's *Radical Geography*.[108] There was considerable tension between the different groups espousing a socially responsible geography. One was exemplified in Dawn Gill's radical critique[109] of the Avery Hill 14–16 Geography project, accusing it of presenting a white, Eurocentric view of global issues, and of indoctrination rather than education. On this occasion the Schools Council was equally unhappy about this radical attack, and refused to publish the Gill Report which it had commissioned.[110] Gill was also closely associated with in the work of the Association for Curriculum Development, an anti-racist organisation publishing the now defunct journal, *Contemporary Issues in Geography and Education* which, among many other issues, offered an issue on anarchist geography, defined as an ideology which argues that we would be better off as a self-organising society without government.[111] Lambert more recently has explored how the values of a radical-Marxist geography, which he regards as reactionary in its fundamentalist form, can be reinterpreted to be of use in mainstream human geography, in seeing such a critique as required in a social and political context which stresses the ideology of individualism.[112] Whether the way to combat one extreme ideology is to confront it with one from the other extreme is a point of debate.

Unfortunately, there again seems little fundamental research to underpin more cogent and consensual development in the welfare geography area. As we have seen, the International Charter for Geographical Education of the IGU is firmly based on international declarations of human rights, though continuing work on images of children in other countries has been undertaken by Haubrich[113] and Kent,[114] under the auspices of the IGU. There is also important related work in Huckle (see note 42) and by Australian geographical educationists, as in *Teaching Geography for a Better World*,[115] which is avowedly evangelical in its purpose, and distances itself not only from conservative, but also liberal ideologies. Whether the entirely laudable purpose of using education to improve the global quality of life requires either an extremist ideology (either from the left or the right) or anything that savours of evangelism is a moot point, as the promotion of good causes is something that has often been abused in the past by the agencies promoting them.[116] As we have seen, in the wrong hands, the good cause has engendered inculcation, indoctrination and an attitudinal rigidity of thought that is surely anti-educational.

The Philosophy of Education

It is doubtful whether today many geographical educationists would produce such an article entitled 'Geography and Philosophy', as Graves co-authored in 1966,[117] followed up by a similar contribution in 1972.[118] The tenor of the time (or so it seems in retrospect) was one of less fevered academic endeavour than at present. The whole status of geography had been attacked both at academic levels by David[119] and, implicitly, in education by Hirst.[120] An epistemological discussion was then timely and, in my view, continues to be necessary, but little is forthcoming. Thus, in recent years there have been important statements about the position of geography as a discipline, among other things redefining the regional concept and re-establishing the primacy of place study. Key texts over the last 15 years by Gregory,[121] Stoddart,[122] Johnston[123] have not been so assiduously perused for their value in schools as were, for example, those of Chorley and Haggett (see note 5), and Harvey[124] in the 1960s. It may be that this failure has been due in part to the priority given to action research and materials production rather than to an engagement in more fundamental thinking. Such writing has, however, probably had some influence, for there has not been too much dispute over the fact that geography in the National Curriculum should be place-based and issues-permeated, rather than issues-based and place-permeated.

As previously indicated, there has been evidence of more basic work in the sphere of values education, written up particularly in the volumes of the Australian journal *Geographical Education* by, for example, Blachford[125] and Smith[126], and also by Watson[127] in *Geography,* and more recently by Fien and Slater (see note 49) and Huckle (see note 50). Unusually for its time, in a paper celebrating Graves' contributions to geographical education, Slater[128] harks back to Peters' metaphor of education not being about arriving at a destination but about travelling with a different view. There is need to capitalise on this more and probing work.

The History of Education

The field of the history of education is perhaps the most neglected in the sphere of geographical education, perhaps because the background of practitioners is more in tune with social science research in the areas of psychology and sociology. A good deal of the writing that exists is like that in school histories: the story of great names and heroic deeds. The positive qualities of the work of pioneers such as Mackinder and Fairgrieve are appropriately extolled: their unacceptable face is left as part of the 'structure of omission'.[129] Too much discussion draws uncritically and highly selectively on the historical record, either to sharpen a contemporary axe or to chronicle a consistent story of progress from past primitivism to the current apogee of achievement. Not learning through this neglect of the past means that wheels are constantly being reinvented.

False consciousness is also generated. In recent times seriously overstretched parallels have been drawn between, for example, the requirements of the National Curriculum and 'capes and bays' geography, which carry little credibility when the evidence is looked at, though the parallels no doubt have some ideological purchase. Similarly, comparisons between the 'place' requirements of the National Curriculum and old-time regional geography are asserted which again could not rationally be envisaged, unless teachers rescued from the cellars old-time copies of Thomas Pickles. The picture regularly painted is also an insult to the past, in which, rather than primitive groups of pioneer teachers doing their limited best, there were complexity, intelligence, involved and contested discussions of pedagogy, differentiated approaches, and scores of journals, some designed for elementary teachers. The discontinuation of the educational codes in the 1920s did not necessarily bring benefits. Thus I have shown that my father's experience of geography at elementary school in the first decade of this century, under a National Curriculum (the Code of 1904), was far in advance of what I received over 30 years later in a 'scholarship' school which was free to choose what it taught, and chose very narrowly.[130]

Perhaps the most important function of historical research, particularly important in an environment in which belief systems and ideology appear to count more than balanced and comprehensive hard evidence, is, as Lawrence Stenhouse put it, to provide a public scholarly tradition that allows a critique of current understandings, drawing on common sense and experience, and thus allowing the researcher and teacher 'to plot better his own educational adventure'.[131] We can also find in history rich stores of tested practice, whether progressive or utilitarian. It illustrates on numerous occasions how the splendidly differentiated thinking of the pioneers was narrowed into a belief system by their disciples. Who would have thought that some of the strongest and most persuasively expressed justifications for geography and history in the primary curriculum came from the arch-progressive, John Dewey?[132]

So far as the substance of historical such work is concerned, the centenary of the Geographical Association has predictably generated an informative history[133] and a series of articles in *Geography*[134] and *Teaching Geography*.[135] There is also work on the influence on geographical education of the Royal Geographical Society,[136] of the National Society for the Study of Education in the United States,[137] of a number of famous names in the history of geographical education (see note 74), and of the regional paradigm (see note 3). There have been reviews of old textbooks by Hanson,[138] Wright,[139] Marsden,[140] and Walford,[141] and of issues of racism in old geography and history textbooks,[142] of racism and gender,[143] of geography and cross-curricular areas, including citizenship education and League of Nations teaching,[144] and of the politicisation of the history and geography curriculum (see note 116). Both Graves (see note 21) and Marsden (see note 22) offered historical overviews by way of contexts for their books, respectively *Geography in Education,* and *Evaluating the Geography Curriculum.* Similarly, Williams included a number of key historical articles as part of his collection *Geography and the Integrated Curriculum* (see note 26).

CONCLUSION: A RETURN TO CURRICULUM THEORY?

To ask a pertinent question, do workers in geographical education have the same stimulus of the quality of a resource base today as those in the early 1970s who had access to the following: Ausubel and Robinson,[145] Bloom (see note 12), Bruner (see note 16), Gagne (see note 13), Hirst,[146] Kerr,[147] Peters,[148] Phenix (see note 17), Taba (see note 15), Tyler (see note 14), Wheeler,[149] Young,[150] White,[151] and Lawton,[152] among others, all of whom could be classed as curriculum theorists or had a very direct influence on curriculum theory?

Rational curriculum planning, though subject to serious criticism at the time, largely addressed to the more extreme behavioural objectives wing of the movement,[153] has been very influential. In its favour, it at least demanded a balanced and interactive approach between the variables of subject content, the needs of the child, and the needs of society. The approach, variously amended, structuring material under headings such as key concepts or key ideas, underpinned all the Schools Council projects in geography. In turn, the secondary phase geography projects, seeking a secure basis for widespread dissemination, successfully achieved co-operation with the nation's examination boards, by now also geared to spelling out aims and objectives for their syllabuses.

The application of the specification of aims and objectives to school geography was perhaps most clearly seen in the early work of Bennetts,[154] which was fleshed out more authoritatively in the *Geography 5–16* document in the HMI *Curriculum Matters* series and elsewhere,[155] and has served as a source of reference for much thinking in geographical education since. It is, indeed, more progressive and wide-ranging in its approach than much of the detail of the National Curriculum on the subject. While the term 'rational' was regarded suspiciously at the time, because it carried the hint of too much science, too much logic and prescription, and not enough of the human, the personal, and the unexpected, to an extent a consensus was offered, not by Stenhouse,[156] who resisted the use of the term 'objectives', but by Skilbeck.[157] Unfortunately, in the multitude of Statements of Attainment in the Attainment Target sections of the pre-Dearing Orders of the National Curriculum subjects can be discerned a return to the more negative features of the behavioural objectives wing of the rational curriculum planning movement.

Notwithstanding the manifest importance of policy and classroom-based research, of government sponsored macro-projects or of action research with teachers, there is surely a need for some return to fundamental thinking in geographical education. Deliberately, I am here again excluding what is specifically classroom-based research, for reasons already given. There are various possible agendas for future work, listed below:

(a) Ideologies of geographical education.

(b) The nature of geographical knowledge today.

(c) Geography's interfaces with (i) other National Curriculum subjects and (ii) cross-curricular areas.

(d) Connecting geography at the frontiers with geography in school.

(e) Systematic historical studies of aspects of geographical education.

(f) Applications of relevant research in other curriculum areas.

(g) Systematic comparative research in aspects of geographical education.

Obviously, the distinction between action research and fundamental research should not be polarised. There are overlaps, for example, in (f) above. To pursue this example, how many in geographical education are aware of the research on using children's misconceptions,[158] or that the application of Ausubel's theories of meaningful learning for work in primary science[159] is of considerable potential relevance for the teaching and learning of geography, or that of art specialists on the development of children's drawing skills?[160] We need, in fact, for reasons of principle and of opportunism, not just to assert that geography is one of the most important bridging subjects in the curriculum, but also to produce more fundamental investigations of the potentially fruitful links with not only core and other foundation subjects, but also with the cross-curricular themes, dimensions and skills,[161] and with other issues, such as assessment,[162] in which the National Curriculum has provoked radical change.

If we take as a starting-point that the important principle in curriculum development and research is to maintain the balance of necessary inputs from the subject, from educational research, and from the broader context of social education, it can be argued that at present the social dimension, whether seen through the élitist lenses of government or the egalitarian ones of many geographical educationists, has slipped out of balance in both teaching and research priorities. Restoring and maintaining the balance will be difficult in the context of the situation in England and Wales where external forces continue to conspire to control and marginalise the more fundamental research agendas.

NOTES

1. C. T. Lukehurst and N. J. Graves, *Geography in Education: a Bibliography of British Sources 1870–1970* (The Geographical Association, 1972).
2. M. C. Naish, *Some Aspects of the Study and Teaching of Geography in Britain: a Review of Recent British Research* (The Geographical Association, 1972).
3. D. S. Biddle, 'Paradigms and Geography Curricula in England and Wales 1882–1972' (1980), reprinted in D. Boardman (ed.), *New Directions in Geographical Education* (The Falmer Press, 1985), pp. 11–33; see also D. Hall, 'The Influence of Culture, Education and Subject Tradition on the Teaching of the Mediterranean in British Schools', in A. Hernando (ed.), *Geographical Education and Society* (IGU Commission on Geographical Education, 1986).
4. W. E. Marsden, *Evaluating the Geography Curriculum* (Oliver & Boyd, 1976).
5. R. Chorley and P. Haggett (eds), *Frontiers in Geographical Teaching,* (Methuen, 1965); and *Models in Geography* (Methuen, 1967).
6. N. Helburn, 'The Educational Objectives of High School Geography', *Journal of Geography,* 67 (1968), pp. 280–82; also N. J. Graves, 'The High School Project of the Association of American Geographers', *Geography,* 53 (1968), pp. 68–73.
7. J. A. Everson and B. P. Fitzgerald, *Settlement Patterns* (Longman, 1969).
8. M. G. Bradford and W. A. Kent, *Human Geography: Theories and their Applications* (Oxford University Press, 1977).
9. K. Briggs, *Introducing Transportation Networks* (University of London Press, 1972).
10. J. P. Cole and N. J. Beynon, *New Ways in Geography* series (Basil Blackwell, 1968ff.).
11. A. Garnett, 'Teaching Geography: Some Reflections', *Geography,* 54 (1969), pp. 385–400.
12. B. S. Bloom (ed.), *Taxonomy of Educational Objectives,* Handbook 1 (Longman, 1956).
13. R. M. Gagne, *The Conditions of Learning* (Holt, Rinehart & Winston, 1965).
14. R. W. Tyler, *Basic Principles of Curriculum and Instruction* (University of Chicago Press, 1949).

15. H. Taba, *Curriculum Development: Theory and Practice* (Harcourt Brace, 1962).
16. J. S. Bruner, *The Process of Education* (Vintage Books, Random House, 1960); and *Towards a Theory of Instruction* (Harvard University Press, 1966).
17. P. H. Phenix, *Realms of Meaning* (McGraw Hill, 1964).
18. M. Long and B. S. Roberson, *Teaching Geography* (Heinemann, 1966).
19. P. Bailey, *Teaching Geography* (David and Charles, 1974).
20. N. J. Graves, *Geography in Education* (Heinemann, 1975).
21. N. J. Graves, *Curriculum Planning in Geography* (Heinemann, 1979).
22. Marsden, op. cit. (1976).
23. D. Hall, *Geography and the Geography Teacher* (George Allen & Unwin, 1976).
24. J. Bale, N. Graves and R. Walford (eds), *Perspectives in Geographical Education* (Oliver & Boyd, 1973).
25. N. Graves (ed.), *New Movements in the Study and Teaching of Geography* (Temple Smith, 1972).
26. M. Williams (ed.), *Geography and the Integrated Curriculum: a Reader*, (Heinemann, 1976).
27. R. Walford (ed.), *New Directions in Geography Teaching* (Longman, 1973).
28. G. Hickman, J. Reynolds and H. Tolley, *A New Professionalism for a Changing Geography* (Schools Council, 1973); and H. Tolley and J. B. Reynolds, *Geography 14–18: a Handbook for School-based Curriculum Development* (Macmillan, 1977).
29. W. A. L. Blyth, K. Cooper, R. Derricott, G. Elliott, H. Sumner and A. Waplington, *Place, Time and Society, 8–13: Curriculum Planning in History, Geography and Social Science* (Collins/ESL, 1976).
30. M. Naish, E. Rawling and C. Hart, *The Contribution of a Curriculum Project to 16–19 Education* (Longman/ SCDC, 1987).
31. See B. MacDonald and R. Walker, *Changing the Curriculum* (Open Books, 1976); C. Parsons, *The Curriculum Change Game: a Longitudinal Study of the Schools Council Geography for the Young School Leaver Project* (The Falmer Press, 1987); and D. Boardman, T*he Impact of a Curriculum Project: Geography for the Young School Leaver* (University of Birmingham, 1988).
32. G. C. Martin and K. Wheeler (eds), *Insights into Environmental Education* (Oliver & Boyd, 1975).
33. S. Fisher and D. Hicks, *World Studies 8–13: a Teacher's Handbook* (Oliver & Boyd, 1985).
34. A. B. Archer and H. G. Thomas, *Geography First Series*, Book 1 (Ginn, 1936).
35. G. Jahoda, 'The Development of Children's Ideas and Attitudes about other Countries', *British Journal of Educational Psychology*, 323 (1963), pp. 47–60.
36. J. Carnie, 'The Development of National Concepts in Junior School Children' (1966), reprinted in Bale, Graves and Walford (eds), op. cit., pp. 101–18.
37. W. E. Marsden, 'Stereotyping and Third World Geography', *Teaching Geography*, 1 (1976), pp. 228–31.
38. D. R. Wright, 'Visual Images in Geography Texts', *Geography*, 64 (1979), pp. 47–61.
39. D. Hicks, 'Global Perspectives in the Curriculum: a Geographical Contribution', *Geography*, 64 (1979), pp. 104-14; and 'The Contribution of Geography to Multicultural Misunderstanding', *Teaching Geography*, 7 (1981), pp. 64-67.
40. D. Hicks and M. Steiner (eds), *Making Global Connections: a World Studies Workbook* (Oliver & Boyd, 1989).
41. G. Pike and D. Selby, *Global Teacher, Global Learner* (Hodder & Stoughton, 1988).
42. J. Huckle (ed.), *Geographical Education: Reflection and Action* (Oxford University Press, 1983).

43. R. Beddis and C. Mares, *School Links International* (Avon County Council/Tidy Britain Group, 1988).
44. See R. Cracknell, 'Putting Geography back into the Primary School Curriculum: Wasn't John Dewey Right?', *Teaching Geography,* 4 (1979), pp. 115–17; and W. E. Marsden, 'Breadth, Balance and Connection in the Primary Curriculum: Bridge-Building, Past and Present', in R. J. Campbell (ed.), *Breadth and Balance in the Primary Curriculum* (The Falmer Press, 1993), pp. 122–36.
45. W. E. Marsden, 'Cartoon Geography: the New Stereotyping?', *Teaching Geography*, 17 (1992), pp. 128–31.
46. M. Naish, 'Geography 16–19', in Boardman (ed.), op. cit. (1985), pp. 99–115.
47. M. Storm, 'Geographical Development Education: a Metropolitan View', in J. Bale (ed.), *The Third World: Issues and Approaches* (The Geographical Association, 1983), pp. 31–39.
48. J. Fien and F. Slater, 'Four Strategies for Values Education in Geography' (1981), reprinted in Boardman (ed.), op. cit. (1985), pp. 171–86.
49. J. Huckle, 'Geography and Values Education', in R. Walford (ed.), *Signposts in Geography Teaching* (Longman, 1981), pp. 147–64.
50. D. Lambert, 'Towards a Geography of Social Concern', in M. Naish (ed.), *Geography and Education: National and International Perspectives* (University of London Institute of Education, 1992), pp. 144-59.
51. W. E. Marsden, 'Recycling Religious Instruction? Historical Perspectives on Contemporary Cross-curricular Issues', *History of Education*, 22 (1993), pp. 321–33.
52. Lord Callaghan, 'The Education Debate I', in M. Williams, R. Daugherty and F. Banks (eds), *Continuing the Great Debate* (Cassell, 1992), pp. 9–16.
53. HMI, *The Teaching of Ideas in Geography: Some Suggestions for the Middle and Secondary Years of Education* (HMSO, 1978).
54. DES, *Primary Education in England: a Survey by HM Inspectors of Schools* (HMSO, 1978).
55. R. Alexander, *Primary Teaching* (Holt, Rinehart & Winston, 1984), pp. 70–2.
56. DES, *Geography from 5–16: Curriculum Matters 7,* an HMI Series (HMSO, 1986).
57. DES, *Aspects of Primary Education: the Teaching and Learning of History and Geography* (HMSO, 1989).
58. D. Boardman (ed.), *Handbook for Geography Teachers* (The Geographical Association, 1986).
59. D. Mills (ed.), *Geographical Work in Primary and Middle Schools* (The Geographical Association, 1988).
60. DES, *The School Curriculum* (HMSO, 1981).
61. See N. Proctor, 'Geography and the Common Curriculum', *Geography,* 69 (1984), pp. 38–45.
62. Sir Keith Joseph, 'Geography in the School Curriculum', *Geography,* 70 (1985), pp. 290–7.
63. P. Bailey and T. Binns (eds), *A Case for Geography* (The Geographical Association, 1987).
64. P. Bailey, 'A Place in the Sun: the Role of the Geographical Association in Establishing Geography in the National Curriculum of England and Wales', *Journal of Geography in Higher Education,* 13 (1989), pp. 149–57.
65. R. Walford, 'Creating a National Curriculum: a View from the Inside', in A. D. Hill (ed.), *International Perspectives on Geographical Education* (Department of Geography, University of Colorado at Boulder/Rand McNally, 1992), pp. 89–100.

66. E. Rawling, 'The Making of a National Geography Curriculum', *Geography*, 77 (1992), pp. 292–309.
67. W. Morgan, 'Making a Place for Geography: The Geographical Association's Initiatives and the Geography Working Group's Experience', in J. Hughes and W. E. Marsden (eds), *Primary School Geography* (David Fulton, 1994), pp.23–36.
68. D. Graham with D. Tytler, *A Lesson for us All: the Making of the National Curriculum* (Routledge, 1993).
69. There is now a burgeoning literature by geographical educationists and teachers on potential fruitful links between geography and other National Curriculum subjects: for example:

    English, V. Banks and S. Hackman, 'Geography and English Liaison', *Teaching Geography*, 18 (1993), pp. 105–7.

    Mathematics, G. Walker and P. Winbourne, 'Linking Geography and Mathematics at Key Stage 3', *Teaching Geography*, 18 (1993), pp. 21–23.

    Science, P. Adamczyk, T. Binns, A. Brown, S. Cross and Y. Magson, 'The Geography–Science Interface: a Focus for Collaboration', *Teaching Geography*, 19 (1994), pp. 11–14.

    Reading and Literature, A. Gadsden, *Geography and History through Stories, Key Stage One* (Cheshire County Council/The Geographical Association, 1991); R. Gerber and N. Stewart-Dore, 'Strategies for Improving Reading and Learning in Geography Lessons', *Teaching Geography*, 9 (1984), pp. 216–22.

    History, H. N. Nicholson, *Geography and History in the National Curriculum: Key Stages One and Two Support Material* (The Geographical Association, 1991).

    Religious Education, 'Relating Subjects in the School Curriculum: Geography and Religious Education – a Discussion Paper', *Teaching Geography*, 6 (1980), pp. 27–39; and D. Rainey, 'Foundation Subject: Geography', in P. D. Pumfrey and G. K. Verma, *The Foundation Subjects and Religious Education in Primary Schools: Cultural Diversity and the Curriculum*, Vol. 3 (The Falmer Press, 1993), pp. 158–71.

    Music, J. Dove and D. Owen, 'Teaching Geography through Music and Sound', *Teaching Geography*, 16 (1991), pp. 3–6.

    Art, E. Brough, 'Geography through Art', in J. Huckle (ed.), op. cit. (1983), pp. 56–63; and P. Howard, 'Art, Design and Landscape', *Teaching Geography*, 5 (1979), pp. 84–6.
70. J. Wolforth, 'Research in Geographical Education', in R. Choquette, J. Wolforth and M. Villenure, *Canadian Geographical Education* (University of Ottawa Press, 1980), pp. 165–78.
71. H. Schrettenbrunner, 'Empirical Methods for Researching Media – a Challenge for more Awareness of Methodology', in H. Haubrich (ed.), *Perception of People and Places through Media*, Vol. 2 (IGU/Pädagogische Hochschule, Freiburg, 1984), pp. 489–99; and 'Memorandum for a Working Group: Empirical Research in the Didactics of Geogra+phy', in R. Gerber and J. Lidstone (eds), *Skills in Geographical Education*, Vol. 1 (IGU/Brisbane College of Advanced Education, 1988a), pp. 322–31.
72. P. Knight, *Primary Geography, Primary History* (David Fulton, 1993), p. 49.
73. J. P. Stoltman (ed.), *International Research in Geographical Education* (IGU/Department of Geography, Western Michigan University, 1976).
74. W. E. Marsden (ed.), *Historical Perspectives on Geographical Education* (IGU/University of London Institute of Education, 1980).
75. N. J. Graves (ed.), *Research and Research Methods in Geography* (IGU/University of London Institute of Education, 1984).

76. Gerber and Lidstone (eds), op. cit. (1988a).
77. Hill (ed.), op. cit. (1992).
78. H. Haubrich, *Newsletter 25* (IGU Commission on Geographical Education, 1992), pp. 4.
79. M. Williams (ed.), *Understanding Geographical and Environmental Education: The Role of Research* (Cassell, 1996).
80. See J. Lidstone, 'Research in Geographical Education', in R. Gerber and J. Lidstone (eds), *Developing Skills in Geographical Education* (IGU Commission on Geographical Education/The Jacaranda Press, 1988b), pp. 273–85.
81. L. Stenhouse, 'Case Study and Case Records: towards a Contemporary History of Education', *British Educational Research Journal,* 4 (1978), pp. 21–39.
82. J. Elliott, *Action Research for Educational Change* (Open University Press, 1991).
83. R. Hebden and E. Fyfe, 'Research in Geographical Education in the United Kingdom', in Gerber and Lidstone (eds), op. cit. (1988b), pp. 286–97.
84. J. Fien, 'What Kind of Research for What Kind of Teaching? Towards Research in Geographical Education as Critical Social Science', in Hill (ed.), op. cit. (1992), pp. 265–75.
85. N. J. Graves, 'The Changing Nature of Research in Geographical Education in the United Kingdom', in Gerber and Lidstone (eds), op. cit. (1988a), pp. 249–58.
86. J. Piaget and B. Inhelder, *The Child's Conception of Space* (Routledge & Kegan Paul, 1956).
87. J. M. Blaut and D. Stea, 'Mapping at the Age of Three', *Journal of Geography,* 73 (1974), pp. 5–9; see also 'Studies of Geographic Learning' (1971) reprinted in Bale, Graves and Walford (eds), op. cit. (1973), pp. 87–99.
88. D. Boardman, *Graphicacy and Geography Teaching* (Croom Helm, 1983); 'Spatial Concept Development and Primary School Map Work', in Boardman (ed.), op. cit. (1985), pp. 119–34; 'The Development of Graphicacy: Children's Understanding of Maps', *Geography,* 74 (1989); 'Graphicacy Revisited: Mapping Abilities and Gender Differences', *Educational Review,* 42 (1990), pp. 57–64.
89. S. Catling, 'Maps and Cognitive Maps: the Young Child's Perception', *Geography,* 64 (1979), pp. 288–96; 'Building Less Able Children's Map Skills', *Remedial Education,* 19 (1984), pp. 21–5; 'Using Maps and Aerial Photographs', in Mills, op. cit. (1988), pp. 99–119.
90. R. Gerber, 'Young Children's Understanding of the Elements of Maps', *Teaching Geography,* 6 (1981), pp. 128–33; 'Competence and Performance in Cartographic Language' (1981), reprinted in D. Boardman (ed.), op. cit. (1985), pp. 153–70; 'Is Mapping in Schools Reflecting Development in Cartography and Geographical Information?', in M. Naish (ed.), op. cit. (1992), pp. 194–211.
91. M. Blades and C. Spencer, 'Map Use by Young Children', *Geography,* 71 (1986), pp. 47–52.
92. M. H. Matthews, 'Children as Map Makers', *The Geographical Magazine,* 58 (1986), pp. 124–26; 'Gender, Graphicacy and Geography', *Educational Review,* 38 (1986), pp. 259–71; *Making Sense of Place: Children's Understanding of Large-Scale Environments* (Harvester Wheatsheaf, 1992).
93. D. G. Watkin, 'Pictures to Plans: Some Early Map Work in the Infant Curriculum', *Early Years,* 11 (1990), pp. 53–66.
94. J. Martland, 'New Thinking in Mapping', in Hughes and Marsden, op. cit., pp. 37–49.
95. P. Gould and R. White, *Mental Maps* (Penguin Books, 1974).
96. R. M. Downs and D. Stea, *Maps in Minds: Reflections on Cognitive Mapping* (Harper & Row, 1977).

97. R. Hart, *Children's Experience of Place* (Irvington, 1979).
98. R. C. Moore, *Childhood's Domain: Play and Place in Child Development* (Croom Helm, 1986).
99. C. Spencer, M. Blades and K. Morsley, *The Child in the Physical Environment: the Development of Spatial Knowledge and Cognition* (John Wiley and Sons, 1989); see also C. Spencer and M. Blades, 'Children's Understanding of Places: the World at Hand', *Geography*, 78 (1993), pp. 367–73.
100. C. Ward, *The Child in the City* (The Architectural Press, 1977).
101. Matthews, op. cit. (1992), p. 8.
102. J. Bale, *Geography in the Primary School* (Routledge & Kegan Paul, 1987).
103. P. Wiegand, *Places in the Primary School: Knowledge and Understanding of Places at Key Stages 1 and 2* (The Falmer Press, 1992).
104. W. L. Brittain, *Creativity, Art and the Young Child* (Collier Macmillan, 1979).
105. H. B. Joicey, *An Eye on the Environment: an Art Education Project* (World Wildlife Fund/Bell & Hyman, 1986).
106. E. Adams and C. Ward, *Art and the Built Environment* (Longman/Schools Council, 1982).
107. See D. M. Smith, 'Who Gets What, Where, and How?: a Welfare Focus for Human Geography', *Geography*, 59 (1974), pp. 289–97; B. E. Coates, 'Towards a Geography of Social Well-Being', in P. Wiegand and K. Orrell (eds), *New Leads in Geographical Education* (The Geographical Association, 1982); J. Huckle, 'Humanistic Geography: an Introduction', in ibid., pp. 14–20; J. Fien, 'Humanistic Geography', in Huckle (ed.), op. cit. (1983), pp. 43–55; J. Bale, 'Welfare Approaches to Geography', in ibid., pp. 64–73; F. Slater, '…to Travel with a Different View', in Naish (ed.), op. cit. (1992), pp. 97–13; D. Hall, 'The National Curriculum and the Two Cultures: Towards a Humanistic Approach', *Geography*, 75 (1990), pp. 313–24.
108. R. Peet (ed.), *Radical Geography* (Methuen, 1977); see also I. Cook, 'Radical Geography', in Huckle (ed.), op. cit. (1983), pp. 74–81.
109. D. Gill, 'GYSL: Education or Indoctrination', *Contemporary Issues in Geography and Education*, 1 (1984), pp. 34–8.
110. D. Gill, *Assessment in a Multi-cultural Society: Geography* (unpublished Schools Council Report, Commission for Racial Equality, 1982).
111. See C. Ward, 'An Anarchist looks at Urban Life', in I. Cook and D. Pepper (eds), *Anarchism and Geography, Contemporary Issues in Geography and Education*, 3 (1990), p. 80.
112. Lambert, op. cit. (1992), pp. 144–59.
113. H. Haubrich (ed.), *How I See my Country: Personal Views of 15 Year Olds from 28 Countries* (IGU Commission on Geographical Education, 1987); 'National Identification and International Understanding', in Naish, op. cit. (1992), pp. 131–43; 'Auto-and heterostereotypes of French, Swiss and German Students', in Hill (ed.), op. cit. (1992), pp. 31–5.
114. W. A. Kent, 'Images of People, Environment and Life', in ibid., pp. 37–48; see also M. Walton, 'The Influence of the World Cup on International Stereotypes', *Teaching Geography*, 9 (1984), pp. 203–7.
115. J. Fien and R. Gerber (eds), *Teaching Geography for a Better World* (Oliver & Boyd, 1988).
116. W. E. Marsden, '"All in a Good Cause": Geography, History and the Politicization of the Curriculum in Nineteenth and Twentieth Century England', *Journal of Curriculum Studies*, 21 (1989), pp. 509–26; see also B. Hudson, 'The New Geography and the New Imperialism', *Antipode*, 9 (1977), pp. 12–19.

117. N. J. Graves and M. Simons, 'Geography and Philosophy' (1966), reprinted in Bale, Graves and Walford (eds), op. cit. (1973), pp. 27–34.
118. N. J. Graves and T. Moore, 'The Nature of Geographical Knowledge', in Graves (ed.), op. cit. (1972), pp. 17–28.
119. T. David, 'Against Geography' (1956), reprinted in Bale, Graves and Walford (eds), op. cit. (1973), pp. 12–26.
120. P. H. Hirst, 'Liberal Education and the Nature of Knowledge' (1965), reprinted in R. S. Peters (ed.), *The Philosophy of Education* (Oxford University Press, 1973), p. 96.
121. D. Gregory, *Ideology, Science and Human Geography* (Hutchinson, 1978); also R. Walford and D. Gregory (eds), *Horizons in Human Geography* (Macmillan, 1989).
122. D. R. Stoddart (ed.), *Geography, Ideology and Social Concern* (Basil Blackwell, 1981); D. R. Stoddart, *On Geography and its History* (Basil Blackwell, 1986).
123. R. J. Johnston (ed.), *The Future of Geography* (Methuen, 1986); also *A Question of Place: Exploring the Practice of Human Geography* (Blackwell, 1991); and R. J. Johnston, J. Hauer and G. A. Hoekveld (eds), *Regional Geography: Current Developments and Future Prospects* (Routledge, 1990); see also T. Unwin, *The Place of Geography* (Longman, 1992).
124. D. Harvey, *Explanation in Geography* (Edward Arnold, 1969).
125. K. Blachford, 'Values and Geographical Education', *Geographical Education,* 1 (1972), pp. 319–30.
126. D. L. Smith, 'Values and the Teaching of Geography', *Geographical Education,* 3 (1978), pp, 147–61.
127. J. W. Watson, 'On the Teaching of Value Geography', *Geography,* 62 (1977), pp. 198–204.
128. Slater, op. cit. (1992), pp. 97–113.
129. W. E. Marsden, '"The Structure of Omission": British Curriculum Predicaments and False Charts of American Experience', *Compare,* 21 (1991), pp. 5–25.
130. W. E. Marsden, 'Researching the History of Geographical Education', in Williams (ed.), op. cit. (1996), pp.264–73.
131. Stenhouse, op. cit. (1978), p. 30.
132. Cracknell, op. cit. (1979), p. 116.
133. W. G. V. Balchin, *The Geographical Association: the First Hundred Years 1893–1993* (The Geographical Association, 1993).
134. See M. Wise, 'The Campaign for Geography in Education: the Work of the GA 1893–1993', *Geography,* 78 (1993), pp. 101–9; S. Catling, 'The Whole World in our Hands', *Geography,* 78 (1993), pp. 340–58; see also for an earlier historical appraisal of geography in school, V. Tidswell, 'Capes, Concepts and Conscience: Continuity in the Curriculum', *Geography,* 75 (1990), pp. 302–12.
135. D. Boardman and M. McPartland, 'A Hundred Years of Geography Teaching', *Teaching Geography,* 18 (1993), pp. 3–6; 'From Regions to Models: 1944–1969', *Teaching Geography,* 18 (1993), pp. 65–8; 'Innovation and Change: 1970–1982', *Teaching Geography,* 18 (1993), pp. 117–20; 'Towards Centralisation: 1983–1993', *Teaching Geography,* 18 (1993), pp. 159–62.
136. W. E. Marsden, 'The Royal Geographical Society and Geography in Secondary Education', in M. H. Price (ed.), *The Development of the Secondary Curriculum* (Croom Helm, 1986).
137. W. E. Marsden, 'The 32nd Yearbook of the National Society for the Study of Education on *The Teaching of Geography*: an External Appraisal', in Hill (ed.), op. cit. (1992), pp. 131–8.

138. J. Hanson, 'Textbooks of the Past: What can we Learn from Them?', *Teaching Geography*, 7 (1982), pp. 124–7.
139. D. R. Wright, 'Applied Text-book Research in Geography', in Gerber and Lidstone (eds), op. cit. (1988), pp. 327–32; '"Colourful South Africa"; an Analysis of Textbook Images', *Multi-racial Education*, 10 (1983), pp. 27–36.
140. W. E. Marsden, 'Continuity and Change in Geography Textbooks: Perspectives from the 1930s to the 1960s', *Geography*, 73 (1988), pp. 327–43.
141. R. Walford, 'On the Frontier with the New Model Army: Geography Publishing from the 1960s to the 1990s', *Geography*, 74 (1989), pp. 308–20.
142. W. E. Marsden, 'Rooting Racism into the Educational Experience of Childhood and Youth in the Nineteenth and Twentieth Centuries', *History of Education*, 19 (1990), pp. 333–53.
143. D. R. Wright, 'They have no Need of Transport...A Study of Attitudes to Black People in Three Geography Textbooks', *Contemporary Issues in Geography and Education*, 1 (1983), pp. 11–15; 'In Black and White: Racist Bias in Textbooks', *Geographical Education*, 5 (1985), pp. 13–17; 'Are Geography Textbooks Sexist?', *Teaching Geography*, 10 (1985); J. Connolly, 'Gender Balanced Geography: Have We Got it Right Yet?' *Teaching Geography*, 18 (1993, pp. 61–4; D. Hicks, op. cit. (1981), pp. 64–7.
144. Marsden, op. cit. (1993), pp. 321–33; and W. Y. Yong and W. E. Marsden, 'Continuity and Change in Geography's Contribution to Citizenship Education', *Paedagogica Historica*, 29 (1993), pp. 483–502.
145. D. P. Ausubel and F. D.Robinson, *School Learning: an Introduction to Educational Psychology* (Holt, Rinehart & Winston, 1969).
146. P. H. Hirst, *Knowledge and the Curriculum* (Routledge & Kegan Paul, 1974).
147. J. F. Kerr (ed.), *Changing the Curriculum* (University of London Press, 1968).
148. R. S. Peters, *Education as Initiation* (Evans, 1963).
149. D. K. Wheeler, *Curriculum Process* (University of London Press, 1967).
150. M. F. D. Young (ed.), *Knowledge and Control: New Directions for the Sociology of Education* (Collier-Macmillan, 1971).
151. J. P. White, *Towards a Compulsory Curriculum* (Routledge & Kegan Paul, 1973).
152. D. Lawton, *Social Change, Educational Theory and Curriculum Planning* (University of London Press, 1973).
153. As represented, for example, by R. F. Mager, *Preparing Instructional Objectives* (Fearon Publishers, 1962).
154. T. Bennetts, 'The Nature of Geographical Objectives', in Walford (ed.), op. cit. (1973), pp. 160–74; 'Objectives for the Teacher', in Graves (ed.), op. cit. (1972), pp. 42–54.
155. DES, op. cit. (1986); 'Geography from 5 to 16: a View from the Inspectorate', *Geography*, 70 (1985), pp. 299–314; 'Progression in the Geography Curriculum', in Walford (ed.), op. cit. (1981), pp. 165–85.
156. L. Stenhouse, *An Introduction to Curriculum Research and Development* (Heinemann, 1975).
157. M. Skilbeck, *School-based Curriculum Development* (Harper & Row, 1984).
158. See, for example, R. Driver, *The Pupil as Scientist?* (Open University Press, 1983); G. Claxton, *Educating the Inquiring Mind: the Challenge for School Science* (Harvester Wheatsheaf, 1991), Ch. 5; and C. Richards, 'The Primary Curriculum and Primary Science', in C. M.Richards and D. Holford (eds), *The Teaching of Primary Science: Policy and Practice* (Falmer Press, 1983).
159. G. McClelland, 'Ausubel's Theory of Meaningful Learning and its Implications for

Primary Science', in Richards and Holford, op.cit., pp. 113–123.

160. See Brittain, op. cit. (1979).

161. The literature on this is too numerous to mention, and some of it is indicated in the references above. But see, for a particularly influential cross-curricular link, predating the National Curriculum, G. Corney, *Teaching Geography for Economic Understanding: the Experience of the Geography Schools and Industry Project* (The Geographical Association, 1990); for a post-National Curriculum discussion, see M. Williams, 'Geography and Cross-curricularity', in Hill, op. cit. (1992), pp. 101–10.

162. See R. Daugherty, 'Assessment in the Geography Curriculum', *Geography,* 75 (1990), pp. 289–301; and 'The Role of Assessment in Geographical Education: a Framework for Comparative Analysis', in Hill (ed..), op. cit. (1992), pp. 111–18. See also W. E. Marsden, *Geography 11–16: Rekindling Good Practice* (David Fulton, 1995), p.99–118.

2

HISTORY

Martin Booth

THE 1960S: HISTORY IN DANGER

There are the strongest reasons for believing that in a great many schools [history] is excruciatingly, dangerously, dull, and what is more, of little apparent relevance to the pupils (Price, 1968, p. 344).

Mary Price's outspoken words on the state of history in schools sounded the alarm bells among history educators, even though her strictures were not supported by any evidence. My own survey of history teaching in five grammar schools in the south of England in 1965–1967 (Booth, 1969) supported her thesis but presented a much fuller picture based on quantitative and qualitative data with questionnaire surveys of both history teachers and students as well as interviews. My conclusion was that change both of syllabus content and of teaching methods was badly needed if history were not to go the way of classical subjects. In particular, I emphasised the need for new teaching techniques to be adopted:

Perhaps the point which emerges most clearly from the investigation is that teaching methods need as much attention as teaching content. We may have exciting syllabuses dealing with recent and world history; we may issue the glossiest and latest of textbooks; but all this can achieve no more that the most reactionary of courses if the methods used fail to illuminate. We are still wedded to techniques which tend to deaden rather than inspire; and so long as we believe that pupils must be told rather than discover for themselves there is little possibility for uncovering their potential for creative, divergent thought (p.122).

Such prognoses were symptomatic of the time, for the late 1960s were proving something of a watershed for all teachers, a period when practices and syllabuses were being questioned and new content and teaching methods being considered. Price's and Booth's writing raised the spectre of 'history in danger, history betrayed'; but education as a whole was now firmly on the public agenda, for the Labour Party had gained office in 1964, determined to push ahead with the abolition of the bi-partite and tri-partite secondary education system and replace it with comprehensive all-ability schools (DES Circular 10/65).

In the early stages, the government and local authorities' emphasis was on structures, organisations and amalgamations; the curriculum was not a matter for debate. As Harold Wilson, the Prime Minister, had declared, the comprehensive schools would provide 'grammar school education for all'; and the grammar school curriculum, with its emphasis on the transmission of knowledge and the teaching of discrete subjects, was tried and tested.

Increasingly, however, the debate began to focus on what was taught and how it was taught. The national Schools Council for the Curriculum and Examinations had been established in October 1964 and quickly became involved in a flurry of activity; a new public examination for school leavers at 16-plus, for whom the General Certificate of Education Ordinary Level was deemed too demanding, was introduced in 1965 to meet the growing demand of the less academic for a leaving certificate. Research and development begin to reflect these concerns. The Nuffield Foundation was carrying out pioneering work in the fields of school mathematics and science; the Schools Council was funding work on science and humanities curricula for the young school leaver (the school leaving age was to be raised from 15 to 16 in 1970–71, formalising the trend in the less academic secondary modern schools for students to stay on beyond the age of 15) as well as curriculum development in English and primary science; and at Southampton University between 1963 and 1967 a group of people came together to research the teaching and assessment of humanities subjects – particularly English, history and geography. Curriculum content, teaching methods and assessment were now increasingly the focus of educational research and policy .

THE EMERGENCE OF THE NEW HISTORY

Whereas Booth's work was high on the practicalities of freeing the history curriculum from an approach which emphasised British history and where teaching was concerned with content, chronology, coverage and note taking, to one in which a more world-orientated syllabus was married with debate, sources and project work (Booth, 1969), the epistemological foundations for his prescriptions were not evident. Curriculum reformers during the 1960s, however, were becoming aware of the significance of the writings of two American educationists, Jerome Bruner and Benjamin Bloom. Bruner's *The*

Process of Education appeared in 1960 and made an impact on curriculum developers with the cogency, succinctness and radicalism of the argument. Bruner made two telling points. An effective curriculum and effective teaching demand a determining of the fundamental understanding of the principles that give structure to the subject. Given that emphasis on structure, on the particular nature of the discipline being taught, Bruner went on to claim 'that any subject can be taught in some intellectually honest form to any child at any stage of development' (Bruner, 1960, p. 33).

Bloom's writing was more prosaic. Bloom and his associates had produced the first volume of their *Taxonomy of Educational Objectives. The Classification of Educational Goals. Handbook 1: Cognitive Domain* in 1956. *Handbook 2: Affective Domain* appeared eight years later (Bloom, 1956; Krathwohl, Bloom and Masia, 1964). The authors believed that too much teaching was concerned with low-level cognitive activities such as comprehension, memorisation and recall, and that the higher level processes of, for example, analysis, evaluation and synthesis were being neglected, in spite of the rhetoric of schools. Similarly, though syllabuses often claimed to be developing attitudes and affective behaviours of, for example, good citizenship or tolerant understanding, the reality was that such ideals were quickly forgotten once teaching was under way; there was a tacit belief among many teachers that imparting the curriculum content would *ipso facto* lead to desirable affective outcomes. Bloom's taxonomies, therefore, attempted to produce two hierarchical frameworks of cognitive and affective goals or assessment objectives applicable to all curriculum subjects which would at once provide a common language and raise standards both of teaching and learning.

Bloom's intentions were worthy though perhaps naive in that they assumed a common *modus operandi* and implied the linear development of cognitive and affective skills and behaviour – a precursor of the assessment model which underpins the English and Welsh National Curriculum. He and Bruner, however, were catalysts for two of the most significant developments in the early 1970s as far as history teachers were concerned. Taking the twin ideas of structure and a range of cognitive objectives, Coltham and Fines produced a framework of objectives specifically for history which they hoped would serve 'as a basis of discussion among teachers who are concerned to establish the relative value and the place of their discipline in the school curriculum' (Coltham and Fines, 1971); and in 1972, the Schools Council commissioned a major new curriculum initiative in England and Wales at the University of Leeds under the direction of David Sylvester – the Schools Council History 13 – 16 Project. The 'new history' had been launched.

EDUCATIONAL OBJECTIVES FOR THE STUDY OF HISTORY AND
THE SCHOOLS COUNCIL HISTORY PROJECT

Though the Coltham and Fines framework is not hierarchical in the
Bloomian sense, it shows the hallmark both of the taxonomies with their
emphasis on precise, measurable learning outcomes and of Bruner's concern
for structure and the distinctive nature of the subject. The four sections of the
framework direct our attention to 'attitudes to the study of history', 'the
nature of the discipline', 'skills and abilities' and 'educational outcomes of
study'. Though it was to come in for some sharp criticism (see Gard and Lee,
1978), there is no doubt that the framework generated lively debate – the
pages, for example, of the Historical Association journal *Teaching History*
(established in 1969 partly in response to the feeling of crisis among history
teachers) are full of references to its influence; and R. Ben Jones'
introduction to his edited collection of papers *Practical Approaches to the
New History* (Jones, 1973) raised its profile even higher. But the influence of
the Coltham and Fines pamphlet pales into insignificance compared with the
impact of the Schools Council project commissioned in 1972 which was
enjoined to develop a history curriculum for students aged 13 to 16. Four
premises underwrote the project. First, the development of the curriculum
and teaching materials would stem from the structure of the subject itself;
second, the needs of student aged 13 to 16 would also determine the focus
and thrust of the new curriculum; third, the project would involve teachers
and students in the development and trialling of material and teaching
approaches, thus avoiding the dangers of a top-down model of curriculum
innovation; fourthly, the effectiveness of the new curriculum would be
assessed by novel means through the public national examination system at
16-plus – the General Certificate of Education (ordinary level) and the more
recently established Certificate of Secondary Education – with course work
playing a significant part in the examination process (Schools Council
History 13–16 Project, 1976).

'What is History?' was the first teaching pack which the project team
developed and tested. With its emphasis on the use of historical sources of a
wide range and their interpretation and evaluation as evidence, the asking of
historical questions and the production of historical explanation which is
recognised as provisional and debatable, the project placed itself squarely in
the Brunerian camp. The varied approaches to the past were underlined
through the subsequent development of units on a modern world study (for
example, Northern Ireland), a study in depth (for example, the American
West), a study in development (medicine through time and later energy
through time) and a local study – 'history around us'. But the mark of Bloom

was also to be found in the search for precise assessment objectives, covering a range of cognitive and affective skills and understandings and the development of new assessment strategies and performance measures that would be both valid and reliable – in particular, criterion-referenced mark schemes (Macintosh, 1987).

RESEARCH AND THE NEW HISTORY

Entries for the Schools Council History Project examination papers at GCE O and CSE levels grew exponentially in the 1970s; one GCE board had 29 candidates in 1976 and 1,900 by 1980. But the influence of the Project was far wider than this, and there was hardly a secondary school history department in England and Wales that was not in some way touched by its philosophy. The pages of the Historical Association's journal *Teaching History* were full of references to the Project and to teaching materials and styles that were directly or indirectly inspired by its approach (see, for example, *Teaching History*, 1979, 25).

The authors of these articles often expressed an evangelical fervour and an unquestioning faith in the powers of the Project to develop genuine historical understanding in students; but what little research evidence there was to give substance to these glowing descriptions of classroom conversions was not encouraging. A number of researchers in the 1950s, 1960s and 1970s had examined the nature and development of students' historical thinking in terms of the developmental framework of Jean Piaget. Between 1957 and 1976, 13 pieces of research were undertaken, all of which indicated that formal operational thought developed considerably later in students when constructing historical discourse based on source materials (Booth, 1994). Most influential was the work of Roy Hallam because it was widely reported (for example, Dickinson and Lee, 1978; Garvey and Krug, 1977; Hallam, 1967, 1969a, 1969b, 1970, 1971; Maitland, 1977; Steele, 1976; Thompson, 1972). Hallam's first piece of research (Hallam, 1966) suggested that formal operational historical thinking developed about the mental age of 16.5 years; his doctoral thesis (1975) showed that though lively and challenging teaching could accelerate the thinking processes of some of his nine- and ten-year-old students, students aged 13 to 14 remained remarkably unaffected and showed no significant improvement in comparison with a control group that was being taught history in a didactic and 'conventional' way. If Hallam were correct in his conclusions, what point then was there in trying to teach the 'new history' with its emphasis on procedural and substantive concepts, empathy and using a range of historical sources as evidence on which to create an historical explanation? What hope was there of teaching the subject effectively 'in some intellectually honest form to any child at any stage of development', as Bruner claimed (1960, p. 33).

Research engendered by the 'new history' in general and the Schools Council 13–16 History Project in particular did much to counter the gloomy prognosis of the Piagetian-based research. My own research (Booth, 1979) was motivated by doubts about the premises and methodology of Hallam as well as my practical experience as a classroom teacher in both grammar and comprehensive schools. Hallam had started with a framework of cognition which was then applied to thinking in history; I took as my starting-point a view of historical thinking such as Gallie (1964), Fischer (1971) and Hexter (1972) advance. Most historians are not concerned with inducing general laws or deducing conclusions from given premises. Rather, they focus on the particular and, by using a range of sources as evidence, attempt to create or *adduce* – to use Fischer's word (Fischer, 1971, p.xv) – an image of the past, an explanation, a discourse, in which there is a blend of evidence and empathy. Portal puts it well:

> Understanding of the importance of empathy as a dimension of *every* historical topic and situation would do a great deal to underline the humane quality of history, as a subject concerned primarily with the intentions and actions of human beings and the ways in which these purposes interact and influence each other...in making history an actively rational subject it is possible to overemphasise the objectivity and the stability of the judgments it may lead us to. Such a positivist interpretation of history is misleading and excludes aspects of intuitive insight into the existence and coherence of mental worlds other than the one we happen to inhabit; aspects of thought and judgment essential to history as such (Portal, 1987, p. 98).

My research was based on a sample of 53 boys and girls aged 14 years in an 11–16 comprehensive secondary school in the south of England who were following a two-year modern world history course. Developing a range of written and oral research instruments, I attempted to map the students' capacity to use historical primary sources as evidence, their understanding of abstract concepts, their attitudes to aspects of the subject and their ability to adduce an historical account based on a number of photographs and extracts from late nineteenth- and twentieth-century British and world history. Their pre- and post-treatment test scores were compared with a group of pupils, matched for age and intelligence, who were not studying history. The research has been reported elsewhere (for example, Booth, 1980, 1983); but it indicated strongly that those who had started with the Piagetian framework had pre-empted their results by looking for thinking which was not specifically historical and had used flawed research instruments. 14- to 16-year-old students, I claimed, are perfectly capable of construing the past in a genuinely historical manner. School history, provided it is taught in a way that exposes students to the unique structure of the subject and involves them in the use of a range of source materials and in active learning, can make a significant difference to students' cognitive and affective behaviour. More than this, my research indicated that historical thinking is largely *sui generis* and that it develops unevenly and in specific contexts; to assess it against an age-related framework in which stages are described in terms of logical structures and hypothetico-deductive thinking is inappropriate – a conclusion that was to be prophetic in the light of later government requirements for the age-stage assessment of the English and Welsh National Curriculum.

THE EVALUATION OF THE SCHOOLS COUNCIL HISTORY 13–16 PROJECT AND SUBSEQUENT BRITISH RESEARCH

Shemilt's rigorous evaluation of the Schools Council History 13–16 Project was a further and highly influential vindication of the effectiveness of the new history (Shemilt, 1980). The research was based on a sample of approximately 500 SCHP students who were compared with 500 students studying history in a conventional way. The results were widely reported (Shemilt,1980, 1983, 1987); they showed that the SCHP students consistently outperformed the control group in their understanding of key concepts having to do with change, causation and development in history. On the basis of his data, Shemilt advanced the notion of broad, decontextualised cognitive understandings in history that developed in a generally hierarchical and progressive manner. Shemilt, however, was at pains to emphasise

> ... an immense variation in the levels of historical conceptualisation achieved by children of similar abilities and social backgrounds. Indeed, in determining the level of a child's conceptual attainment, the character and quality of the teaching he receives is, if anything, more important than his measured intelligence (Shemilt, 1980, p.85).

Subsequent British research seemed to reinforce the optimistic message of Booth and Shemilt by fleshing out still further the nature and development of students' historical thinking. The work of Dickinson and Lee (1984) and Ashby and Lee (1987) has been important here. Using quite complicated but stimulating and controversial materials (for example, written documents relating to an Anglo-Saxon oath helping and the ordeal–methods of establishing the innocence or guilt of an accused by submitting the person to divine judgement), they demonstrated the capacity of young people (particularly the less able), aged between eight and 18 to come to terms with the strangeness of the past, provided that ample time is given for the students to explore the materials in their own way and to express themselves orally. The transcripts of the students' interactive discussions show that they were immersed in the materials they were considering. Sometimes they were confused by the issues, sometimes their thinking was anachronistic; but what clearly emerged was their ability to think effectively in history, with imagination playing a central role.

Dickinson and Lee are pursuing these ideas in a new research project funded by the Economic and Social Research Council for the period 1991–95. The project, with the cosy acronym of CHATA (Concepts of History and Teaching Approaches at Key Stages 2 and 3 [the National Curriculum terms designating the seven to 11 and 11 to 14 age groups]), is divided into three phases. In phase 1, the project is looking at the progression of students' ideas of *historical enquiry* and *historical explanation* between the ages of seven and 14 years. In phase 2, instruments are being developed for investigating teaching approaches in history and for categorising the way in which history is seen in relation to the wider context. Phase 3 sees the exploration of the relationship between students' concepts of enquiry and explanation, on the one hand, and curriculum contexts and differences in teaching approach, on the other (Dickinson and Lee, 1994). Underpinning the research project are two fundamental assumptions: first, students' ideas about the nature of history and what is involved in understanding the past and creating historical discourse must be fully investigated and understood – 'such ideas are the constructs by which each child makes sense of the world, past and present' (Dickinson and Lee, 1994, p. 79). Second, through such ideas come concepts such as evidence and explanation which produce the keys to progression. Notions of progression therefore will arise from what the students can in practice reveal of their historical thinking in specific contexts rather than imposing a preconceived hierarchy.

The collection and analysis of the data is still in its early stages and Dickinson and Lee's writing to date comes to no firm conclusions. But they are moving towards seven hierarchical clusters of ideas which students aged seven to 14 seem likely to bring to bear when confronting historical materials which contain an apparent paradox. The first phase they call 'the baffling past' where the student finds it hard even to get to grips with the historical issue with which he or she is being confronted – it is simply baffling. The second phase is 'the divi past' – actions they find strange are dismissed as 'divi' ('stupid', in the youth argot of today) with the implicit assumption of our superiority. In the third phase, 'the ignorant past', students explain behaviour in terms of the characters being hindered by what they cannot yet do – they are not as clever as us. 'Stereotypical generalising', the fourth phase, assumes that people in the past were much like people today, and that the past can be understood by conventional, commonsense reference to people's intentions, values and goals. In the fifth phase, students show 'everyday empathy'. They assume that there is a point in trying to reciprocate positions, 'making a genuine attempt to work out salient features but relying on some form of personal projection and generalisations of how people react'. It is only in the sixth and seventh phases – 'restricted historical empathy' and 'contextualised historical empathy' – that genuine historical thinking begins to show itself. Here the student accepts that people in the past were acting within different contexts, though it is only in the seventh phase that he or she can place a paradoxical issue in the contemporary context of the wider values, goals and habits of the age, in contrast to those of today. The Project team is continuing to explore this model of thinking; the team members believe these hierarchies are holding up well and are optimistic that they will be able to come up with a sharper, clearer picture of how students' understanding of explanation in history develops. They are also developing models of students' concepts of evidence, causation and plausibility in history.

The CHATA project research, like Booth's (1979) and Shemilt's (1980), relies heavily on paper and pencil tests and interviews to investigate the nature of students' historical thinking; others have concentrated on the effects of using particular teaching strategies on deepening historical understanding. Of especial interest and influence has been the writings of history educator, John Fines and drama specialist, Ray Verrier (Fines and Verrier, 1974). Their immensely readable book chronicles their work in the classroom with a range of ages where drama and role play become powerful ways of exploring complex and baffling historical concepts such as authority and power. Of particular note is the way the authors stress that the drama is not an end in itself but a means to historical understanding, and that role play must stem from and lead to a consideration of the evidence and the search for further sources and knowledge.

Though not research in the conventional sense of the word, Fines and Verrier's book has all the hallmarks of authenticity – we hear the students speaking, we empathise with teachers and students struggling to make sense of the past or searching for new information. In a small-scale research project, Rogers and Aston tried to quantify the effects of the 'enactive mode of representation' in enabling students to get to grips with the past (Rogers and Aston, 1977). They devised a series of games to help a group of 48 students aged nine to 11 understand the layout and purpose of a ruined castle, comparing their performance on a written test with that of a control group of 35 students who were taken round the castle in a more conventional manner. The higher scores of the research group in comparison with those of the control group proved to be statistically highly significant. More recently, Goalen and Hendy conducted a similar though more substantial and long-term piece of research (Goalen and Hendy, 1993). Taking as their proposition that history through drama is a means of developing children's historical thinking, they worked for 12 weeks in a primary school with two parallel classes of students aged nine to ten (year 5) on the topic of 'Explorations and Encounters 1450–1550'. For most of the term the classes were engaged in broadly similar activities; but one class was taught by the researchers for six Friday afternoons using drama and role play as a means of deepening and broadening the students' understanding of the Aztecs and their encounters with the Europeans. The experimental group performed slightly less well than the control group on the pre-test; 'the post-test, however, showed that a proportion of the experimental group had begun to out-perform their peers in the control group in a statistically significant way. This increase was particularly marked for students in the middle range of ability, 'the section of the class so often left uninspired by less active approaches to [history] classroom management and organisation' (Goalen and Hendy, 1993, p.365).

RESEARCH IN NORTH AMERICA

This plethora of British activity was not matched by research in North America. As Wineburg shows, there was a brief period in the early twentieth century when historians and psychologists addressed the question of historical understanding. Behaviourism, however, took over and questions to do with the historical sense and historical understanding were considered – if they were viewed at all – 'as misguided and wrongheaded' (Wineburg, 1994, p.57). The special issue of the *Educational Psychologist* which focuses on the teaching and learning of history (1994, 29, 2), however, marks a resurgence of interest in matters to do with the teaching and learning of history in schools. Such renewal was partly a reaction to calls for excellence, following the perception that American educational standards had declined – the Reagan administration was creating a right-wing backlash similar to that of the Thatcher government in the United Kingdom. For example, writers such as Ravitch and Finn castigated the historical knowledge base of 17-year-old students (Ravitch and Finn, 1987); E. D. Hirsch advanced the idea that there is a corpus of essential factual knowledge, much of it historical, which every adult should be in possession of to be able to function effectively in American society (Hirsch, 1987). State and federal governments reacted by producing new social studies syllabuses (California State Department of Education, 1988; US Government Printing Office, 1992). In particular, a private foundation, the Bradley Commission on History in Schools, also reacted to the perceived inadequacy in the quality and quantity of the history taught in American schools, coming up with its own solution (Bradley Commission on History in Schools, 1988).

Such unsubstantiated claims and activity spurred a number of researchers to respond. Dale Whittington called into question the conclusions of Ravitch and Finn's study, even arguing that today's students know *more* about American history than did their age peers of the past (Whittington, 1991). Others took issue with Diane Ravitch's earlier call for more history and less social studies, and the need for a return, according to Education Secretary Bennett to a 'golden age – there truly was such a time' (Kaestle, 1986). In addition, a number of researchers, particularly in the Universities of Washington, Wisconsin-Madison and British Columbia, began turning their attention to the realities of the classroom: what were students learning and how were they learning it? There are now a number of active researchers. What characterises their work is the meticulous and finely crafted explorations of particular classrooms and groups of students and teachers. All are reluctant to generalise; all stress the need for the interaction between knowledge and teaching strategy and the pre-eminently important role of the history teacher.

Foremost in this work is Samuel S. Wineburg at the University of Washington; typical of his research and writing is his detailed and convincing analysis of and reflection on the lessons of two history teachers, whom peers had designated 'expert' (Wineburg and Wilson, 1991). His aim here is to focus on the significance of the teacher's knowledge of history in classroom practice. While recognising that historical knowledge alone does not dictate the teacher's pedagogical approach, Wineburg postulated that what teachers know must influence not only *what* they teach but *how* they choose to teach it. Elizabeth Jensen and John Price on first meeting are very different history teachers. Jensen seems to take a backstage role, setting up the situation, giving out the materials and then allowing her students to debate the issue of the authority of the eighteenth-century British government to tax the American colonies:

> For three days, Elizabeth Jensen has been an invisible presence, nestled in the corner, scribbling notes on her pad. Sometimes, unable to contain her delight, she would flash a smile to a student after a particularly incisive point about Salutary Neglect or the imperatives of Natural Rights. But the only words she uttered (with the exception of 'Hold still!') were to the judges, reminding them every so often to sound their gavels and maintain order. During these classes, Jensen did little that would conventionally be called 'teaching' – she did not lecture; she did not present information; she did not write on the blackboard; she did not intercede when students became confused; she did not hand out a worksheet, a quiz or a test... The impression that Jensen played a small role in this event is a testament to her artistry. For just as we do not see the choreographers of a Broadway musical standing on stage next to a group of

dancers, neither do we see the hand of Elizabeth Jensen as her students shape ideas and craft arguments in a debate on the legitimacy of taxation. Choreographers work on and off stage with their dancers for months, helping them prepare for the moment when they are center stage, alone. In much the same way, during her years of experience with this activity, Jensen has learned to help students prepare to be loyalists, rebels and judges ... (Wineburg and Wilson, 1991, pp. 314–315).

Price on the other hand is much more up front, a far more visible teacher:

A casual observer peering into Price's classroom door might claim to have seen what Goodlad and other researchers have observed – teacher dominated whole-group discussion, with activities centered on the teacher's questions and explanations.

But these is something that makes this class different from those described by researchers. There is electricity in the air. Students lean forward in their seats, ask thoughtful and stimulating questions, and stay in the room to continue the discussions after the bell has rung. Price is pure energy – laughing, pacing the room, bantering with students, gesturing excitedly. No ordinary teacher, John Price is a master performer who has seized the collective imagination of 35 adolescents, and led them on to an expedition into the past (Wineburg and Wilson, 1991, p. 322).

I have quoted at some length from Wineburg's article so that the flavour of his research methodology and style can be conveyed. Here is no neatly packaged research project with pre- and post-tests, attitude and bi-polar construct questionnaires and statistical tables showing significant differences. Rather, Wineburg presents us with a rich ethnographic study which captures the sights and sounds of two very different series of lessons but which ultimately achieve the same ends. For what Wineburg is at pains to emphasise is the similarity between the two teachers and the students, despite Jensen's and Price's marked differences in styles and classroom organisation. Both have created students who are deeply committed to history, prepared to stay on debating the issues after class has finished; students in both classes are able to address issues of evidence, uncertainty, debate, and historical knowledge which is positioned and determined by contexts, institutions, societies, beliefs and attitudes. Above all, what characterises both Elizabeth Jensen and John Price is their profound knowledge of the period they are teaching, their continued reading and thinking, their continuous re-evaluation and revision over 20 years. The message for history teachers is deceptively simple: know and be committed to your subject and constantly challenge, revise and reassess your historical knowledge base.

THE HISTORY NATIONAL CURRICULUM FOR ENGLAND

It was in the midst of this ferment of debate and research that the British Parliament passed one of its most far-reaching pieces of educational legislation, the Education Reform Act of 1988. The Act, which was born in a climate of increasing right-wing concern for standards and a fear of the left-wing policies of some local authorities, transformed the educational scene in England and Wales (Northern Ireland and Scotland have their own separate educational systems) by giving primary and secondary state (public) schools control of their own management and budgets, guaranteeing parents greater choice of schools and feedback on standards, as well as cutting back on the powers of the local education authorities in the shires and metropolitan districts. Standards were to be raised by the creation of a national, centralised curriculum. For the first time in the history of education in Britain, the government would determine the aims, objectives and content of the curriculum, and decide the methods for assessing, recording and reporting the achievement of all students aged five to 16 in state schools (Great Britain: Laws and Statutes, 1988). The government determined that the curriculum, which would be compulsory for all five- to 16-year-olds, would consist of ten subjects: three core (mathematics, English and science) and seven further or foundation subjects, including history and geography – an arbitrary decision for which there was little or no justification (White, 1988).

The History Working Group charged to draw up proposals for the new History National Curriculum five–16 for England was personally selected by the Secretary of State for Education and Science, Kenneth Baker.[1] It was significant that out of the twelve original members, only two were practising classroom teachers (one from the primary, the other from the secondary phase); no one who had been to the fore in history education debate, research and innovation was included. Observers particularly noted the absence of Alaric Dickinson, John Fines, Peter Lee and Denis Shemilt. The Group, therefore, though sympathetic to the new history, lacked the expertise to apply the fruits of a decade of work by history educators.

To be fair, the framework for the Group's deliberations was heavily circumscribed by the Secretary of State and was increasingly to feel the pressures of right-wing activists who sympathised with the views of E. D. Hirsch and others in believing that too much emphasis was being placed on skills and not enough on content (see, for example, the newsletters of the Campaign for Real Education). Content was clearly to be at the centre of members' discussions, a substantial proportion of which had to focus on British history.

The supplementary guidance to the Chairman of the History Working

Group made clear that 'The programmes of study should have at their core the history of Britain, the record of its past, and in particular, its political, constitutional and cultural heritage'. But Mr Baker was also anxious that the programmes should 'take account of Britain's evolution and its changing role as a European, Commonwealth and world power, influencing and being influenced by ideas, movements, and events elsewhere in the world', as well as provide a study of classical civilization. Overall, 'they should help students to acquire and develop an historical approach based on objective analysis of evidence' (DES, 1990, p.189).

The syllabus should provide possibilities for cross-curricular work – for example, the discussion of equal opportunities and multicultural issues, environmental education, industrial and economic awareness, citizenship and the skills of communication and problem solving, as well as study and thinking skills. Information technology was something which should permeate the curriculum (DES, 1990).

REACTIONS TO THE HISTORY NATIONAL CURRICULUM

Such a brief clearly called for putting a quart into a pint pot; and some teachers were dismayed about the amount of content to be covered. Even though the final version of the history curriculum, approved by Parliament in early 1991, cut back the detail in the programmes of study (DES, 1991a), what was seen as excessive coverage of content was still an issue. Inevitably, too, the message which came across on reading the British core study units (which constituted over 50 per cent of the core units in keys stages 2 and 3) was that British history is essentially about the white indigenous population and is the 'whiggish' story of the political and economic improvement of the great British people, even though writers such as Keith Jenkins and Peter Brinkley pointed to the unintended opportunities that the History National Curriculum framework opens up (Jenkins and Brinkley, 1991). In a similar vein, in a chapter in a book on the multicultural dimension of the national curriculum published in 1993, I argued that the history curriculum, far from being a recipe for top-down, whiggish history, in fact provides many opportunities (admittedly implicit) for history teachers to bring out the multicultural character of our past history (Booth, 1993).

Though worries still remained about the amount to be covered, it was the assessment proposals which caused greatest dismay. The government-appointed Task Group on Assessment and Testing (TGAT) had established an assessment framework within which achievement and progression would be measured against assessment objectives or Attainment Targets (ATs), as they were to be called. A student's progression in the subject would be determined by the ten hierarchical Statements of Attainment (SoAs) which would accompany each AT. The Attainment Targets and their associated Statements of Attainment, in the words of the History Group's Final Report, constituted the 'backbone of the National Curriculum', the means by which standards would be promoted and enhanced and the framework within which assessment, recording and reporting on and comparison between the achievement levels of schools would be conducted (DES, 1990).

From the start the History Working Group was unhappy about the assessment framework within which they had to work. They had enough sensitivity to the 'new history' and its adoption by many history teachers, to be determined that history should not be allowed to revert to the 'Gradgrindery' of former days; and they knew that if content were to be specifically written into the Statements of Attainment, not only would this be to assert that some facts were by definition 'simpler' than others but also to allow teaching for content to dominate the curriculum. The three Attainment Targets – originally four but reduced to three in the Final Order on the recommendation of the National Curriculum Council (National Curriculum Council, 1990) – attempt to capture something of the spirit of the 'new history' with their stress on 'knowledge and understanding of history (AT 1), 'interpretations of history (AT 2) and 'the use of historical sources' (AT 3). The progressive hierarchy of the ten Statements of Attainment which go with each Attainment Target make no mention of content, defining the criteria for each level in terms of what are supposed to be increasingly sophisticated and demanding generalised criteria. The sop to the lobby who were pushing for history teaching to become more content orientated was the injunction, repeated like a litany at the head of each list of Statements of Attainment: 'Demonstrating their knowledge of the historical content in the programmes of study, pupils should be able to [for example]: Level 1 (AT 1) a) place in sequence events in a story about the past b) give reasons for their own actions.'

Neither side was satisfied with this compromise. History teachers and educators pointed out that an assessment system based on 45 separate hierarchical statements was going to be cumbersome and bureaucratic to operate. More tellingly, it was argued that research had shown that progression in history is not a smooth, linear process, and that historical thinking could not be targeted as discrete cognitive skills and concepts. Above all, the Statements of Attainment – the criteria for each level – could only make sense within the context of specific contexts, specific sources, specific questions, specific historical knowledge (Booth, 1993). Dismay was compounded when in January 1992, the then government council for examinations and assessment (SEAC), published its *Specification for the Development of Tests in History for Pupils at the End of the Third Key Stage of the National Curriculum* (School Examinations and Assessment Council, 1992). The *Specification* looked for 'probably no more than two tests, each lasting approximately one hour'; the tests had to include opportunities for extended writing and should cover all the attainment targets, including the three strands of Attainment Target 1. They were to be based on the programme of study for key stage 3 and should be capable of showing whether students had acquired sufficient historical knowledge to demonstrate attainment in all the attainment targets at the level appropriate for their age and ability. As teachers were to be responsible for the marking, the overall marking load should not be too heavy and it was suggested that the total time spent on any one student's papers should not exceed 25 minutes.

Such a framework for the development of the key stage 3 tests seemed unduly prescriptive; a small-scale research project cast further doubts on the capacity of such standardised assessment to reveal useful information about the attainment of students in history (Booth and Husbands, 1993). The project was concerned with devising and administering simple 'paper-and-pencil' tests which focused on the three history national curriculum attainment targets and could be easily and reliably marked. Given to students in years 7, 9 and 11 in key stages 3 and 4 (age range 11–16 years old), the test scores seemed superficially to give some endorsement to the principle of external standardised assessment in history. In practice, they revealed the problems which testing along National Curriculum lines would generate. The authors pointed to the fact that the tests were summative and can tell us nothing about the reasons for success or failure in learning or how the students had acquired their historical knowledge and understanding. Second, though taken as a whole the test scores suggest that between the ages of 11 and 16 significant gains are made in both the knowledge base and the conceptual understandings of the students, the mean scores for each age group hide considerable variation within groups, once again underlining the uneven, non-linear and context-specific nature of progression in historical knowledge and understanding. As the authors emphasise:

> ... the span of scores at each age suggest that pupils' understanding of historical sequencing and concepts may be extremely sophisticated at the age of 11 or 12 (Booth and Husbands, 1993, p. 31).

They conclude:

> The statements of attainment clearly must not be regarded as a series of hoops of increasing difficulty, through which pupils must be trained to jump at particular ages; little will be achieved by treating them in this way and much of the pupils' potential for developing real historical insight and understanding will be lost. But the attainment targets and their associated statements are in

danger of being seen in this light, particularly from those looking outside the classroom at the formal structure of the Statutory Orders for history – and this danger becomes all the greater if National Curriculum testing is conducted in the spirit of the *Specification*, with quick responses, global scores and grading being the main consideration (Booth and Husbands, 1993, p. 32).

The 'content' lobby too was dissatisfied with the proposed test but for different reasons; its members claimed that though

> the government has tried to disguise this surrender [to the 'new history' lobby] by pretending that historical knowledge will be tested at the same time as the 'skills',

in fact,

> there is no proper provision for the testing of historical knowledge, and if knowledge is not systematically tested it will not be systematically taught (Campaign for Real Education *Newsletter.* CRE, 18 Westlands Grove, Stockton Lane, York YO3 0EF, 13 July 1991).

THE DEARING REVIEW OF THE NATIONAL CURRICULUM

As dissatisfaction with National Curriculum assessment and content overload in all subjects mounted, the government made piecemeal attempts to reform the curriculum. Mathematics, science and English were slimmed down; and history became an alternative to geography at key stage 4 (ages 14 to 16). In 1993, the then Secretary of State, John Patten, ordered a complete review and Sir Ron Dearing was charged with simplifying the assessment structures and reducing content (Dearing, 1994). New working groups were established; draft proposals for history were published in May 1994 (School Curriculum and Assessment Authority, 1994). The page-proof copy of text and layout of the National Curriculum Orders for history at key stages 1, 2 and 3, sent to every school in November 1994, follows very closely the May proposals. It reduces the number of units to be covered within each programme of study and sketches their content even more briefly than in the current Statutory Order. The most notable change is in the assessment framework. Gone are the three Attainment Targets of the Statutory Order; they are replaced by a single target named, disarmingly, 'history'. The nine level descriptors (the linear TGAT-model has not been abandoned) are such a rag-bag of decontextualised skills, concepts and knowledge that it will be impossible to use them as anything more than the broadest, most general of profiles against which to determine the level of a student's performance.

Though many may welcome the lack of prescription of the history proposals, there is no denying the fact that history has suffered a set-back. The 1988 Education Reform Act looked to a broadly based and balanced curriculum for the five to 16 age-range, in which arts and science subjects would be studied by all. That has now given way to a situation in which history becomes an option after the age of 14; there is to be no national assessment; and for the post-14 age group, the curriculum will concentrate on a core of mathematics, English and science to which will be added short courses in technology and a single modern foreign language, with religious education, sex education and physical education remaining statutory compulsory subjects. Increasingly, too, the government is stressing the parallel routes of the academic advanced level curriculum and vocational education with an increasing number of bridges linking them (Taylor, 1994).

THE FUTURE OF HISTORY

What place then for history in this brave new world? Have all our efforts been in vain? Is history to become a marginalised subject, as it was in danger of becoming in the late 1960s? History, of course, will still be taught to all five- to 14-year-olds in English and Welsh state schools; and the gains in understanding about history teaching and learning styles and opportunities that research has provided can still inform and refine our classroom practice. The use of information technology in history teaching may also continue to gain ground. But whether or not the levels of debate – often acrimonious, sometimes ill-informed but usually productive and thought-provoking, and keeping history to the fore of the educational agenda – that we have seen over the past six years will be maintained, will depend largely on the history teachers and educators themselves. One promising aspect of the new order lies with the changing provisions for the training of new history teachers. Since 1992, the government has decreed that this should take place increasingly in schools, with practising teachers acting as mentors. The move to school-based training and the development of teachers as mentors has generated considerable research and a large literature base; and though much of it points to the difficulties of implementing the change or of determining the function of the mentor, most commentators and researchers agree that the new situation is forcing many teachers to reconsider their own practice in the light of their role as trainer (see, for example, Bridges and Kerry, 1993; and specifically with the focus on history, John and Lucas, 1994).

This move to empower history teachers by giving them a real stake in the training of future recruits may be one way of ensuring the survival of history in schools; all the exhortations and research papers can do little unless those at the chalk face are committed to their subject and their students. For, at the end of the day, it is the calibre of individual teachers which will be crucial, as Wineburg's research so graphically reminds us. With history teachers like Elizabeth Jensen and John Price, we need have no fears for the future. As Price so movingly states:

> ... I am seeking a balance between their understanding of the potential excitement of how historians do their work, and on the other hand, I fully understand where history is as a priority [in this school]. So *I've got to get to the exciting conclusions*...My mission...is to get them really excited about some of the characters along the way so that they have some interest in the past. Second, that there is real excitement in how this information was discovered... These are the two things I constantly have in mind (Wineburg and Wilson, 1991, p. 329).

Is history teaching then simply a matter of the individual teacher doing his or her 'own thing' in whatever ways seem best? Is there no place for further research? Of course, the history teacher is at the heart of the enterprise; but good research can illuminate and strengthen the pratice. I would point to three related areas where there is considerable scope for further investigation. First, I would favour more work along the lines pioneered by Samuel Wineburg – detailed ethnographic analyses of classroom practice which expose effective teaching and learning-studies where we can hear and see students and teachers at work, construing history and making sense of the past. Second, I believe the whole area of professional development is of crucial importance to teaching, particularly in relation to the training needs of neophytes. We need less rhetoric, exhortation and prescription and more analysis of the language of professionalism and the ways in which experts, whether history or science teachers, can articulate and pass on their subject-specific and generic professional craft knowledge to beginners. Third, I would favour continued work on the concept of making progression in history, partly because it is a key idea in the National Curriculum, partly because it is invariably cast in merely cognitive terms with little or no reference to contexts, affective behaviours and the notion of 'engagement' with the subject. Finally, and closely linked, there is still much work to be done on the issue of assessment, recording and feedback in history. The assessment and recording requirements for the current History National Curriculum have manifestly failed and are shortly to be replaced. The new requirements, I believe, will be little more satisfactory. It would be a major advance both to define more sensitively what the nature of the student's historical progression is and to propose ways of assessing and recording it.

NOTE

1. A separate Working Group was established to draw up proposals for Wales. Members worked closely with the Working Group for England and within the same centrally imposed framework. The final Statutory Order for Wales (DES, 1991b) is very similar in structure to the Order for England (DES, 1991a), though the programmes of study stress Welsh rather than English history.

REFERENCES

Ashby, R. and Lee, P. J. (1987). 'Discussing the evidence', *Teaching History,* 48, 6, pp. 13–17.

Bloom, B. S. (ed.) (1956). *Taxonomy of Educational Objectives: The Classification of Education Goals. Handbook One: Cognitive Domain.* New York: David McKay.

Bridges, D. and Kerry, T. (1993). *Developing Teachers Professionally. Reflections for Initial and In-service Trainers.* London: Routledge.

Booth, M. B. (1969). *History Betrayed?* London: Longman.

— (1979). *A Longitudinal Study of Cognitive Skills, Concepts and Attitudes of Adolescents Studying a Modern World History Syllabus and an Analysis of their Adductive Historical Thinking.* Unpublished doctoral thesis, University of Reading.

— (1980). 'A modern world history course and the thinking of adolescent students', *Educational Review,* 32, 3, pp. 245–57.

— (1983). 'Skills, concepts and attitudes; the development of adolescent children's historical thinking', *History and Theory,* 22, pp. 101–17.

— (1993). 'History', in A. S. King and M. J. Reiss (eds), *The Multicultural Dimension of the National Curriculum.* Lewes: Falmer.

— (1993). 'Students' historical thinking and the national history curriculum in England', *Theory and Research in Social Education,* 21, 2, pp.105–27.

— (1994). 'Cognition in history; a British perspective', *Educational Psychologist,* 29, 2, pp. 61–9.

Booth, M. B. and Husbands, C. (1993). 'The history national curriculum in England and Wales: assessment at key stage 3', *The Curriculum Journal,* 4, 1, pp. 21–36.

Bradley Commission on History in Schools (1988). *Building a History Curriculum.* Washington, DC: Education Excellence Network.

Bridges, D. and Kerry, T. (1993). *Developing Teachers Professionally. Reflections for Initial and In-sevice Trainers.* London: Routledge.

Bruner, J. S. (1960). *The Process of Education.* Cambridge, MA: Harvard University Press.

Coltham, J. and Fines, J. (1971). *Educational Objectives for the Study of History: A Suggested Framework.* London: Historical Association.

California State Department of Education (1988). *History–Social Science Framework for Public Schools, K-12.* Sacramento, California.

Campaign for Real Education. *Newsletters.* York: Campaign for Real Education, 18 Westlands Grove, Stockton Lane, York.

Dearing, R. (1994). *The National Curriculum and its Assessment: Final Report.* London: School Curriculum and Assessment Authority.

Department of Education and Science (1965). *The Organisation of Secondary Education.* London: DES circular 10/65 12 July.

— (1990). *History for ages 5 to 16. Proposals of the Secretary of State for Education and Science.* London: Department of Education and Science.

— (1991a). *History in the National Curriculum (England).* London: HMSO.

— (1991b). *History in the National Curriculum (Wales).* London: HMSO.

Dickinson, A. K. and Lee, P. J. (1978). 'Understanding and research', in A. K. Dickinson and P. J. Lee (eds), *History Teaching and Historical Understanding.* London: Heinemann Educational, pp. 21–38.

Dickinson, A. K. and Lee, P. J. (1984). 'Making sense of history', in A. K. Dickinson, P. J. Lee and P. J. Rogers, *Learning History.* London: Heinemann Educational, pp. 117–53.

Dickinson, A. K. and Lee, P. J. (1994). 'Investigating progression in children's ideas about history: the CHATA project', in P. John and P. Lucas (eds), *Partnership and Progress. New Developments in History Teacher Education and History Teaching* (pp. 78–115). Sheffield: Standing Conference of History Teacher Educators in association with The Division of Education: University of Sheffield.

Fines, J. and Verrier, R. (1974). *The Drama of History.* London: New University Education.

Fischer, D. H. (1971). *Historians' Fallacies: Towards a Logic of Historical Thought.* London: Routledge & Kegan Paul.

Gallie, W. B. (1964). *Philosophy and the Historical Understanding.* London: Chatto & Windus.

Gard, A. and Lee, P. J. (1978). 'Educational objectives for the study of history reconsidered', in A. K. Dickinson and P. J. Lee (eds.), *History Teaching and Historical Understanding.* London: Heinemann Educational, pp. 21–38.

Garvey, B. and Krug, M. (1977). *Models of History Teaching in the Secondary School.* Oxford: The Clarendon Press.

Goalen, P. and Hendy, L. (1993). 'It's not just fun, it works! Developing children's historical thinking through drama', *The Curriculum Journal,* 4, 3, pp. 363–83.

Great Britain: Laws and Statutes (1988). *Educational Reform Act.* London: HMSO.

Hallam, R. N. (1966). 'An investigation into some aspects of the historical thinking of children and adolescents'. Unpublished master's thesis, University of Leeds.

— (1975). 'A study of the effect of teaching method on the growth of logical thought with special reference to the teaching of history'. Unpublished doctoral thesis, University of Leeds.

— (1967). 'Logical thinking in history', *Educational Review,* 19, 3, pp.183–202.

— (1969a). 'Piaget and moral judgments in history', *Educational Research,* 11, 3, pp. 200–6.

— (1969b). 'Piaget and the teaching of history', *Educational Research,* 12, 1, pp. 3–12.

— (1970). 'Piaget and thinking in history', in M. Ballard (ed.), *New Movements in the Teaching of History.* London: Temple Smith, pp 162–78.

— (1971). 'Thinking and learning in history', *Teaching History,* 2, 8, pp. 337–46.

Hexter, J. (1972). *The History Primer.* London: Allen Lane.

Hirsch, E. D. (1987). *Cultural Literacy: what every American needs to know.* New York: Vintage Books.

Jenkins, K. and Brinkley, P. (1991). 'Always historicise: unintended opportunities in national curriculum history', *Teaching History,* 62, pp. 8–14.

John, P. and Lucas, P. (eds) (1994). *Partnership and Progress. New Developments in History Teacher Education and History.* Sheffield: Standing Conference of History Teacher Educators in association with The Division of Education: University of Sheffield.

Jones, R. B. (ed.) (1973). *Practical Approaches to the New History.* London: Hutchinson Educational.

Kaestlen C.F. (1986). *Comments on a paper by Diane Ravitch,* 'The erosion of history in American schools with especial attention to the elementary school curriculum'. National Academy of Education, Fall Meeting, Harvard Graduate School of Education. Typed paper. University of Wisconsin-Madison.

Krathwohl, D. R., Bloom, B. S. and Masia, B. B. (1964). *Taxonomy of Educational Objectives: The Classification of Education Goals. Handbook two: Affective Domain.* New York: David McKay.

Macintosh, H. G. (1987). 'Testing skills in history', in C. Portal (ed.), *The History Curriculum for Teachers.* Lewes: Falmer, pp. 183–213.

Maitland, J. (1977). 'Child development and history', in N. Little and J. Mckinolty (eds) *A New Look at History Teaching.* New South Wales: History Teachers' Association, pp. 23–31.

National Curriculum Council (1990). *Consultation Report.* York: National Curriculum Council.

Portal, C. (1987). 'Empathy as an objective for history teaching', in C. Portal (ed.), *The History Curriculum for Teachers.* Lewes: Falmer, pp. 89–99.

Price, M. (1968). 'History in danger', *History,* 58, pp. 342–7.

Ravitch, D. and Finn, C. E. (1987). *What do our 17-year-olds know?* New York: Harper & Row.

Rogers, P. J. and Aston, F. M. (1977). 'Play, enactive representation and learning', *Teaching History,* 19, pp. 18–21.

School Curriculum and Assessment Authority (1994). *History in the National Curriculum. Draft Proposals.* London: SCAA Offices.

School Examinations and Assessment Council (1992). 'Specification for the development of tests in history for pupils at the end of the third key stage of the national curriculum', Unpublished typescript.

Schools Council History 13–16 Project (1976). *A New Look at History.* Edinburgh: Holmes McDougall.

Shemilt, D. (1980). *Evaluation Study: Schools Council History 13–16 Project.* Edinburgh: Holmes McDougall.

— (1983). 'The devil's locomotive', *History and Theory,* 22, pp. 1–18.

— (1987). 'Adolescent ideas about evidence and methodology in history', in C. Portal (ed.), *The History Curriculum for Teachers.* Lewes: Falmer, pp. 39–61.

Steele, I. (1976). *Developments in History Teaching.* London: Open Books.

Taylor, L. (1994). 'Responses to the Dearing report: history post-19', *Teaching History,* 75, pp. 7–8.

Thompson, D. (1972). 'Some psychological aspects of history teaching', in W. H. Burston, C. W. Green *et al.* (eds), *Handbook for History Teachers.* London: Methuen, pp. 18–36.

US Government Printing Office (1992). *America 2000.*

White, J. (1988). 'An unconstitutional curriculum', in D. Lawton and C. Chitty (eds), *The national curriculum.* London: Institute of Education, pp. 113–22.

Whittington, D. (1991). 'What have 17-year-olds known in the past?' *American Educational Research Journal,* 28, 4, pp. 759–80.

— (1994). 'Introduction: out of our past and into our future – the psychological study of learning and teaching history', *Educational Pyschologist,* 29, 2, pp. 57–60.

Wineburg, S. S. and Wilson, S. M. (1991). 'Subject-matter knowledge in the teaching of history', in J. E. Brophy (ed.), *Advances in Research on Teaching.* Greenwich, CT: JAI, pp. 305–47.

3

ENGLISH

Tony Burgess

INTRODUCTION

English teaching is continually evolving. The subject taught in school will probably always be too much on the move in its activities – and too diversely influenced by various research interests – for any one approach or research tradition to encompass all there is to be said. An interest in language and learning has predominated. in post-war years, in school English teaching. However, the interest was never exhaustive and there have been notable elaborations of new perspectives in linguistics, literary studies and education, which have also helped to shape the subject. Many influences, then, have interacted at different points in empirical explorations of the whole loose alliance of skills and concerns and knowledge and interest which English teaching comprises. An awareness of these wider theoretical influences is a necessary point of entry for understanding research concerning English teaching; and it is also helpful to bear in mind an underlying narrative of change as new interests have emerged and been incorporated. and as old continuities of the subject have been redescribed.

In the years since the Second World War, it is possible to see two phases of developments within English teaching. Through to the publication of the Bullock Report in 1975, many new initiatives were undertaken, and encouragement was given to curriculum oriented research. The main lines of work in language and learning were laid down in that period, and their influence shaped the Bullock Report. The Report's publication, however, coincided with the wider change in educational policy signalled by James Callaghan's speech, at Ruskin College, in 1976. From this point to the present, during the run up to the new educational framework of the 1988 Education Act and in the subsequent implementation of the National Curriculum, the influence of curriculum-oriented research has probably weakened. However, some enquiries have continued. and there have been new developments in literary theory, and a growing influence from media and cultural studies, which have helped to fill the vacuum.

National policy changes have overlapped with intellectual changes in ways that are partly coincidental. The growing interest in cultural perspectives and literary theory in recent years has been in many ways incidental to the changes taking place in the management and organisation of schools. However, developments in cultural and literary discussion have been met by traditionalist literary and linguistic arguments; and in due course these have been echoed in debates on the National Curriculum. At times, though, these literary arguments have seemed to have more to do with what was going on in universities than developments actually taking place in schools. It is arguable, also, that the increasing influence of cultural work in the 1980s has been a consequence in part of the limits placed on educational work in the same period, and the relatively greater freedom to develop fundamental perspectives outside the framework of schooling.

In thinking about research in English, it is necessary to recognise the existence of research influences of different kinds and it is helpful to take some account of the subject's movement and trajectory. With this in mind, I shall begin with a brief account of developments in English in post-war years. I shall then try to disentangle the broad perspectives which have emerged and relate these to the empirical investigations to be found in contemporary work.

ENGLISH IN POST-WAR YEARS

The common and accepted aims of contemporary English teaching are probably still much those of the Bullock Report's (DES, 1975) synthesising account, published 20 years ago: a priority for children *using* language and an emphasis on the role of language in learning. Built into English teaching tradition from the work leading up to that Report are concerns for pupils' talk, for audience and function and intentionality in writing, for confidence, autonomy and range in reading, together with an awareness of diversity and language variety and of the principle of working with the language and experience which the children bring. More teachers will be influenced by these concerns than will have read the Bullock Report, or the writings of a post-war generation of English teachers, such as James Britton, Nancy Martin, Harold Rosen, Douglas Barnes, Andrew Wilkinson, John Dixon, Paddy Creber, Margaret Meek. However, whatever the actual currency of this founding work may be, the relevant consideration is its surviving impact.

The Bullock Report drew on what was by then a quarter century of development. After the Second World War, the London Association for the Teaching of English, newly formed in 1947, embarked on a series of studies of comprehension, marking, talk in classrooms and language across the curriculum. A pattern of working was developed which was conducted through study groups and drew on research carried out in classrooms. Both these themes and the working methods were influential. Other local associations followed. leading to the formation of the National Association for the Teaching of English (NATE) in 1963. By that date, a research orientation had become characteristic of the way in which English teaching developed. together with assumptions of a base in local studies carried out by teachers, collaboration between teachers and academics and a continuing interest in developing a wider, English teaching rationale; and a number of distinctive points of investigation had emerged.

Events in the 1960s consolidated and drew on this tradition. The formation of the Schools Council for Curriculum and Examinations (1964) encouraged curriculum-oriented educational research in a way for which there has been no parallel, before or since. Also, in 1966, an international seminar of British and American educators was held at Dartmouth, New Hampshire. John Dixon's resulting book, *Growth through English* (Dixon, 1967), has been highly influential, and its title provides a kind of epitaph for what was central in the approach. Historically, the Dartmouth seminar, the first meeting of its kind, was important in generating an international community of English teachers. The two events together ensured a wide dissemination of a rationale for English teaching, based on language and learning, abroad and in the UK.

By 1965, the Schools Council had recognised the need for 'a major initiative in the field of English teaching' and had produced its Working Paper 3: *English – A Programme for Research and Development in English Teaching* (HMSO, 1965). Following this, in 1966, several new researches were initiated. Some others were taken over from other funding bodies. It is worth pausing briefly to consider the themes. The list marks out, in effect, a new field of English educational research; and the continuing influence of the topics which were proposed is still apparent.

Oracy was to be studied by Andrew Wilkinson, in Birmingham, also continuing work originally funded by Gulbenkian (Wilkinson, 1965). A project on writing, *The Development of Writing Abilities, 11–18*, was set up by James Britton, in London (Britton *et al.*, 1975). A survey of approaches to English was to be undertaken by Bill Mittins, in Newcastle. Meanwhile, themes in teaching literature were taken up by Frank Whitehead, in Sheffield, who was to pay special attention to patterns of reading (Whitehead *et al.*, 1974) and by Douglas Barnes, at Leeds, who, in a project to be developed in conjunction with NATE, set out to look at children as readers

(1967–73). There was also to be an investigation of relations between linguistics and English teaching, work which had already been begun by Michael Halliday, and which was transferred from Nuffield to Schools Council funding (see Doughty *et al.*, 1972). I shall refer later to these projects in greater detail.

The Council also took some steps towards developing the teaching of English as a second language. June Derrick was invited to enquire into the *Teaching of English to Immigrants* (Derrick, 1966), an enquiry whose title is indicative of the ways in which questions of English second-language teaching and of minority languages were first perceived. In due course, a full project, SCOPE, was initiated. This was directed by June Derrick, together with colleagues Josie Levine and Hilary Hester. It was to play an important role in disseminating information about Britain's new populations and in developing a distinctive practice in the teaching of English as a second (rather than foreign) language. There was relatively little co-ordination at this stage between the English (mother tongue) projects just described and the work of the SCOPE team (Levine *et al.*, 1972). Greater co-ordination in the teaching of English as a first and a second language has developed later (see Brumfit *et al.*, 1985; Levine, 1990).

The substantial achievement of the Bullock Report was to weave together, in its central statement, the confidence in a 'new English' which had been won in everyday classroom teaching and the literary, linguistic and educational strands of thought which had underwritten the researches of the 1960s and early 1970s. Initiated amid the criticisms being made of English teaching by the writers of the Black Papers (1968–77), the Report may be read, in some ways, as 'new English teaching's' reply. The central rationale for theorising English as 'language and learning' reflects the hand of James Britton (see Britton, 1970). Meanwhile, the recent work on oracy, linguistics and language study, writing development, English second language teaching and language across the curriculum all received support.

A note of dissent by Stuart Froome (pp. 556–9) voiced the continuing concerns of the Black Paper writers. However, a more substantial difficulty for the authors was that the Bullock Report's publication coincided with the financial recession following the oil crisis (1973), and was shortly followed by the new directions set for education in the Ruskin speech. No national action was taken on its main recommendations. Much has since changed during the 1980s, change which has included the ending of the Schools Council and, relatedly, reduction of support for curriculum-oriented research. However, the priorities of this time for attention to pupils' learning and for teachers' involvement in researching their own classrooms still remain.

Subsequent work has been undertaken in a different and changing educational climate. One consequence of the ending of the Schools Council has been a reduction in support for curriculum research which aimed to develop fundamental perspectives. Thus, in the 1980s, the main funded projects which were undertaken – in oracy and writing – were essentially development work, though these played an important role in disseminating research findings more widely. The limits placed on fundamental work were also characteristic of the Language in the National Curriculum (LINC) project (Carter, 1990), a third initiative. The project was set up following the report of the Kingman Committee (HMSO, 1988), with the brief to disseminate findings about language. In its theoretical work, the team went further than many in confronting tensions between the linguistic and the psychological ends of English teaching tradition, ones which had always been present to some degree but which emerged more strongly following the Bullock Report. The whole public context, however, with its discovery of grammar as an issue, limited the development of fundamental arguments, and led finally to the suppression of the project's materials. The work, though, gave 'knowledge about language' a new and welcome prominence.

Building on the Bullock Report, however, some new work has been undertaken and some fresh themes have emerged. The teaching of reading, neglected in some ways in the first round of Schools Council projects, has received widespread attention. Among various initiatives, Margaret Meek's work (1978; 1982) has been influential, both for its dissemination of psycholinguistic perspectives and for the bearing it has had on the teaching on the literature. The teaching of literature has also been the subject of development, in its own right, influenced by new insights from literary theory (Corcoran and Evans, 1987; Hayhoe and Parker, 1990). Meanwhile, sociolinguistic perspectives, together with the experience of new populations entering schooling as a result of migrations of the 1950s and 1960s, have led to work on language diversity. While initiatives in this area have also been subject to fluctuations in national policy, a new awareness of responsibilities towards bilingual populations has resulted (Rosen and Burgess, 1980; The Linguistic Minorities Project, 1985).

Seen from the vantage of the 1990s, what is most striking is an underlying shift towards social and cultural perspectives, replacing the more psychological orientation of earlier work. It is the tension in these different, broad perspectives that will occupy us in the section which follows. To anticipate, Dell Hymes's influential concept of communicative competence (1972) has led on to establishing rules of use in heterogeneous language communities and to cross-cultural studies of literacy and speech events. Halliday's work in language, similarly, has begun from context of culture and situation, rather than from developing learners. Although his *Learning How to Mean* (1973) is a widely read study of language acquisition, the focus of this work is on confirming a functional description of language rather than the child's learning processes. Meanwhile, the tendency in both British cultural theory and literary theory has been to emphasise the cultural construction of signs and language and the social nature of forms of representation. In recent linguistic, literary and cultural work, there has been a common concentration on the social nature of texts of any kind and on developing the concepts which will link utterances and texts to underlying circumstances of their production.

It will be apparent from this history that there have been several evolving lines of empirical work, with their roots in the developments of post-war years. Also, though, a number of general perspectives frame the present picture of research in English, and it will be best to proceed by examining them in more detail.

GENERAL PERSPECTIVES

An approach to children's learning, and to language's role in this, is probably still the main research perspective informing research in English teaching. The interest here has been in elaborating general principles of development in children's learning and their use of language as a way of grounding English work. An integrating study of development in communication, though never actually carried out, was central to the proposals of the Schools Council outline of future research in English teaching (1965, op. cit.). The Bullock Report's celebrated Chapter 4 is similarly conceived. constructing a rationale for English teaching based in an account of the symbolic nature of language and its role in learning. While the levels and key stages of the National Curriculum suppose a different, curriculum-centred approach, the actual descriptions of these levels cannot escape developmental assumptions and detailed commentary has not unnaturally focused on whether drafters and working parties have got these right. Thus, the main official accounts of the subject have then been preoccupied with the nature of development in English, and this has both reflected and legitimated research concentrations of this kind.

The close of Chapter 4 of the Bullock Report still offers one of the most cogent statements of the role of language in learning. Three propositions are briefly stated. They are inferences, in the Committee's view, to be drawn from a study of the relationship of language and learning. The heart of this approach to English is still powerfully captured by them:

(1) All genuine learning involves discovery, and it is as ridiculous to suppose that teaching begins and ends with 'instruction' as it is to

suppose that 'learning by discovery' means leaving children to their own resources;

(2) language has a heuristic function; that is to say a child can learn by talking and writing as certainly as he can by listening and reading.

(3) to exploit the process of discovery through language in all its uses is the surest means of enabling a child to master his mother tongue. (*A Language for Life*, The Bullock Report, HMSO, 1975).

It is worth pausing on these splendid, interlocking statements, and noting their cumulative force. The account begins from learning, with language seen connectedly, as having a role in thinking, not as just fulfilling a communicative function. Learning is assimilated to discovery, since 'what is known', as has been said earlier in the report, 'must in fact be brought to life afresh within every "knower" by his own efforts'. The emphasis can then be placed on an active, inward process, which is used to steer between the two antinomies of straightforward instruction and merely *laissez faire*. Linked into the account of learning (and instruction) are the exploratory possibilities of language, derived especially from the interior force of words in shaping pupils' thought. Finally, learning language and learning *through* language are brought together, in a connected vision of language as acquired through use.

The drafting of this section of the Report was James Britton's. A major influence on school English teaching in post-war years, Britton sought for more than three decades to draw together the disparate activities of English teaching within a unifying account of language's role in learning. Britton's work had at its centre a long engagement with Vygotskian thought, to which he added a notion of representation developed from an account of symbolising given by Ernst Cassirer and Susanne Langer (Britton, 1970, op. cit.). The account drew on the psychology of the time, especially the new cognitive psychology arriving from America and British developmental work influenced by Piaget, since all sought an alternative to behaviourism and existing experimental traditions. The agency of children learning was placed at the centre of the picture, and learning and literature were brought together since both could be related to the work of representation, to children working on their picture of the world. This account of language and learning is still influential, and I shall return to it at various points. However, Britton's work must now be set beside some other approaches which have their origin in the study of language in society rather than in development and learning.

A relatively general influence has been that of sociolinguistics. Developing in the 1960s, sociolinguistics initially made a strong impact on educational debates about language and inequality. In this country, Basil Bernstein's theory of the way cultural codes work within social control had been a continuing line of argument (Bernstein, 1971). Replacing earlier dialect studies, there came the well-known work on vernaculars by Labov (1972) in America, and by Trudgill (1974) and the Milroys (Milroy, J. and Milroy, M., 1985) in the UK. However, British educators have tended to regard sociolinguistic research principally in the context of debates about dialects and Standard English, and while this has given the work immediate relevance, at the same time it limited the attention paid to wider theoretical understandings. What has been at issue is more than a particular debate, however vital. Behind the attention paid to dialect and standard language has been a whole larger aim for the development of a study of language in society.

The major theoretical formulations have come from Dell Hymes's revival of the tradition of American anthropological linguistics (Hymes, 1972; 1977). His concepts of communicative competence, speech communities and speech events, and his emphasis on ethnography have marked out a new vocabulary for the social exploration of language, reflected also in the work in literacy by Shirley Brice Heath (1983) and Brian Street (1984). Hymes recognises that speech communities are normally heterogeneous, and that communicative competence may often extend to use of different languages, as well as to different dialects of a single language and to various registers and styles. He has written, characteristically, at a high level of generality and theoretical density, and for this reason also has had less direct impact than some other formulations of issues of language diversity. However, his work brings together bilingualism and the command of different dialects within a single conceptual framework which assumes heterogeneity and the need for ethnographies of language use. In doing so, he has also helped to bring these issues back from the margins of attention to which they are often consigned in British discussion, dominated as this usually is by normative expectations about language and majority assumptions of a monolingual nation.

Another approach to language in society has been that of Michael Halliday. As is often noted, Firthian linguistics were also anthropological in origin, and set out from an approach to language in the context of situation and the context of culture. Michael Halliday's development of this has in some ways contrasted with American sociolinguistic work, in its stress on what he has called 'inter-organism' perspectives in contrast to 'intra-organism' ones. In Hymes's linguistics the speaker/listener remains at the centre of the theoretical picture through the stress on 'communicative competence'. Halliday's interest has been in the meaning potential and functions of language as these are realised in a network of social situations, accumulating in the end to total social semiotics (Halliday, 1978). In a later development of this work the focus has been on the text, spoken or written, as the site where the social semiotic can be explored (Halliday, 1985).

Michael Halliday's contribution to educational insights into language has also extended over many years, from the work in the 1960s on language awareness and knowledge about language, through his study of language acquisition (1973), to his authoritative *Functional Grammar* (1985) and contemporary influence on Australian genre theory. It is interesting to note Gordon Wells, in recent commentary, drawing connections between a Hallidayan approach and that of Vygotsky (Wells, 1994), though Halliday himself has resisted the psychologising tendencies of much work on language. Despite the common interest in genre of both Hymesian ethnography and Hallidayan accounts of texts, there seems at present to have been few attempts to link the different foci of these two approaches to language in society. It seems in principle likely, though, that educational work can benefit from both approaches in linguistics.

The interest in a social theory of language has been complemented by a parallel movement in literary studies. In his *The Long Revolution* (1963), Raymond Williams outlined, 30 years ago, an account of social change in British society, connecting politics and culture. The central thesis marked processes of democratisation, changing institutions and ways of life. As important, though, was that the analysis was also extended to language, literacy and literature, and to new media and forms of communication. The accompanying thesis of a common culture may require some later qualification. But the widening of literary work which Williams signalled, and the connection made by him between politics and culture, remain fundamental to a whole range of newer English studies. The main period of this influence has been from the mid 1970s onwards, carried forward by Williams's own further cultural writings (Williams, 1980) and by those of Stuart Hall (Hall *et al.*, 1980). Its consequences will require a slightly more extended treatment.

Williams's rereading of Marxist literary and cultural theory has been among a number of influences which lie behind the new voices and the new cultural perspectives that have emerged in recent years. There have also been the influence of French structuralist theory, with its sustained critique of humanism, and an anti-historicism in writers like Foucault (1981) and Derrida (1976) used to destabilise conventional western histories. This has been accompanied. in Britain, by the labour history of writers such as E. P. Thompson (1963) and Eric Hobsbawm (1964), recovering lost voices and struggles, and putting at issue, though from a different point of view, versions of a national past. Work from feminist and anti-racist perspectives has also both contributed within these broader directions and paid specific attention to developing an account of social and cultural difference.

In British cultural studies, a movement from within literature towards a more general cultural history has been joined by sociologists interested in new social and cultural developments. The interests of the Birmingham Centre for Contemporary Cultural Studies, a main centre for this work, have been wide ranging. These have included popular culture and youth culture, education, feminist and anti-racist critiques and also media, literature and language. Theoretical perspectives have been drawn from sociology and history as well as literary and linguistic theory, and there has been a sustained effort to achieve synthesis, especially in the writings of Stuart Hall (Hall *et al.*, 1980). The work has been conducted on many levels. Many specific and empirical studies have been reported in the various collections which have been produced (Clarke *et al.*, 1978; Hall *et al.*, 1980, op. cit; McRobbie and Mica Nava, 1984). Attention has been paid also to the development of fundamental theory, within which the diverse concerns implied by studies of contemporary culture may be integrated.

The impact of new theoretical developments on literary studies, more specifically, has revived old hopes for the role of criticism and ushered in new ones. Works like Catherine Belsey's *Critical Practice* (1980) or Terry Eagleton's *Literary Theory* (1983) do not dispute the need for judgement or for close reading. The argument is, rather, for a criticism which does not leave implicit its own theoretical bases and for a widened view of the concerns of literary studies.

To take just one example, Colin MacCabe's *Futures for English* (1988) introduces a collection of such new studies. The anthology includes essays on several Shakespeare plays, his sonnets, Stevenson, Conrad, Eliot and Pound, as well as on soap operas and popular music. As will be clear from such a list of contents, the newer literary studies have not advocated the abandonment of these powerful texts. Rather, they seek a rereading of these texts against the background of a different, critical relation to literary tradition and a changed relation to the past. As MacCabe notes in his introduction, 'The necessity of engaging with contemporary culture and the urgency of interrogating the assumptions of our cultural past should not, however, be identified with a simple rejection of that past.' Instead, he calls for a rereading – 'a past understood not as a tradition to be transmitted but a set of contradictions to be used' (MacCabe, 1988, pp. 12–13).

MacCabe goes on to make the argument for a widening of literary studies to include attention both to 'crucial contemporary cultural forms' and to the 'various communication technologies'. The underlying perception connects literary and media studies, and indicates the broader range of considerations characteristic of newer literary approaches. What will also be apparent is that the perspective which MacCabe proposes need not be confined to literary studies, and is capable of wider application. MacCabe's interest here is in claiming for literary study the broad ground of writing in society as a necessary co-ordinate of an adequate approach to literary texts and literary tradition. Clearly, on such wider ground, an interest in texts, arising in a reconceptualised literary studies, converges with a wider account of language as a social semiotic, originating in linguistics; and there are possibilities for drawing on both perspectives.

In the revised sociolinguistics of Norman Fairclough (1989), Gunther Kress (Hodge and Kress, 1986) and Theo Van Dijk (1985), it is indeed such a wider approach to text which has been taken. Distinctively, these writers and researchers draw on an eclectic range of theoretical sources, including cultural and literary theory and European as well as Anglo-American accounts of discourse, ideology and meaning. Their interpretation of 'text', as an object of study, is, similarly, a wide one. Their work extends to spoken and written language and to media texts of different kinds, and also to purely visual representations. The common insight, shared with literary and cultural studies (and with other forms of analysis in the arts), is that texts are culturally produced, concealing and excluding meanings as well as revealing them, bearing complex, underlying relationships to institutional frameworks and the exercise of power by different social groups.

These, then, have been the main directions in the development of a wider rationale for English teaching and for English studies. How different tendencies of this kind are to be articulated provides a complex set of issues in the ongoing development of a wider rationale for English work. Given that teachers' main concern lies in their work with children in classrooms, the priority for work on development and learning seems likely to remain. Undoubtedly, though, there is a need for these developmental concentrations to be reshaped by wider understandings about language in culture and society, which call into question the exclusive focus on processes and cognition characteristic of the dominant tradition of developmental work.

What have been at issue, perhaps, are more than just new theoretical developments. Driving these, there has been a search for usable accounts of language and literature, appropriate for a society that is meeting new demands and experiencing change. Included in such changes have been a widening diversity of language and populations within national boundaries, an increasing awareness of the international dimensions of culture, literatures and languages, new technologies of communication, and the need for strategies to combat, in Chomsky's phrase, 'the manipulation of consent'. In an apparent contrast to the more individualised and inward focus of earlier work on language and learning, the shared tendency in all these newer strands of thought is, perhaps, towards an 'anthropological' turn of mind. In this, an emphasis on culture, and on the lives of children within cultural settings, has been accompanied by an urgent recognition that British institutions and traditions are, and should be, as open for interrogation as those of any other society.

EMPIRICAL INVESTIGATIONS AND DEVELOPMENT WORK

The main concentrations of empirical work have been on oracy and spoken language, writing, children's reading, and the teaching of literature. I shall give these areas priority in what follows, though I should also mention that, from Bullock to the Assessment of Performance Unit, there have been investigative surveys which have been concerned to monitor standards and evaluate the provisions made for English teaching. I shall not do justice to drama and media studies. I have no doubt that these have been a part of English teaching as well as curriculum subjects in their own right and that it would better reflect present developments in the subject were I able to include them adequately. Unfortunately, the resulting canvas would be too large. In addition, there have been explorations of a further range of topics such as knowledge about language, language diversity, bilingual learners, language across the curriculum and assessment as a continuing thread in all these various interests which will remain in the background of my account.

In all the following work, research by teachers has played an important part, in addition to that contributed by universities and by funded projects. Even if relations between teachers and researchers have sometimes been hierarchical and not always successful, there has been a real history of collaboration from the London Association for the Teaching of English study groups of the 1950s, through to the era of the Schools Council, and on to the national projects, in oracy, writing and knowledge about language, initiated in the 1980s.

Talk and Oracy

Some of the most effective studies of pupils' talk were conducted in the 1960s by teachers staggering into classrooms, carrying cumbersome and less than secret reel-to-reel tape recorders, and recording lessons. Typically, this work contrasted talk in formal lessons managed by the teacher with what pupils were able to achieve on their own in small groups. As just one example, the supportive, spiralling talk of the Norwood girls in south London discussing Yevtushenko's poem, 'The Companion', which can be found in Nancy Martin's *Understanding Children Talking*, plainly takes their learning further than the question and answer format of the contrasting, teacher-led lesson (Martin *et al.*, 1975). Douglas Barnes's larger-scale investigation of talk in different curriculum subjects, reported in *Language. the Learner and the School* (1969), hypothesised a 'language of secondary education', which was at odds with the informal discussion needed when encountering new concepts. With Frankie Todd, he went on to study talk in pupil groups (Barnes and Todd, 1977). This later work continued the demonstration of what can be achieved by pupils working on their own, and also developed the helpful analytic concepts of 'cognitive and interaction frames'.

Work of this kind – small-scale, focused on pupil learning, attentive to group processes – has continued fruitfully, facilitated by more manageable equipment and providing a point of entry into studying classroom language which can be powerful in generating language policies. Predominantly the focus has been Vygotskian, influenced by James Britton's (1970) account of language and learning, already mentioned; and Britton himself contributed to the developing analysis in his *Talking and Writing* (1967) and in his chapter in *Language, the Learner and the School* (Barnes *et al.*, 1969, op. cit.). Investigations of pupil language of this kind are always illuminating, and can be a corrective to some of the wilder statements about poor spoken English which are regularly made in public debate.

Other perspectives and interests have been added in the 1970s and 1980s. Harold Rosen's work on language and class (1972; and see also the journal, *Language and Class*, 1972–4, occasional) added a further sociolinguistic dimension to investigations of informal, pupil language. The investigation of pupil dialect and of switching between different codes is well illustrated in John Richmond's work in Vauxhall Manor School in the early 1980s (1982). John Hardcastle has explored talk in the multicultural setting, evolving over time (1985). Accounts of talk in multilingual classrooms, and proposals for managing jointly the development of bilingual and monolingual pupils, can be found in Neil Mercer's *Language and Community* (1981) and in the projects developed by Josie Levine, Hilary Hester and Jean Bleach (Levine, 1990; Hester, 1983; Bleach and Riley, 1985). Jane Miller's *Many Voices* (1983) is a sustained study of bilinguals' experience in UK, based on interviews with a diverse sample of informants. Feminist work has explored the interaction between girls and boys, showing the usual dominance of boys in formal classroom settings but also the different and successful classroom strategies pursued by girls (Swann and Graddol, 1988; Bousted. 1989; Maybin, 1991).

There has also been a continuing elaboration of frameworks for understanding classroom discourse, the role of teachers' questions, and pupil/teacher interaction. Sinclair and Coulthard's (1975) proposals for the analysis of classroom discourse contribute some conceptual tools, but arguably founder on the assumption of the formal setting. Michael Stubbs's (1976) account of language in classrooms concentrates usefully on teachers' handling of metalinguistic aspects of classroom discourse. Edwards and Westgate's (1978) investigation of teacher/pupil interaction in informal talk is illuminating about the complicities which can develop in managing classroom tasks. Neil Mercer and Derek Edwards have undertaken useful recent studies of classroom discourse and more specifically of the scaffolding for classroom tasks which teachers can supply (see Edwards and Mercer, 1987; Maybin *et al.*, 1992).

Much of this work informed the National Oracy Project, administered by the then newly formed National Curriculum Council, from 1987–88 to 1992–93. Like its companion project, the National Writing Programme, the aims of the Project were more concerned with development and dissemination than with fundamental, investigative research. The work was conducted by a small central team, supported by local co-ordinators, with a brief for enhancing the role of speech in the learning process and developing the skills of teachers and methods of assessment. Much of this development work, however, took the form of initiating small-scale research, and Kate Norman's (1992) edited account is alive with transcripts, conversations and dialogues and studies of pupils working. This record of the work also brings together the voices of teachers and academics in the field, and provides an excellent introduction to the lines which are currently being followed.

Writing

The major study of children's writing has been Britton's (1975) account of the development of writing abilities from 11 to 18. The work described development in writing as becoming progressively more able to write in different functions for different audiences, outlining the threefold division into expressive, transactional and poetic functions which has influenced much subsequent work. Equally, the awareness that different audiences pose different problems for the writer has its origin in Britton's work. Britton sampled the written output of pupils of four different age groups (years 7, 9, 11 and 13 in contemporary descriptions) in different subjects, in 65 secondary schools. With minor variations, informative writing, usually for an examining audience, counted for around 80 per cent of the writing produced in every year in all curriculum subjects, except English. The level of abstraction moved slowly up from report to classification and stayed there. This finding about the narrow range of secondary writing lay behind the attention to language across the curriculum which was subsequently called for in the Bullock Report. Subsequent work in writing, such as Harpin's (1976) on the primary school and Martin's (1976) investigations of writing across the curriculum, together with that of the National Writing Programme, referred to below, has taken its cue from Britton in emphasising variety and the role which writing plays in learning.

It is still not generally recognised how recent has been an informed encouragement in schools for children to explore the possibilities of written language and to use writing for real purposes. The elementary schools taught handwriting and copying, rather than writing, and it was not until the highest grades that children were expected to compose short pieces in their own words. In more recent educational practice, writing may often enough be employed in the course of everyday classroom teaching and learning, but without opportunities being offered for authentic communication or for writing at any length. Early twentieth-century reformers challenged the teaching of composition at the time; and their counterparts in the years following the Second World War promoted the cause of 'free writing' (Pym, 1957), and more generally 'creative writing' (Clegg, 1964), as an antidote to questions and answers, tests, short exercises, blackboard copying and ever-present worksheets. But 'creative writing' was an indifferent substitute for an informed approach, and has since become part of the rhetoric of educational debate. It is worth stressing, then, that it is the attempt to ground the teaching of writing in a principled description of development in language which has been characteristic of recent research, rather than the advocacy of particular teaching methods or support for specific movements.

Work from perspectives other than Britton's has included James Moffett's (1968) account of the Universe of Discourse and James Kinneavy's (1971) development of rhetoric, approaches originating in the United States but also influential in the UK. Andrew Wilkinson's Crediton Project developed a different, wider approach to the study of development in writing (Wilkinson, 1987). Gunther Kress's study of *Learning to Write* (1982) was the first account to be written from a Hallidayan perspective. Kress's work shows children gradually differentiating written from spoken grammar, and has something in common with Katherine Perera's *Children's Writing and Reading* (1985), written from a different grammatical perspective. Kress also introduced the notion of 'genre' in written language, which has since been widely influential in other Australian work. Marie Clay's 'developmental writing' (1975) offered a coherent way of working in the teaching of writing in the early years, reconciling the claims of development with the need for children to master the grammar, orthography and spellings of the written system. Donald Graves's approach to drafting and peer editing became influential in both the US and the UK from the late 1970s onwards (see Graves, 1983). In America, also, what began as the Bay Area Project evolved into the National Writing Programme and provided a highly successful model for in-service education and the development of teaching practices.

These developments influenced Britain's National Writing Project, initiated, like the Oracy Project mentioned earlier, with the aim of enhancing practice and disseminating understanding. Again, much of the best work of this project was undertaken locally, and its success is to be judged by the engagement of teachers in development work rather than in published outcomes. In relation to these criteria, the several booklets produced in the closing stages of the project (1989–90) provide evidence of powerful and successful work. There are records here of countless different investigations conducted by teachers and a convincing demonstration of the effectiveness of new approaches in the quality of pupil work. It is perhaps slightly disappointing that this work presupposes fundamental research arguments without seeking to explore them further, since even in development work such explorations have their place. Pam Czerniewska's own account of writing (1992), however, is a fine compensation.

Reading

Trends in reading standards have been close to the centre of the national educational debate, ever since the National Foundation for Educational Research (NFER) Report of Start and Wells (1972) suggested evidence of possible decline. As importantly, this original NFER work drew attention to the inadequate base existing for a comparative analysis of this kind. In their work, Start and Wells compared evidence from national surveys initiated since 1948 with a comparable survey of their own. As they themselves pointed out, however, achieving comparability required them to rely on sentence completion tests standardised at a much earlier date, and the evidence was uncertain.

The difficulties for research of this kind remain, not greatly different from those identified in the NFER review, in commentary at the time. What is and should be tested by reading tests is not straightforward; and comparability between tests of different kinds administered in different local conditions is difficult to establish. Whether specific instruments reveal something about general reading ability is always debatable, as is the validity to be accorded to data gathered under test conditions without normal reading supports. The question is whether the statistical significance of findings gathered in this manner is actually of educational significance in the real world.

A discussion of such issues is to be found in the Bullock Report which was set up shortly after the NFER Report. Bullock made proposals for a rolling programme of national monitoring to be undertaken by the newly formed Assessment and Performance Unit (APU) (1974) and questioned the validity of evidence drawn from existing forms of testing. The APU subsequently conducted national surveys in English, Maths and Science between 1978 and 1984, and again in 1988. Following Bullock's guidance, new measures of a more naturalistic kind were developed and a battery of tests applied to a 2 per cent sample of ten-year-olds in each year. This work is summarised in the APU's *Language Performance in Schools* (1988). A useful critique of APU work is Rosen (1982). As it happens, little evidence of change in either direction seems to have been found by the APU during the period.

The APU has now been disbanded but the pattern of argument and counter-argument has continued in recent years. Recent work includes Martin Turner's *Sponsored Reading Failure* (1991), which sought to link changes in methods of teaching to a decline in standards, based on results of tests administered in the 1980s in nine local education authorities. This has been followed by a substantial NFER survey (1991) and HMI reports on the teaching of reading in both primary and secondary schools (DES, 1990, 1992). A good discussion of these more recent surveys is to be found in Reed *et al.* (1995). In brief, there has been little further evidence to support Turner's claims.

Turner's advocacy of phonics in the teaching of reading illustrates a long-standing controversy over teaching methods, which is still best described by Jeanne Chall in her authoritative account, *Learning to Read: the Great Debate* (1967). However, it seems unlikely that there could in principle be a straightforward validation of one method in preference to another; and, equally, any decline in reading standards is unlikely to be attributable to a single cause. Meanwhile, the evidence of HMI investigations (DES, op. cit.) has been that mixed methods are used by the vast majority of primary teachers concerned with initial literacy. Many children plainly learn to read from mixed and different methods; and a significant proportion have continuing difficulties, whatever method is employed. More illuminating than the method debates have been the continuing explorations of how children learn to read, new accounts of reading process, and specific examinations of causes of reading failure.

Recent accounts of learning to read, with summaries of research, include Meek (1982), Clark (1985), Beard (1987, 1990) and Oakhill and Garnham (1988). Reading theory was influenced in the 1970s by the psycholinguistic accounts of reading process developed in the US by Frank Smith and Kenneth and Yetta Goodman (Smith, 1972; Goodman, 1982). Balancing their examination of what it is that fluent readers are able to do, there has been a continuing examination of children's reading problems (see Bryant and Bradley, 1985). Among possible variables leading to 'backwardness' in reading, Bryant and Bradley propose as most important 'that backward readers tend to find it difficult to disentangle the sounds in words'. Other influential work on learning to read and on reading difficulties includes that by Marie Clay (1979a, 1979b, 1982). The field, though, is a large one, and is best approached through one of the introductory texts which have been mentioned above.

While studies of initial literacy predominate in research in reading, there has been some influential work on reading at higher age levels and on developing skills. Two major Schools Council projects were Southgate *et al.*, *Extending Beginning Reading* (1981) and Lunzer and Gardner's work, *The*

Effective Use of Reading (1979; and see also Lunzer and Gardner, 1984). Drawing on a wide set of fact-finding investigations, Southgate's special recommendations concern the resourcing of books for the 7–9 age group and the effective use of teacher time. Lunzer and Gardner opened up a range of issues concerning comprehension, reading strategies and coming to read new and more complex texts, and their proposals include the influential 'directed activities related to texts' (DARTs). Their studies of reading across the curriculum parallel those made for talk and writing, with findings not dissimilar to those for writing, concerning the limited extent of sustained. silent reading in the secondary curriculum. Like the work on writing, these findings were based on close investigations of work in classrooms which it is also possible to conduct on a small scale in an individual school.

For historical reasons, there has been a strong interest in psychology concerning questions of reading, an interest that has not been developed to the same degree for talk and writing or for other aspects of research in English. Anthropological work from the 1970s onwards has begun to reconsider issues about reading in the more general context of literacy and society (Goody and Watt, 1972). Dell Hymes's influence in this field has led to characteristic emphases on communities and literacy events and, further, on issues of variety in literacy. Shirley Brice Heath's well-known study of literacy in South Carolina (1983, op. cit.) shows different literacies and different literacy events existing in the black and white communities of Trackton, Stockton and Maintown. Brian Street's work is based similarly in ethnography (Street, 1984, op. cit.). Such studies have opened up a new attention to the literacy of children outside school, studies on an ethnographic or case-study basis, and Hilary Minns's *Read It To Me Now* (1990) is a recent study of this kind.

There also now exists a body of work influenced by Margaret Meek's concern to bring studies of reading more closely together with the insights derived from the tradition of research in language and learning. Meek's own writings have always made subtle connections between reading, development and the part played in this by story-telling and children's literature (Meek *et al.*, 1978, Meek *et al.*, 1983); and these links are to be found explored in other work of this kind. Notable studies have been those by Henrietta Dombey (1992) and Carole Fox (1992); and also by Eve Gregory (1992), where special attention is paid to bilingual literacy, investigated in the classroom setting.

Teaching of Literature

The new criticism of I. A. Richards, F. R. Leavis and others in the *Scrutiny* group in the 1920s and 1930s remains the starting-point for work on the teaching of literature. Cambridge English rediscovered literature, wresting it from the hands of a previous generation's historical and textual scholarship, and substituting the aim of alert and critical reading. The aim also made reading much more difficult. Richards's *Practical Criticism* (1929) revealed how difficult even the highly educated found reading poetry. Now, an emphasis on tone, style, artistic structure, symbol, irony – the imaginative qualities of texts – replaced biographical information and the noticing of rhetorical figures. Despite the recent impact of literary theory, the perspective remains influential and deserves to do so.

Drawing on this inheritance, educational work in English has sought a general account of literature and its purposes, with a view to bridging specialist and developmental concerns. James Britton's account (1970) embraces an account of literature and a view of language within a general theory of the role of the symbols in forming a representation of experience. His theory of the spectator role sees the making and reading of stories and poems as continuous, and he also links gossip and reflection on one's picture of the world with the work of the literary artist. Britton's work on literature draws on Susanne Langer's (1954) distinction between discursive and presentational symbolism; and he was influenced by D. W. Harding's parallel conception of the role of the onlooker (1937) and by his attention to psychological processes in reading fiction and turning experience into words (Harding, 1963). These emphases on reading and the reader, and on the role of narrative in everyday life, are brought together in Margaret Meek's *The Cool Web* (Meek *et al.*, 1977), an important collection of themes in post-war British work.

Louise Rosenblatt's *Literature as Exploration* (1938) places a similar emphasis on the reader in American work, which has made its way more slowly in the UK but has steadily become more influential. Rosenblatt studies the 'transactions' between works and readers, distinguishing between types of readings, and argues for a case-study method in investigating literary response. In her later (1978) work on poetry, she distinguishes between 'text' and 'reader' and 'poem'. The poem is the event which happens in the transaction between reader and text. 'As with the elements of an electric circuit, each component of the reading process functions by virtue of the presence of the others. A specific reader and a specific text at a specific time and place; change any of these, and there occurs a different circuit, a different event – a different poem' (quoted in Benton, 1992, p. 72).

In the last decade, there have been several excellent books on the teaching of literature (Benton and Fox, 1985; Griffith, 1987; Stibbs, 1991; Benton, 1992), written in the light of these concerns for reading and the reader. Each of these attempts also to draw on more recent literary theory, offering a restatement of English teaching approaches and illustrative accounts of classroom work. Collections of articles and essays, similarly exploring new forms of work with literature, include Miller (1984), Corcoran and Evans (1987), Lee (1987), and Hayhoe and Parker (1990). There is much to be learned from the accounts of work in progress assembled in these volumes, and important conceptual writing is being done in winnowing ideas from academic literary theory and adapting them for the school setting. As yet, though, there has been no sustained empirical research study of children's development as readers of literary texts, of the kind which Rosenblatt indicates. Arguably, one is overdue.

Robert Protherough's *Developing Response to Fiction* (1983) moves in this direction. The work is based on a number of 'linked. small-scale classroom investigations', carried out from Hull University over a number of years, involving local teachers and research students. A four stage model of development in response is suggested. and five case-studies are reported. Other work by Protherough (1986) includes investigations of teaching literature at 'A' level and enquiries into children's developing sense of stories. This work points towards the need for a larger-scale investigation, as Protherough himself noted. one which crosses educational phases, and combines case-studies with a broad, developmental enquiry.

It is also clear that a focus on reading and the reader is a starting-point which can then be further conceptualised in different ways, with different emphases. It is possible to point to more or less literary, psychological or cultural strands within the recent commentary, with more culturally oriented researchers indicating ways in which readings are constrained by wider discursive formations and by specific textual structures. Calling for an awareness of 'passive, active and resistant' dimensions of reading, Corcoran (1990) points out that 'Vigilance may still be needed to see whether the teacher continues to send subtle but firm messages about whose readings and which reading strategies or heuristics are valued and supported. As various critics of personal growth teaching and reader-response theory have argued … commitment to a plurality of readings is no guarantee that the classroom remains unmarked by privileged modes of analysis, privileged values and privileged ways of reading' (Corcoran, 1990, p. 143). Similar, delicately illustrated arguments about the positioning of readers and readings within classroom traditions of literary study can be found, from a feminist perspective, in Miller (1991) and Turvey (1992).

Contemporary English practice regularly juxtaposes literary texts and texts of other kinds in ways that are ahead of both full theoretical description and research study. Andrew Stibbs's work (1992) on narrative draws at points on film as well as literary text; and Michael Benton's recent work (1992) has broken new ground in integrating painting and the visual image into teaching literature. Meanwhile, there has been a developing tradition of media studies teaching in schools and of school-focused research studies

(Bazalgette, 1988; Buckingham, 1990). Studies of children's development as television viewers, ethnographies of classroom teaching of cultural studies and accounts of the construction of TV audiences have been developing lines of work. Related studies of popular culture include those by Moss of children's use of popular fiction (Moss, 1989) and recent work by Charles Sarland (1992) on gaps and overlaps between popular culture and school. As English teaching has engaged with developing traditions of work in media and cultural studies, there has been a profitable interaction and some pioneering research studies have resulted. It does seem clear, however, that the work of rethinking and development is still taking place. We are perhaps still some way from a fully articulated account, adequate to ensure a balance between work in depth of different kinds which can be undertaken in school. On this, unfortunately, the National Curriculum barely makes a beginning.

Other Themes

While these have been the main themes of research in English, there is a need to close this summarising account by indicating that it has not been exhaustive. In all these areas – talk, writing, reading, teaching of literature – there are further windows to be opened at points where a circle drawn by educational interest can profitably be illuminated by wider studies. An investigation into talk, for example, leads naturally on to issues of language acquisition, language variety, different institutional contexts and ultimately to power and social structure; or alternatively to issues of description at different linguistic levels, to pragmatics or phonology. The point will be well taken; and the same process of expansion or sub-division could be illustrated in all the areas mentioned. above.

In concentrating on these areas, I have also tended to limit illustration to research of certain kinds – broadly, research relevant to processes for which English teachers have responsibility in schools and classrooms. I should mention, then, research of other kinds which could as easily have been included. Most prominently, I have said little about evaluation work (except the APU's on reading), or about the different forms in which this can be undertaken. Also, as I indicated at the opening of this section, work has been included in the areas mentioned which might have been afforded independent treatment. An omission of this kind is examining and assessment as topics for English research. From the introduction of the Certificate of Secondary Education in 1966 to the General Certificate of Secondary Education (1984) and on to the development of National Curriculum assessment, English teachers and researchers have been profoundly interested in issues of this kind. More could have been said too about bilingualism, biliteracy and second-language teaching in the mainstream classroom, though I have indicated some lines which could be further followed.

AGENCIES AND SUPPORT FOR RESEARCH

The agencies and sources behind the work that I have mentioned have been of various kinds. Many of the earlier projects were made possible by Schools Council funding, and usually were carried forward by research teams formed in university departments of education. Funding of this kind is now rarer. The Economic and Social Research Council. however, funds curriculum-oriented work, though not development projects; and other agencies, such as Gulbenkian and Leverhulme, support specific kinds of work. The tendency, though, has been for policy-oriented and evaluation work to predominate in recent years, funded by the Department for Education or by government agencies such as the School Curriculum and Assessment Authority (SCAA).

A notable development of the 1980s was the co-ordination of local authority financing in the (then) National Curriculum Council's sponsoring of the National Oracy and Writing Projects (1986–92); and the use of a special Educational Support Grant to attract work in local areas in the Language in the National Curriculum Project (1989–92). Such initiatives brought together possibilities of fundamental work, development and dissemination in a national undertaking and opened up possibilities for research by teachers in ways which could contribute to developments in schools. Apart from these national projects, many local authorities are still in a position to support local initiatives and there are possibilities for schools through Grant for Educational Support and Training (GEST) bids and in-service education funding.

Directly or indirectly, the influence of university departments of education remains important in encouraging research more widely, as I have indicated. As well as funded work, there is the personal research of staff, often conducted in collaboration with local authorities and local schools. An important development in recent years has been to tailor work on higher degrees, both at Masters and PhD levels, more closely to the needs of individual students and researchers working in their own settings. While PhDs remain the main academic route, a number of MA dissertations have become influential books in recent years (Moss, 1989; Scafe, 1989; Minns, 1990; Fry, 1985), and many more have made useful articles. The provision of more studentships, both by separate institutions and by the Economic and Social Science Research Council, would undoubtedly assist the process.

For English teachers, the National Association for the Teaching of English plays an important central role, both in the focus for dissemination in its national conferences and through the work of its local associations. The tradition of study groups remains. Moreover, NATE is sometimes in a position to make special grants available for development work, as in its recent association with the Arts Council. NATE's journal, *English in Education,* is still a main publishing outlet for work in English and regularly carries accounts of new teaching approaches or classroom research, contributed by members. I should mention also the British Association for Applied Linguistics and the British Reading Association for their work in related fields.

CONCLUSION

In this introduction to research in English teaching, I have tried to give a picture of a subject which is always moving, pushed by different research perspectives and new interests and always shifting its borders. It was for this reason that I dwelt a little on English's post-war history. It is necessary to sense where the subject has come from in order to see its present and its future. While English always changes, there are also important continuities in its central research problems. There is nothing as old as language and literature as matters for investigation, after all. A new investigation is always in a sense a rediscovery and a rereading of a former history. We have seen a little of this continuity in some of English's key empirical areas.

Notwithstanding the present form of the National Curriculum in English, a curriculum which has been steadily narrowed in its implementation, there are signs of a changing intellectual and educational climate. These changes are what seem likely to be most significant in the long run. The level of concentration on curriculum implementation in recent years may of itself have limited the development of educational projects. In a different sphere the influence of newer work in cultural, literary and media theory, and in linguistics and social semiotics, has extended the interest in language, thinking and learning processes, characteristic of earlier work, and in places has actively challenged some of its presuppositions. There is a growing concern to look towards a new synthesis, and especially towards a richer view of English than has emerged in the description finally arrived at in the National Curriculum.

REFERENCES

Adams, A. (1974). *Every English Teacher.* Oxford: Oxford University Press.
Andrews, R. (ed.) (1989). *Narrative and Argument.* Milton Keynes: Open University Press.

Bakhtin, M. (1981). *The Dialogic Imagination* (ed. Michael Holquist, trans. Caryl Emerson and Michael Holquist). Austin: University of Texas Press.

Barnes, D. (1976). *From Communication to Curriculum.* Harmondsworth: Penguin.

Barnes, Dorothy and Barnes, Douglas (1984). *Versions of English.* London: Heinemann Educational Books.

Barnes, D., Britton, J. and Rosen, H. (1969). *Language, the Learner and the School.* Harmondsworth: Penguin.

Barnes, D. and Todd, F. (1977). *Communication and Learning in Small Groups.* London: Routledge & Kegan Paul.

Barrs, M., Ellis, S., Hester, H. and Thomas, A. (1988). *The ILEA Primary Language Record.* ILEA Centre for Primary Language Education.

Bazalgette, C. (1988). '"They Changed the Picture in the Middle of the Fight": New Kinds of Literacy', in Meek, M. and Mills, C. (eds), *Language and Literacy in the Primary School.* Lewes: Falmer Press.

Beard, R. (1987). *Developing Reading 3–13.* London: Hodder & Stoughton.

Belsey, C. (1980). *Critical Practice.* London: Methuen.

Benton, M., (1992). *Secondary Worlds: Literature Teaching and the Visual Arts.* Buckingham: Open University Press.

Benton, M. and Fox, G. (1985). *Teaching Literature, Nine to Fourteen.* Oxford: OUP.

Benton, M., Teasey, J., Bell, R. and Hurst, K. (1988). *Young Readers Responding to Poems.* London: Routledge.

Bernstein, B. (1971). *Class, Codes and Control. Vol 1: Theoretical Studies towards a Sociology of Language.* London: Routledge & Kegan Paul.

Bleach, J. and Riley, S (1985). 'Developing and extending the literacy of bilingual pupils through the secondary years'. *English in Education*, 19, 3, pp. 28–40.

Bousted, M. (1989). 'Who talks?' *English in Education*, 23, 3, pp. 41–51.

Britton, J. (ed.) (1967). *Talking and Writing.* London: Methuen.

— (1970). *Language and Learning.* London: Allen Lane.

— (1982). *Prospect and Retrospect: Selected Essays of James Britton* (ed. G. Pradl). London: Heinemann.

Britton, J., Burgess, T., Martin, N., McLeod, A. and Rosen, H. (1975). *The Development of Writing Abilities, 11–18.* London: Macmillan.

Brown, R. (1973). *A First Language.* Harmondsworth: Penguin.

Brumfit, C., Ellis, R. and Levine, J. (1985). *ESL in the UK: Educational and Linguistic Perspectives.* ELT document 121. Oxford: Pergamon.

Bryant, M. and Bradley, L. (1985). *Children's Reading Problems.* Oxford: Basil Blackwell.

Buckingham, D. (ed.) (1990). *Watching Media Learning: Making Sense of Media Education.* London: Falmer.

Cameron, D. (1985). *Feminism and Linguistic Theory.* London: Macmillan.

Carter, R. (ed.) (1990). *Knowledge about Language and the Curriculum, The LINC Reader.* London: Hodder & Stoughton.

Cato, V. and Whetton, C. (1991). *An Enquiry into LEA Evidence on Standards of Reading of Seven-Year-Old Children.* Windsor: NFER.

Chall, J. (1967). *Learning to Read: The Great Debate* (2nd edition, 1983). New York: McGraw Hill.

Clark, M. (ed.) (1985). *New Directions in the Study of Reading.* Lewes: Falmer Press.

Clarke, J., Critcher, C. and Johnson, R. (eds) (1979). *Working Class Culture: Studies in History and Theory.* London: Hutchinson.

Clay, M. (1975). *What Did I Write?* Auckland, NZ: Heinemann.
— (1979a). *Reading: The Patterning of Complex Behaviour* (2nd edition). London: Heinemann Educational.
— (1979b). *The Early Detection of Reading Difficulties*. London: Heinemann Educational.
— (1982). *Observing Young Readers: Selected Papers*. Exeter, New Hampshire: Heinemann Educational.
Clegg, A. (1964). *The Excitement of Writing*. London: Chatto & Windus.
Corcoran, W. (1990). 'Reading, re-reading, resistance: versions of reader response', in Hayhoe, M. and Parker, S. (eds). *Reading and Response*. Buckingham: Open University Press.
Corcoran, W. and Evans, E. (eds). (1987). *Readers, Texts, Teachers*. Upper Montclair, NJ: Boynon/Cook.
Creber, J. P. (1965). *Sense and Sensitivity*. London: ULP.
Crystal, D. (1976). *Child Language, Learning and Linguistics*. London: Arnold.
Currie, W. (1973). *New Directions in Teaching English Language*. London: Longman.
Czerniewska, P. (1992). *Learning about Writing: The Early Years*. Oxford: Blackwell.
Derrick, J. (1966). *Teaching English to Immigrants*. London: Longman.
Derrida, J. (1976). *Of Grammatology* (trans. G. C. Spivak). Baltimore: Johns Hopkins University Press.
Dixon, J. (1967). *Growth through English*. Oxford: OUP.
— (1991). *A Schooling in 'English'*. Milton Keynes: Open University Press.
Dombey, H. (1992). 'Lessons Learnt at Bed-time', in Kimberley, K., Meek, M. and Miller, J. (eds), *New Readings: Contributions to an Understanding of Literacy*. London: A. & C. Black.
Doughty, P., Pearce, J. and Thornton, G. (1972). *Language in Use*. London: Arnold.
Eagleton, T. (1984). *Literary Theory*. Oxford: Blackwell.
Edwards, A. and Westgate, D.(1988). *Investigating Classroom Talk*. Lewes: Falmer Press.
Edwards, D. and Mercer, N. (1987). *Common Knowledge*. London: Methuen.
Fairclough, N. (1989). *Language and Power*. London: Longman.
Foucault, M. (1981). 'The Order of Discourse', in Young, R. (ed.), *Untying the Text: A Post-Structuralist Reader*. London: Routledge & Kegan Paul.
Fox, C. (1992). '"You Sing So Merry Those Tunes". Oral storytelling as a window on young children's language learning', in Kimberley, Meek, and Miller (eds), op. cit.
Fry, D. (1985). *Children Talk about Books: Seeing Themselves as Readers*. Milton Keynes: Open University Press.
Gannon, P. and Czerniewska, P. (1980). *Using Linguistics, An Educational Focus*. London: Arnold.
Goodman, K. S. (1982). *Language and Literacy: The Selected Writings of Kenneth S. Goodman* (ed. F. V. Gollasch), Vols. 1 and 2. London: Routledge & Kegan Paul.
Goody, J. and Watt, I. (1972). 'The Consequences of Literacy', in Giglioli, P. (ed.), *Language and Social Context*. Harmondsworth: Penguin.
Gregory, E. (1992). 'Learning codes and contexts: a psychosemiotic approach to beginning reading in school', in Kimberley, Meek, and Miller (eds.), op. cit.
Griffith, P. (1987). *Literary Theory and English Teaching*. Milton Keynes: Open University Press.
Hall, S., Hobson, D., Lowe, A. and Willis, P. (eds) (1980). *Culture, Media, Language*. London: Hutchinson.
Halliday, M. (1973). *Explorations in the Functions of Language*. London: Arnold.
— (1975). *Learning How to Mean*. London: Arnold.

— (1978). *Language as a Social Semiotic*. London: Arnold.
— (1985) *An Introduction to Functional Grammar*. London: Arnold.
Halliday, M., McIntosh, A. and Strevens, P. (1964). *The Linguistic Sciences and Language Teaching*. London: Arnold.
Hardcastle, J (1985). 'Classrooms as sites for cultural making', *English in Education*, 19, 3, pp. 8–22.
Harding, D.W. (1937). 'The Role of the Onlooker'. *Scrutiny*, Vl, (3), pp. 247–58.
— (1963). *Experience into Words*. London: Chatto & Windus.
Harpin, W. (1976). *The Second 'R'*. London: Allen & Unwin.
Hayhoe, M. and Parker, S. (1990). *Reading and Response*. Milton Keynes: Open University Press.
Heath, S. B. (1983). *Ways with Words*. Cambridge: CUP.
Hester, H. (1983.) *Stories in the Multilingual Primary School*, London: ILEA.
Hobsbawm, E. (1964). *Labouring Men*. London: Weidenfeld & Nicolson.
Hodge, R. and Kress, G. (1988). *Social Semiotics*. Cambridge: Polity Press.
Holbrook, D. (1961). *English for Maturity*. Cambridge: CUP.
Hourd, M. (1949). *The Education of the Poetic Spirit*. London: Heinemann.
Hymes, D. (1972). 'On communicative competence', in Pride J. B. and Holmes, J. (eds), *Sociolinguistics: Selected Readings*. Harmondsworth: Penguin.
— (1977). *Foundations in Sociolinguistics: an Ethnographic Approach*. London: Tavistock.
Jackson, D. (1987). *Continuity in Secondary English*. London: Methuen.
Jones, K (ed.) (1992). *English and the National Curriculum: Cox's Revolution*. Bedford Way Papers. London: Kogan Page, in association with the Institute of Education, University of London.
Kinneavy, J. (1971). *A Theory of Discourse*. New York: Prentice Hall.
Kress, G. (1982). *Learning to Write*. London: Routledge & Kegan Paul.
Labov, W. (1972). *Language in the Inner City: Studies in the Black English Vernacular*. Philadelphia: University of Philadelphia Press.
Langer, S. (1954). *Philosophy on a New Key*. Cambridge, MA: Harvard University Press.
Leavis, F. R. (1930). *Mass Civilisation and Minority Culture*. Cambridge: CUP.
Leavis, F. R. and Thompson, D. (1933). *Culture and Environment*. London: Chatto & Windus.
Leith, Dick (1983). *A Social History of English*. London: Routledge & Kegan Paul.
Levine, J. (ed.) (1990). *Bilingual Learners and the Mainstream Curriculum*. London: Falmer.
Levine, J., with Hester, H. and Skirrow, G. (1972). *Scope: Stage 2*. London: Longman, for the Schools Council.
Linguistic Minorities Project (1985.) *The Other Languages of England*. London: Routledge.
Lunzer, E. and Gardner, K. (eds) (1979). *The Effective Use of Reading*. London: Heinemann/Schools Council.
Lunzer, E and Gardner, K. (1984). *Learning from the Written Word*. Edinburgh: Oliver & Boyd.
MacCabe, C. (ed.) (1986). *Futures for English*. Manchester: Manchester University Press.
Mackay, D., Thompson, B. and Schams, P. (1970). *Breakthrough to Literacy*. London: Longman/Schools Council.
Marenbon, J. (1987). *English Our English*. London: Centre for Policy Studies.
Martin, N. (1983). *Mostly about Writing*. New Jersey: Heinemann.
Martin, N., D'Arcy, P., Newton, B. and Parker, R. (1976). *Writing and Learning Across the Curriculum*. London: Ward Lock.

Maybin, J. (1991). 'Children's informal talk and the construction of meaning', *English in Education*, 25, 2, pp. 34–49.

Maybin, J., Mercer, N. and Stierer, B. (1992). '"Scaffolding" Learning in the Classroom', in Norman, K. (ed.), *Thinking Voices*. London: Hodder & Stoughton.

McRobbie, A. and Mica Nava (eds) (1984). *Gender and Generation*. London: Macmillan.

Medway, P. (1980). *Finding a Language*. London: Writers and Readers.

Meek, M. (1982). *Learning to Read*. London: The Bodley Head.

— (1988) *How Texts Teach What Readers Learn*. Stroud: Thimble Press.

Meek, M., Warlow, A. and Barton, G. (eds) (1977). *The Cool Web*. Oxford: The Bodley Head.

Meek, M. with Armstrong, S., Austerfield, V., Graham, J. and Plackett, E. (1983). *Achieving Literacy: Longitudinal Case Studies of Adolescents Learning To Read*. London: Routledge & Kegan Paul.

Mercer, N. (ed.) (1981). *Language in School and Community*. London: Edward Arnold.

Miller, J. (1983). *Many Voices. Bilingualism, Culture and Education*. London: Routledge & Kegan Paul.

— (ed.) (1984). *Eccentric Propositions. Essays on Literature and the Curriculum*. London: Routledge & Kegan Paul.

— (1986). *Women Writing about Men*. London: Virago.

— (1991). *Seductions. Studies in Reading and Culture*. London: Virago.

Milroy, J. and Milroy, M. (1985). *Authority in Language: Investigating Language Prescription and Standardisation*. London: Routledge & Kegan Paul.

Minns, H. (1990). *Read it to me Now!* London: Virago.

Moffett, J. (1968). *Teaching the Universe of Discourse*. Boston: Houghton-Mifflin.

Morris, J. M. (1966). *Standards in Reading*. London: NFER.

Moss, G. (1989). *Un/popular Fictions*. London: Virago.

Muller, H. J. (1967). *The Uses of English*. New York: Holt, Rinehart & Winston.

National Writing Project (1989–1990). *Issues from the National Writing Project*. London: Nelson. (See booklets published in this series).

Norman, Kate (ed.) (1992). *Thinking Voices, The Work of the National Oracy Project*. London: Hodder & Stoughton.

Oakhill, J. and Garnham, A. (1988). *Becoming a Skilled Reader*. Oxford: Basil Blackwell.

Perera, K. (1984). *Children's Writing and Reading*. Oxford: Blackwell.

Protherough, R. (1983). *Developing Response to Fiction*. Milton Keynes: Open University Press.

— (1986) *Teaching Literature for Examinations*. Milton Keynes: Open University Press.

Pym, D. (1956). *Free Writing*. London: ULP.

Reed, M., Webster, A. and Beveridge, M. (1995). 'The Conceptual Basis for a Literacy Curriculum', in Owen, P. and Pumphrey, P. (eds), *Children Learning to Read: International Concerns, Vol.1. Emergent and Devleoping Readings: Messages for Teachers*. London: Falmer Press.

Richards, I. A. (1929). *Practical Criticism*. London: Routledge.

Richmond, J. (ed.) (1982). *Becoming Our Own Experts: Studies in Language and Learning made by the Talk Workshop Group at Vauxhall Manor School*. London: ILEA English Centre.

Rosen, C. and Rosen, H. (1973). *The Language of Primary School Children*. Harmondsworth: Penguin.

Rosen, H. (1972). *Language and Class*. Bristol: Falling Wall Press.

— (1982). *The Language Monitors: A Critique of the APU's Primary Survey Report 'Language Performance in Schools'*. Bedford Way Papers, University of London Institute of Education.

Rosen, H. and Burgess, T. (1980). *The Languages and Dialects of London Schoolchildren*. London: Ward Lock.

Rosenblatt, L. (1938). *Literature as Exploration*. New York: Modern Language Association.

— (1978). *The Reader, The Text, The Poem: The Transactional Theory of the Literary Work*. Carbondale, IL: Southern Illinois University Press.

Sarland, C. (1992). *Young People Reading*. Buckingham: Open University Press.

Scafe, S. (1989). *Teaching Black Literature*. London: Virago.

Sinclair, J. and Coulthard, M. (1975). *Towards an Analysis of Discourse: The Language of Teachers and Pupils*. London: Oxford University Press.

Smith, F. (1972). *Understanding Reading*. New York: Holt, Rinehart & Winston.

— (1982). *Writing and the Writer*. London: Heinemann.

Southgate, V. *et al.* (1981). *Extending Beginning Reading.* London: Heinemann Educational, for the Schools Council.

Start, K. B. and Wells, B. K. (1972). *The Trend of Reading Standards*. Windsor: NFER.

Stibbs, A. (1992). *Reading Narrative as Literature: Signs of Life*. Buckingham: Open University Press.

Street, B. (1984). *Literacy in Theory and Practice*. Cambridge: CUP.

Stubbs, M. (1987). *Educational Linguistics*. Oxford: Blackwell.

— (1976). *Language, Schools and Classrooms*. London: Routledge & Kegan Paul.

Swann, J. and Graddol, D. (1988). 'Gender inequalities in classroom talk', *English in Education*, 22, 1, pp. 48–65.

Thompson, E. P. (1963). *The Making of the English Working Class*. London: Victor Gollancz (Pelican Books edition, 1968).

Torbe, M. (ed.) (1980). *Language Policies in Action*. London: Ward Lock.

Trudgill, P. (1974). *Sociolinguistics: An Introduction*. Harmondsworth: Penguin.

Turner, M. (1990). *Sponsored Reading Failure*. Warlingham: Education Unit.

Turvey, A. (1992). 'Interrupting the lecture: "Cox" seen from a classroom', in Jones, K. (ed.), *English and the National Curriculum*. op. cit.

Van Dijk, T. (ed.) (1985). *Handbook of Discourse Analysis,* 4 Vols. London: Academic Press.

Vygotsky, L. (1986). *Thought and Language* (ed. Kozulin, L). Cambridge, MA: Harvard University Press.

Wells, G. (1994) 'The Complimentary Contributions of Halliday and Vygotsky to a "Language-Based Theory of Learning"', *Linguistics and Education*, 6, 1, pp. 41–90.

Wertsch, J. V. (1985). *Vygotsky and the Social Formation of Mind*. Cambridge, MA: Harvard University Press.

Whitehead, F. (1966). *The Disappearing Dais*. London: Chatto.

Whitehead, F, Capey, A. C. and Maddren, W. (1974). *Children's Reading Interests*. London: The Schools Council.

Widdowson, Peter (ed.) (1982). *Re-Reading English: Essays on Literature and Criticism in Higher Education*. London: Methuen.

Wilkinson, A. (1965). *Spoken English*, Educational Review Occasional Publications No. 2. Birmingham: University of Birmingham School of Education.

— (1971). *The Foundations of Language*. Oxford: OUP.

— (1987). *The Writing of Writing*. Milton Keynes: Open University Press.

Williams, R. (1963). *The Long Revolution*. Harmondsworth: Penguin.

— (1980). *Problems in Materialism and Culture. Selected Essays*. London: Verso.

REPORTS

1921: *The Teaching of English in England* (The Newbolt Report). HMSO.
1954: *Language*. HMSO.
1959: *15–18* (The Crowther Report). HMSO.
1963: *Secondary School Examination Council: Final Report*. HMSO.
1964: *Half Our Future* (The Newsom Report). HMSO.
1965: *Working Paper No.3: English*. Schools Council. HMSO.
1975: *A Language for Life* (The Bullock Report). HMSO.
1984: *Education for All* (The Swann Report). HMSO.
1985: *English 5–16*. HMSO.
1987: *Report of the Task Group on Assessment and Testing* (The TGAT Report). HMSO.
1988: *Report of the Committee of Inquiry into the Teaching of English Language* (The Kingman Report). HMSO.
1989: *English from 5–16, Report of the English Working Party* (The Cox Report). HMSO.
1990: *The Teaching and Learning of Reading in Primary Schools: A Report by HMI*. DES.
1992: *The Teaching and Learning of Reading in Primary Schools 1991*. DES.
1995: *English in the National Curriculum*. SCAA.

4

MUSIC

Piers Spencer

INTRODUCTION

> Standard Five girls were having a singing lesson, just finishing the lah-me-doh la exercises and beginning a sweet children's song'. Anything more unlike song, spontaneous song, would be impossible to imagine: a strange bawling yell that followed the outlines of a tune. It was not like savages: savages have subtle rhythms. It was not like animals: animals *mean* something when they yell. It was like nothing on earth, and it was called singing...What could possibly become of such a people, a people in whom the intuitive faculty was dead as nails...? (D. H. Lawrence, 1928, p. 158).

It would seem that music in schools has been in trouble for longer than most of us remember. However, it was not until the 1960s that statistics became available to confirm Lawrence's bleak snapshot of the failure of school music to awaken the 'intuitive faculty'. The Newsom Report (DES, 1963) and *Enquiry 1, Young School Leavers* (Schools Council, 1968) painted a devastating picture of music's low status in the curriculum and poor esteem in the eyes (and ears) of secondary pupils. The Plowden Report (DES, 1967) found a shortage of expertise among primary teachers. This had led to the subject 'lagging behind' as a stimulus for creative work compared with observed achievements in art, dance and drama. Further surveys (Witkin, 1974, Schools Council, 1975) confirmed these findings and highlighted music's isolation within the curriculum. There were two areas of tangible success. One was the excellence of bands, orchestras and choirs in many schools. The other was the development of instrumental teaching in local education authorities (LEAs) which had led to the formation of high-quality youth orchestras. These involved only a minority of talented youngsters who pursued ensemble activities outside the timetable. In the eyes of the general public, local politicians, the press and, above all, parents, a school or LEA that was 'good for music' meant one that had the resources and the management skills to deliver instrumental teaching and high-profile performing activities rather than one that paid attention to the quality of day-to-day classroom music.

After briefly setting a context for the survey, the writer gives an account of curriculum initiatives since the 1960s and emphasises a significant new development in music education research: evaluative accounts of pupils' classroom achievements, particularly in composing. The significance of black American styles (jazz and rock) is highlighted, as is the contribution research into these has made to the understanding of musical teaching and learning processes. Sections on primary education and on the role of LEAs are followed by an account of the contributions that the social sciences have, directly or indirectly, made to the field. Finally, following two major curriculum developments: the General Certificate of Secondary Education (GCSE) and the National Curriculum, the writer looks at the state of music education in the mid-1990s and suggests four possible areas for future research. Although it deals mainly with schools and LEAs, the chapter does touch upon some recent innovations in conservatoires and universities.

THE CONTEXT

In the background to its failure as a school subject lay a crisis within music itself:

> We are no longer, have long ceased to be in fact, an aural society, one which communicates mainly by hearing. Our entire system of values, of the things we accept to be true, is based on the visual sense (Stockhausen, 1989, p. 25).

There is a certain irony in the fact that Stockhausen's words come from a composer whose music lay at the heart of another controversy: the freezing of the concert repertoire and the failure of most 'serious' composers since 1920 to find favour with the public. Classical music has become increasingly dominated by the performance of a repertoire reflecting a nostalgia for the past rather than celebrating the achievements of the present. Small (1987, p. 343) saw this as a crisis resulting from four disjunctions:

> between creator and performer, between producer and consumer, between classical and vernacular traditions and between composer and potential audience (the last I believe to be a consequence of the other three).

These were clearly present in music education in the 1960s. The disjunction between producer and consumer was reflected in the fact that lessons often consisted of information about music, rather than experience of it. 'Music appreciation' largely aimed to train an informed but passive audience rather than to make people musically responsive through actually working with sounds. Brace (1970) showed that in secondary schools music *making* tended to take place mostly outside the classroom, during voluntary, extra-curricular rehearsals directed by teachers. The disjunction between creator and performer meant that the idea of encouraging pupils to compose or even improvise their own music was quite alien to the training of most music teachers.

The other disjunctions, between composer and audience and between the classical and the vernacular, were largely the consequences of the development of modernism. A hundred years ago, the salon waltzes of Scott Joplin and the late piano intermezzi of Brahms could be said to share a common language. This could no longer be said of the relationship between pop and the music of 'serious' composers of the 1960s.

Bunting (1977) pointed out that an individual's musical development depends on a healthy equilibrium between the *vernacular* – the absorption and use of a 'common language' of music, which in the West depends on tonal harmony and periodic rhythm and the *speculative*, which Paynter (1977, p. 10) called 'the unprejudiced acceptance of sound as the basic material of music'. The disjunction between the vernacular and the speculative became wider after 1945, with composers of the European and American *avant garde* becoming entirely preoccupied with the latter. They seemed to regard progress in composition as the exploration of sounds in an autonomous and abstract system of relationships having little affinity with the common experience of music. Music's traditional function of binding communities together with a sharing of emotions and a reinforcement of identity had little significance for the work of these composers. On the other hand, the tonal-harmonic vernacular was maintained and enriched within the black American tradition: the music of jazz and its derivatives including pop and rock. Despised as 'commercial' by the *avant garde* (many of whom, it has to be said, subsisted on fat grants from the state), these styles never lost touch with music's social function. Since the late 1960s, many composers (including even Stockhausen himself) have, in differing ways, returned to tonality and now see progress in music as including, rather than excluding, the natural listening habits of a majority. For three-quarters of the century, music historians had assumed that it was the modernist composers who were the natural heirs of the 'great tradition'. Today, such confidence seems misplaced. There are still critically acclaimed pieces composed in the first decade of the century that have yet to find favour with audiences in the last. The possibility is dawning that the idioms and performing practices of black American musicians have made a more significant contribution to the development of music world-wide than the modernists and that it is these styles, rather than those of the post-war *avant garde,* that will survive, loved by audiences and respected by historians, into the millennium.

THE NEW CURRICULUM IMPETUS OF THE LATE 1960s
AND EARLY 1970s

However, that was not how people involved at the forefront of music education saw things at the end of the 1960s. Just as Herbert Read (1943) (developments in music always seem to lag behind those in art) had seen modernism in art as a natural ally of progressivism in education, composer-educators in England and Canada were beginning to use the idioms of the *avant garde* as a basis for their classroom practice. They saw audience alienation from contemporary 'serious' music and pupil alienation from classroom music as problems that could be solved together. They conveniently forgot the contempt for ordinary people expressed by the Godfather of modernism, Arnold Schoenberg (1946, p. 124): 'If it is art, it is not for all, and if it is for all, it is not art.'

Read's approach found kinship in the work of the composer-educator Peter Maxwell Davies in the early 1960s. The compositions of some of Davies' senior pupils at Cirencester Grammar school (heard on the recording supporting Davies, 1962) were clearly influenced by their teacher's interests and preoccupations. However, Davies (1962, p. 109), always stressed the importance of the tonal-harmonic vernacular as a starting-point, calling this 'the common denominator of experience and communication'.

The work of Self (1967) and Dennis (1970) marked a more radical departure from the vernacular. The aim stated on the first page of Dennis's book was to introduce pupils to 'truly modern music'. What was presented, however, was a ring-fenced idiom that forbade as much as it allowed. The use of a regular pulse, triadic harmonies and diatonic scales was discouraged for the reason that they trained 'for the past and for pop music' (Self, 1967, p. 2). Dennis's title *Experimental Music in Schools* inevitably provokes the question: for whom is this an experiment? For the children being taught, or for the adults who are keen to promote a style that sounds 'experimental'? Children's compositions that explore diatonic tonality (and the evidence of work collected over a period of 20 years indicates that many more choose to compose in this way) may be just as experimental for the pupils concerned as those whose explorations take them closer to the preoccupations of the *avant garde.* It is to their credit, however, that the work of Self and Dennis and the Canadian Murray Schafer (1975), placed composition for the first time at the heart of the classroom agenda.

The most powerful advocacy for composing as integral to the general curriculum came from Paynter and Aston (1970). Here was a more balanced view of what counted as musical creativity. This seminal book, originally entitled *Sound and Silence*, and recently republished in a revised form as *Sound and Structure* (Paynter, 1991), saw the experience of music from both the teacher's *and* learner's points of view. They valued the vernacular vocal harmonies improvised by a group of teenagers singing a traditional song round a camp fire as much as they appreciated the speculative approach of a pair of students exploring the sonorities in a piano frame. Paynter and Aston grasped the nature of empirical musical encounters and understood that teachers and textbooks often rationalise musical experience by introducing alien-sounding terminology for musical phenomena which children have absorbed and understood quite intuitively:

> None of the children has heard of a dominant seventh or a perfect cadence and most of them cannot read music: yet they are responding to the harmonic implications of the melody by improvising other parts around it....
>
> They will not have been *taught* anything: can we say how much music they will have learned? (Paynter and Aston, 1970, p. 1).

'Creative' music was not a new idea. The systematic teaching schemes of Kodály and Orff encouraged children to improvise. But *Sound and Silence* struck a new note. It did not propose a new 'method' as much as aim to change the hearts and minds of teachers. The most significant aspect of this inspiring book was the research findings it conveyed. The close and sympathetic analysis of pupil compositions that occurred throughout was, at the time, new to music education. Writers about children's work in the other arts, such as Read (1943) and Holbrook (1967), had drawn attention to the fact that it was possible and indeed necessary to write in this way about children's work.

RESEARCH INTO PUPILS' ACHIEVEMENT

Analysis and evaluation of children's compositions have, in the writer's view, made the most important contribution to research in music education in the past 20 years. However, their contribution also stands in danger of being the most undervalued, owing to the lack of a suitable published format in which to present musical work. This is a particular weakness of the presentation of research that considers the arts generically. A recent book on assessment in the arts (Ross *et al.*, 1993) focuses on 'assessment dialogues' between teachers and pupils. The text features examples of children's writing and reproductions of their art work. However, it is difficult to gauge the appropriateness of the discussions of the musical work as the reader has no way of knowing what it sounds like.

Since Paynter and Aston (1970) produced an LP record of compositions to accompany *Sound and Silence*, a number of analytical and evaluative accounts have been produced with supporting recorded illustrations and sometimes notated transcriptions. Spencer (1976) gives a detailed analysis of the song-writing progress of a 15-year-old pupil who started by imitating stock harmonic and melodic patterns, but who gradually developed a distinctive expressive style of his own. Bunting (1987 and 1988) gave similar analyses of the gradual development of composing fluency and confidence with the handling of sound materials by individual pupils. Loane (1984) dealt with the symbolic processes at work in children's compositions and showed that the 'process of skill learning and the act of musical education are closely connected, even in some senses, identical'. Davies (1986 and 1992) looked closely at songs composed by children aged five to seven and showed how very young children acquire a sense of structure and pattern in articulating their musical thoughts. A substantial investigation by Swanwick and Tillman (1986) constructed a theory of musical development based on Bunting's (1977) ideas about a 'common language' of music. Swanwick and Tillman found that as children grew up, the musical preoccupations revealed in their compositions changed and developed in a predictable pattern. These findings have echoes in observations of children's work in the visual arts made by Richardson (1948) and Plaskow (1964).

POPULAR MUSIC IN SCHOOLS

The 'progressive' educational climate of the 1960s was originally hostile to pop music. Schafer (1975, p. 4) saw pop as a 'social more than a musical phenomenon and ... therefore unsuitable as an abstract study, which music must always be if it is to remain an art and a science in its own right'. However, musicians and social scientists were increasingly to challenge the notion of music as an autonomous sphere unrelated to social context.

Swanwick (1968) made a thoughtful analysis of the black American tradition and the reasons that jazz and the popular styles derived from it have had such a potent and lasting appeal to young people since the beginning of the century. However, it was not until the mid-1970s that a substantial publication appeared (Vulliamy and Lee, 1976) suggesting practical approaches and supported by evidence of pupils' achievements in pop and related styles. The work of Vulliamy and Lee and later research by Spencer (1982) presented and analysed learning processes of pupils engaged in making music in black styles such as rock, blues and reggae. They demonstrated that the distinctive features of this music-making tradition, a tradition that did not readily separate the act of composing from the act of performing, offered unique opportunities for the development of worthwhile practical skills and useful musical insights. It was not the 'popularity' of pop that these writers regarded as significant, but its potential for inventive and expressive work in music for a large number of pupils who might have otherwise rejected the subject.

MUSIC IN PRIMARY SCHOOLS

A major difficulty for pupils and teachers lay in the lack of co-ordination and alignment between the different phases of education. The wide disparity between GCSE and A-level has proved irksome for both students and teachers (Spencer, 1993, p. 83). However, the discontinuity between primary and secondary schooling had the most widespread negative impact on progress. Here the vicious circle created by Western élitism could be seen to be operating in its most damaging manifestation. Students training to be generalist primary teachers had been so alienated by their experience of music as pupils that few wished to teach the subject. This reluctance resulted in very patchy provision for music in primary schools (Mills, 1989). The National Curriculum Music Working Group (1991, p. 5) pointed out that observations by HMI in primary schools during the 1980s had shown that 'the least well developed aspect of the work seen was composing'. One possible solution was to train musically confident primary teachers to act as 'consultants', sharing and disseminating their expertise among colleagues and aiming to conquer the 'fear of music' that so many of them had (Kemp, 1984.) In her accounts of early developments of the primary consultancy scheme, Allen (1988 and 1989) found that there needed to be a two-way process, with the success of the consultant depending crucially on the support given by heads and colleagues in facilitating the dissemination of music teaching skills. More recent research by Lawson *et al.* (1994) found that the decline in mutual support networks and help in the form of LEA-based in-service training was hindering the full implementation of the National Curriculum in primary schools.

THE ROLE OF LOCAL EDUCATION AUTHORITIES

The most striking success story in music education was the significant role of LEAs and their advisers in the promotion of borough or county-wide activities. According to the Bullock Report (DES, 1975, p. 238), in the early 1970s there were nationally more advisers for music than for any other subject, apart from physical education. However, it was not until the late 1980s that researchers started to survey the musical work of LEAs. Cleave and Dust (1989) found many authorities lacking in clear statements about their instrumental policies and called for a greater involvement of instrumental teachers in the day-to-day work of classrooms.

Despite excellent performances and prestigious tours organised by LEAs over the years, the privilege of free instrumental teaching was confined to a few, often less than 10 per cent of the school population. The National Curriculum Music Working Group (1991, p. 55) also pointed out that 'twice as many girls as boys learn instruments, and the proportions are yet more out of balance in woodwind and strings. So it may be that the opening up of a lifetime's enjoyment of music is being denied to many boys in particular'. The range of instruments available for loan and tuition also tended to reflect the make-up of concert bands and symphony orchestras rather than the wishes of parents and pupils. Cleave and Dust (1989, p. 45) showed that all LEAs lent bassoons and provided bassoon teaching to preserve the orchestral tradition. However, only one third of the 93 authorities surveyed provided tuition in instruments and styles that would have proved more popular, such as the electric guitar. Witkin (1974, p. 128) conveys the exasperation and frustration of a teacher overwhelmed with requests for folk guitar lessons. She sees the LEA adviser as 'a man who wants an élitist society of musicians and what about the majority? – just let 'em go! – How can you let 'em go when they're burning to play?'

The government implemented the policy of Local Management of Schools in 1990. Budgets previously held centrally were devolved to schools, with the result that many LEAs were no longer able to fund and administer music services. However, the most recent research (Sharp, 1991, and Coopers and Lybrand, 1994) points to a continuing rise in the numbers learning instruments. The much feared decline has not yet started to happen, despite the fact that parents now pay both for the tuition and for the instruments. The independent agencies that replaced LEA-run services now have to sell their instrumental teaching schemes to schools. This means having to do market research into exactly what schools, parents and pupils really want. As a consequence, there may in future be a closer matching of supply to need than in the past. But the divide between the classroom and the extra-curricular remains, and its impact on music education as a whole remain damaging and negative. Pupils not selected for instrumental training, or whose parents cannot afford the commitment now that schools are charging, will feel excluded from what many perceive, rightly or wrongly, as the mainstream of musical activity, with its emphasis on the development of skills including, not least, the learning of notation. They will inevitably perceive the music teacher as an agent promoting inequality.

MUSIC AND SOCIETY

Music is primarily a commodity for consumption, and most people do not have the talents required to perform or compose it. This attitude is prevalent in Western industrialised countries. The mass media have turned music of all styles into a passive recreation – to be taken in without being listened to, heard without really being experienced. Benjamin Britten (1964, p. 20) once condemned the loudspeaker as 'the principal enemy of music'. The stagnated classical concert repertoire is as much a product of western industrialised society as muzak or the standard commercial dissemination of pop.

Some relevant insights have come from musicians (Small, 1977), anthropologists (Blacking, 1976) and from sociologists (Vulliamy and Shepherd, 1984). They point to the very different notions of 'musicality' in societies and cultures less industrialised than our own. Mills (1991, p. 102) describes some New Zealand research about singing where children from ethnic Polynesian backgrounds showed greater confidence and accuracy of pitching than their white counterparts. Clearly music-making was very much alive and seen both as important and as something everyone could do within the families and the culture of the close-knit communities of these children:

> Singing is an integral part of Polynesian culture...Children of European ethnic background, on the other hand, often arrive at school with little background in singing. Consequently, the educational needs of the two groups differ. The European children often need systematic help, whereas the Polynesian children just need practice.

It might be argued that the absence of 'system' was the key to the success of the Polynesians. Their evident musicality is surely something that has been 'caught' rather than 'taught'. To recall Paynter and Aston again (1970, p. 2) 'They will not have been *taught* anything: can we say how much music they will have learned?'

The emphasis on intensive teaching characterises the Western conservatoire system that has trained many specialists working in schools. Sloboda (1994, p. 167) concludes a survey of the development of 'classically' trained instrumentalists with the observation that 'Musical learning is sustained primarily through a constructed environment in which practice levels may be increased and sustained.' However, he realises that this is not the only route to musical achievement:

> Finally, it is necessary to point out that there exist many cultures, especially traditional non-Western cultures, where the spread of musical accomplishment in the population is much more even than it is in modern Western culture. In

such cultures, participation in musical activity is often more rooted in the whole life and work of society, rather than being something separate (Blacking, 1976). In the long view it may turn out to be modern western society that is unusual in its capacity to inhibit musical development in all but a small minority. Rather than looking within a small number of individuals for signs of genetic superiority in 'musicality', we may need to look more closely at the way our culture operates to inhibit the majority of people form becoming the fully expressive musical performers that they could be.

The sustained periods of isolated practice that conservatoire students undertake can take a toll of their personal lives. They often prevent students from reflecting on what music is *for*. The conservatoire (the word itself has overtones both of tradition and of the hothouse) often isolates them from the very people with whom they should be learning to communicate. Kushner (1985) and Renshaw (1986) have produced fascinating reports on efforts to overcome these tendencies among music students. The 'Music Performance and Communication Skills Project' at the Guildhall School of Music and Drama in London has sought to encourage students to share their skills with a range of people in special schools, hospitals prisons and community centres:

> The project works from within the teaching programme of the [Guildhall] school and has among its aims to turn the face of élite music education to a wider public than the conservatoire would otherwise meet (Kushner, 1986, p.1).

PSYCHOLOGY AND EAR TRAINING

During the 1980s, some college lecturers began to question the content of the purely musical parts of conservatoire and university courses. At the same time, psychologists and musicians interested in each others' disciplines were starting to probe assumptions about the nature of musical perception and its relationship to what was traditionally known as 'ear training'. Such questions originally arose out of psychologists' interest in the problems associated with audience alienation from modernism in music. Lerdahl (1988) and Sergeant (1994) found that the pitch patterns defined by serial composers were not readily perceptible, even by trained musicians. However, Gotlieb and Konecni (1985) showed that the mismatch between what musicians defined as structurally significant and what people actually perceived (and more importantly, enjoyed) when they listened extended to a more familiar repertoire. Cook (1990) found that seemingly everyday concepts such as the notion of a piece being 'in C major' were, on close examination, problematic. The received notion that listeners, consciously or intuitively, hear every sound as relating to and somehow aiming purposefully towards the goal of an ending in the 'home' key did not stand up to experimental verification. Cook's findings have implications for music theory as they challenge many of the claims of musical analysis as having psychological validity. They also have implications for education, from university degree courses, through the whole 'set works' industry of GCSE and A-level to what the American composer Virgil Thompson once sourly called the 'appreciation-racket'.

Another assumption ripe for challenging was that *pitch* was the touchstone of musical aptitude. In the 1960s, following the work of Seashore (1938), there was much preoccupation with the measurement of musical abilities. Bentley (1967) and, later, Mills (1988) devised ingenious batteries of tests for this purpose. These testing strategies took no account of people's aesthetic responses, or of the possession of an aural imagination as opposed to aural accuracy in responding to specific test items. The model for their *modus operandi* was the sterile approach of 'ear training'. Cook (1994, p. 67) has been highly critical of this:

> Such training – called ear training, aural training or aural analysis – creates the interface between musical sound and the theoretical knowledge in terms of which musicians create, notate and reproduce music. So we have a lot of psychological studies of ear training. The trouble is that they are not called studies of ear training. They are called studies of musical listening. And as such they are thoroughly unsatisfactory, because they begin with the premise that people hear in terms of music-theoretical categories. They assume what music theory assumes; that music is made out of notes.

Another challenge to conventional notions of ear training came from Pratt (1990), who pointed out that in the past 'aural testing' served only to alienate rather than support students' learning as it tended to concentrate on the easily assessable, rather than musically useful. Pratt's project, known as Research into Applied Musical Perception (RAMP), was conducted with students at the University of Huddersfield. It extended the scope of aural training into areas that, while less amenable to testing, relate more usefully to what musicians do (or indeed, ought to do) in their daily work as performers and composers: 'vocal and instrumental tessitura, the density and distribution of sounds within musical textures, timbre, dynamics, articulation and phrasing, the location of sounds, and, above all, the variations in pace at which all these elements may occur'.

Like Cook, Pratt is trying to acknowledge a more holistic mode of listening, one that is truer to the experience of making or listening to music. Both writers emphasise that a truly musical engagement often lies outside rationalised frameworks, such as notation, which musicians construct for their own convenience. For example, it is the use of rhythmic *rubato* and the tiny adjustments in intonation singers and players make according to harmonic context that breathe expressive life into performing and give it its essentially aesthetic quality.

The psychology of music has developed rapidly in recent years and is now a much livelier field of enquiry. Sloboda (1985) and Hargreaves (1986) have contributed useful surveys of recent developments.

THE GCSE AND THE NATIONAL CURRICULUM

It was not until 1985 that the outcomes of innovation and research finally had an opportunity to influence the formal framework for the curriculum. In that year, the government published criteria for the GCSE. The proposals for music were among the most radical, using an epistemological model proposed by Swanwick (1979) that placed listening, performing and composing into the mainstream of musical activity for the first time. This seemingly self-evident 'common core' is also the foundation for the Attainment Target structure of the National Curriculum.

The National Curriculum Music Working Group (1991) based their proposals for attainment targets and programmes of study on established good principles and reported good practice. The group produced an imaginative scheme, ambitious in scope and demanding of teacher expertise. Like nearly every other subject, their 'interim report' aroused a fair share of controversy. What most distressed the teachers and educationists who had worked for over 20 years to widen the scope of the classroom was the enduring belief among politicians and their advisers that the main aim should be to educate a consumer society *about*, rather than getting children to know and understand, music through making it:

> Hence, the disparagement of the so-called 'passive' appreciation of music and the arts, which we saw in the controversy over the music curriculum; as if the human spirit were somehow more actively engaged in a child's participation in a school rock band than in the same child closely and silently attending to a performance of a Beethoven quartet (O'Hear, 1993, p. 54).

O'Hear does not explain how 'closely and silently attending' to music is to be assessed. Like the other critics who attacked the proposals, he offers no evidence from either the work of teachers or the achievement of pupils to support his case.

The story of how the National Curriculum Council rewrote the Working Group's proposals (1992) at the behest of these advisers and of the extraordinary protest that this drew from many distinguished musicians is well-documented in Graham (1993, pp. 75–82) and Swanwick (1993). The 'final' National Curriculum Order for music (DES, 1992) was an uneasy compromise between the views of the teaching and music professions and of government advisers from groups such as the Centre for Policy Studies. Despite their brevity, the further revisions following Sir Ron Dearing's review (DFE, 1995) are truer to the spirit of the original proposals.

MUSIC EDUCATION IN THE 1990s

We now know and understand a great deal more about music education than we did back in the 1960s. We know much more about how children develop musically. We know that they can compose as well as perform and a growing body of research supports this claim. There is clearer thinking about the possible structure and mode of delivery of the curriculum. Anthropologists and sociologists have delivered healthy challenges to notions of what counts as 'musical' and the subject has widened its repertoire to embrace different styles and cultures. New technologies have had their impact on music as they have affected every other subject. By the end of the 1980s, most secondary departments possessed a minimum of electronic hardware and software. This was in stark contrast to the way many of them were equipped at the start of that decade. A diversification of extra-curricular activities was also apparent, with instruments reflecting a growing range of musical cultures increasingly in evidence.

The GCSE has emphasised course work and practical achievement. Teachers, examiners and psychologists intending to investigate and develop aural perception have increasingly drawn materials from the living repertoire rather than from musically impoverished exercises artificially designed for testing purposes. The reduced curriculum (DFE, 1995) contains a manageable basis for teachers to teach and for pupils to learn.

With all these reforms and new approaches, one would expect music to have shown a dramatic improvement particularly in popularity among pupils. Yet recent surveys (Frances, 1987 and Hannam, 1993) still show the subject in secondary schools at the bottom of the league:

> There is no evidence I am aware of that recent changes in music education – e.g., the stress upon practical, creative work and the new attachment to composition – have done anything to remove the stigma visited upon music teachers twenty years ago, that, of all subjects in the secondary school curriculum, music was the most boring and the most useless (Ross, 1992, p. 174).

Hannam (1993) re-ran the 'Arts in the Adolescent' survey of pupil attitudes to school subjects and came out with virtually identical findings about the status of music:

The similarity of the relative rejection of Music is especially depressing...
because certainly three out of the five departments concerned were doing their
best to be practical and progressive in their practice...Sadly music once again
takes on the profile of a 'failed art' recorded in Witkin (1974) with as many as
30% finding nothing interesting in the lessons and feeling that they have
learned nothing of importance to them, while over 40% complain of
'boredom'. Expressions of negativity were a quantum leap higher for music
compared to the other subjects, the boredom factor rising to over 60% for the
boys in three of the schools (Hannam, 1993, pp. 100–1).

One reason for these disappointing outcomes may lie in the fact that
reforms in music came too late to catch the current of progressivism that
dominated the rest of the curriculum in the 1960s and early 1970s. During
the next decade, a mood of disillusion had set in:

> Culture and education during the past two decades have been typical in their
> having been in stress. But these twenty years have also been unusual in the
> degree and severity of tension caused by a remarkably wide swing between
> tradition and change. The irony of the situation is the fact that the direction of
> this stunning change has been toward tradition, beginning with a 10-year
> period of great innovation starting some 20 years ago, and ending with a
> conservative revolt in which we find ourselves today. The disjunctions caused
> by this change are no less powerful for having come from a reversal of
> direction, the new traditionalism and the older progressivism crashing against
> each other in waves of controversy (Reimer, 1982, p. 42).

Reimer's image of 'crashing waves' is particularly apt for music.
Developments in the subject have always tended to 'lag behind' those in the
other arts. The creative music momentum was gathering steam in the early
1980s, particularly through the in-service dissemination work of the Schools
Council Project *Music in the Secondary School Curriculum* (Paynter, 1982).
However, at the same time, theorists who took a generic view of the arts were
beginning to question notions such as 'creativity' and 'self expression'. Abbs
(1987, p. 10) was to provide a scathing critique of Read's marriage of
modernism and progressivism that had led, in his view. 'to the present
impasse and disorientation' in arts education. The change in the educational
climate may have led to a loss of confidence among music teachers who were
just beginning to develop their practice along 'progressive' lines.

TEACHING QUALITY

Despite these reasons, the issue of teaching quality emerges uncomfortably
from research findings and continues to disturb. There have been profound

changes in content and method, but the quality of class music teaching remains poor in many schools. Her Majesty's Inspectors (HMI, 1991, p. 26) found 'two persistent and related weaknesses in the music curriculum of many primary schools: a lack of progression in the work and under-expectation of the children's musical abilities'. In a survey conducted from the University of London Institute of Education (1988), researchers in both primary and secondary classrooms found teachers responding to the growing diversification of pupils' musical interests through differentiated classroom organisation and the judicious deployment of resources. However, there seemed to be little sense of progression in the work planned for the pupils to do. The tasks did not make demands:

> School music lessons rarely seem to lead students on with any strong feeling of purpose...Class music seems to be about 'enjoyment', a word frequently used by music teachers and others who contributed to our curriculum study (Swanwick *et al.*, 1988a, p. 144).

What these observers rarely saw, however, was 'the enjoyment of *achievement*: a sense of mastery; travelling further from where we begin; the feeling of moving forward that can be experienced through good science or English teaching'. Only exceptionally in this survey of classroom practice in over 30 schools did the researchers observe work where 'the children were challenged to extend themselves musically' or where 'the behaviour of the teacher was musically sensitive at all times' (Swanwick, 1988b, p. 69).

Poor teaching was even found at Key Stage 4, where the subject is an elective option and usually taught in groups smaller than the normal class size of 25–30 pupils. Spencer (1993) conducted a survey of GCSE students who were among the first to take the new examination and who went on to further specialist musical study at A-level and in conservatoires and universities. The majority of this high-achieving cohort found the GCSE undemanding and saw an inappropriate alignment between the examination and the demands of subsequent study, particularly at A-level. The survey revealed a picture of many teachers ill-prepared for GCSE, either to teach the course with conviction, or to conduct the necessary administration efficiently. There were complaints about unclear objectives and sloppy assessment procedures in both composing and performing components. They fell disappointingly short of the ideals stated in the Criteria (1985):

> 1.1 To encourage imaginative teaching in schools and foster a greater understanding of music through more direct experience of the creative processes involved (DES, GCSE Criteria, 1985).

It may be of some comfort to know that music education in other countries is in similar trouble. Szemere (1982, p. 128) found that in her native Hungary, the Kodály method of vocal training, 'one of the most profitable cultural export articles of our country', has not in practice worked out as successfully as many would have us believe. According to Szemere, there are 'only a few schools in Hungary where music teachers can make children love and understand music'. By the early 1980s, Hungarian adolescents were beginning to reject Kodály's tamed, sanitised version of Hungarian folk music, rationalised into sol-fa, in favour of more authentic performing styles being promoted by a folk revival among the young.

It is not just pupils in a range of countries who are rejecting music. Staff, it seems, don't like teaching it either. A survey of secondary teachers in Australia (Hodge, Jupp and Taylor, 1994) points to low morale among music teachers compared to that of their colleagues in mathematics. Low subject status, lack of purpose in lessons, professional isolation and the absence of peer group support have all contributed to their poor professional self-esteem. The issues of isolation, the pressure of extra-curricular activities and of teaching too many pupils for too little of the time afflict both British and Australian music teachers similarly, it seems.

What, then, constitutes good practice? It is salutary to go back to Witkin (1974) and to reflect on the best lessons his research team observed as part of the Arts in the Adolescent Project. A generally pessimistic picture of music in the curriculum as practised in the 1970s emerges from Witkin's book. He found that 'Music is on the whole rejected by the majority of pupils in secondary schools and is in any case poorly provided for within the curriculum. The pupils' evaluations reveal it to be a very poor position in relation to art or drama' (Witkin, 1974, p. 149). However, Witkin singles out two schools from his survey where attitudes were more positive. These showed highly contrasting teaching styles. One was broadly 'progressive' in approach, described by Witkin as 'modern, free, creative'. He sums up the other as conveying a spirit of participation in a rousing 'let the people sing' approach. The finding that the more directed approach of the second school was considerably more successful with the pupils (music was third from the top in popularity in this school whereas it was third from the bottom in the other) would seem to go against the grain of Witkin's own preconceptions. As he says, the 'progressive' department gave 'greater opportunity for creative expression' and 'I personally believe the future lies with the relatively less successful (in terms of pupil evaluations) of the two departments'. However, his observations told him that while the 'progressive' teacher gave children the opportunity to explore sounds, they had no clear idea where this exploration ultimately was leading them, or of how, ultimately, it would enrich their musical understanding. By contrast, the other department relies strongly on rule-directed control of the medium. The pupils are given the opportunity to feel in control as they make music simply because they are left in no doubt about the way to begin, how to proceed, and where it is all leading. There is a great atmosphere of warmth and enthusiasm and the pupils seem to know what they are 'making' and how to make it. On the whole there is a great deal less opportunity for individualism and self-expression...but what opportunity there is can actually be utilised fully by the pupils (Witkin, 1974, p. 153).

Reports from HMI (1991) and the National Curriculum Working Group (DES, 1991) offer further descriptive examples of good practice. However, while these may show what *is* possible given the right teacher and the right conditions, they remain anecdotal. Given that the sampled statistical outcomes continue to indicate the low popularity of music, it would seem that such lessons remain the exception rather than the norm. The more practical character of the GCSE has indeed resulted in a steady rise in the numbers opting since it replaced O-level in 1986. However, music remains the one foundation subject most children drop at the age of 14. Figures from the School Curriculum and Assessment Authority (1994) show that drama, which is not a National Curriculum foundation subject, recruits nearly *twice* the number of GCSE students that music does. Art recruits nearly *six* times the number, perhaps confirming Stockhausen's point about the hegemony of the visual in our culture. Most music teachers, it seems, do not have the time, energy and motivation to work at improving their classroom practice. Their energies remain principally committed to extra-curricular rehearsal leading to public performance. The situation today is no different from a quarter of a century ago, when Geoffrey Brace (1970, p. 11) wrote:

So the music teacher finds himself in the extraordinary position of having far more expected of him *outside* his working day than in it. He also expects more *of himself* outside school than in the classroom; he is more likely to be assessed by others on his extra-curricular work and, what is more, he is tacitly obliged to agree to this arrangement if he wishes to be considered for preferment.

This distortion of teaching priorities applies at all levels of education. Universities and colleges encourage their staff to see prestige and status in the production of research or composition rather than in teaching. Many former LEA advisers were keen to develop curriculum music, but their political masters took more interest in the promotion of prestigious public performance. The ignominious way in which so many advisers' jobs disappeared once council politicians found the financial going getting tough (Thomas, 1993, p. 27) is an example of gross ingratitude towards a group of people who contributed much to the public profile of LEAs.

Many working in music education look wistfully at the success of art as a curriculum subject even with teachers and pupils of seemingly average ability:

> The reasons why pupils, even with few talents in this domain, enjoy art lessons are several. Each pupil has a high degree of autonomy in a task which challenges one's creative powers. Each lesson tends to have a clear product as an end in itself; every picture is complete in itself, not just an isolated exercise as part of a complex syllabus which exists only in the teacher's mind. Moreover, there is no 'right answer' already known to the teacher; there is no absolute standard of what makes a good drawing or painting....The teacher can advise, guide, suggest and support; he rarely makes the dogmatic statements to pupils that are common in other lessons....I suspect art lessons have their own special magic to many pupils (Hargreaves, 1982, p. 157).

POSSIBILITIES FOR FUTURE RESEARCH

Music education is a highly challenging area for research. If the present picture seems gloomy and disappointing, it only goes to show that more research is needed to improve the quality of learning for the majority of pupils and that more precise and searching questions need to be formulated. Above all, we need evidence to counter the potential damage to progress in musical teaching and learning that politicians (of whatever party persuasion) could inflict by acting out of ignorance and ideological prejudice rather than for educational reasons. The campaign to reinstate the National Curriculum Music Working Group's original proposals succeeded precisely because the musicians and teachers involved could draw upon research to support their defence.

The disturbing findings about music's continuing failure as a classroom subject come from fairly small-scale surveys. There is, therefore, a pressing need for a nationally based project to confirm or refute these. There is also a need for further vigilant country-wide surveys of instrumental provision as LMS-related changes start to have a longitudinal impact on the range and number of pupils learning instruments. However, this chapter will conclude with suggestions for smaller-scale investigations that nevertheless could cast highly relevant light on the state of music education.

At the start of this chapter, the writer quoted Small's 'four disjunctions': between creator and performer, producer and consumer, classical and vernacular and composer and potential audience. Four parallel disjunctions, the writer suggests, still characterise music education. These could form the basis for some useful future research, and a number of the questions raised under these headings could be addressed through locally based projects

undertaken by students or teachers.
The disjunctions are:

*(1) Between how music is rationalised by those who teach it and how it
is experienced by those who learn;*

Investigations under this heading raise both psychological and epistemological questions. They could be informed by the methodologies adopted by
Cook (1990) and Pratt (1990), in dealing with matters such as ear-training
and its relationship to the development of a *musical imagination.* In
particular, researchers could explore the problematical notion of musical
'understanding' and its promotion. They could enquire into the relationship
between teachers' stated intentions and the outcomes in the form of musical
behaviour by pupils. The ever-thorny issue of the relationship between sound
and symbol (musical notation) could also be a fruitful topic for investigation.

(2) Between specialist and generalist notions of music education;

To quote HMI (1991, p. 26) again:

> Musical talent is sometimes associated with small numbers of children who are
> often described as 'gifted' and considered markedly more able than others,
> There are such children, and an effective school policy for music will result in
> their talent being spotted and provision being made for them to excel.
> However, such provision should not result in the neglect of a broad and
> balanced music curriculum for all pupils.

This disjunction is not entirely the fault of schools, conservatoires or
individual teachers. It arises from deeply embedded assumptions about the
nature of musicality. What can be done to encourage participation by more
pupils? What can be done to mitigate the stigma of élitism that still taints our
work as teachers? Can further evidence be drawn from pupils in, for
example, ethnic minority communities to show that these cultures have a
great deal to teach us both about the relationship between music and people
and between teaching and learning?

*(3) Between what is learnt in the classroom and what is publicly
exhibited as musical achievement;*

One has only to step through the entrance of a typical primary school to see
words and pictures produced in the classroom on visible display. Yet
classroom music remains undervalued. Much has changed in the content and
organisation of curriculum music in the past 25 years. Yet it is often seen as

something quite separate from those prestigious and possibly more visible activities known as 'extra-curricular' music. How can children's musical work best be exhibited and celebrated so that other teachers, governors and, above all, parents, can be helped to value the general music curriculum for all pupils?

Assessment is another area where much research needs to be done. Teachers and pupils need not only to be able to use *musical* criteria to evaluate outcomes, such as a finished composition or performance. They also need to be able to identify the *learning* that takes place while the work is in progress, For example (as is often the case in the classroom), how do pupils working in a group interact as they work together preparing a performance? How do they use language to convey their musical ideas? How do they arrive at decisions? What is the quality of their listening? Such questions would be particularly suitable for investigation by either a practising experienced teacher or a student on teaching practice. The writer has highlighted the significance of the growing literature about children's classroom achievements, particularly in composing. The tapes that accompany this literature contain pieces that are every bit as fascinating and moving as the more publicly known body of children's work in art and writing.

(4) Between music and the other arts in the curriculum with which it should share similar aims.

Music tends to be isolated from other subjects and, in primary schools, tends to be taught by specialists. It is even isolated from the other aesthetic subjects. Art, dance, drama and music all share similar fundamental aims: the awakening of the senses, the fostering of sensitivity and the ability to articulate and work within structures that relate to feeling. Yet very often the 'aesthetic' seems to be missing from music classrooms and research has shown that musically sensitive work in lessons tends to be rare. What can music teachers learn from classroom interactions in the other arts? Equally importantly, can other arts teachers learn from the unique expertise and experience of musicians? If, in our culture, hearing really is less valued than seeing, then research that explores ways of righting the balance could have a really significant impact upon education as a whole.

REFERENCES

Abbs, P. (1987). *Living Powers: The Arts in Education.* London: Falmer Press.
Aiello, R. (ed.) (1994). *Musical Perceptions.* Oxford: Oxford University Press.
Allen, S. (1988). 'Music consultancy in primary education', *British Journal of Music Education*, 5, 3, pp. 217–40.

Allen, S. (1989). 'Case studies in music consultancy', *British Journal of Music Education*, 6, 2, pp. 139–54.

Bentley, A. (1966). *Musical Ability in Children and its Measurement*. London: Harrap.

Blacking, J. (1976). *How Musical is Man?* London: Faber.

Brace, G. (1970). *Music and the Secondary School Timetable*. University of Exeter.

Britten, B. (1964). *On receiving the Aspen Award*. London: Faber.

Bunting, R. (1977). *The Common Language of Music*, a discussion paper, Schools Council Project: Music in the Secondary School Curriculum, Working Paper 6, York, Schools Council Publications.

— (1987). 'Composing music: case studies in the teaching and learning process', *British Journal of Music Education*, 4, 1, pp. 25–32.

— (1988). 'Composing music: case studies in the teaching and learning process', *British Journal of Music Education*, 5, 3, pp. 269–310.

Cleave, S., and Dust, K. (1989). *A Sound Start*. Windsor, NFER.

Cook, N. (1990). *Music, Imagination and Culture*. Oxford: Oxford University Press.

— (1994). 'Perception: a perspective from music theory', in Aiello, R. (ed.), op. cit.

Coopers and Lybrand (1994). *Review of Instrumental Music Services*. London: Incorporated Society of Musicians.

Davies, C. (1986). 'Say it till a song comes', *British Journal of Music Education*, 3, 3, pp. 279–93.

— (1992). 'Listen to my song: a study of songs invented by children aged 5 to 7 years', *British Journal of Music Education*, 9, 1, pp. 19–48.

Davies, P. M. (1962). 'Music composition by children', in Grant (ed.), *Music in Education*, London: Butterworth.

Dennis, Brian (1970). *Experimental Music in Schools: Towards a New World of Sound*. Oxford: Oxford University Press.

Department for Education (1995). *Music in the National Curriculum*. London: HMSO.

Department of Education and Science (1963). *Half our Future* (The Newsom Report). London: HMSO.

— (1967). *Children and their Primary Schools* (The Plowden Report). London: HMSO.

— (1975). *A Language for Life*, (The Bullock Report). London: HMSO.

— (1985). *The GCSE Music Criteria*. London: HMSO.

— (1991). *Music for ages 5 to 14: Proposals of the Secretary of State for Education and Science and the Secretary of State for Wales*. London: HMSO.

— (1992). *Music in the National Curriculum*, statutory order. London: HMSO.

Frances, L. J. (1987). 'The decline in attitudes towards religious education among 8 to 15-year olds', in *Educational Studies*, 13,2.

Gottlieb, H., and Konecni, V. (1985). 'The effects of instrumentation, playing style and structure in the Goldberg Variations by Johann Sebastian Bach', *Music Perception*, 3, pp. 87–101.

Graham, D., (1993). *A Lesson for Us All: The Making of the National Curriculum*. London: Routledge.

Hannam, D, (1993). 'Arts in the Adolescent Revisited', in Ross, M. (ed.), *Perspectives 49: Wasteland Wonderland: the Arts in the National Curriculum*. University of Exeter School of Education.

Hargreaves, D. (1982). *The Challenge for the Comprehensive School*. London: Routledge.

Hargreaves, D. J. (1986). *The Developmental Psychology of Music*. Cambridge: Cambridge University Press.

Her Majesty's Inspectors (HMI) (1991). *Aspects of Education: The Teaching and*

Learning of Music. London: HMSO.

Hodge, G., Jupp, J. and Taylor, A. (1994). 'Work stress, distress and burnout in music and maths teachers', *British Journal of Educational Psychology*, 64, 1, pp. 65–76.

Holbrook, D., (1967). *Children's Writing*. Cambridge: Cambridge University Press.

— (1973). *English in Australia now*. Cambridge: Cambridge University Press.

Kemp, A. (1984). 'Music consultancy in primary schools', in *Schools Music Association Bulletin*, 95, pp. 3–4.

Kushner, S. (1985). *Working Dreams*. Centre for Applied Research in Education, University of East Anglia.

Lawrence, D. H. (1928). *Lady Chatterley's Lover*, unabridged edition. Harmondsworth: Penguin, 1960.

Lawson, D., Plummeridge, C., and Swanwick, K. (1994). 'Music and the National Curriculum in primary schools', *British Journal of Music Education*, 11, 1, pp. 3–14.

Lerdahl, F. (1988). 'Cognitive constraints on compositional systems', in Sloboda, J. (ed.), *Generative Processes in Music: the Psychology of Performance, Improvisation and Composition*. Oxford: Oxford University Press.

Loane, B. (1984). 'Thinking about children's compositions', *British Journal of Music Education*, 1, 3, pp. 205–31.

Mills, J. (1988). *Group Tests of Musical Abilities*. Slough: NFER.

— (1989). 'The generalist primary teacher of music: a problem of confidence', *British Journal of Music Education*, 6, 2, pp. 125–38.

— (1991). *Music in the Primary School*. Cambridge: Cambridge University Press.

National Curriculum Council (1992). *Consultation report: Music in the National Curriculum*. York: NCC.

National Curriculum Music Working Group (1991). *Interim Report*. London: DES.

O'Hear, A. (1993). 'Art and ideas: naturally creative?', *Modern Painters*, 6.1, pp. 52–5.

Paynter, J. and Aston, P. (1970). *Sound and Silence*. Cambridge: Cambridge University Press.

Paynter, J. (1977). 'The role of creativity in the school music curriculum', in Burnett (ed.), *Music Education Review*, Vol. I. London: Chappell.

— (1982). *Music in the Secondary School Curriculum*. Cambridge: Cambridge University Press.

— (1992). *Sound and Structure*. Cambridge: Cambridge University Press.

Plaskow, D. (1964). *Children and Creative Activity*. London: The Society for Education through Art.

Pratt, G. (1990). *Aural Awareness*. Milton Keynes: Open University Press.

Read, H. (1943). *Education through Art*. London: Faber.

Reimer, B. (1982). 'Tradition and change in education', in Dobbs (ed.), *International Society for Music Education (ISME) Yearbook*, 1982/IX.

Renshaw, P. (1986). 'Towards the changing face of the conservatoire curriculum', *British Journal of Music Education*, 3, 1, pp. 79–90.

Richardson, M. (1948). *Art and the Child*. London: University of London Press.

Ross, M. (1993). Open peer commentary on Swanwick, K. (1993), *Psychology of Music*, 20, pp. 162–79.

Ross, M., Radnor H., Bierton, C. and Mitchell, S. (1993). *Assessing Achievement in the Arts*. Milton Keynes: Open University Press.

Schoenberg, A. (1946). 'New music, outmoded music, style and idea', in Stein (ed.) (1975), *Style and Idea*. London: Faber.

Schools Council (1968). *Enquiry 1, Young School Leavers*. London: HMSO.

— (1975). *The Arts and the Adolescent*. London: Schools Council Publications.

Seashore, C. (1938). *The Psychology of Music*. New York: McGraw-Hill.

Self, G. (1967). *New Sounds in Class*. London: Universal Edition.

Sergeant, D. (1994).'The perception of verticalization in serial music', in *Bulletin of the Council of Research in Music Education*, 119, pp. 3–9.

Sharp, C. (1991). *When Every Note Counts: The Schools Instrumental Service in the 1990s*. Slough: NFER.

Sloboda, J. (1985). *The Musical Mind*. Oxford: Oxford University Press.

— (1994). 'Music performance: Expression and the Development of Excellence' in Aiello (ed.), op. cit.

Small, C. (1977). *Music – Society – Education*. London: John Calder.

— (1987). *Music of the Common Tongue*. London: John Calder.

Spencer, P. (1976). 'An Individual develops', in Vulliamy, G. and Lee, E. (eds), *Pop Music in School*. Cambridge: Cambridge University Press.

— (1982). 'Different Drummers: The case for Afro-American music-making in the school curriculum', unpublished D. Phil. thesis, University of York.

— (1993). 'GCSE Music: A survey of undergraduate opinion', *British Journal of Music Education*, 10, 1, pp. 73–84.

Stockhausen, K. (1989). 'On the musical gift', in Maconie (ed.), *Stockhausen on Music*. London: Marion Boyars.

Swanwick, K. (1968). *Popular Music and the Teacher*. Oxford: Pergamon Press.

— (1979). *A Basis for Music Education*. Windsor: NFER.

— and Tillman, J. (1986). 'The sequence of musical development', *British Journal of Music Education*, 3,3, pp. 305–39.

— (1988a). *Music, Mind and Education*. London: Routledge.

— (ed.) (1988b). *Music in Schools: A Study of Context and Curriculum Practice*. University of London Institute of Education.

— (1992).'Open Peer Commentary: Musical Knowledge: the Saga of Music in the National Curriculum', *Psychology of Music*, 20, pp. 162–79.

— (1994). *Intuition, Analysis and Music Education*. London: Routledge.

Szemere, A. (1982). 'The role of folk music in young people's life', in Dobbs (ed.), op. cit.

Thomas, S. (1994). 'Diminuendo', *Times Educational Supplement*, 9 July.

Vulliamy, G. and Lee, E. (eds) (1976). *Pop Music in School*. Cambridge: Cambridge University Press.

Vulliamy, G. and Shepherd, J. (1984). 'The application of critical sociology to music education', *British Journal of Music Education*, 1,3, pp. 247–66.

Witkin, R. (1974). *The Intelligence of Feeling*. London: Heinemann.

5

RELIGIOUS EDUCATION

Leslie J. Francis

A NEW ERA

A new impetus for research in religious education emerged in Britain during the early 1960s, heralded by seven key figures: Harold Loukes (reader in education, University of Oxford), Violet Madge (senior tutor, Rolle College of Education), Ronald Goldman (lecturer in educational psychology, University of Reading), Kenneth Hyde (senior lecturer in divinity, Furzedown College of Education), Edwin Cox (lecturer in education, University of Birmingham), R. J. Rees (researcher, University College of North Wales, Bangor) and Colin Alves (lecturer in divinity, King Alfred's College, Winchester), each of whom published a major study between 1961 and 1967. This new impetus for research was driven by some very practical concerns. Under the terms of the 1944 Education Act (Dent, 1947) religious instruction was a compulsory component of the school curriculum throughout the maintained sector. Twenty years later significant shifts in the social, political, educational, moral, religious and theological climates were raising questions about the appropriateness and effectiveness of this statutory provision (Mathews, 1966; Cox, 1966). Research was seen as useful both to understand the situation and to underpin the case for change.

Before 1960 a few other researchers had made a start on charting the field. Daines (1958, 1964) provides an overview of unpublished theses between 1918 and 1963. Studies of particular interest from this early period include the following unpublished dissertations: Glassey (1943), on the attitude of grammar-school pupils and their parents to education, religion and sport; Forrester (1946), on a study of the attitudes of adolescents to their own intellectual, social and spiritual development; Bradbury (1947), on the religious development of the adolescent; Daines (1949), on a psychological study of the attitude of adolescents to religion and religious instruction; Bradshaw (1950), on a psychological study of the development of religious beliefs among children and young people; Dawes (1954), on the concept of God among secondary school pupils; Rixon (1959), on an experimental and critical study of the teaching of scripture in secondary schools. Of note, also, is the report by the Institute of Christian Education (1954) on religious education in schools. Loukes, Madge, Goldman, Hyde, Cox, Rees and Alves, however, each found his or her own distinctive starting-point.

LISTENING TO TEENAGERS

In his study *Teenage Religion*, Loukes (1961) arranged for six schools to tape-record discussions held by 14 year olds in the presence of a class teacher or researcher during ordinary lessons on religious topics. In this way he attempted to catch the authentic and spontaneous voices of young people frankly expressing their own convictions, confusions and struggles. Recognising that this method may only have captured the views of the more vocal members of the class, Loukes' project included a second stage. A number of typical quotations were selected from the recorded discussions and submitted to 502 pupils within a further eight schools for their written comments. This study was clearly successful in allowing the views of some teenagers to be more widely heard. What it lacked, however, were any sound theoretical or methodological groundings.

On the basis of these data Loukes concluded that in their response to religious education, 14 year olds were confused, rather than hostile, ambivalent rather than rejecting. The subject matter, they agreed, was interesting and important: the manner and method of teaching were totally boring.

In his next book, *New Ground in Christian Education*, Loukes (1965) built on his earlier study in two ways. First, he set out to identify schools in which religious education was thought to be successful, by writing to all Local Education Authorities, training colleges and university departments. In this way some 500 schools were nominated. A questionnaire sent to these schools to profile their religious education curriculum elicited a 60 per cent response. Then these schools were asked to let some of their pupils complete a test originally developed by a project undertaken in the University of Sheffield Institute of Education (Sheffield, 1961). While this method provides a more statistically secure base of knowledge it is weakened by the nature of the sample. The practical outcome of Loukes' research was a new view of the religious education curriculum being life-centred or problem-centred.

Loukes' third study applied the same basic approach of tape-recording classroom discussions to the question of *Teenage Morality* (Loukes, 1973).

LISTENING TO CHILDREN

Madge's (1965) study, *Children in Search of Meaning*, offers a window into the religious ideas and feelings of primary school children. It is a less systematic and less disciplined enquiry than Loukes' study among teenagers, but is rich in illustrative material. Madge explained that the material was gathered together in a variety of ways, including observations involving 200 children. She wrote:

> Whenever opportunities occurred during my year's secondment, personal observations were made of children engaged in spontaneous activities, but I have also drawn on previous observations made over a period of years. In addition, I have included some observations contributed by parents and teachers, as well as recollections of childhood by adults.

In her next book, *Introducing Young Children to Jesus*, Madge (1971) examined children's statements about Jesus and developed implications for curriculum design.

CLINICAL INTERVIEWS

Goldman's (1964) study, *Religious Thinking from Childhood to Adolescence*, based on an earlier doctoral dissertation (Goldman, 1962), was grounded in both a recognised research methodology and a theoretical framework. The theoretical framework was provided by Piagetian developmental psychology (Flavell, 1963; Modgil and Modgil, 1982); the methodology employed the clinical interview. This approach had already been explored in the USA and in Europe to study the development of the child's concepts of divine protection (Godin and van Roey, 1959), sacraments (Godin and Marthe, 1960) and denominational identity (Elkind, 1961, 1962, 1963, 1964).

Goldman interviewed 200 pupils, ten boys and ten girls within each year group between the ages of six and 17, treating 15, 16 and 17 year olds as one age group. Two main devices were used in these interviews. First, the pupils were asked to listen to three tape-recorded bible stories: Moses and the burning bush, crossing the red sea, and the temptations of Jesus. After each story they were asked questions about their understanding of the narratives. Second, the pupils were asked questions about three pictures, used as projective devices: family going to church, boy or girl at prayer, and boy or girl looking at mutilated bible.

Using the statistical technique of scalogram analysis, Goldman interpreted the findings of these interviews as evidence for the view that religious thinking develops through an invariant sequence of stages during childhood and adolescence. This analysis was based on answers to just five of the many questions asked in the interviews. Goldman's conclusion was that before the onset of formal operational thinking, occurring from the age of 13 or 14 upwards, religious thinking was seriously restricted.

In his second book, *Readiness for Religion*, Goldman (1965a) proposed a fresh approach to religious education, based not on scripture, but on life-themes, and subtitled 'a basis for developmental religious education'. This approach was influential in changing the face of religious education in county schools, beginning with the new West Riding Agreed Syllabus (West Riding, 1966).

Like Loukes, in his more recent work Goldman's interests shifted from religion to morality. He applied the same basic approach of the clinical interview method to *Children's Sexual Thinking* (Goldman and Goldman, 1982), which was followed by the more practical sequel *Show Me Yours* (Goldman and Goldman, 1988). Goldman's work was also closely followed by Bull (1969) in his study of *Moral Judgement from Childhood to Adolescence* and by a series of other studies which attempted to apply the method and theoretical framework to specific aspects of religious development, including Brisco (1969), Kingan (1969), Miles (1971), Greer (1972c), Whitehouse (1972), Richmond (1972), Fagerlind (1974) and Morley (1975).

For example, Whitehouse (1972) selected the biblical narrative of Zacchaeus, to avoid the emphasis on miraculous events which was present in the three stories used by Goldman, and interviewed 20 first year and 20 fourth year junior pupils from two closely matched county and Roman Catholic schools. Related studies have used the clinical interview technique to explore the child's ideas of eucharistic presence (Jaspard, 1971), the priest's occupations (Dumoulin, 1971), themes of resurrection and hell (Darcy and Beniskos, 1971), and the concept of God (Nye and Carlson, 1984).

QUESTIONNAIRES

Hyde's (1965) study, *Religious Learning in Adolescence*, also based on an earlier doctoral dissertation (Hyde, 1959), brought quantitative methods to religious education. Hyde developed four pencil and paper tests, concerned with image of God, religious concepts, religious knowledge and attitude towards religion. The attitude towards religion measure contained six subscales, measuring attitude towards God, bible, religion, institutional church, local church and churchgoing. From the responses of over 3,500 pupils to these tests Hyde concluded that, while religious attitudes consistently fell over the 11–16 age range, and while girls consistently showed more favourable attitudes than boys, pupils who attended church once a month or more were much less inclined to experience erosion of positive attitudes with age, and such erosion as did occur was greatly retarded.

In a second stage of his study, Hyde examined the effect of student teachers applying four different approaches to teaching the same syllabus, testing pupils before and after the experiment. He found little difference that could be attributed to teaching methods. A major conclusion drawn from the study, as pointed by Jeffreys in his foreword to the book was that 'religious learning depends significantly on religious attitudes, and attitudes are closely connected with churchgoing'.

Hyde's work did not result in significant changes in religious education, but it did influence the future trend of research in that field. Hyde's instruments were subsequently employed by other researchers, including Miles (1971), Richmond (1972) and Mark (1979).

SIXTH FORM RELIGION

Cox's (1967) study, *Sixth Form Religion*, also employed quantitative methods, although in a less sophisticated way than Hyde. Cox's questionnaire was content to gauge opinions rather than attempt to scale attitudes. This project, sponsored by the Christian Education Movement, was concerned to discover what the élite group of young people in the second year of the grammar school sixth form thought about the following issues: existence of God, Jesus, life after death, bible, church, religious education, personal religious behaviour and a series of moral behaviours. In total 96 grammar schools contributed up to 25 pupils each, making a total sample of 2,276 completed questionnaires.

In his analysis, Cox presented the percentages of pupils holding positive and negative opinions on the various topics and then gave extracts from the pupils' more extended responses to open-ended questions to demonstrate how they had come to their conclusions. The findings confirmed the general approval of religious education by pupils, although their answers also indicated a desire for reform. Subsequent analyses explored the relationship between co-education and religious belief (Wright and Cox, 1967a) and between moral judgement and religious belief (Wright and Cox, 1967b).

Like Hyde's work, Cox's study helped to shape a future trend in research in religious education. Two particular sets of studies are of particular significance. Cox's original data were collected in 1963. In collaboration with Derek Wright, the study was replicated seven years later in 1970 and reported in two papers concerned with changes in attitudes towards religious education and the bible and changes in moral belief (Wright and Cox, 1971a,

1971b). Both analyses demonstrated that traditional values were changing among sixth formers. For example, while in 1963 77.3 per cent of the girls and 57.5 per cent of the boys agreed with the statutory provision of religious education, by 1970 the proportions had fallen to 45.6 per cent of the girls and 28.5 per cent of the boys.

Second, Cox's questionnaire was administered among second year sixth-form pupils attending county and Protestant voluntary schools in Northern Ireland during 1968 by Greer (1972a, 1972b). This enabled a comparison to be made between England and Northern Ireland. Of even greater significance, however, Greer (1980a) replicated his study ten years later in 1978 and Greer (1989) conducted a second replication in 1988. This provides a unique study of change over a 20-year period. In Northern Ireland pupil support for religious education was increasing, not declining. The proportion of boys in favour of statutory religious education rose from 47.1 per cent in 1968 to 54.6 per cent in 1988. The proportion of girls in favour rose from 63.0 per cent in 1968 to 69.8 per cent in 1988.

LOOKING BACK

Rees' (1967) study, *Background and Belief*, provided a rather different perspective by asking third-year students at Oxford, Cambridge and Bangor to assess their experience of religious education in the sixth form, alongside a survey of their current religious beliefs and practices. From an original address list of 583 names, 433 questionnaires were returned. The analysis is a simple presentation of statistics enlivened by illuminating quotations from the respondents' answers to open-ended questions. Rees found that 23 per cent of the students who had attended boarding school and 21 per cent of the students who had attended day school were 'generally bored or resentful of time wasting', in sixth-form religious education, while 49 per cent of boarding school and 48 per cent of day school students had 'enjoyed lessons, and particularly valued them for the discussion they included'. A similar retrospective view of religious education was conducted by Daines (1962) among students at three Colleges of Education.

COMPARING SCHOOLS

Alves' study (1968), *Religion in the Secondary School*, was the third major enquiry in religious education during the 1960s to use questionnaires. Undertaken on behalf of the Education Department of the British Council of Churches, this was a project of considerable ambition. The first aim of the project was to discover where religious education was meeting with success and to identify the factors underlying such success. Loukes' list of about 300 schools characterised by successful religious education was complemented by a random list of schools. Altogether 637 schools were invited to participate and 539 accepted the invitation. In 1965 20,000 questionnaires were despatched for completion by the highest ability stream of their fourth formers. Only 13 of the schools failed to return the completed questionnaires. The pupils' questionnaires were scored to rank order the schools, stratified into 12 groups according to three criteria: mixed, boys and girls, large and small, grammar and modern. For the next stage of the project the seven or eight top and bottom scoring schools were identified within each of the 12 categories, and questionnaires were sent to the headteachers and religious education staff. For the third stage of the project, a further batch of questionnaires was completed within the top scoring schools by the pupils who had spent longest in those schools (sixth formers in grammar schools and fifth formers in modern schools).

Alves' questionnaire contained a test of pupils' knowledge of the New Testament, pupils' insight into the meaning of New Testament quotations, belief and attitude items about Jesus, the bible and the church rated on a five-point Likert scale, items relating to moral choices and questions about personal religious identity and practice.

These data were employed in a number of imaginative ways to explore the correlates of positive pupil responses to religious education. Had the project been conducted a decade later with the advantages of computer-generated multi-variate analyses so much more could have been learnt from the database. One of the main conclusions to which Alves drew attention concerned the importance of geography in shaping responses to religious education. Alves concluded that, 'generally speaking the nearer one gets to London the less favourable the attitude to Christianity becomes'. Alves also reported a more positive attitude towards religious education in girls' single sex schools than in boys' single sex schools or mixed schools. Alves' questionnaire has not been taken up by other researchers.

LAYING FOUNDATIONS

Alongside the books published by Loukes, Madge, Goldman, Hyde, Cox, Rees and Alves, the 1960s also saw a number of other significant initiatives in research in religious education which put in place foundations for future studies. Examples of note include: Wright (1962) on a study of religious beliefs in sixth form boys; Dale and Jones (1964) on an investigation into the comparative response of boys and girls to scripture as a school subject in certain co-educational grammar schools in industrial south Wales; Marratt (1965) on the attitudes of sixth formers to the retention of the legal provision of religious education.

LOCATING RELIGIOUS EDUCATION

There has been a long history of research concerned with locating pupils' attitudes towards religious education alongside their attitudes towards other areas of the curriculum, going back to the early study by Lewis (1913). Studies enabling this comparison undertaken since 1960 include Garrity (1960), Williams and Finch (1968), Povall (1971), Greer and Brown (1973), Ormerod (1975), Keys and Ormerod (1976), Harvey (1984) and Francis (1987b).

A relatively unambiguous picture emerges from these disparate studies, locating religious education among the lowest positions, at the least favourable end of the attitudinal continuum. For example, Williams and Finch (1968) reported that religious education was assigned the thirteenth-rank position by boys and the eleventh-rank position by girls with regard to usefulness and the thirteenth-rank position by both boys and girls with regard to interest. Their study embraced fourteen school subjects. Harvey (1984) reported that religious education was assigned, among 18 school subjects, sixteenth place by boys and seventeenth place by girls. Francis (1987b) found that religious education jostled with music lessons to occupy the place of the least preferred school subject in each year from the third year of the junior school to the fourth year of the secondary school.

Another set of studies has explored the range of factors which may influence pupils' responses to religious education. A number of studies have found that girls take a more positive view of religious education than boys. Archer and Macrae (1991) took this issue of sex differences one step further and asked 60 children, aged 11–12 years, to rate 17 school subjects on a seven-point semantic differential scale from masculine to feminine. They found that religious education was rated in third place towards the feminine end of the continuum, closely followed by home economics and typing. A number of studies have also reported a less positive view of religious education among older pupils in comparison with younger pupils. For example, McQuillan (1990) invited 1,724 pupils to respond to the question, 'How much do you learn about religion at school?' on a three-point scale: a lot, something and nothing. She found that the response 'a lot' declined from 50 per cent in year seven to 27 per cent in year eleven. A third important predictor of a more positive response to religious education has been found to be religious affiliation. This was shown to be the case, for example, by

Lewis (1974) in a study conducted among 320 fourth-year secondary pupils in 13 co-educational comprehensive schools in south Wales.

During the 1960s, 1970s and 1980 several studies reported on adults' attitudes towards religious education, including a national probability sample (Goldman, 1965b) and surveys of parents (May, 1967; May and Johnston, 1967; Greer, 1970). Other studies explored the attitudes of teachers, including May (1968), Kay (1973), Bedwell (1977) and Burgess (1975, 1980), and the provision made within schools, including local studies in Lancashire (Benfield, 1975), Lincolnshire (Bailey, 1979) and Gloucestershire (Francis, 1987a).

Orchard (1991, 1994) has analysed HMI reports on religious education between 1985 and 1991. In the first study, Orchard tested the proposition that the problems of religious education in schools were largely due to the multi-faith content of lessons, and concluded that the weakness of religious education lay much more in the lack of time and skilled teaching. In the second study, Orchard concluded that the 1988 Education Act had done little to reverse the poor standing of the subject. In spite of reassurances from government that religious education enjoyed parity with other subjects in the basic curriculum, schools have failed to allocate time and resources for its delivery.

RELIGIOUS THINKING

The most influential of the studies conducted during the 1960s was that of Ronald Goldman. When research is influential, it is also subjected to scrutiny and to criticism. The debate about Goldman's research included studies by Howkins (1966), Hyde (1968, 1984), Godin (1968), Cox (1968), Langdon (1969), Attfield (1974), Murphy (1977b), Roy (1979), Greer (1980b), McGrady (1982), Maas (1985), Gobbel and Gobbel (1986), Petrovich (1988) and Slee (1986a, 1986b, 1990). These studies have criticised Goldman for over-reliance on the Piagetian framework or for misuse of this framework; for distorting the biblical material used to stimulate the interviews or for failing to select a proper range of biblical material; for confusing analysis of stages of thinking with styles of theological preference or for giving unfair preference to a liberal theological perspective; for misunderstanding or misapplying statistical techniques to qualitative data; for failing to demonstrate a sound link between his research findings and curriculum recommendations.

For example, Slee (1986b) examined the two methods of data analysis which formed the basis of Goldman's developmental theory of religious thinking: content analysis and scalogram analysis. She concluded that both methods were subject to grave limitations and weaknesses and cannot substantiate Goldman's theory of religious thinking development. Francis (1979a) suggested that more careful consideration be given to the meaning of the phrase 'the development of religious thinking'. He argued that current use of this phrase disguises three very different notions which he distinguishes as *thinking about religion, thinking religiously* and *thinking in religious language*. Each of these different constructs requires a different research method. Goldman's research, he argued, was concerned solely with thinking about religion and should not be generalised as if it also embraced the other two notions.

A number of empirical studies, working within a range of research traditions, have suggested that primary school children are capable of a much richer and more developed understanding of religious ideas and concepts than those with which Goldman credited them, including Van Bunnen (1965), Gates (1976) and Murphy (1979). Streib (1994) gives attention to the continuing place of magical feeling and thinking in adolescence and adulthood.

MEASURING RELIGIOUS THINKING

Goldman's research raised a number of questions about the correlates of the development of religious thinking, concerning issues like the comparative influence of home background and school curriculum on promoting or inhibiting the development from one stage to the next. The problem with Goldman's method of the clinical interview is that, since each interview takes so long, it becomes very costly to build up a database of sufficient size to enable the statistical modelling of potential influences. Peatling (1973, 1974, 1977) proposed an imaginative solution to this problem by developing a criterion referenced, multiple-choice pencil and paper test, known as *Thinking About the Bible* (TAB). This instrument was designed to generate scores on six scales of religious thinking. Two scales represented developmentally sequential levels of concrete religious thinking; two scales represented developmentally sequential levels of abstract religious thinking; two scales represented overall levels of concrete and abstract religious thinking. The original study, based on 1,994 pupils in the USA, suggested that abstract religious thinking was not attained until later than Goldman's estimate of 14 years two months. Peatling (1976) discussed a similar approach to the assessment of moral judgement.

Peatling's *Thinking About the Bible* measure has been reapplied in the USA by Peatling and Laabs (1975), Peatling, Laabs and Newton (1975) and Hoge and Petrillo (1978); in Finland by Tamminen (1976, 1991); in Northern Ireland by Greer (1981a, 1982a); in Eire by McGrady (1990, 1994a, 1994b);

and in England, Northern Ireland and Eire by Kay (1981e).

Peatling's measure, *Thinking About the Bible,* has been significantly criticised from both conceptual and psychometric perspectives. For example, Greer (1983a) argued that item selection within the forced choice format might be influenced not only by preferences for stages of thinking but also by variability in readability and in theological perspective. He also maintained that, while the test appears to give a useful measure of the level of religious thinking in which groups are operating, it does not seem to be a valid indicator of the level of religious thinking revealed by the interview of individual pupils. McGrady (1983) argued that the six scales of instrument seek to measure underlying developmental constructs that misrepresent Goldman's categories, and to quantify the results of the measurement in a manner inconsistent with Piagetian stage theory.

RELIGIOUS LANGUAGE

One particularly significant response to Goldman's research was a renewed interest in religious language. In a paper entitled 'A new approach to the study of the development of religious thinking in children', Murphy (1978) argued that researchers in the area of religious education should draw on the experimental techniques at present associated with 'the study of children's language and word meaning development'. He supported his case by discussing two techniques employed to investigate the meanings which certain religious words hold for children by Deconchy (1965, 1968) and Murphy (1979).

Murphy's ideas are developed further by Francis (1979a) who built on traditions in the philosophy of religious language (Ramsey, 1957; Van Buren, 1972) to argue that research regarding the development of religious language needs to undertake a systematic investigation of two things: the way in which religious discourse uses language in an odd fashion to convey a special experience; and existing research regarding the child's ability to use language in ways which point beyond the constraints of the literal meaning of the individual words themselves. In a secular context, examples of research into using language in special ways include studies of similes (Malgady, 1977), metaphors (Billow, 1975, 1981), verbal humour (Brodzinsky, 1975), jokes (Brodzinsky, 1977), riddles (Fowles and Glanz, 1977) and proverbs (Honeck, Sowry and Voegtle, 1978). In a religious context some studies have begun to explore the child's response to religious allegory (Greenacre, 1971), parables (Ainsworth, 1961; Gregory, 1966, Debot-Sevrin, 1968; Beechick, 1974; Murphy, 1977a) and metaphor (McGrady, 1990, 1994a, 1994b).

For example, Murphy (1977a) explored the understanding of 200 pupils, drawn from four schools, between the ages of seven and 11, making 40 for each year group. Although the project was concerned with six parables (the two houses, the rich fool, the good Samaritan, the sower, the Pharisee and the tax collector, and the lost sheep), each child was read just four of the parables. Although the research method was based on the semi-structured interview, some pupils were given a multiple-choice questionnaire instead. Three levels of understanding were applied. At the first level, the child can only repeat facts or elements of the parable, and shows no more than a literal application of the parable. At the second level, the child can make an application in a simple way that shows a movement in the direction of understanding the allegorical meaning of the parable. At the third level ,the child shows an understanding of the allegorical meaning of the parable.

McGrady (1990, 1994a, 1994b) explored the metaphorical and operational aspects of religious thinking among a sample of 117 Irish Catholic pupils. In this study McGrady proposed a paradigm of six capabilities relating to the metaphorical component of religious thinking, which he defined as recognition, comprehension, production, elaboration, interrelation and validation. Fifty-eight of the pupils completed semi-clinical interviews based on McGrady's *Metaphor and Model Test of Religious Thinking*, consisting of seven sections. Section one required subjects to complete and explain four common religious metaphors drawn from biblical and liturgical sources. Section two required recognition and comprehension of four, probably unfamiliar, religious metaphors. Section three required recognition, comprehension and interrelation of two parabolic statements of Jesus. Section four examined parental metaphors of the divine, inviting subjects to explore images of God as a father and as a woman feeding her child. Section five discussed the subject's personal metaphors of the divine and required subjects to interrelate these with other metaphors presented during the interview. Section six explored three important religious questions, namely, the meaning of life, the meaning of suffering, and belief in an afterlife, and required subjects to select metaphors from among those discussed previously and to elaborate on them in terms of their usefulness in approaching the three questions. Section seven invited the subjects to consider why metaphors are used as part of religious discourse.

For the other 59 pupils the interviews were based on Goldman's use of the story of the temptations of Jesus. McGrady's findings contradicted Goldman's view that the use of biblical material should be restricted before the onset of formal operations by demonstrating that pupils were able to think metaphorically before the onset of formal operations. McGrady argues that rather than enhancing readiness for the examination of biblical material, formal operations may actually inhibit the pupils' appreciation by limiting the realm of that which is perceived as truthful. On these grounds, McGrady concluded that, rather than waiting for the emergence of formal operations before introducing young people to biblical material, it may be necessary to strengthen their metaphorical capabilities to withstand the reductionist aspects of early formal operations.

Another, very different, perspective on assessing religious language is provided by Turner (1978) who developed a standardised test of religious language comprehension. This test has been used by Turner (1980) and Jamison (1989).

FAITH DEVELOPMENT

A much more ambitious theory of religious development was advanced by Fowler (1981) in his book, *Stages of Faith*. While Goldman's view of religious development was grounded on one psychological perspective, Fowler's view of faith development attempts to synthesise seven aspects which he defines as form of logic, perspective taking, form of moral judgement, social awareness, relation to authority, form of world-coherence and symbolic function. On the basis of the detailed coding and scoring of faith development interviews, Fowler defined six stages and a pre-stage. He defined the stages as follows: stage zero, *primal faith*; stage one, *intuitive-projective faith*; stage two, *mythic-literal faith*; stage three, *synthetic-conventional faith*; stage four, *individuative-reflective faith*; stage five, *conjunctive faith*; stage six, *universalising faith*. By the time *Stages of Faith* was published in 1981, 359 interviews had been conducted.

Fowler's faith development interviewing technique has been used by a number of other researchers, like Leavey and Hetherton (1988). The underlying theory has been used to influence the churches' approaches to Christian education (Astley, 1991), pastoral counselling (Droege, 1984), ministry among the mentally retarded (Schurter, 1987), work with older adults (Shulik, 1988), campus ministry (Chamberlain, 1979) and pastoral care (Fowler, 1987).

Just as Peatling tried to translate Goldman's theory into a pencil and paper test, so Barnes, Doyle and Byron (1989) attempted to develop a Fowler scale. This is a simple instrument inviting respondents to make a forced choice selection among nine sets of paired statements. This scale may be a useful indicator of faith style preference, although it fails to capture the full nuances of Fowler's seven aspects of faith. Another attempt to assess faith stages by a pencil and paper test is exampled by Green and Hoffman (1989). In view of its wide application, Fowler's theory has been subject to theological and psychological scrutiny. Some theologians would argue that what Fowler means by faith is not what their religious tradition means by faith. Some psychologists would argue that Fowler's method of research fails to establish empirically that the seven aspects of faith cohere into a meaningful structure, that there are in fact six distinct forms of styles of faith (or seven including primal faith), or that these styles of faith necessarily unfold in a stage structure. Further helpful commentary on faith development theory is provided in collections of essays edited by Dykstra and Parks (1986), Astley and Francis (1992) and Fowler, Nipkow and Schweitzer (1992).

RELIGIOUS JUDGEMENT

Oser's theory of religious development is much less well known in the English speaking world than Fowler's theory. His key text, *Religious Judgement: a developmental perspective*, first published in German in 1984, was not available in English translation until 1991 (Oser and Gmünder, 1991). Oser's concern with religious judgement is both much more narrowly and precisely defined than Fowler's concern with faith.

Oser and Gmünder began their work by developing a clear theoretical perspective on what they mean by religious judgement. Their concern is not in discussing 'religion' in its historical forms, but 'religiosity' as a 'special subjective form of coping with the contingencies of life'. They maintain that, in this sense, religiosity is an essential, universal and irreducible anthropological category or 'mother-structure'. Second, they clarify their use of the term 'religious judgement' as being concerned with the linguistic form through which individuals resolve the tensions implicit in religious dilemmas. According to their conceptual analysis, religious judgement is a structural form, abstracted from content, characterised by the tensions between seven polarities: the sacred versus the profane, the transcendent versus the immanent, freedom versus dependency, hope versus absurdity, trust versus anxiety, eternity versus ephemerality, and functional transparency versus opaqueness. Third, they propose that the 'equilibrium' between these poles characterise five different stages of development in religious judgement. According to the theory, the individual stages are characterised by qualitative differentiation, irreversible sequentiality, structural wholeness, and hierarchical differentiation and integration.

At stage one (absolute heteronomy) the Ultimate, or God, interferes actively and unmediated in the world. At stage two ('Do Ut Des') the Ultimate, still viewed as external, can be influenced. At stage three (absolute autonomy) the Ultimate is being pushed out of the world. At stage four (mediated autonomy and salvation-plan) subjects surrender again to an Ultimate. At stage five (inter-subjective religiosity) subjects occupy a totally religious standpoint but feel no need to be grounded in a plan of salvation or a religious community. Prior to stage one, Oser and Gmünder posit a pre-religious attitude (stage zero). After stage five, they raise the possibility of a further stage which tends towards universal communication and solidarity (stage six).

Alongside this clearly developed theory Oser and Gmünder propose an empirical methodology for the 'validation' of the stage-concept of religious judgement. They develop the semi-clinical interview technique to explore the responses of individuals to 'religious dilemma' narratives designed to allow the interviewees to be located on the seven polarities of religious judgement. At the time when their book was published, however, all this theoretical structure rested on just 112 interviews, and as yet insufficient statistical detail is given regarding the analysis of the interview data to permit an objective independent assessment of what these data actually demonstrate.

COMPLEMENTARITY IN RELIGIOUS THINKING

The conflict between science and religion has been noted by a number of studies concerned with adolescent religiosity, including Poole (1983), Gibson (1989a), Reich (1991) and Fulljames, Gibson and Francis (1991). A valuable theoretical framework for understanding this conflict is provided by Reich (1989) who argues that:

> It is the maturity of children's thinking which influences the way they see the relationship between science and religion. We must therefore study the stages of cognitive development to see how the crisis in the views of the world develops. The crucial factor is whether alternative structures of interpretation can be understood as complementing each other, and we shall suggest that it is the achievement of this 'complementarity' which enables young people to pass through critical stages of their development. Complementarity enables people to co-ordinate 'conflicting' statements and to arrive at synoptic points of view.

According to Reich's theoretical schema, the development of complementarity, if fully formulated, would consist of five consecutive levels of thinking. When confronted by two alternative theories, at the first level of thinking it is characteristic that either one or the other theory is declared correct. At the second level of thinking there is some examination of the possibility that both theories are correct. At the third level of thinking both theories are regarded as necessary for a satisfactory description or explanation. Reich regards this third level as the appearance of genuine complementarity in thinking. At the fourth level of thinking both theories are immediately understood as complementary, and the mutuality of their relationship is discussed. At the fifth level the problem is considered afresh starting from basic principles and a sophisticated synopsis of logically possible explanations and relationships is presented.

An empirical study by Oser and Reich (1987) concluded that about two-thirds of the decisions made by six- to ten-year-olds were at level one, while about 80 per cent of the decisions made by the 20–25-year-olds in their sample were at level four.

MEASURING ATTITUDES

In a rather different critique of Goldman's work, Francis (1976) drew attention to the way in which the link between his programmes of research and curriculum development hinged on a series of untested assumptions regarding the relationships between pupil attitudes and stages of thinking and between pupil attitudes and curriculum content. This critique led to a new initiative concerned with promoting a series of interrelated studies into the development of attitudes towards Christianity during childhood and adolescence.

After reviewing previous research in the area, Francis (1979b) recognised that, while a series of studies had explored aspects of pupil attitudes towards religion in recent years (Garrity, 1960; Jones, 1962; Johnson, 1966; Alatopoulos, 1968; Esawi, 1968; Taylor, 1970; Turner, 1970; Povall, 1971; Lewis, 1974; Westbury, 1975; Russell, 1978), the problem in integrating and synthesising the findings from these studies resulted from the diversity of measuring instruments used. As a consequence, in a paper entitled 'Measurement reapplied', Francis (1978a) invited other researchers to collaborate with him in using the same measuring instrument, the Francis scale of attitude towards Christianity described by Francis (1978b).

This 24-item scale was developed after systematically testing the five different approaches to attitude scaling proposed by Thurstone (1928), Likert (1932), Guttman (1944), Edwards (1957) and Osgood, Suci and Tannenbaum (1957) among different age groups. The Likert method of scaling emerged as the most reliable and robust over the school age population. The items are concerned with the pupils' affective responses to God, Jesus, bible, prayer, church and religion in school, assessed on a five-point scale, ranging from *agree strongly*, through *not certain*, to *disagree strongly*. Considerable evidence is now available on the reliability and validity of this instrument during childhood and adolescence (Francis, 1988) and on the influence of different test conditions (Francis, 1979c, 1981). The scale has been modified for use among adults by Francis and Stubbs (1987) and Francis (1992a). Short forms of the instrument have been developed for use among young people (Francis, Greer and Gibson, 1991; Francis 1992b) and among adults (Francis, 1993a). The scale has also been subjected to significant scrutiny and criticism, for example by Greer (1982c, 1983b) and Levitt (1995).

LOCATING ATTITUDES

The Francis scale of attitude towards Christianity has now been employed in upwards of 80 published studies which integrate to provide a cumulative picture of the personal, social and contextual factors relating to attitudes towards Christianity during childhood and adolescence. These studies fall into seven main groups (Francis, 1993b).

First, a series of descriptive studies has charted how attitudes towards Christianity change as children grow up, how attitudes differ between boys and girls, and how the situation varies between different cultures. Examples of such studies are provided in England (Francis, 1989a), Scotland (Gibson, 1989b), Northern Ireland (Francis and Greer, 1990a), Kenya (Fulljames and Francis, 1987b) and Nigeria (Francis and McCarron, 1989). Other studies have extended the jigsaw into Catholic schools in England (Francis, 1987c), Scotland (Gibson and Francis, 1989) and Northern Ireland (Greer and Francis, 1991).

Second, a series of studies has been conducted throughout the same schools at four-yearly intervals since 1974. Such replication allows careful monitoring of how the young person's response to Christianity is changing over time (Francis, 1989b, 1989c, 1992c).

Third, several studies have concentrated on identifying the character and influence of denominational schools, at primary (Francis, 1984, 1986a, 1987a) and secondary level (Francis and Carter, 1980; Francis, 1986b; Long, 1989; Francis and Greer, 1990b). Boyle (1984) explored the relative influence of Catholic middle and secondary schools among 12 year olds.

Fourth, a group of studies has focused specifically on the influence of home and parents. Gibson, Francis and Pearson (1990) and Francis, Pearson and Lankshear (1990) isolated the role of social class. Francis and Gibson (1993a) isolated the relative influence of mothers and fathers on sons and daughters at two different stages in development. Kay (1981a) explored the relationship between parental marital happiness and their children's attitudes towards religion. Francis, Gibson and Lankshear (1991) charted the influence of Sunday school attendance.

A fifth set of studies has modelled the influence of personality on individual differences in religious development, including the function of neuroticism (Francis, Pearson, Carter and Kay, 1981a; Francis, Pearson and

Kay, 1983a; Francis and Pearson, 1991), extraversion (Francis, Pearson, Carter and Kay, 1981b; Francis, Pearson and Kay, 1983b; Francis and Pearson, 1985a) and psychoticism (Kay, 1981b; Francis and Pearson, 1985b; Francis, 1992d). Francis, Pearson and Kay (1983c, 1988) and Pearson and Francis (1989) explored the relationship between religiosity and lie scale scores or truthfulness. Francis and Pearson (1987) charted the role of religion in the development of empathy during adolescence. Pearson, Francis and Lightbown (1986) modelled the relationship between religion and impulsivity and venturesomeness during adolescence. Other studies in this tradition are exampled by Francis, Pearson and Stubbs (1985), Francis and Pearson (1988), Francis, Lankshear and Pearson (1989) and Francis and Montgomery (1992).

A sixth set of studies has explored the relationship between attitudes towards Christianity and attitudes towards science, giving particular attention to the ideas of scientism and creationism (Fulljames and Francis, 1987a, 1988; Francis, Gibson and Fulljames, 1990; Fulljames, Gibson and Francis, 1991; Francis, Fulljames and Gibson, 1992).

Other studies have employed the attitude scale to explore issues like the religious significance of denominational identity (Francis, 1990), the impact of popular religious television (Francis and Gibson, 1992), the influence of pop culture (Francis and Gibson, 1993b), the contribution of conversion experiences (Kay, 1981c) or religious experience (Greer and Francis, 1992; Francis and Greer, 1993), the relationship between religion and prejudice (Greer, 1985), and the impact of teaching world religions on adolescent attitude towards Christianity (Kay, 1981d).

RELIGIOUS EXPERIENCE

Although studies of religious experience conducted among adults often draw attention to remembered events during childhood and adolescence (Robinson, 1977a, 1977b, 1978), comparatively little attention has been given to researching religious experience among school pupils. Five notable exceptions are provided by Elkind and Elkind (1962), Paffard (1973), Miles (1983), Robinson and Jackson (1987) and a set of studies by Greer (1981b, 1982b), Greer and Francis (1992) and Francis and Greer (1993).

Elkind and Elkind (1962) found that a high percentage of a group of 144 high school pupils in the USA had 'recurrent' and 'acute' experiences in which they had felt close to God. In England, Paffard (1973) produced evidence of the common occurrence of 'transcendental experiences' among 400 sixth-form pupils and undergraduates. Miles (1983) undertook a detailed study among 137 sixth form students to test three hypotheses: that transcendental experience forms an element in the experience of adolescents; that teaching can improve students' understanding of transcendental experience; and that understanding improves students' attitudes towards transcendental experience. Comparisons were made between a group of 82 students who followed a taught programme about transcendental experience and a control group of 55 students. Attitudes were assessed by semantic differential tests, while levels of understanding were assessed by Piagetian type interviews. Robinson and Jackson (1987) conducted a questionnaire survey among 6,576 pupils from the age of 16 upwards. Factor analysis identified ten potential scales within the questionnaire, including measures of numinous experience and mystical experience. The survey also presented the pupils with two model passages presenting accounts of religious experiences. These examples were then followed by questions probing the pupils' own understanding and experiences.

Greer (1981b) reported on a survey conducted among 1,872 upper-sixth form pupils at controlled or Protestant voluntary schools in Northern Ireland in 1978. The data demonstrated that 38 per cent of the boys and 51 per cent of the girls replied 'yes' to the question, 'Have you ever had an experience of God, for example, his presence or his help or anything else?' Over a quarter of the pupils described this experience, and Greer classified their descriptions under nine headings, namely, guidance and help, examinations, depression and sickness, death, answered prayer, God's presence, conversion experiences, good experiences and miscellaneous. Greer (1982b) reported on the findings of including the same question in a survey conducted in 1981 among 940 Roman Catholic and 1,193 Protestant pupils between the ages of 12 and 17 in Northern Ireland. The answer 'yes' was given to this question by 31 per cent of the Protestant boys, 39 per cent of the Protestant girls, 35 per cent of the Roman Catholic boys and 64 per cent of the Roman Catholic girls. Greer and Francis (1992) and Francis and Greer (1993) employed two different samples to explore the contribution of religious experience to the development of positive religious attitudes among secondary school pupils in Northern Ireland. They concluded that the acknowledgement and naming of personal religious experience was associated with the formation of more positive attitudes towards Christianity.

Hay (1988, 1990) discussed the bearing of empirical studies of religious experience on education.

IMAGES OF GOD

A significant strand in the empirical psychology of religion has been concerned with the relationship between parental images and representations of God (Vergote and Tamayo, 1981). Differences in research methods used, populations examined, and concepts employed by these studies, however, led to four different and conflicting views. First, the pioneering study by Nelson and Jones (1957) drew attention to a strong relation between the concept of God and the mother image for both male and female subjects. A second group of studies by Strunk (1959), Godin and Hallez (1965) and Deconchy (1968) indicated that the relation between God and mother (or the feminine image) was pre-eminent in men, whereas in women the relation between God and father (or the masculine image) predominated. Third, Vergote, Tamayo, Pasquali, Bonami, Pattyn and Custers (1969) found that, in their American samples, both males and females emphasised the paternal image of God rather than the maternal image and that this tendency was even stronger in males than females. The paternal image of God was also emphasised by both boys and girls within the two Asian communities reported by Vergote and Aubert (1973). Fourth, Vergote, Bonami, Custers and Pattyn (1967) found that, in their French-speaking Belgian sample, both males and females emphasised the parental image of God corresponding to their own sex.

A very different research tradition concerned with images of God was pioneered by Harms (1944) who asked children to imagine God or 'the highest being they thought to exist' and then to draw or paint what they imagined. From his analysis of these drawings Harms discerned three stages of development, described as fairy tale, realistic and individualistic. This tradition has been carried on by Pitts (1976, 1977, 1979). Heller (1986) also employed drawings, alongside letters to God, doll play and interviews.

A third research tradition is used by Hilliard (1959) who asked 608 pupils in four secondary schools to write on the topic, 'My idea of God'. They were given no prompting or assistance 'in the hope that what they wrote would be a spontaneous expression of their own ideas'. More recently, Oger (1970) and Ludwig, Weber and Iben (1974) invited children to write letters to God and analysed their content.

A fourth research tradition in this area is illustrated by Claerhout and Declercq (1970) who employed a photo-test to explore adolescents' images of Jesus among 1,200 pupils attending Catholic schools. Forty photos were used. The pupils were asked to identify the images they would be inclined to prefer and the images they would be inclined to reject, and then to justify their choices.

LIFE QUESTIONS

Tamminen (1977) pioneered a research programme in Finland to explore the place of pupils' own questions and problems in religious education, between the ages of seven and 16. In charting the pupils' life questions, three different measuring instruments were used. The first instrument was a projective test consisting of eight photographs of children. The photographs were followed by captions like: 'Sometimes we think of something that is difficult to understand. This is Pekka. Just now he is thinking of something that he has thought of many times before and that he would really like to understand. Pekka is reflecting on ... .' The second instrument presented a list of 35 experiences and problems like 'I am afraid of failing at school' or 'I am wondering whether life goes on after death.' The pupils were asked to rate how often such experiences or problems occurred in their lives. The third instrument presented 65 topics of religious education and asked the pupils to rate their level of interest in these topics. Over 1,500 pupils participated in this initial project from four different geographical areas. Other aspects of this project are discussed by Tamminen (1991).

PRAYER

Research concerned with prayer during childhood and adolescence falls into three main strands. The first strand, grounded in developmental psychology, has attempted to discover stages in the development of the concept of prayer. For example, Long, Elkind and Spilka (1967) identified three stages in their sample of 160 boys and girls between the ages of five and 12. In the first stage, between the ages of five and seven, children had a global conception of prayer in the sense that their comprehension of the term was both vague and fragmentary. In the second stage, between the ages of seven and nine, children had a concrete differentiated conception of prayer and recognised that it involved verbal activity. At this stage, however, prayer was still an external activity, a routine form, rather than personal and internal. In the third stage, between the ages of nine and 12, children had an abstract conception of prayer in the sense that it was regarded as an internal activity deriving from personal conviction and belief. Other studies in this tradition include Elkind, Spilka and Long (1968), May (1977; 1979), Worten and Dollinger (1986), Rosenberg (1990) and Scarlett and Perriello (1991).

A second strand of research has concentrated on mapping changing patterns of belief in the causal efficacy of prayer during childhood and adolescence. For example, Brown (1966) explored the responses of 398 boys and 703 girls between the ages of 12 and 17 to seven situations: success in a football match, safety during battle, avoidance of detection of theft, repayment of a debt, fine weather for a church fête, escape from a shark and recovery of a sick grandmother. In relation to each situation, he addressed two questions: is it right to pray in this situation? Are the prayers likely to have any effect? The data demonstrated a consistent age-related trend away from belief in the causal efficacy of petitionary prayer. Other studies in this tradition include Godin and van Roey (1959), Thouless and Brown (1964), Brown (1968) and Tamminen (1991).

A third strand of research, grounded in social psychology, has attempted to discover the social and contextual influences on individual differences in the practice of prayer during childhood and adolescence. For example, Francis and Brown (1990) examined the influence of home, church and denominational identity on an attitudinal predisposition to pray and the practice of prayer among 4,948 11-year-old children in England. Francis and Brown (1991) replicated this study among 711 16-year-olds. They demonstrate that among 16-year-olds the influence of church is stronger and the influence of parents is weaker than among 11-year-olds. Another study in this tradition by Janssen, de Hart and den Draak (1989, 1990) demonstrated significant differences in praying practices according to religious affiliation among 16- and 17-year-old Dutch high school pupils.

SCHOOL WORSHIP

In spite of its central place in school life in England and Wales, the daily act of worship has received little research in its own right, although a number of surveys concerned with the broader issue of religious education include some reference to school worship. For example, Greer (1972b) found that 93 per cent of parents agreed with the school day beginning with an act of worship. Among sixth-form pupils, however, the proportion fell to 62 per cent among girls and 40 per cent among boys. A recent survey of religion and values among more than 13,000 13- to 15-year-olds in England and Wales found that only 6 per cent of this age group agreed with the view that schools should hold a religious assembly every day. Even among those pupils who attended church every week, the proportion rose no higher than 17 per cent (Francis and Kay, 1995).

Brimer (1972) set out to explore the practices and attitudes of primary school headteachers and fourth-year junior pupils in the city of Birmingham. He found that, while 61 per cent of headteachers rated assemblies as very important, this view was shared by only 27 per cent of their pupils. Pritchard (1974) undertook case studies of worship in Church of England primary schools.

A major study into school worship and assemblies was initiated within the University of Southampton in the early 1980s. The report of the pilot survey by Souper and Kay (1982) described the situation in Hampshire on the basis on an 83 per cent response rate from a total survey of the secondary schools and a 72 per cent response rate from a survey of one in four of the primary schools. The analysis considered issues like who conducts the assemblies, where assemblies are held, how assemblies relate to the religious education syllabus and the general curriculum, the use of prayer and singing, drama and audio-visual aids, withdrawal from assemblies and pressure for change.

Souper and Kay (1983) followed this pilot study with a survey in independent schools. No report emerged, however, from this major study in state maintained schools.

CATHOLIC SCHOOLS

Research in religious education is also concerned with the wider issues of the religious distinctiveness and effectiveness of denominational schools. Here, the international nature of the Catholic Church has generated a wide international literature. Key studies are provided as follows: in the USA by Neuwien (1966), Greeley and Rossi (1966), Greeley, McCready and McCourt (1976), Greeley (1982), Lesko (1988), Marsh and Grayson (1990), Francis and Egan (1990), Marsh (1991) and Bryk, Lee and Holland (1993); in Australia by Leavey (1972), Flynn (1975, 1985), Fahy (1976, 1978, 1980, 1992), De Vaus (1981), and Francis and Egan (1987); and in Canada by McLaren (1986).

Research into the distinctiveness and effectiveness of Catholic schools in the UK has its roots in studies by Brothers (1964), Spencer (1968), Hornsby-Smith and Petit (1975) and Hornsby-Smith (1978). More recent studies on Catholic schools in the UK have employed three main techniques. Participant observation was employed by Burgess (1983, 1987) to make a detailed case study of one Catholic comprehensive school in England and by Murray (1985) to compare a Catholic and a Protestant school in Northern Ireland. Dent (1988) used unstructured interviews to profile five different Catholic schools. Francis and colleagues employed psychometric techniques to assess the influence of Catholic schools on the pupils. For example, in a comparative study of ten- and 11-year-old pupils attending county, Anglican and Catholic primary schools in 1974, 1978 and 1982, Francis (1986a) concluded that Catholic schools contribute to the development of positive religious attitudes among pupils of this age, after controlling for the influence of home and church. A similar conclusion is suggested by Francis (1987a) among 11- year-old pupils. In a study of 2,895 pupils attending five Catholic secondary schools, Francis (1986b) drew attention to the way in which these schools had a less positive influence on pupils from non-Catholic backgrounds, even when they were practising members of other denominations. Egan and Francis (1986) and Egan (1988) went one step further in their study of the fifth-year pupils attending 15 of the 16 Catholic secondary schools in Wales and highlighted the different influence of these schools on non-Catholic, lapsed Catholic and practising Catholic pupils. In a study in Scotland, Rhymer (1983) and Rhymer and Francis (1985) drew attention to the equal influence of separate Catholic schools and separate Catholic religious education provision within non-denominational schools, in comparison with Catholic pupils who attended non-denominational schools in which separate religious education provision was not available.

Other recent research perspectives on Catholic schools in Britain are provided by Hanlon (1989) on provisions for religious education, by Arthur (1992, 1993, 1994a, 1994b), including studies of parental involvement, policy perceptions of headteachers and governors, admissions policies and curriculum, by Morris (1994) on the academic performance of Catholic schools, and by Tritter (1992) on the effect of religious schools on their students' moral values.

ANGLICAN SCHOOLS

There is considerably less research on the distinctiveness and effectiveness of Anglican schools than on Catholic schools. Francis (1986c) explored the attitudes of teachers in Anglican primary schools and found that the younger teachers were less sympathetic to the church school system than older teachers. Kay, Piper and Gay (1988) and Francis and Stone (1995) reported on the attitudes of governors of Anglican schools. Francis (1987a) compared the provision for religious education in Anglican and county primary schools. He found that the church schools adopted a more church-related approach to religious education. In two studies into the impact of Anglican primary schools on the pupils' attitudes towards religion, Francis (1986a) found that Church of England voluntary-aided schools exerted a negative influence compared with county schools, while Francis (1987a) found that Church of England voluntary-controlled schools exerted a negative influence compared with county schools. In two studies exploring the impact of Anglican secondary schools on pupil attitudes, Francis and Brown (1991) identified a negative influence on attitude towards prayer, while Francis and Jewell (1992) found no influence, either positive or negative, on attitude towards the church. In two studies exploring the impact of Anglican primary schools on local church life, Francis and Lankshear (1990, 1991) identified a significant positive influence in both rural and urban settings. O'Keeffe (1986) explored the role of church schools in a multi-cultural, multi-racial context. She drew on information from 103 Church of England and county schools of both primary and secondary level in Greater London, the north west and the West Midlands, including interviews with 102 headteachers, 67 religious education teachers and 139 parents whose children were attending church schools. Two other studies provide profiles of Anglican primary and secondary schools in the diocese of London (Gay, Kay, Newdick and Perry, 1991a, 1991b).

In a study concerned with multi-cultural education, Ball and Troyna (1987) concluded that both Anglican and Catholic schools have lagged behind county schools in promoting multi-cultural education. Cox and Skinner (1990) reported an early stage of a curriculum development project based in five church aided primary schools in a north Warwickshire town. It set out to uncover the attitudes of the teachers to multi-faith religious education and to assess the impact of in-service training. The authors concluded that the teachers had welcomed and reported favourable to a multi-faith approach to religious education, and they found the change less difficult than they had expected. Higgins (1989) analysed the ways in which the syllabuses of religious education developed for use in Church of England voluntary-aided schools treat the role of women in the context of the current social and ecclesiastical debate. He found the syllabuses uninformed by these contemporary perspectives.

INDEPENDENT SCHOOLS

Most British research in religious education has been conducted within the state maintained sector of schools. The major exception is the report of the Bloxham Project Research Unit, *Images of Life*, by Richardson and Chapman (1973). This project set out to enquire into the ways in which English boarding schools 'communicate the Christian ideas and values to which they are historically committed', through the use of interviews and questionnaires among headteachers, chaplains and pupils. The analysis focused on four themes: images of God, images of self and society, images of school and images of change.

Following on from their study of assemblies within state maintained schools, Souper and Kay (1983) provided a detailed profile of worship in the independent day school, including analyses of the use of prayer and song, music and drama, audio and visual aids.

Two more recent studies by Brenda Gay examined the Church of England's role in the independent sector, with particular emphasis on religious education, school worship and the involvement of clergy in the life of the school (Gay, 1993a) and the wider religious factor in girls' independent schools (Gay, 1993b).

THE WAY AHEAD

Looking back over the past three decades, three main points can be made about research in religious education. First, the social, political, religious and educational climate of the early 1960s generated a range of fresh initiatives in this field. From a positive perspective, these initiatives influenced practice and stimulated changes. From a less positive perspective, however, they failed to develop a sufficiently broadly based range of theoretical and methodological foundations to establish sustainable research traditions in religious education. Second, religious educators themselves still tend to undervalue the potential contribution which educational research can make to their discipline. This may be illustrated, for example, by the comparative dearth of empirically-based projects undertaken for research degrees in the field. Third, the field has been significantly shaped by the pioneering work of just a handful of skilled and committed researchers, as exampled by John Greer in the University of Ulster.

If research in religious education is to mature in the next decade, three issues now need to be addressed. To begin with, religious educators need to be adequately equipped with the appropriate range of interdisciplinary skills to critique and to promote research. Good research in religious education needs to be both theologically informed and methodologically grounded. Second, diverse initiatives in the field need to be more professionally co-ordinated and integrated. The time is right for the development of a graduate school of research in religious education capable of drawing together a balance of research skills. Third, research in religious education needs to be adequately funded and supported. A government apparently committed to the value of religious education within schools needs also to recognise the value of a research base for this subject.

The research agenda for the next decade is likely still to be dominated by studies in four areas: religious development, religious language, religious understanding and religious attitudes. If basic research in these areas could lead to greater conceptual clarity and improved techniques of assessment, the next generation of researchers in religious education would inherit a much stronger foundation on which to build.

FURTHER READING

Two thorough reviews of empirical research in aspects of religious development are provided by Strommen (1971) and Hyde (1990). A collection of new essays assembled under the title *Research in Religious*

Education is edited by Francis and Campbell (1996).

REFERENCES

Ainsworth, O. (1961). 'A study of some aspects of the growth of religious understanding of children aged between 5 and 11 years', unpublished Dip.Ed. dissertation, University of Manchester.

Alatopoulos, C. S. (1968). 'A study of relationship between religious knowledge and certain social and moral attitudes among school leavers', unpublished M.Phil. dissertation, University of London.

Alves, C. (1968). *Religion and the Secondary School*. London: SCM.

Archer, J. and Macrae, M. (1991). 'Gender-perceptions of school subjects among 10–11 year olds', *British Journal of Educational Psychology*, 61, pp. 99–103.

Arthur, J. (1992). 'The Catholic school and its curriculum', *British Journal of Religious Education*, 14, pp. 157–68.

— (1993). 'Policy perceptions of headteachers and governors in Catholic schooling', *Educational Studies*, 19, pp. 275–87.

— (1994a). 'Parental involvement in Catholic schools: a case of increasing conflict', *British Journal of Educational Studies*, 42, pp. 174–90.

— (1994b). 'Admissions to Catholic schools: principles and practice', *British Journal of Religious Education*, 17, pp. 35–45.

Astley, J. (1991). *How Faith Grows: faith development and Christian Education*, London, National Society and Church House Publishing.

Astley, J. and Francis, L. J. (eds) (1992). *Christian Perspectives on Faith Development: a reader*. Leominster: Gracewing.

Attfield, D. (1974). 'A fresh look at Goldman: the research needed today', *Learning for Living*, 14, pp. 44–9.

Bailey, J.R. (1979). 'Religious education in Lincolnshire secondary schools', *British Journal of Religious Education*, 1, pp. 89–94.

Ball, W. and Troyna, B. (1987). 'Resistance, rights and rituals: denominational schools and multicultural education', *Journal of Educational Policy*, 2, pp. 15–25.

Barnes, M., Doyle, D. and Byron, J. (1989). 'The formulation of a Fowler scale: an empirical assessment among Catholics', *Review of Religious Research*, 30, pp. 412–20.

Bedwell, A. E. (1977). 'Aims of religious education teachers in Hereford and Worcester', *Learning for Living*, 17, pp. 66–74.

Beechick, R. A. (1974). 'Children's understanding of parables: a developmental study', unpublished D.Ed. dissertation, Arizona State University.

Benfield, G. (1975). 'Religious education in secondary schools: a close look at one area', *Learning for Living*, 14, pp. 173–8.

Billow, R. M. (1975). 'A cognitive developmental study of metaphor comprehension', *Developmental Psychology*, 11, pp. 415–23.

— (1981). 'Observing spontaneous metaphor in children', *Journal of Experimental Child Psychology*, 31, pp. 430–45.

Boyle, J. J. (1984). 'Catholic children's attitudes towards Christianity', unpublished M.Sc. dissertation, University of Bradford.

Bradbury, J. B. (1947). 'The religious development of the adolescent', unpublished M.Ed. dissertation, University of Manchester.

Bradshaw, J. (1950). 'A psychological study of the development of religious beliefs among children and young persons', unpublished M.Sc. dissertation, University of London.

Brimer, J. (1972). 'School Worship with Juniors', *Learning for Living*, 11, 5, pp. 6–12.

Brisco, H. (1969). 'A study of some aspects of the special contribution of Church of England aided primary schools to children's development', unpublished M.Ed. dissertation, University of Liverpool.

Brodzinsky, D. (1975). 'The role of conceptual tempo and stimulus characteristics in children's humour development', *Developmental Psychology*, 11, pp. 843–50.

— (1977). 'Children's comprehension and appreciation of verbal jokes in relation to conceptual tempo', *Child Development*, 48, pp. 960–7.

Brothers, J. (1964). *Church and School: A study of the impact of education on religion.* Liverpool: University of Liverpool Press.

Brown, L.B. (1966). 'Ego-centric thought in petitionary prayer: a cross-cultural study', *Journal of Social Psychology*, 68, pp. 197–210.

— (1968). 'Some attitudes underlying petitionary prayer', in Godin, A. (ed.), *From Cry to Word: contributions towards a psychology of prayer.* Brussels: Lumen Vitae Press, pp. 65–84.

Bryk, A. S., Lee, V. E. and Holland, P. B. (1993). *Catholic Schools and the Common Good.* Cambridge, MA: Harvard University Press.

Bull, N. J. (1969). *Moral Judgement from Childhood to Adolescence.* London: Routledge & Kegan Paul.

Burgess, B.G. (1975). 'A study of the attitudes of primary school teachers in Essex and Walsall to religious education and worship', unpublished M.Phil. dissertation, University of London, Institute of Education.

— (1980). 'a further study of opinions of Essex primary teachers about religious education and school assembly in the context of contemporary controversy', unpublished Ph.D. dissertation, University of London, Institute of Education.

Burgess, R.G. (1983). *Experiencing Comprehensive Education: A Study of Bishop McGregor School.* London: Methuen.

— (1987). 'Studying and restudying Bishop McGregor School', in G. Walford (ed.), *Doing Sociology of Education.* Barcombe: Falmer Press, pp. 67–94.

Chamberlain, G. L. (1979). 'Faith development and campus ministry', *Religious Education*, 74, pp. 314–24.

Claerhout, J. and Declercq, M. (1970). 'Christ in the mind of the adolescent: photo-test and enquiry in Catholic education', *Lumen Vitae*, 25, pp. 243–64.

Cox, E. (1966). *Changing Aims in Religious Education.* London: Routledge & Kegan Paul.

— (1967). *Sixth Form Religion.* London: SCM.

— (1968). 'Honest to Goldman: an assessment', *Religious Education*, 63, pp. 424–8.

Cox, E. and Skinner, M. (1990). 'Multi-faith religious education in church primary schools', *British Journal of Religious Education*, 12, pp. 102–9.

Daines, J. W. (1949). 'A psychological study of the attitude of adolescents to religion and religious instruction', unpublished Ph.D. dissertation, University of London.

— (1958). 'Religious education: a series of abstracts of unpublished theses in religious education', Part 1, 1918–1957. Nottingham, University of Nottingham Institute of Education.

— (1962). *An Enquiry into the Methods and Effects of Religious Education in Sixth Forms.* Nottingham, University of Nottingham, Institute of Education.

— (1964). 'Religious education: a series of abstracts of unpublished theses in religious education', Part 2, 1958–1963. Nottingham, University of Nottingham Institute of Education.

Dale, R. R. and Jones, J. A. (1964). 'An investigation into the comparative response of boys and girls to scripture as a school subject in certain co-educational grammar schools in industrial South Wales', *British Journal of Educational Psychology*, 34, pp. 132–42.

Darcy, F. and Beniskos, J. M. (1971). 'Some people say: the themes of resurrection and hell as perceived by 6 to 8 year old children receiving religious instruction', *Lumen Vitae*, 26, pp. 449–60.

Dawes, R.S. (1954). 'The concept of God among secondary school children', unpublished M.A. dissertation, University of London.

Debot-Sevrin, M.R. (1968). 'An attempt in experimental teaching: the assimilation of a parable by normal and maladjusted children of the 6–7 age group', in Godin (ed.), *From Cry to Word*, pp. 135–58.

Deconchy, J. P. (1965). 'The idea of God: its emergence between 7 and 16 years', in Godin (ed.), *From Religious Experience to a Religious Attitude*. Chicago: Loyola University Press, pp. 97–108.

— (1968). 'God and the parental images', in Godin (ed.), *From Cry to Word*, pp 85–94.

Dent, H. J. (1947). *The Education Act 1944: provisions, possibilities and some problems* (3rd edn.). London: University of London Press.

Dent, R. (1988). *Faith of Our Fathers: Roman Catholic schools in a multifaith society.* Coventry: City of Coventry Education Department.

De Vaus, D. A. (1981). 'The impact of Catholic schools on the religious orientation of boys and girls', *Journal of Christian Education*, 71, pp. 44–51.

Droege, T.A. (1984). 'Pastoral counselling and faith development', *Journal of Psychology and Christianity*, 3, 4, pp. 37–47.

Dumoulin, A. (1971). 'The priest's occupations as perceived by 6-12-year-old children', *Lumen Vitae*, 26, pp. 316–32.

Dykstra, C. and Parks, S. (eds) (1986). *Faith Development and Fowler*. Birmingham, Alabama: Religious Education Press.

Edwards, A. L. (1957). *Techniques of Attitude Scale Construction*. New York: Appleton-Century-Crofts.

Egan, J. (1988). *Opting Out: Catholic schools today*. Leominster: Fowler Wright.

Egan, J. and Francis, L. J. (1986). 'School ethos in Wales: the impact of non-practising Catholic and non-Catholic pupils on Catholic secondary schools', *Lumen Vitae*, 41, pp. 159–73.

Elkind, D. (1961). 'The child's conception of his religious denomination I: the Jewish child', *Journal of Genetic Psychology*, 99, pp. 209–25.

— (1962). 'The child's conception of his religious denomination II: the Catholic child', *Journal of Genetic Psychology*, 101, pp. 185–93.

— (1963). 'The child's conception of his religious denomination III: the Protestant child', *Journal of Genetic Psychology*, 103, pp. 291–304.

— (1964). 'The child's conception of his religious identity', *Lumen Vitae*, 19, pp. 635–46.

Elkind, D. and Elkind, S. (1962). 'Varieties of religious experience in young adolescents', *Journal for the Scientific Study of Religion*, 2, pp. 102–12.

Elkind, D., Spilka, B. and Long, D. (1968). 'The child's conception of prayer', in Godin (ed.), *From Cry to Word*, pp. 51–64.

Esawi, A. R. M. (1968). 'Ethico-religious attitudes and emotional adjustment in children aged 11-18 years', unpublished Ph.D. dissertation, University of Nottingham.

Fagerlind, T. (1974). 'Research on religious education in the Swedish school system', *Character Potential*, 7, pp. 38–47.

134 A GUIDE TO EDUCATIONAL RESEARCH

Fahy, P. S. (1976). 'School and home perceptions of Australian adolescent males attending Catholic schools', *Our Apostolate*, 24, pp. 167–88.
— (1978). 'Religious beliefs of 15,900 youths: attending Australian Catholic schools, years 12, 10, 8, 1975–1977', *Word in Life*, 26, pp. 66–72.
— (1980). 'The religious effectiveness of some Australian Catholic high schools', *Word in Life*, 28, pp. 86–98.
— (1992). *Faith in Catholic Classrooms*. Homebush, New South Wales: St Paul Publications.
Flavell, J. H. (1963). *The Developmental Psychology of Jean Piaget*. New York: Van Nostrand Reinhold Company.
Flynn, M. F. (1975). *Some Catholic Schools in Action*. Sydney: Catholic Education Office.
— (1985). *The Effectiveness of Catholic Schools*. Homebush, New South Wales: St Paul Publications.
Forrester, J. F. (1946). 'A study of the attitudes of adolescents to their own intellectual, social and spiritual development', unpublished Ph.D. dissertation, University of London.
Fowler, J. W. (1981). *Stages of Faith: the psychology of human development and the quest for meaning*. San Francisco: Harper & Row.
— (1987). *Faith Development and Pastoral Care*. Philadelphia: Fortress Press.
Fowler, J. W., Nipkow, K. E. and Schweitzer, F. (1992). *Stages of Faith and Religious Development*. London: SCM.
Fowles, B. and Glanz, M. E. (1977). 'Competence and talent in verbal riddle comprehension', *Journal of Child Language*, 4, pp. 433–52.
Francis, L. J. (1976). 'An enquiry into the concept "readiness for religion"', unpublished PhD dissertation, University of Cambridge.
— (1978a). 'Measurement reapplied: research into the child's attitude towards religion', *British Journal of Religious Education*, 1, pp. 45–51.
— (1978b). 'Attitude and longitude: a study in measurement', *Character Potential*, 8, pp. 119–30.
— (1979a). 'Research and the development of religious thinking', *Educational Studies*, 5, pp. 109–15.
— (1979b). 'The child's attitude towards religion: a review of research', *Educational Research*, 21, 1 pp. 103–8.
— (1979c). 'The priest as test administrator in attitude research', *Journal for the Scientific Study of Religion*, 18, pp. 78–81.
— (1981). 'Anonymity and attitude scores among ten and eleven year old children', *Journal of Experimental Education*, 49, pp. 74–76.
— (1984). 'Roman Catholic schools and pupil attitudes in England', *Lumen Vitae*, 39, pp. 99–108.
— (1986a). 'Denominational schools and pupil attitudes towards Christianity', *British Educational Research Journal*, 12, pp. 145–52.
— (1986b). 'Roman Catholic secondary schools: falling rolls and pupil attitudes', *Educational Studies*, 12, pp. 119–27.
— (1986c). *Partnership in Rural Education: church schools and teacher attitudes*. London: Collins Liturgical Publications.
— (1987a). *Religion in the Primary School: partnership between church and state?*. London: Collins Liturgical Publications.
— (1987b). 'The decline in attitude towards religion among 8-15 year olds', *Educational Studies*, 13, pp. 125–34.

— (1987c). 'Measuring attitudes towards Christianity among 12- to 18-year-old pupils in Catholic schools', *Educational Research*, 29, pp. 230–33.

— (1988). 'The development of a scale of attitude towards Christianity among 8-16 year olds', *Collected Original Resources in Education*, 12, fiche 1, A04.

— (1989a). 'Measuring attitude towards Christianity during childhood and adolescence', *Personality and Individual Differences*, 10, pp. 695–8.

— (1989b). 'Drift from the churches: secondary school pupils' attitudes towards Christianity', *British Journal of Religious Education*, 11, pp. 76–86.

— (1989c). 'Monitoring changing attitudes towards Christianity among secondary school pupils between 1974 and 1986', *British Journal of Educational Psychology*, 59, pp. 86–91.

— (1990). 'The religious significance of denominational identity among eleven year old children in England', *Journal of Christian Education*, 97, pp. 23–8.

— (1992a). 'Reliability and validity of the Francis scale of attitude towards Christianity (adult)', *Panorama*, 4, 1, pp. 17–19.

— (1992b). 'Reliability and validity of a short measure of attitude towards Christianity among nine to eleven year old pupils in England', *Collected Original Resources in Education*, 16, 1, fiche 3, A02.

— (1992c). 'Monitoring attitudes towards Christianity: the 1990 study', *British Journal of Religious Education*, 14, pp. 178–82.

— (1992d). 'Is psychoticism really a dimension of personality fundamental to religiosity?' *Personality and Individual Differences*, 13, pp. 645–52.

— (1993a). 'Reliability and validity of a short scale of attitude towards Christianity among adults', *Psychological Reports*, 72, pp. 615–18.

— (1993b). 'Attitudes towards Christianity during childhood and adolescence:assembling the jigsaw', *The Journal of Beliefs and Values*, 14, 2, pp. 4–6.

Francis, L. J. and Brown, L. B. (1990). 'The predisposition to pray: a study of the social influence on the predisposition to pray among eleven year old children in England', *Journal of Empirical Theology*, 3, 2, pp. 23–34.

— (1991). 'The influence of home, church and school on prayer among sixteen year old adolescents in England', *Review of Religious Research*, 33, pp. 112–22.

Francis, L. J., Kay, W. F. and Campbell, W. S. (eds.) (1996). *Research in Religious Education*. Leominster: Gracewing.

Francis, L. J. and Carter, M. (1980). 'Church aided secondary schools, religious education as an examination subject and pupil attitudes towards religion', *British Journal of Educational Psychology*, 50, pp. 297–300.

Francis, L. J. and Egan, J. (1987). 'Catholic schools and the communication of faith', *Catholic School Studies*, 60, 2, pp. 27–34.

— (1990). 'The Catholic school as "faith community": an empirical enquiry', *Religious Education*, 85, pp. 588–603.

Francis, L. J., Fulljames, P. and Gibson, H. M. (1992). 'Does creationism commend the gospel? a developmental study among 11–17 year olds', *Religious Education*, 87, pp. 19–27.

Francis, L. J. and Gibson, H. M. (1992). 'Popular religious television and adolescent attitudes towards Christianity', in Astley, J. and Day, D. V. (eds), *The Contours of Christian Education*. Gt Wakering: McCrimmons, pp. 369–81.

— (1993a). 'Parental influence and adolescent religiosity: a study of church attendance and attitude towards Christianity among 11-12 and 15-16 year olds', *International Journal for the Psychology of Religion*, 3, pp. 241–53.

— (1993b). 'Television, pop culture and the drift from Christianity during adolescence',

British Journal of Religious Education, 15, pp. 31–7.

Francis, L. J., Gibson, H. M. and Fulljames, P. (1990). 'Attitude towards Christianity, creationism, scientism and interest in science among 11-15 year olds', *British Journal of Religious Education*, 13, pp. 4–17.

Francis, L. J., Gibson, H. M. and Lankshear, D. W. (1991). 'The influence of Protestant Sunday Schools on attitude towards Christianity among 11-15 year olds in Scotland', *British Journal of Religious Education*, 14, pp. 35–42.

Francis, L. J., and Greer, J. E. (1990a). 'Measuring attitudes towards Christianity among pupils in Protestant secondary schools in Northern Ireland', *Personality and Individual Differences*, 11, pp. 853–6.

— (1990b). 'Catholic schools and adolescent religiosity in Northern Ireland: shaping moral values', *Irish Journal of Education*, 24, 2, pp. 40–7.

— (1993). 'The contribution of religious experience to Christian development: a study among fourth, fifth and sixth year pupils in Northern Ireland', *British Journal of Religious Education*, 15, pp. 38–43.

Francis, L. J., Greer, J.E. and Gibson, H.M. (1991). 'Reliability and validity of a short measure of attitude towards Christianity among secondary school pupils in England, Scotland and Northern Ireland', *Collected Original Resources in Education*, 15, 3, fiche 2, G09.

Francis, L. J. and Jewell, A. (1992). 'Shaping adolescent attitude towards the church: comparison between Church of England and county secondary schools', *Evaluation and Research in Education*, 6, pp. 13–21.

Francis, L. J. and Kay, W. K. (1995). *Teenage Religion and Values*. Leominster: Gracewing.

Francis, L. J. and Lankshear, D. W. (1990). 'The impact of church schools on village church life', *Educational Studies*, 16, pp. 117–29.

— (1991). 'The impact of church schools on urban church life', *School Effectiveness and School Improvement*, 2, pp. 324–35.

Francis, L. J., Lankshear, D. W. and Pearson, P. R. (1989). 'The relationship between religiosity and the short form JEPQ (JEPQ-S) indices of E, N, L and P among eleven year olds', *Personality and Individual Differences*, 10, pp. 763–9.

Francis, L. J. and McCarron, M. M. (1989). 'The measurement of attitudes towards Christianity among Nigerian secondary school students', *Journal of Social Psychology*, 129, pp. 569–71.

Francis, L. J. and Montgomery, A. (1992). 'Personality and attitudes towards religion among 11-16 year old girls in a single sex Catholic school', *British Journal of Religious Education*, 14, pp. 114–19.

Francis, L. J. and Pearson, P. R. (1985a). 'Extraversion and religiosity', *Journal of Social Psychology*, 125, pp. 269–70.

— (1985b). 'Psychoticism and religiosity among 15 year olds', *Personality and Individual Differences*, 6, pp. 397–8.

— (1987). 'Empathic development during adolescence: religiosity the missing link?' *Personality and Individual Differences*, 8, pp. 145–8.

— (1988). 'Religiosity and the short-scale EPQ-R indices of E, N and L, compared with the JEPI, JEPQ and EPQ', *Personality and Individual Differences*, 9, pp. 653–657.

— (1991). 'Religiosity, gender and the two faces of neuroticism', *Irish Journal of Psychology*, 12, pp. 60–8.

Francis, L. J., Pearson, P.R., Carter, M. and Kay, W.K. (1981a). 'The relationship between neuroticism and religiosity among English 15- and 16-year olds', *Journal of Social Psychology*, 114, pp. 99–102.

— (1981b). 'Are introverts more religious?' *British Journal of Social Psychology*, 20, pp. 101–4.

Francis, L. J., Pearson, P. R. and Kay, W. K. (1983a). 'Neuroticism and religiosity among English school children', *Journal of Social Psychology*, 121, pp. 149–50.

— (1983b). 'Are introverts still more religious?' *Personality and Individual Differences*, 4, pp. 211–12.

— (1983c). 'Are religious children bigger liars?' *Psychological Reports*, 52, pp. 551–4.

— (1988). 'Religiosity and lie scores: a question of interpretation', *Social Behaviour and Personality*, 16, pp. 91–5.

Francis, L. J., Pearson, P. R. and Lankshear, D. W. (1990). 'The relationship between social class and attitude towards Christianity among ten and eleven year old children', *Personality and Individual Differences*, 11, pp. 1019–27.

Francis, L. J., Pearson, P. R. and Stubbs, M. T. (1985). 'Personality and religion among low ability children in residential special schools', *British Journal of Mental Subnormality*, 31, pp. 41–5.

Francis, L. J. and Stone, E. A. (1995). 'The attitudes of school governors towards the religious ethos of Church of England voluntary aided primary schools', *Educational Management and Administration*, 23, pp. 176–87.

Francis, L. J., and Stubbs, M. T. (1987). 'Measuring attitudes towards Christianity: from childhood to adulthood', *Personality and Individual Differences*, 8, pp. 741–3.

Fulljames, P. and Francis, L. J. (1987a). 'Creationism and student attitudes towards science and Christianity', *Journal of Christian Education*, 90, pp. 51–5.

— (1987b). 'The measurement of attitudes towards Christianity among Kenyan secondary school students', *Journal of Social Psychology*, 127, pp. 407–9.

— (1988). 'The influence of creationism and scientism on attitudes towards Christianity among Kenyan secondary school students', *Educational Studies*, 14, pp. 77–96.

Fulljames, P., Gibson, H. M. and Francis, L. J. (1991). 'Creationism, scientism, Christianity and science: a study in adolescent attitudes', *British Educational Research Journal*, 17, pp. 171–90.

Garrity, F. D. (1960). 'A study of the attitude of some secondary modern school pupils towards Religious Education', unpublished M.Ed. dissertation, University of Manchester.

Gates, B. E. (1976). 'Religion and the developing world of children and young people', unpublished Ph.D. dissertation, University of Lancaster.

Gay, B. (1993a). 'The Church of England and the independent schools: a survey,' in Francis, L. J. and Lankshear, D. W. (eds), *Christian Perspectives on Church Schools: a reader*. Leominster: Gracewing, pp. 345–61.

— (1993b). 'Religion in the girls' independent schools', in G. Walford (ed.), *The Private Schooling of Girls: Past and Present*. London: Woburn Press, pp. 187–206.

Gay, J., Kay, B., Newdick, H. and Perry, G. (1991a). *A Role for the Future: Anglican primary schools in the London diocese*. Abingdon: Culham College Institute.

— (1991b). *Schools and Church: Anglican secondary schools in the London diocese*. Abingdon: Culham College Institute.

Gibson, H. M. (1989a). 'Attitudes to religion and science among school children aged 11 to 16 years in a Scottish city', *Journal of Empirical Theology*, 2, pp. 5–26.

— (1989b). 'Measuring attitudes towards Christianity among 11-16 year old pupils in non-denominational schools in Scotland', *Educational Research*, 31, pp. 221–7.

Gibson, H. M. and Francis, L. J. (1989). 'Measuring attitudes towards Christianity among 11-to 16-year old pupils in Catholic schools in Scotland', *Educational Research*, 31, pp. 65–9.

Gibson, H. M., Francis, L. J., and Pearson, P.R. (1990). 'The relationship between social class and attitude towards Christianity among fourteen- and fifteen-year-old adolescents', *Personality and Individual Differences*, 11, pp. 631–5.

Glassey, W. (1943). 'The attitude of grammar school pupils and their parents to education, religion and sport', unpublished M.Ed. dissertation, University of Manchester.

Gobbel, R. and Gobbel, G. (1986). *The Bible: a child's playground*. London: SCM.

Godin, A. (1968). 'Genetic development of the symbolic function: meaning and limits of the works of Goldman', *Religious Education*, 63, pp. 439–45.

Godin, A. and Hallez, M. (1965). 'Parental images and divine paternity', in A. Godin (ed.), *From Religious Experience to a Religious Attitude*. Chicago: Loyola University Press, pp. 65–96.

Godin, A. and Marthe, S. (1960). 'Magic mentality and sacramental life', *Lumen Vitae*, 15, pp. 277–97.

Godin, A. and van Roey, B. (1959). 'Imminent justice and divine protection', *Lumen Vitae*, 14, pp. 129–48.

Goldman, R. J. (1962). 'Some aspects of religious thinking in childhood and adolescence', unpublished Ph.D. dissertation, University of Birmingham.

— (1964). *Religious Thinking from Childhood to Adolescence*. London: Routledge & Kegan Paul.

— (1965a). *Readiness for Religion*. London: Routledge & Kegan Paul.

— (1965b). 'Do we want our children taught about God?' *New Society*, 5, 139, pp. 8–10.

Goldman, R. J. and Goldman, J. (1982). *Children's Sexual Thinking*. London: Routledge.

— (1988). *Show Me Yours*. Harmondsworth: Penguin.

Greeley, A. M. (1982). *Catholic High Schools and Minority Students*. New Brunswick: Transaction Books.

Greeley, A. M., McCready, W.C. and McCourt, K. (1976). *Catholic Schools in a Declining Church*. Kansas City: Sheed and Ward.

Greeley, A. M. and Rossi, P. H. (1966). *The Education of Catholic Americans*. Chicago: Aldine Publishing Company.

Green, C. W. and Hoffman, C. L. (1989). 'Stages of faith and perceptions of similar and dissimilar others', *Review of Religious Research*, 30, pp. 246–54.

Greenacre, I. (1971). 'The response of young people to religious allegory', unpublished Dip.Ed. dissertation, University of Birmingham.

Greer, J. E. (1970). 'The attitudes of parents and pupils to religion in school', *Irish Journal of Education*, 4, pp. 39–46.

— (1972a). 'Sixth-form religion in Northern Ireland', *Social Studies*, 1, pp. 325–40.

— (1972b). *A Questioning Generation*. Belfast: Church of Ireland Board of Education.

— (1972c). 'The child's understanding of creation', *Educational Review*, 24, pp. 94–110.

— (1980a). 'The persistence of religion: a study of adolescents in Northern Ireland', *Character Potential*, 9, pp. 139–49.

— (1980b). 'Stages in the development of religious thinking', *British Journal of Religious Education*, 3, pp. 24–28.

— (1981a). 'Religious attitudes and thinking in Belfast pupils', *Educational Research*, 23, pp. 77–189.

— (1981b). 'Religious experience and Religious Education', Search, 4, 1, pp. 23–34.

— (1982a). 'Growing up in Belfast: a study of religious development', *Collected Original Resources in Education*, 6, 1, fiche 1, A14.

— (1982b). 'The religious experience of Northern Irish pupils', *The Irish Catechist*, 6, 2, pp. 49–58.

— (1982c). 'A comparison of two attitudes to religion scales', *Educational Research*, 24, pp. 226–7.

— (1983a). 'A critical study of "Thinking about the Bible"', *British Journal of Religious Education*, 5, pp. 113–25.

— (1983b). 'Attitude to religion reconsidered', *British Journal of Educational Studies*, 31, pp. 18–28.

— (1985). 'Viewing "the other side" in Northern Ireland: openness and attitude to religion among Catholic and Protestant Adolescents', *Journal for the Scientific Study of Religion*, 24, pp. 275–92.

— (1989). 'The persistence of religion in Northern Ireland: a study of sixth form religion, 1968–1988', *Collected Original Resources in Education*, 13, 2, fiche 20, G9.

Greer, J. E. and Brown, G.A. (1973). 'The effects of new app.roaches to Religious Education in the primary school', *Journal of Curriculum Studies*, 5, pp. 73–8.

Greer, J. E. and Francis, L. J. (1991). 'Measuring attitudes towards Christianity among pupils in Catholic secondary schools in Northern Ireland', *Educational Research*, 33, pp. 100–3.

— (1992). 'Religious experience and attitude towards Christianity among secondary school children in Northern Ireland', *Journal of Social Psychology*, 132, pp. 277–9.

Gregory, H. M. (1966). 'Parables in the secondary school', unpublished Diploma in Religious Education dissertation, University of Nottingham.

Guttman, L. (1944). 'A basis for scaling qualitative data', *American Sociological Review*, 9, pp. 139–50.

Hanlon, K. (1989). 'A survey on Religious Education in Roman Catholic secondary schools in England and Wales', *British Journal of Religious Education*, 11, pp. 154–62.

Harms, E. (1944). 'The development of religious experience in children', *American Journal of Sociology*, 50, pp. 112–22.

Harvey, T. J. (1984). 'Gender differences in subject preference and perception of subject importance among third year secondary school pupils in single-sex and mixed comprehensive schools', *Educational Studies*, 10, pp. 243–53.

Hay, D. (1988). 'The bearing of empirical studies of religious experience on education', unpublished Ph.D. dissertation, University of Nottingham.

— (1990). 'The bearing of empirical studies of religious experience on education', *Research Papers in Education*, 5, 1, pp. 3–28.

Heller, D. (1986). *The Children's God*, Chicago, University of Chicago Press.

Higgins, J. L. (1989). 'Gender and Church of England diocesan syllabuses of Religious Education', *British Journal of Religious Education*, 1, pp. 8–62.

Hilliard, F. H. (1959). 'Ideas of God among secondary school children', *Religion in Education*, 27, 1, pp. 14–19.

Hoge, D. R. and Petrillo, G. H. (1978). 'Development of religious thinking in adolescence: a test of Goldman's theories', *Journal for the Scientific Study of Religion*, 17, pp. 139–54.

Honeck, R. P., Sowry, B. M. and Voegtle, K. (1978). 'Proverbial understanding in a pictorial context', *Child Development*, 49, pp. 327–31.

Hornsby-Smith, M. P. (1978). *Catholic Education: the unobtrusive partner*. London: Sheed and Ward.

Hornsby-Smith, M. P. and Petit, M. (1975). 'Social, moral and religious attitudes of secondary school students', *Journal of Moral Education*, 4, pp. 261–72.

Howkins, K. G. (1966). *Religious Thinking and Religious Education*. London: Tydale Press.

Hyde, K. E. (1959). 'A study of some factors influencing the communication of religious

ideas and attitudes among secondary school children', unpublished PhD dissertation, University of Birmingham.
— (1965). *Religious Learning in Adolescence*. University of Birmingham Institute of Education, Monograph No. 7. London: Oliver & Boyd.
— (1968). 'A critique of Goldman's research', *Religious Education*, 63, pp. 429–35.
— (1984). 'Twenty years after Goldman's research', *British Journal of Religious Education*, 7, pp. 5–7.
— (1990). 'Religion in Childhood and Adolescence: a comprehensive review of the research'. Birmingham, Alabama: Religious Education Press.
Institute of Christian Education (1954). *Religious Education in Schools*. London: SPCK.
Jamison, H. E. (1989). 'Religious understanding in children aged seven to eleven', unpublished Ph.D. dissertation, The Queen's University of Belfast.
Janssen, J., de Hart, J. and den Draak, C. (1989). 'Praying practices', *Journal of Empirical Theology*, 2, 2, pp. 28–39.
— (1990). 'A content analysis of the praying practices of Dutch youth', *Journal for the Scientific Study of Religion*, 29, 99–107.
Jaspard, J. M. (1971). 'The 6-12 year old child's representation of the Eucharistic presence', *Lumen Vitae*, 26, pp. 237–62.
Johnson, W. P. C. (1966).' The religious attitudes of secondary modern county school pupils', unpublished M.Ed. dissertation, University of Manchester.
Jones, J. A. (1962). 'An investigation into the response of boys and girls to scripture as a school subject in certain co-education grammar schools in industrial South Wales', unpublished M.A. dissertation, University of Wales (Swansea).
Kay, B. W., Piper, H. S. and Gay, J. D. (1988). *Managing the Church Schools: a study of the governing bodies of Church of England aided primary schools in the Oxford diocese*. Abingdon: Culham College Institute Occasional Paper 10.
Kay, W. (1973). 'Some changes in primary school teachers' attitudes to religious and moral education', *Journal of Moral Education*, 3, pp. 407–11.
Kay, W. K. (1981a). 'Marital happiness and children's attitudes to religion', *British Journal of Religious Education*, 3, pp. 102–5.
— (1981b). 'Psychoticism and attitude to religion', *Personality and Individual Differences*, 2, pp. 249–52.
— (1981c). 'Conversion among 11-15 year olds', *Spectrum*, 13, 2, pp. 26–33.
— (1981d). 'Syllabuses and attitudes to Christianity', *Irish Catechist*, 5, 2, pp. 16–21.
— (1981e). 'Religious thinking, attitudes and personality amongst secondary pupils in England and Ireland', unpublished Ph.D. dissertation, University of Reading.
Keys, W. and Ormerod, M. B. (1976). 'Some factors affecting pupils' subject preferences', *The Durham Research Review*, 7, pp. 1109–15.
Kingan, B. A. (1969). 'The study of some factors hindering Religious Education of a group of primary school children', unpublished M.Ed. dissertation, University of Liverpool.
Langdon, A. A. (1969). 'A critical examination of Dr Goldman's research study on religious thinking from childhood to adolescence', *Journal of Christian Education*, 12, 1, pp. 37–63.
Leavey, C. (1972). 'The transmission of religious moral values in nine Catholic girls' schools', *Twentieth Century*, 27, pp. 167–84.
Leavey, C. and Hetherton, M. (1988). *Catholic Beliefs and Practices*. Melbourne, Australia: Collins Dove.
Lesko, N. (1988). *Symbolizing Society: stories, rites and structure in a Catholic high school*. London: Falmer Press.
Levitt, M. (1995). '"The church is very important to me." A consideration of Francis'

attitude towards Christianity scale to the aims of Church of England aided schools', *British Journal of Religious Education*, 17, pp. 100–7.

Lewis, E. O. (1913). 'Popular and unpopular school subjects', *Journal of Experimental Pedagogy*, 2, pp. 89–98.

Lewis, J.M. (1974). 'An examination of the attitudes of pupils towards the content and method of teaching Religious Education in certain co-educational comprehensive schools in Wales', unpublished M.Ed. dissertation, University of Wales (Swansea).

Likert, R. A. (1932). 'A technique for the measurement of attitudes', *Archives of Psychology*, 140, pp. 1–55.

Long, D., Elkind, D. and Spilka, B. (1967). 'The child's concept of prayer', *Journal for the Scientific Study of Religion*, 6, pp. 101–9.

Long, J. F. (1989). 'A study of Catholic secondary schools in the Archdiocese of Armagh with special reference to RE', unpublished D.Phil. dissertation, University of Ulster.

Loukes, H. (1961). *Teenage Religion*. London: SCM.

— (1965). *New Ground in Christian Education*. London: SCM.

— (1973). *Teenage Morality*. London: SCM.

Ludwig, D. J., Weber, T. and Iben, D. (1974). 'Letters to God: a study of children's religious concepts', *Journal of Psychology and Theology*, 2, pp. 31–5.

McGrady, A. G. (1982). 'Goldman: a Piagetian based critique', *The Irish Catechist*, 6, pp. 19–29.

McGrady, A. G. (1983). 'Teaching the bible: research from a Piagetian perspective', *British Journal of Religious Education*, 5, pp. 126–33.

McGrady, A. G. (1990). 'The development of religious thinking: a comparison of metaphoric and operational paradigms', unpublished Ph.D. dissertation, University of Birmingham.

— (1994a). 'Metaphorical and operational aspects of religious thinking: research with Irish Catholic pupils (part 1)', *British Journal of Religious Education*, 16, pp. 148–63.

— (1994b). 'Metaphorical and operational aspects of religious thinking: research with Irish Catholic pupils (part 2)', *British Journal of Religious Education*, 17, pp. 56–62.

McLaren, P. (1986). *Schooling as a Ritual Performance*. London: Routledge & Kegan Paul.

McQuillan, M. (1990). 'An analysis of Religious Education provision, in one town, for children aged seven to sixteen years', unpublished M.Phil. dissertation, University of Manchester.

Maas, R. M. (1985). 'Biblical catechesis and religious development: the Goldman project twenty years later', *Living Light*, 22, pp. 124–44.

Madge, V. (1965). *Children in Search of Meaning*. London: SCM.

— (1971). *Introducing Young Children to Jesus*. London: SCM.

Malgady, R. G. (1977). 'Children's interpretation and appreciation similes', *Child Development*, 48, pp. 1734–8.

Mark, T. J. (1979). 'A study of cognitive and affective elements in the religious development of adolescents', unpublished Ph.D. dissertation, University of Leeds.

Marratt, H. (1965). 'Religious Education: the sixth former's view', *Learning for Living*, 4, 5, pp. 10–12.

Marsh, H. W. (1991). 'Public, Catholic single-sex, and Catholic coeducational high schools: their effects on achievement, affect and behaviour', *American Journal of Education*, 99, pp. 320–56.

Marsh, H. W. and Grayson, D. (1990). 'Public/Catholic differences in the High School and Beyond data: a multigroup structural equation modelling approach to testing mean differences', *Journal of Educational Studies*, 15, pp. 199–236.

142	A GUIDE TO EDUCATIONAL RESEARCH

Mathews, H. F. (1966). *Revolution in Religious Education*. Oxford: Religious Education Press.

May, P. R. (1967). 'Why parents want religion in school', *Learning for Living*, 6, 4, pp. 14–18.

— (1968). 'Why teachers want religion in school', *Learning for Living*, 8, 1, pp. 13–17.

— (1977). 'Religious judgements in children and adolescents: a research report', *Learning for Living*, 16, pp. 115–22.

— (1979). 'Religious thinking in children and adolescents', *Durham and Newcastle Research Review*, 8, 24, pp. 15–28.

May, P.R. and Johnston, D.R. (1967). 'Parental attitudes to RE in state schools', *Durham Research Review*, 18, pp. 127–38.

Miles, G. B. (1971). 'The study of logical thinking and moral judgements in GCE bible knowledge candidates', unpublished M.Ed. dissertation, University of Leeds.

— (1983). 'A critical and experimental study of adolescents' attitudes to and understanding of transcendental experience', unpublished Ph.D. dissertation, University of Leeds.

Modgil, S. and Modgil, C. (1982). *Jean Piaget: consensus and controversy*. London: Holt, Rinehart & Winston.

Morley, H. C. (1975). 'Religious concepts of slow learners: an application of the findings of Ronald Goldman', *Learning for Living*, 14, pp. 107–10.

Morris, A. B. (1994). 'The academic performance of Catholic schools', *School Organisation*, 14, pp. 81–9.

Murphy, R. J. L. (1977a). 'Does children's understanding of parables develop in stages?' *Learning for Living*, 16, pp. 168–72.

— (1977b). 'The development of religious thinking in children in three easy stages?' *Learning for Living*, 17, pp. 16–19.

— (1978). 'A new approach to the study of the development of religious thinking in children', *Educational Studies*, 4, pp. 19–22.

— (1979). 'An investigation into some aspects of the development of religious thinking in children aged between 6 and 11 years', unpublished Ph.D. dissertation, University of St Andrews.

Murray, D. (1985). *Worlds Apart: segregated schools in Northern Ireland*. Belfast: Appletree Press.

Nelson, M. O. and Jones, E. M. (1957). 'An application of the Q–technique to the study of religious concepts', *Psychological Reports*, 3, pp. 293–7.

Neuwien, R. A. (ed.) (1966). *Catholic Schools in Action*. Notre Dame, Indiana: University of Notre Dame Press.

Nye, W. C. and Carlson, J. S. (1984). 'The development of the concept of God in children', *Journal of Genetic Psychology*, 145, pp. 137–42.

Oger, J. H. M. (1970). 'Letters to God', *Lumen Vitae*, 25, pp. 93–115.

O'Keeffe, B. (1986). *Faith, Culture and the Dual System: a comparative study of church and county schools*. Barcombe: Falmer Press.

Orchard, S. (1991). 'What was wrong with Religious Education? an analysis of HMI reports 1985–1988', *British Journal of Religious Education*, 14, pp. 15–21.

Orchard, S. (1994) 'A further analysis of HMI reports 1989–1991', *British Journal of Religious Education*, 16, pp. 21–27.

Ormerod, M. B. (1975). 'Subject preference and choice in co-educational and single sex secondary schools', *British Journal of Educational Psychology*, 45, pp. 257–67.

Oser, F. and Gmünder, P. (1991). *Religious Judgement: a developmental approach*. Birmingham, Alabama: Religious Education Press.

Oser, F. and Reich, K. H. (1987). 'The challenge of competing explanations: the development of thinking in terms of complementarity', *Human Development*, 30, pp. 178–86.

Osgood, C. E., Suci, G. J. and Tannenbaum, P. H. (1957). *The Measurement of Meaning*. Urbana: University of Illinois Press.

Paffard, M. (1973). *Inglorious Wordsworth*. London: Hodder & Stoughton.

Pearson, P.R. and Francis, L. J. (1989). 'The dual nature of the Eysenckian lie scales: are religious adolescents more truthful?' *Personality and Individual Differences*, 10, pp. 1041–8.

Pearson, P.R., Francis, L. J. and Lightbown, T. J. (1986). 'Impulsivity and religiosity', *Personality and Individual Differences*, 7, pp. 89–94.

Peatling, J. H. (1973). 'The incidence of concrete and abstract religious thinking in the interpretation of three bible stories by pupils enrolled in grades four through twelve in selected schools in the Episcopal Church in the United States of America', unpublished Ph.D. dissertation, University of New York.

— (1974). 'Cognitive development in pupils in grades four through twelve: the incidence of concrete and abstract religious thinking', *Character Potential*, 7, 1, pp. 52–61.

— (1976). 'A sense of justice: moral judgment in children, adolescents and adults', *Character Potential*, 8, 1, pp. 25–34.

— (1977). 'On beyond Goldman: religious thinking and the 1970s', *Learning for Living*, 16, pp. 99–108.

Peatling, J. H. and Laabs, C. W. (1975). 'Cognitive development of pupils in grades four through twelve: a comparative study of Lutheran and Episcopalian children and youth', *Character Potential*, 7, pp. 107–17.

Peatling, J. H., Laabs, C. W. and Newton, T. B. (1975). 'Cognitive development: a three sample comparison of means on the Peatling scale of religious thinking', *Character Potential*, 7, pp. 159–62.

Petrovich, O. (1988). 'Re–review: Ronald Goldman's Religious Thinking from Childhood to Adolescence', *Modern Churchman*, 30, 2, pp. 44–9.

Pitts, V. P. (1976). 'Drawing the invisible: children's conceptualisation of God', *Character Potential*, 8, 1, pp. 12–24.

— (1977). 'Drawing pictures of God', *Learning for Living*, 16, pp. 123–129.

— (1979). *Children's Pictures of God*. Schenectady, NY: Character Research Press.

Poole, M. W. (1983). 'An investigation into aspects of the interplay between science and religion at sixth form level', unpublished M.Phil. dissertation, University of London, King's College.

Povall, C. H. (1971). 'Some factors affecting pupils' attitudes to Religious Education', unpublished M.Ed. dissertation, University of Manchester.

Pritchard, C. B. (1974). 'Worship in the primary school: case studies in Church of England schools', unpublished M.Ed. dissertation, University of Liverpool.

Ramsey, I. T. (1957). *Religious Language*. London: SCM.

Rees, R. J. (1967). *Background and Belief*. London: SCM.

Reich, H. (1989). 'Between religion and science: complementarity in the religious thinking of young people', *British Journal of Religious Education*, 11, pp. 62–70.

— (1991). 'Beliefs of German and Swiss children and young people about science and religion', *British Journal of Religious Education*, 13, pp. 65–73.

Rhymer, J. (1983). 'Religious attitudes of Roman Catholic secondary school pupils in Strathclyde region', unpublished Ph.D. dissertation, University of Edinburgh.

Rhymer, J. and Francis, L. J. (1985). 'Roman Catholic secondary schools in Scotland and pupil attitude towards religion', *Lumen Vitae*, 40, pp. 103–10.

Richardson, R. and Chapman, J. (1973). *Images of Life: problems of religious belief and human relations in school.* London: SCM.

Richmond, R. C. (1972). 'Maturity of religious judgements and differences of religious attitudes between ages of 13 and 16 years', *Educational Review*, 24, pp. 225–36.

Rixon, L. D. (1959). 'An experimental and critical study of the teaching of scripture in secondary schools', unpublished Ph.D. dissertation, University of London.

Robinson, E. (1977a). *The Original Vision*. Oxford: Religious Experience Research Unit.

— (1977b). *This Time-Bound Ladder*. Oxford: Religious Experience Research Unit.

— (1978). *Living the Questions*. Oxford: Religious Experience Research Unit.

Robinson, E. and Jackson, M. (1987). *Religion and Values at 16+*. Oxford: Alister Hardy Research Centre and CEM.

Rosenberg, R. (1990). 'The development of the concept of prayer in Jewish-Israeli children and adolescents', *Studies in Jewish Education*, 5, pp. 91–129.

Roy, P. R. (1979). 'Applications of Piaget's theory of cognitive development to religious thinking, with special reference to the work of Dr R.G. Goldman', unpublished M.Ed. dissertation, University of Liverpool.

Russell, A. (1978). 'The attitude of primary school children to Religious Education', unpublished M.Phil. dissertation, University of Nottingham.

Scarlett, W. G. and Perriello, L. (1991). 'The development of prayer in adolescence', *New Directions for Child Development*, 52, pp. 63–76.

Schurter, D.D. (1987). 'Fowler's faith stages as a guide for ministry to the mentally retarded', *Journal of Pastoral Care*, 41, pp.234–40.

Sheffield (1961). *Religious Education in Secondary Schools*. London: Nelson and Sheffield Institute of Education.

Shulik, R. N. (1988). 'Faith development in older adults', *Educational Gerontology*, 14, pp. 291–301.

Slee, N. M. (1986a). 'Goldman yet again: an overview and critique of his contribution to research' *British Journal of Religious Education*, 8, pp. 84–93.

— (1986b). 'A note on Goldman's methods of data analysis with special reference to scalogram analysis', *British Journal of Religious Education*, 8, pp. 168–75.

— (1990). 'Getting away from Goldman: changing perspectives on the development of religious thinking', *Modern Churchman*, 32, 1, pp. 1–9.

Souper, P. C. and Kay, W. K. (1982). *The School Assembly in Hampshire*, Southampton, University of Southampton Department of Education.

— (1983). *Worship in the Independent School*, Southampton, University of Southampton Department of Education.

Spencer, A. E. C. W. (1968). 'An evaluation of Roman Catholic educational policy in England and Wales 1900–1960', in Jeff, P. (ed.), *Religious Education: drift or decision?*. London: Darton, Longman & Todd, pp. 165–221.

Streib, H. (1994). 'Magical feeling and thinking in childhood and adolescence: a developmental perspective', *British Journal of Religious Education*, 16, pp. 70–81.

Strommen, M. P. (ed.) (1971). *Research on Religious Development: a comprehensive handbook*. New York: Hawthorn Books.

Strunk, O. (1959). 'Perceived relationship between parental and deity concepts', *Psychological Newsletter*, 10, pp. 222–26.

Tamminen, K. (1976). 'Research concerning the development of religious thinking in Finnish students', *Character Potential*, 7, pp. 206–19.

— (1977). 'What questions of life do Finnish school children reflect on?' *Learning for Living*, 16, pp. 148–55.

— (1991). *Religious Development in Childhood and Youth: an empirical study.* Helsinki: Suomalainen Tiedeakatemia.

Taylor, H. P. (1970). 'A comparative study of the religious attitudes, beliefs and practices of sixth formers in Anglican, state and Roman Catholic schools and an assessment of religious opinion upon them asserted by home and school', unpublished M.Phil. dissertation, University of London.

Thouless, R. H. and Brown, L. B. (1964). 'Petitionary prayer: belief in its appropriateness and causal efficacy among adolescent girls', *Lumen Vitae*, 19, pp. 297–310.

Thurstone, L. L. (1928). 'Attitudes can be measured', *American Journal of Sociology*, 33, pp. 529–54.

Tritter, J. (1992). 'An educated change in moral values: some effects of religious and state schools on their students', *Oxford Review of Education*, 18, pp. 29–43.

Turner, E. B. (1970). 'Religious understanding and religious attitudes in male urban adolescents', unpublished Ph.D. dissertation, The Queen's University of Belfast.

— (1978).' Towards a standardised test of religious language comprehension', *British Journal of Religious Education*, 1, pp. 14–21.

— (1980). 'Intellectual ability and the comprehension of religious language', *Irish Journal of Psychology*, 4, pp. 182–90.

Van Bunnen, C. (1965). 'The burning bush: the symbolic implications of a bible story among children from 5-12 years', in Godin (ed.), *From Religious Experience to a Religious Attitude*, pp. 171–82.

Van Buren, P. (1972). *The Edges of Language*. London: SCM.

Vergote, A. and Aubert, C. (1973). 'Parental images and representations of God', *Social Compass*, 19, pp. 431–44.

Vergote, A. Bonami, M., Custers, A. and Pattyn, M. (1967). 'Le symbole paternel et sa signification religieuse', *Revue de Psychologie et des Sciences de l'Education*, 2, pp. 191–213.

Vergote, A. and Tamayo, A. (1981). *The Parental Figure and the Representation of God*. The Hague: Mouton.

Vergote, A., Tamayo, A., Pasquali, L., Bonami, M., Pattyn, M-R. and Custers, A. (1969). 'Concept of God and parental images', *Journal for the Scientific Study of Religion*, 8, pp. 79–87.

West Riding (1966). *Suggestions for Religious Education*: West Riding Agreed Syllabus, Wakefield, County Council of the West Riding of Yorkshire.

Westbury, J. I. (1975). 'Religious beliefs and attitudes of pupils in east London comprehensive school: factors influencing the pupils and implications for Religious Education', unpublished M.Ed. dissertation, University of Leicester.

Whitehouse, E. (1972). 'Children's reactions to the Zacchaeus story', *Learning for Living*, 11, 4, pp. 19–24.

Williams, R. M. and Finch, S. (1968). *Young School Leavers*. London: HMSO.

Worten, S. A. and Dollinger, S. J. (1986). 'Mothers' intrinsic religious motivation, disciplinary preferences, and children's conceptions of prayer', *Psychological Reports*, 58, p. 218.

Wright, D. S. (1962). 'A study of religious belief in sixth form boys', *Researches and Studies*, 24, pp. 19–27.

Wright, D. and Cox, E. (1967a). 'Religious belief and co-education in a sample of sixth form boys and girls', *British Journal of Social and Clinical Psychology*, 6, pp. 23–31.

— (1967b). 'A study of the relationship between moral judgement and religious belief in a sample of English adolescents', *Journal of Social Psychology*, 72, pp. 135–44.

— (1971a). 'Changes in attitudes towards Religious Education and the bible among

sixth form boys and girls', *British Journal of Educational Psychology*, 41, pp. 328–31.
— (1971b). 'Changes in moral belief among sixth form boys and girls over a seven year period in relation to religious belief, age and sex differences', *British Journal of Social and Clinical Psychology*, 10, pp. 332–41.

6

SCIENCE

Jon Ogborn

STARTING POINTS

To begin: two obvious remarks.

First, science is not terribly popular. It commands respect, but not affection. Only a few per cent of the population are needed as qualified scientists or engineers. Many of the remainder stop studying science at the earliest opportunity – which until recently in England and Wales could be as early as the age of 14. The coverage of science in newspapers and radio and television programmes is minuscule in proportion to that of books, plays and films. Many a cultured person is not at all ashamed to claim to lack all understanding of science. These obvious facts set the scene for much discussion about science education, and cast into harsh relief some of its more inflated ambitions.

Second, teaching science is a practical everyday activity. It cannot wait upon a full understanding of students and their learning and its context, but has to be done today, as best one can. This obvious fact makes research and argument in science education very different from research or argument in science itself. The sciences operate with a strong notion of having found – or of having not yet found – answers to problems. If an answer is not known, that is all there is to it, and those who want one must wait. But science education has to find answers as they are wanted, and to use them more in hope than in certainty of doing the right thing. Thus many urgings to action in science education are – necessarily – more like ideological or rhetorical appeals than like well-founded proposals based on secure understanding.

CURRICULUM REFORM

At the moment of writing, the science curriculum in England and Wales is going through a quiescent, even slightly self-satisfied phase. After five years of turbulent change with the introduction of a National Curriculum, and frequent radical overhauls of its demands, a period of minimal further change is promised. This is widely welcomed by science teachers, but not because the most recent form of the science curriculum is obviously right; rather, they welcome the simple absence of change for a time. Certainly some of the worst anomalies have gone, most notably the replacing of a narrow and ludicrously limiting vision of what should be taught about the nature of scientific investigation by a wider, more generous and more practicable vision. But the content of the curriculum remains a tour through a number of 'fundamental scientific concepts', with little attempt to offer a whole world-picture of scientific knowledge and its limits and possibilities.

The picture in the United States is very different. The current high level of activity may have been stimulated by evidence from international comparisons suggesting that American pupils' scientific knowledge was substantially inferior to that of pupils in many other countries – the USA tending to come below the median, while Japan, Korea and Hungary tended to come very high (Rosier, 1990). Britain did little better in tests at age 14, scoring well only at age 17 where the only pupils tested were those who had by then specialised narrowly in science. These tests are, however, open to many objections, notably their focus on narrow theoretical concepts and formal problem solving. Nor are Japanese educators happy with the intensive and competitive test-oriented curriculum culture in Japan (Ryu, 1994).

Whatever the causes, science education in the USA is undergoing a period of intense debate and reforming activity (Atkin and Helms, 1993; Feldman and Atkin, 1993; Good, 1992; Linn, 1992; Raizen, 1991). Project 2061, named for the next return of Halley's comet, is supported by the American Association for the Advancement of Science, and has produced benchmarks for improved scientific literacy for the whole American population. Two billion additional dollars are being spent on science teacher training and retraining.

There is not, however, wide agreement about how to proceed. Some regard the problems of a capitalist society as the key issue to be addressed (Apple, 1992). Some stress the need for science education to be set in a wider social context (O'Loughlin, 1992), a view seen by others as opening the door to relativism (Fosnot, 1993). Most arguments are more conservative, and mainly focus on trying to define 'scientific literacy' in some way (Atkin and Helms, 1993; Bingle and Gaskell, 1994; Champagne and Newell, 1992; Klopfer and Champagne, 1991).

The key issue is very simple. We have some idea how to teach science so as to train the small percentage of the next generation that will become scientists and technicians. Nearly all such science curricula have a strongly hierarchical structure, building on what are seen as the 'foundations' of 'basic concepts' – typically, force and motion, solids, liquids and gases, chemical elements and compounds, and simple biological functions and structures. We have, by contrast, very little idea how to think about a science curriculum for the whole population. To rely on the same 'basic concepts' is like starting to build a house knowing that it will never be finished or lived in.

It seems to me that one essential component of a solution is to think about science education in schools as part of a lively social system for popularising (or vulgarising, as the French call it) science (Marx, 1994; Ogborn, 1994b). That is, a central function must be to make as accessible and as attractive as possible those stories about the nature of the world – about the origins and nature of life, about the origin and nature of the universe, about matter and what it is made of, about the engineered world around us, and about the use and control of information – which the sciences have to tell. Many of these stories are indeed those that feature in popular radio and television programmes and in newspapers, journals and popular books – and rightly so for they are what is interesting about science. Teachers of literature are not ashamed to teach (and to examine) for enthusiasm for and committed attention to great works of cultural interest and importance; teachers of science do so at best as an occasional by-product or for 'motivation', not as the core of what they are doing. Scientific knowledge, so the rhetoric goes – and no rhetoric could be more false – stands in no need of persuasion or emotional commitment. The facts are supposed to speak for themselves. The lesson that science involves a personal and passionate commitment (Polanyi, 1958) needs to be relearned. There are examples of how to work this vision into the curriculum (Tóth, 1994), but they are few.

WHAT IS SCIENCE?

The name 'Science' has a peculiar mythological force. But those who praise it most seem sometimes to be those who understand it least. For more than two centuries, science has been promoted as the one sure and certain knowledge, mistaking the very definite but also limited achievements of the physical and biological sciences for a generalisable royal road to knowledge. The disease of scientism – the over-valuation of the actual achievements and potential possibilities of science – became serious in the nineteenth century with attempts to model new sciences of society on the physical sciences, and became terminal in our century with the rejection by logical positivists of all but scientific knowledge as meaningless. A number of philosophers are regularly called in aid of a radical critique of science (Feyerabend, 1975; Feyerabend, 1987; Goodman, 1978; Rorty, 1991; Wittgenstein, 1922; Wittgenstein, 1953).

In many educational circles, scientism is in retreat, pursued by accusing cries of 'positivism' and 'objectivism'. Scientific knowledge is written of apologetically as 'scientists' science', as opposed to 'children's science' or to 'everyday science'. It has become scarcely possible to say that common salt is made of the dangerous metal sodium and the poisonous gas chlorine without adding, 'or so we currently suppose'. That scientific knowledge is always revisable – and so it is – has become its most emphasised feature, instead of the remarkable resistance of much of it to any imaginable revision. It has become not uncommon to speak of 'imposing' scientific knowledge on children. Meanwhile, in scientific circles, the attempt to gain a little more solid ground from the swamp of unknowing proceeds, largely in ignorance of the turmoil and confusion without.

RECOVERING REALISM

Without question, scientific knowledge is a human product – there is nothing else for it to be. And anything made by humans can be changed by them, so scientific knowledge is all, in principle, revisable. Further, human beings are social animals and knowledge is a social category, not something attributable simply to individuals.

To some, these obvious facts seem like large and drastic concessions. If knowledge of reality is socially constructed, they suppose that it cannot then be knowledge of reality. If truths of the matter are arrived at through social processes it seems they cannot really concern truths of the matter, but must instead concern social relations of power or some such. If all scientific knowledge is revisable, then seemingly it cannot be certain. Scientific knowledge seems to become fiction; stories told to suit the interests of a particular group, among whose interests are the concealment of this fact.

All this is to make an elementary mistake. The mistake is to judge the attainable against the unattainable; to set impossible standards and reject everything which fails to attain them – as everything then of course does. It is the same mistake as denying the goodness of a person because nobody can be perfect. The unattainable is a bad yardstick because it makes everything measure zero.

Thus it is with certainty. So called 'absolute certainty', certainty for ever and ever, is simply an unattainable fantasy. But that does not leave the word 'certainty' without any sensible use. We use it when we can envisage no possible alternatives, having tried as hard as possible to identify and eliminate them. And this is how certainties in scientific knowledge are achieved – in the cases where this has turned out to be possible – namely by a long and slow, wholly social, process of seeking and eliminating alternatives.

There is nothing guaranteed about the success of this process. It requires luck as well as hard work, and it cannot work without knowledge on which to begin. Thus, although there are some areas in which it has to some extent succeeded, there are many in which it has not. We may have a good idea of what water is made of, but we have only the faintest glimmering of what consciousness is made of. We may know a good deal about the body's immune system but much of curative medicine remains mysterious. Science is perhaps best thought of as islands of solid knowledge set in a sea of uncertainty. For this reason, the best scientists become connoisseurs of flavours of certainty and uncertainty:

> Science is a way to teach how something gets known, what is not known, to what extent things *are* known (for nothing is known absolutely), how to handle doubt and uncertainty, what the rules of evidence are, how to think about things so that judgments can be made, how to distinguish truth from fraud, and from show (Richard Feynman (Gleick, 1992) p. 285).

So far as working scientists are concerned, this knowledge is unproblematically about an existing external reality. Realism is their policy (Harré, 1986), since only by attributing reality to the latest fancy idea can that idea be pursued to see if only it and no other alternative survives, no matter what the context of investigation. Reality has a perfectly clear and simple meaning: that which is as it is regardless of what we would like, hope or think.

Yet doubts about realism are endemic in much current writing in science education. Their sources go back to the positivists who denied reality to everything which was not immediately present to the senses. The scientist, by contrast, talks freely (and rightly) of electrons existing, of the blood really circulating, of DNA actually being copied, of stars really having nuclear furnaces inside, or of continents actually drifting. No 'convenient summaries of sense-experience' are these, but full-blooded denizens of the real world.

Realism is not just a policy, but is also the foundation of a strong, even puritanical, moral order:

> I believe that the scientific community exhibits a model or ideal of rational co-operation set within a strict moral order, the whole having no parallel in any other human activity. And this despite the all-too-human characteristics of the actual members of that community seen as just another social order ... that very community enforces standards of honesty, trustworthiness and good work against which the moral quality of say Christian civilisation stands condemned (Harré, 1986, p. 1).

A more detailed and careful account of these issues can be found in Ogborn (1995). Several philosophers have written helpfully about realism (Bhaskar,

1978; Hacking, 1983; Harré, 1986; Popper, 1979; Ziman, 1967; Ziman, 1978).

THE SOCIAL CRITIQUE OF SCIENCE

The most radical critique of science, and one which lends force to current doubts about the worth and point of teaching science, comes from the so-called 'strong programme' of the sociology of science (Bloor, 1976; Collins, 1992; Latour, 1987; Latour and Woolgar, 1986; Pickering, 1984). This work is largely based on original and well-conducted fieldwork and historical study, observing scientific work as it actually happens. As such, it has many important insights to offer.

However, I see in this body of work a crucial and fundamental defect. As a result the conclusions for which it is best known appear to me to evaporate to nothing. These conclusions are, broadly, that science is in the end not at all about truths of the matter concerning reality, but rather that 'truths of the matter' are an outcome of social bargaining and contest, and are made to seem otherwise by these very social processes, which include the use of rhetorical linguistic 'truth effects' such that social agreements are made to seem like 'natural facts'. The crucial defect is that such 'results' are 'established', not by showing that science works like this. Instead, science is compared with an impossible vision of an algorithmic machine devoted to generating context-free, human-independent and absolutely certain knowledge. It never was so and never could have been. But nothing at all follows from this fact, about the actual nature of science.

One or two examples must suffice here – for a detailed discussion see Ogborn (1995); for a more spirited if sometimes immoderate critique see also Gross and Levitt (1994). One example is the claim (Collins, 1992) to 'show' that scientific work is not, despite its rhetoric, full of careful replication. What Collins describes, it may therefore seem odd to learn, are a number of case-studies each involving much careful and sustained replication. His conclusion follows, not from his interesting and careful observations, but from his beliefs. Collins 'knows' beforehand that replication is in principle impossible, in that one can never know with absolute certainty that one has controlled and checked everything. He points out, rightly, that judgement is called for and that judgements cannot be given an absolutely secure basis. But all that is going on here is that replication is being measured using an impossible yardstick, that of a mechanised absolute certainty, against which actual practice must register zero.

Even more controversial is the claim (Pickering, 1984) that the 'discovery' of neutral Z bosons at CERN, on which much current high-energy physics rests, was not made because there were actually Z bosons there to be found, but because the experimenters changed their arbitrary ways of deciding which events should be taken as evidence or not, thus 'producing' a 'discovery' and in the process generating plenty of future work for themselves and others. Everything in Pickering's argument hinges on the notion of 'arbitrary practice' supported only by 'judgment'. The experimenters did, of course, construct sophisticated principles intended to exclude false instances. As techniques improved, these principles changed. Pickering's argument is merely that these principles could have no absolutely secure basis; that they depend irreducibly on judgements. Again we have the application of an impossible yardstick, against which the best available technical and professional judgements are made to seem nothing at all. It is hardly news that judgments are not mechanical; it is more startling to find that this makes them worthless.

It is hard to know how seriously to take this and related work. Philosophers largely ignore it, and few scientists care about it. But it has been influential with those concerned with cultural or critical theory and with reflection on social science. In this way it has begun to influence science education. The more recent writings seem to have abandoned the close and careful observation of the earlier work, and to have descended into generalities, whimsy and in-fighting (see, for example, Pickering, 1992). The more the pity for a field which started so promisingly with Ravetz's seminal work (Ravetz, 1971).

CONSTRUCTIVISM

Very remarkably, a philosophical-cum-educational position (or rather, a loose collection of positions) has in the last decade swept through science and mathematics education like a bush fire. At its heart are a number of praiseworthy and attractive principles:

- the importance of pupils' active involvement in learning

- the importance of respect for the child and for the child's own ideas;

- that science consists of ideas created by human beings;

- that teaching should give high priority to making sense to pupils, in terms of what they currently know and understand.

All these one may cheerfully accept, and their good sense and decency no doubt helps to account for the broad attractiveness of constructivism.

Much constructivist writing, however, seeks a foundation for these principles in a set of much less acceptable, even absurd ideas. One is the tenet that strictly speaking it is impossible to tell anybody anything (Glasersfeld, 1989, pp. 131–2). The argument offered for this is a misunderstanding of Shannon's theory of communication. Shannon shows that one can measure the channel capacity required to transmit any signal independently of its meaning. But it by no means follows that signals have no meaning. Meaning is given to signs by the interaction, interpersonal and cultural, of the makers and receivers of signs. Both maker and receiver participate actively in constructing meaning. Every sign is at once established and systematic, relying on a stable set of ways of making sense, and yet is at the same time fresh-minted, in need of creatíve interpretation. Thus learning by being told depends both on creative acts of interpretation and on knowing the cultural rules which give signs their regularity. Once a system has been mastered (say the way chemical equations are represented) it is indeed possible to tell people things using that system. That is its very point. We must not neglect the pupil's active participation in coming to master sign-systems and in interpreting messages within them, but we must equally not neglect the reasons for having such sign-systems at all, among which is to tell each other how things are.

Regrettably, much constructivist writing also shares the anti-realism discussed above. It often takes on board a simple-minded empiricism which sees all knowledge as resting on individual 'experience'. This has two consequences. One, in common with positivist accounts, is that the real world becomes a fiction. Experience is just not the right kind of stuff out of which to make sticks and stones, let alone electrons or stars. The other is that knowledge is radically individualised. Every individual is seen as having to create the universe alone and all over again. The work of science is presented in a way deformed beyond recognition, as the private constructing of schemes to make sense of the individual scientist's personal experiential world. Such a view wholly ignores the social nature of knowledge and knowledge-making (Ziman, 1967; Ziman, 1978). It is as if Popper (1979) had never existed. There are examples too numerous to discuss in any detail (Confrey, 1990; Davis, McCarty, Shaw, and Sidani-Tabbaa, 1993; Driver, 1989; Driver and Oldham, 1986; Glasersfeld, 1987; Glasersfeld, 1989; Nadeau and Desautels, 1984; Osborne and Whitrock, 1985; Roth, 1993; Wheatley, 1991). There are, however, a few useful antidotes available (Matthews, 1992; Ogborn, forthcoming; Suchting, 1992).

Finally, it must be emphasised that some constructivist claims to derive from the work of Piaget are deeply misleading. Piaget was indeed a constructivist, but one who sought a way between the simple empiricism and the naive mentalism into which most educational constructivists simultaneously fall. There are clear accounts of his views to which one can turn (Bliss, 1993; 1994); see also his own later writing (Piaget and Garcia, 1983; 1987).

INDIVIDUAL LEARNERS

By far the greatest part of the research effort in science education in the last 20 years has gone into the investigation of knowledge and learning in individuals, with relative neglect of the social dimensions of knowledge and learning. The task has mainly been seen as one of describing how individuals conceptualise aspects of the world which are important for science, and of understanding how we should think about the process of conceptual change.

Conceptions and Conceptual Change

Starting about 15 years ago, a movement towards trying to understand students' ideas about the world in their own terms, began to gather strength. One of the first examples, and still one of the best, is Viennot (1979a; 1979b). Since then there have been many hundreds of studies, catalogued in their increasing numbers by Pfundt and Duit (1994). As a result we have a rather reliable picture of common ways in which pupils and students across a range of ages think about various phenomena of interest to science. We know that across a wide age range, from the primary school years to the end of secondary school and beyond, ideas about force and motion remain very much the same, little affected by any tales told about Galilean and Newtonian mechanics, and reverting back to the original form when formal schooling in physics ends. Quite a detailed account of the structure of these ideas can be given, and one can speculate about their origin in early childhood (Bliss and Ogborn, 1990; 1992; 1993a; 1993b; 1994; Bliss, Ogborn, and Whitelock, 1989; Law, 1988; Law, 1990; Ogborn, 1985; 1992; Whitelock, 1990; 1991). Similarly, we have quite detailed pictures of pupils' ideas about light and colour, about changes of state, about chemical reactions, about several life processes including respiration and digestion, about electric circuits, and about the seasons and the solar system (Pfundt and Duit, 1994).

The topic of energy has been intensively investigated (Boyes and Stanisstreet, 1990; Kesidou and Duit, 1993; Nicholls, 1991; Nicholls and Ogborn, 1993; Trumper, 1990; 1991; 1993). It has been the area in which there has been the strongest insistence on the social dimensions of understanding (Lijnse, 1991; Solomon, 1983a; 1992).

Work in Europe has often tended to focus on describing students' conceptions, whereas work in the USA has had a stronger focus on changing them. The problem is then to identify a suitable model for what might drive conceptual change. The main models are of two kinds, psychological and epistemological, though they often combine the two. The main psychological model is one of cognitive fit or misfit, of change driven by conflict between what one thinks and what one experiences. Versions of this idea appear in various forms (diSessa, 1993; Driver, Squires, Rushworth, and Wood-Robinson, 1994; Guidoni, 1985; Novak, 1988; Osborne and Freyberg, 1985; Osborne and Whitrock, 1985; Reif and Larkin, 1991; Ross and Munby, 1991; Rowell and Dawson, 1989). Epistemological models vary more widely, thinking of conceptual change as analogous to paradigm change (Kuhn, 1962), or as involving shifting ideas from one ontological type to another (Chi, 1992; Duschl and Gitomer, 1991; Strike and Posner, 1982a; 1982b). Note has recently begun to be taken of the importance of language, analogy and metaphor in forming or reshaping concepts (Bloom, 1990; 1992; Brown, 1994; Clement, 1993; Dagher, 1994; Flick, 1991; Thagard, 1992).

The startling feature of this work has been the difficulty of getting students to change their minds. Promising methods have often yielded less than expected. In my own opinion, the most likely cause is the unrealistic expectation of getting pupils to commit themselves to ideas to which they are not yet even accustomed, especially when these ideas are counter-intuitive. We should be aiming more modestly, that these ideas be entertained: that pupils can talk intelligibly if not acceptingly of them. When my daughter was at school she had heard weird tales about the atmosphere: 'They say it goes up ever so high and presses down ever so hard all over you, but you can't feel it.' 'Do you believe them?' 'No, not really, though they do say it.'

Nature of Commonsense Understandings

Most work on students' understandings has been done either by posing problems ('What do you think would happen if...?') or by asking directly what students understand by a given idea ('What is energy, for you?'). In our research group at the University of London Institute of Education we have tried what may be a more fundamental approach. We ask very simple 'ontological' questions, that is, questions about the basic nature of things. Examples would be: 'Can you touch it?', 'Can you see it?', 'Can it do anything by itself?', 'Can it be changed into something else?'. These questions have a systematic basis in Piaget's theory of meaning: that the meaning of an object or event is what you can do to it, what it can do, and what it is made of.

Ideas about the nature of things are now not evidenced by single responses to questions, but patterns of responses to sets of questions. Asked about a wide range of objects and events, including abstract entities such as energy or force, patterns of responses fall into intelligible clusters or lie along interpretable dimensions (Mariani, 1992; Mariani and Ogborn, 1990; 1991; Ogborn and Mariani, 1995). One such cluster is 'passive objects', another is 'actions which are sources of change'. The dimensions identified so far are, roughly: place-like versus localised, dynamic versus static, discrete versus continuous, cause versus effect, and necessary versus contingent. Space and time are place-like, but space is static and time is dynamic. Material objects and actions are localised, the first being static and the second dynamic. Events – for example, the summer, or the moon going round the earth – can be thought of as place-like rather than as usual as being localised (e.g., an explosion). Even actions (e.g., 'thinking') can be understood as time/place-like rather than localised (set something alight). A related line of work (Gutierrez and Ogborn, 1992) investigated the nature of ideas about causality.

LEARNING IN SOCIAL AND CULTURAL SETTINGS

In the past decade, attention has shifted from the learner in lonely confrontation with scientific concepts, towards taking fuller account of the social and cultural context of learning and understanding. This shift has involved paying greater attention to the public understanding of science, to informal sources of scientific understanding, and to language and imagery.

Public Understanding of Science

The issue of the public understanding of science was returned to prominent public attention by a report of the Royal Society in 1985 (Royal Society, 1985). This led to surveys of the scientific knowledge of 'the general public' (Durant, Evans, and Thomas, 1989). More interesting, it also led to investigations of the meanings and uses of science for specific social groups. Examples have included studies of people involved in dealing with radioactive hazards (Wynne, 1991) ; studies of parents of children with Down's syndrome, of elderly people dealing with keeping warm in winter, of councillors deciding waste disposal policy, and of responses to an official report on cancer risk (Layton, Jenkins, MacGill, and Davey, 1993) ; and investigations of primary teachers discussing science seen on television (Hann, Brosnan, and Ogborn, 1992) and of students discussing social issues related to science (Solomon, 1990). An excellent and insightful discussion of the nature and implications of this work is given in Layton et al. (1993). Perhaps the key point is that there is no single homogeneous 'public' for science, but rather a plurality of publics each with their own specific interests.

Informal Learning of Science

From being almost wholly concerned with science in schools, science education has recently paid more attention to informal sources of knowledge (Lucas, 1983; Lucas, 1991). Much interest has centred on learning science from museums and active science centres, partly as a result of the creation by Frank Oppenheimer of The Exploratorium in San Francisco, by Richard Gregory of The Exploratory in Bristol, together with the setting up of 'Launch Pad' in the London Science Museum. Investigations of visitor behaviour (Dierking and Falk, 1994; Ramey-Gassert, Walberg, and Walberg, 1994) tend to show rather brief interactions with exhibits and equivocal evidence about learning from exhibits. One very interesting study (Stevenson, 1991) showed, however, that members of family groups still had clear and vivid memories of many exhibits three to six months after a visit. Thus the potential for learning by reflection on previous experience is clearly there.

There is a key issue hidden here for school science education. The events of a visit to a museum are plainly remembered in what psychologists call 'episodic' or 'autobiographical' memory – memory of particular occasions – which is quite distinct from the conceptual or 'semantic' memory used for thinking more generally about things. A little reflection shows that most of what is gained in a given science lesson must at first be episodic – the experiment seen or the activity undertaken – and will not immediately or automatically become part of a pupil's semantic knowledge. Thus the question of long-term learning of concepts from science lessons is much more like that of long-term learning from informal events than is usually supposed.

Language and Imagery in Science

Recent special issues of science education journals reflect the burgeoning interest in the role of language, including analogy and metaphor, in science teaching (Good, 1993; Yore and Holliday, 1994). Previous work tended to focus mainly on words, whether on the technical vocabulary of science or on the imaginative construction involved in creating new terms ('gas' from the Greek 'chaos'; 'ion' from the Greek 'traveller'). An excellent overview of this style of work is (Sutton, 1993a; 1993b).

However, language is much more than words. A useful theoretical foundation can be found in the perspective of social semiotics (Halliday and Martin, 1993). Their book also gives examples of the specific kinds of grammatical structure characteristic of scientific writing, and analyses how such language structures and their associated social meanings can present difficulties for pupils. This kind of work takes the analysis of 'scientific literacy' well beyond the relatively trivial level of the understanding of scientific terms. Other useful work on writing in science includes Sheeran and Barnes (1991); Sutton (1991).

School science is as much a matter of talk as of writing. And certainly one would expect talk to be crucial in getting into new and strange ideas. Following early work on classroom discussion in science (Barnes, 1972), recent work (Lemke, 1990) has taken up the social semiotic perspective pioneered by Halliday. We find in such work attempts to co-ordinate and relate aspects of classroom talk related to how ideas are structured and developed in discourse, and to how that discourse reflects shifting relations of power. We may be led to reflect on the connection between the teacher's view (often implicit) of the nature of science, and the stance he or she takes towards what constitutes 'teaching science'.

Where traditionally the job of the science teacher in explaining ideas was mainly seen as 'being clear and precise', one outcome of the interest in language has been to shift attention much more to the importance of analogy and metaphor in explanation, and, more generally, to attempts to understand the making of new meanings in the classroom context (Brown, 1994; Clement, 1993; Dagher, 1994; Duit, 1991; Flick, 1991; Ogborn and Martins, 1994a; 1994b; Thagard, 1992; Thiele and Treagust, 1994).

However, 'explanation' still remains a largely unexplicated notion, and I believe that giving a better, clearer and fuller account of what explaining is in the science classroom is a current task of urgency and importance. It will involve collaborating with linguists, and taking account of how philosophers, social psychologists and others deal with explanation (Achinstein, 1983; Antaki, 1988; 1994; Hesse, 1963; Hilton, 1988; Körner, 1975; Pitt, 1988; Ruben, 1990; Schank, 1986). A very useful source of inspiration is recent work in linguistics which recognises metaphor and analogy, not as decorative grace-notes in language, but as fundamental to the way both language and thought actually work (Johnson, 1987a; Lakoff, 1987; Lakoff and Johnson, 1980; 1981). We need better accounts of teachers' explanations in the classroom, and of their relation to what in science counts as an explanation (Ogborn, 1994a).

NATURE OF SCIENCE AND TECHNOLOGY

One of the most vigorous movements in science education over recent years has been for the reform of the science curriculum to take account of science as a human activity, including aspects of its history and philosophy and of the social relations of science and technology. Some regard this as a useful and motivating embellishment of the curriculum; others – among whom I count myself – see it as fundamental to any even half-way reasonable curriculum. For the latter, to study disembodied and decontextualised science is not to study science at all.

History and Philosophy of Science

No fewer than three special issues of science education journals have relatively recently been devoted to discussion of the possible role of history and philosophy of science in the curriculum (Bybee, Ellis and Matthews, 1992; Matthews, 1990; Matthews and Winchester, 1989), together with some recent books (Matthews, 1994; Millar, 1989). Such calls have a long history, going back at least to the 1950s and 1960s, for example, in Harvard Project Physics The key problem has always been giving science teachers, trained in a different tradition, the confidence and the knowledge needed to handle historical and philosophical ideas in science lessons. This issue has been repeatedly analysed and debated (Brickhouse, 1989; Burbules and Linn, 1991; Jenkins, 1990; 1994; Lakin and Wellington, 1994; Matthews, 1990; Solomon, 1989).

A leading research problem naturally became to understand better how teachers themselves understand the nature of science: it turns out that they do have views, that they are not, as is widely thought, simply naive inductivists, and that views shift according to the context (Bloom, 1989; Koulaidis and Ogborn, 1989). Students' conceptions of the nature of science have been similarly investigated (Good, 1991; Larochelle and Désautels, 1991; Ryan and Aikenhead, 1992; Solomon, Duveen, and Scott, 1994; Driver, Leech, Miller and Scott, 1996), and there is evidence that progression is possible (Solomon, 1994). There is still a lack of suitable curriculum materials for dealing with the history and philosophy of science, though some exist (for example, Conant, 1957; Harré, 1981; Nuffield-Chelsea-Curriculum-Trust, 1990; Ziman, 1976).

Science, Technology and Society

More progress has been made with incorporating aspects of science, technology and society into the curriculum, perhaps because the problem is easier and almost certainly because it is closer to the interests of industrialists and others who may fund such developments (Hunt, 1988; Lewis, 1980; Solomon, 1983b).

There has been much debate about how the relationships of science and technology to each other and to society are to be represented (Holman, 1988). The common simplistic view, that technology provides interesting applications of scientific ideas in response to social demands, will clearly not do. More sophisticated and better thought-through positions are available (Layton, 1988; 1991; Medway, 1989; Solomon, 1988; Ziman, 1980). These see both science and technology as social structures, changing in time and having complex and changing relationships. Barely yet taken into account, for example, is the fact that science in this century has largely become 'industrialised', that is, pursued in a systematic, planned, large-scale fashion in specialised technical institutions. It is no longer the preserve of the isolated genius of text-book mythology. More important still, for the future, may be the necessary halting of the incessant growth science and technology have experienced for the past two centuries or more (Ziman, 1994).

Technology Education

The place of technology, within and in relation to the science curriculum is, in my opinion, nothing short of scandalous. The science taught in schools is absurdly disregarding and disrespectful of the technical. Being able to do things is just as important as being smart, and in the purest of branches of science at that. The CERN accelerators may be devoted to the highest level of intellectualism in their discoveries, but their creation has involved engineering of the highest possible order, in precision, power and creative imagination. Nor does the present science curriculum seriously address the needs of future technicians, needed in considerably greater numbers than the scientists around whose needs it is largely constructed.

The historical sources of the bias in British education towards the pure sciences and away from the technical are well documented (Donnelly, 1989; McCulloch, 1987; McCulloch, Jenkins, and Layton, 1985). The current British National Curriculum effects an undesirably sharp division between the two, and – worse – treats technology merely as a branch of design, and all too often as only craft design. Debate continues on how to think about a better set of connections between science and technology which simultaneously respect their close relationship and their deep differences – differences of purpose, outlook and even of language (Allsop and Woolnough, 1990; Black and Harrison, 1985; Gardner, 1994; Jenkins, 1992; Layton, 1991; Medway, 1989). Here is one of the most urgent problems facing science education today.

USING COMPUTERS IN SCIENCE EDUCATION

The advent of personal computers has opened up many opportunities for science education, including simulation, modelling, automated data acquisition, data analysis, and robotics and control. There is space here only for a brief selection.

Computational Modelling

In British science education, at least, there is a strong tradition of exploratory practical work for pupils to do themselves, but there is much less confidence in teaching theory. One possible way of introducing theorising as an essential part of science is through the use of computational modelling. The examples below draw on a recent book about all aspects of modelling in the curriculum (Mellar, Bliss, Boohan, Ogborn, and Tompsett, 1994).

The obvious starting, point is the use of the computer to do the numerical equivalent of solving differential equations, and indeed modelling of this kind is now an essential feature of science and engineering. The mathematics of differential equations is thought of as difficult, suitable at best for the very end of secondary school and for university work. But the computer makes it seem much easier, calculating 'what will happen next' from 'what is happening now', a step at a time. The quickest way to start is to use a spreadsheet programme (suitable ones are widely available for all types of personal computer). 'Cells' in the spreadsheet just need to be told how to get their value from combining values in other cells. Such models can be very simple, and can help understanding of basic relationships. Alternatively, a specially written modelling programme can be used, simplifying the problems of producing models and getting output from them.

It is, however, possible to make useful models without any mathematics at all, and this offers an introduction to modelling for much younger pupils. One way is to use a computational tool which allows the student or teacher to make models just by linking objects on the screen representing variables with arrows representing links between them. For example, one can tell a model that a population of rabbits rises for a positive birth-rate and falls for a positive death-rate. Such a system allows quite young pupils, only just beginning to get used to thinking about the world in terms of variables, to model quite complex situations about which they know something already, such as health and diet, traffic congestion, or keeping a shop in profit.

Another way to model without mathematics is to use a modelling programme in which the pupil or teacher makes 'objects' on the screen and draws picture-rules telling them what they do (Boohan and Ogborn, forthcoming). Rabbit populations are now represented by computer 'rabbits', not by a variable called 'number of rabbits'. Birth is represented by rules showing when baby rabbits can appear; death by rules for rabbits vanishing or being eaten (if the model also has computer 'foxes'). Such models are accessible to pupils from about age nine or ten, but continue to be useful in much more advanced work (for example, chemical equilibrium).

Data Analysis

Another important aspect of theoretical work in science is the handling and picturing of data. This old and for many not very interesting aspect of teaching science has been given a face-lift through some fundamental developments in statistical thinking, namely the movement for exploratory data analysis (Tukey, 1977). The stress is on simple – and often very original – paper-and-pencil ways of analysing and picturing data, which, aided by suitable computer programmes, can make exploring and presenting data a rapid and pleasurable affair, recruiting artistic talent as well as analytical ability. A collection of materials suitable for use in schools has been prepared and tested (Boohan, 1994; Boohan and Ogborn, 1991).

ATTITUDES TO SCIENCE

Research into attitudes towards science, or into the development of 'scientific attitudes', has consistently proved to be a minefield (Schibeci, 1984). Appropriate frameworks for thinking about the nature of attitudes or about how to influence them are difficult to come by (Crawley and Koballa, 1994; Koballa, 1992). There are ideas about how attitudes develop and change (Head, 1985; Head and Ramsden, 1990), but the area remains difficult to investigate.

Some of the liveliest – and the most controversial – work has concerned gender differences in science education. Scientists are still overwhelmingly male, and in Britain (though not in other countries) so are teachers of physics and chemistry. Girls showed a strong tendency to avoid physics and chemistry where this was permitted. More hopefully, at the present time, girls are beginning to show higher scores than boys in many areas of education, including science.

However, for a decade the issue was girls' under-achievement or under-representation in science (Kelly, 1987). Analyses of the nature of the underlying issues have drawn on sociological and feminist perspectives (Bentley and Watts, 1994; Delamont, 1989; Dunne and Johnston, 1992; Harding, 1986; Kelly, 1981). Explanations in terms of differential treatment of girls in science lessons have proved difficult to support with evidence (Hacker, 1991; 1992). Recently, the accent has been on understanding success; on seeing where and why girls can be attracted to science and succeed in it (Delamont, 1994).

ASSESSMENT

The fundamental problems of assessment in science education, as a powerful force for good or evil in influencing the curriculum and teaching, have never been put more powerfully or humanely than by Rogers (1969), recently reprinted (Jennison and Ogborn, 1994). They have, however, been restated very effectively by Black (1994), who draws on evidence from all around the world. The issue is very simple: for assessment to be helpful it must ask students to do what you actually want them to be able to do, not some cheap or artificial surrogate for it. If you want them to think, you must ask them to think. If that is hard or expensive to assess, then accept the cost, or pay the price of sacrificing what you actually want to achieve.

There are several substantial reviews of assessment theory and practice (Champagne and Newell, 1992; Hodson, 1986; Johnson, 1987b). They lay particular stress on the need for, and the scarcity of, assessment used to diagnose what may be wrong before it is too late, as opposed to assessment used to measure what went wrong at the end of the day. The pity is that National Curriculum testing in science in Britain has moved further and further away from accepting such obvious needs, all in the interests of a cheap system which does not even serve the narrow interests it is meant to serve in anything but appearance.

PERSONAL SCIENCE

What is for many one of the least sympathetic features of science is at the same moment its saving grace. Its impersonal qualities mean that we cannot identify with any idea because we admire its originator, because it satisfies our deep moral impulses, or because it just seems so beautiful. Ideas have to meet a sterner test: to be in the end the only possibility apparently left about how things actually are. That which makes scientific knowledge what it is also makes it heartlessly disregarding of our wishes, likings and hopes.

Worse, this means that what knowledge finally gets filtered through by this process is not necessarily the knowledge we want or need; it is just the knowledge we happen to have. In this way, too, science seems to count as nothing our most passionate impulses to know.

Some seek a way out by destroying 'objectivity'. They may then feel better about what they claim to know, but they may suffer from relying on it. And yet science is, as Polanyi so powerfully reminded us (Polanyi, 1958), an affair of passionate commitment. How can science be made to seem personal in this way for students, whilst accepting that this personal passion is for those fragments of knowledge which can by great effort be made impersonal?

It is fitting to close with an example (Martin and Brouwer, 1993). In this paper, an astronomer, recognising our problem, tells of his astronomical way of life, linking its sharp and narrow astronomical passions to the other less unintelligible ones of family, friends and countryside. Some extracts must suffice. The astronomer's friend, Tom, coming with him to the observatory, had just managed to identify what he had come to try to see: a nova in Andromeda.

'I found it!' Tom's enthusiastic announcement preceded his entrance...Nova Andromeda had finally yielded to his searching...

'See it? To the bottom right, about ninth magnitude.'...I agreed that indeed this was likely Nova Andromeda. 'Too bad you don't have a photometer on this', I offered.

'Why do you always have to measure? Isn't it enough just to find it, to see it?... I don't know how you can do this night after night... just sitting there watching numbers. It seems so boring.'

'It's nights like this that make it worthwhile...Look at the noise level, less than 3 millimagnitudes; that's excellent. With this data, I may be able to say something definite about HD 32655...Look at it this way. I'm looking at a star that probably no one else in the world cares about (yet)...This star might be a rapid oscillator. Only good-quality data like this will help tell me...'

HD 32655 has puzzled me for the past six months. Is there a short period variation present in this data? I do not know. Some days I am convinced there is; on other days it is less clear. The road from hunch or hopeful guess to that of published 'fact' is a long and convoluted one.

The story continues with an account of how, co-operating in an international programme of observation with a world expert, the astronomer began to suspect that another star, one of the 'steady' comparison stars assigned by the expert to be used to help detect a variable one, was itself variable. Tentatively, the astronomer sent a telex to the expert asking if anyone had noticed anything unusual about the 'comparison' star. No answer. Was the expert insulted? After some months the astronomer wrote a note about the star for a journal, and sent the expert a copy. The expert replied, apologising for the silence, and saying that others had also found variation in this star. But it was just the type of star that, according to present theory, ought not to be variable – which was why it had been chosen as a standard for comparison. So all the others had thought they must have made a mistake too.

I will not burden the reader with underlining the moral too heavily. A passion for knowing led to uncovering a tiny new fact, through a shared, communal and slow process of eroding alternatives. The scientific passion is a peculiar one, and one we have no right to require everyone to share. But what we must do is to let those who will listen know what it feels like to us. If science teaching, through such examples, could be more personal without being less truthful, I believe that more people might sympathise with the scientific passion even if they would not choose it for themselves.

REFERENCES

Achinstein, P. (1983). *The Nature of Explanation*. Oxford: Clarendon Press.
Allsop, T., and Woolnough, B. (1990). 'The relation of technology to science in British schools', *Journal of Curriculum Studies*, 22, 2, pp. 127–36.
Antaki, C. (ed.). (1988). *Analysing Everyday Explanation*. London: Sage.
— (1994). *Explaining and Arguing: The Social Organisation of Accounts*. London: Sage.
Apple, M. (1992). 'Educational reform and educational crisis', *Journal of Research in Science Teaching*, 29, 8, pp. 779–90.
Atkin, J. M., and Helms, J. (1993). 'Getting serious about priorities in science education', *Studies in Science Education*, 21, pp. 1–20.
Barnes, D. (1972). *From Communication to Curriculum*. London: Penguin.
Bentley, D., and Watts, M. (1994). 'Humanizing and feminizing school science: reviving anthropomorphic and animistic thinking in constructivist science education, *International Journal of Science Education*, 16, 1, pp. 83–98.
Bhaskar, R. (1978). *A Realist Theory of Science*. London: Harvester Wheatsheaf.
Bingle, W. H., and Gaskell, P. J. (1994). 'Scientific literacy for decision-making and the social construction of scientific knowledge', *Science Education*, 78, 2, pp. 185–201.
Black, P. J. (1994). 'Humane and helpful assessment', in Jennison, B. and Ogborn, J. (eds), *Wonder and Delight: Essays in Science Education in honour of the life and work of Eric Rogers 1902–1990*. Bristol: Institute of Physics Publishing, pp. 63–74.
— and Harrison, G. B. (1985). *In Place of Confusion*. London: Nuffield-Chelsea Curriculum Trust.
Bliss, J. (1993). 'The relevance of Piaget to research into children's conceptions', in Black, P. J. and Lucas, A. M. (eds), *Children's Informal Ideas in Science*. London: Routledge.
— (1994). 'Children learning science', in Jennison and Ogborn (eds), *Wonder and Delight*, pp. 45–61.
— and Ogborn, J. (1990). 'A psycho-logic of motion', *European Journal of Psychology of Education*, Vol. 4, pp. 379–90.
— and Ogborn, J. (1992). 'Steps towards the formalisation of a psycho-logic of motion', in Tiberghien, A. and Mandl, H. (eds), *Intelligent Learning Environments and Knowledge Acquisition in Physics*. Berlin: Springer Verlag.
— and Ogborn, J. (1993a). 'A common-sense theory of motion', in Black and Lucas (eds), *Children's Informal Ideas in Science*. London: Routledge.
— and Ogborn, J. (1993b). 'Steps towards the formalisation of a psycho-logic of motion', *Journal of Intelligent Systems*, 3, 1, pp. 3–48.
— and Ogborn, J. (1994). 'Force and motion from the beginning', *Learning and Instruction*, 4, pp. 7–25.
— Ogborn, J., and Whitelock, D. (1989). 'Secondary school pupils' commonsense theories of motion', *International Journal of Science Education*, 11, 3, pp. 261–72.
Bloom, J. W. (1989). 'Pre-service elementary teachers' conceptions of science: science, theories and evolution', *International Journal of Science Education*, 11, 4, pp. 401–16.
— (1990). 'Contexts of meaning: young children's understanding of biological

phenomena', *International Journal of Science Education*, 12, 5, pp. 549–62.
— (1992). 'The development of scientific knowledge in elementary school children: a context of meaning perspective', *Science Education*, 76, 4, pp. 399–413.
Bloor, D. (1976). *Knowledge and Social Imagery*. London: Routledge & Kegan Paul.
Boohan, R. (1994). 'Starting from data: a different approach to making models', in Mellar, H., Bliss, J., Boohan, M., Ogborn, J. and Tompsett, C. (eds), *Learning with Artificial Worlds: Computer-Based Modelling in the Curriculum*. London: Falmer Press, pp. 104–14.
— and Ogborn, J. (1991). *Making Sense of Data: Nuffield Exploratory Data Analysis Project*. Harlow: Longman.
Boohan, R., and Ogborn, J. (forthcoming). *WorldMaker*. London: Institute of Education
Boyes, E., and Stanisstreet, M. (1990). 'Pupils' ideas concerning energy sources', *International Journal of Science Education*, 12, 5, pp. 513–30.
Brickhouse, N. (1989). 'The teaching of the philosophy of science in secondary classrooms: case studies of teachers' theories', *International Journal of Science Education*, 11, 4, pp. 437–50.
Brown, D. E. (1994). 'Facilitating conceptual change using analogies and metaphors', *International Journal of Science Education*, 16, 2, pp. 201–14.
Burbules, N. C., and Linn, M. C. (1991). 'Science education and philosophy of science: congruence or contradiction?', *International Journal of Science Education*, 13 3, pp. 227–42.
Bybee, R. W., Ellis, J. D., Matthews, M. R. (eds) (1992). Special Issue: 'Teaching about the History and Nature of Science and Technology', *Journal of Research in Science Teaching*, 29,4.
Champagne, A., and Newell, S. T. (1992). 'Directions for research and development: Alternative methods of assessing scientific literacy', *Journal of Research in Science Teaching*, 29, 8, pp. 841–60.
Chi, M. (1992). 'Conceptual change within and across ontological categories, in Giere, R. (ed.), *Cognitive Models of Science: Minnesota Studies in the Philosophy of Science*. Minneapolis: University of Minnesota Press, pp. 129–60.
Clement, J. (1993). 'Using bridging analogies and anchoring intuitions to deal with students' preconceptions in physics', *Journal of Research in Science Teaching*, 30, 10, pp. 1241–58.
Collins, H. (1992). *Changing Order: Replication and Induction in Scientific Practice*. Chicago: Chicago University Press.
Conant, J. B. (1957). *Harvard Case Histories in Experimental Science Volumes 1 and 2*. Cambridge, MA: University of Harvard.
Confrey, J. (1990). 'What constructivism implies for teaching', in Davis, R., Maher, C., and Noddings, N. (eds), *Constructivist Views on the Teaching and Learning of Mathematics*. Reston, Virginia: National Council of Teachers of Mathematics.
Crawley, F. E., and Koballa, T. R. (1994). 'Attitude research in science education – contemporary models and methods', *Science Education*, 78, 1, pp. 35–55.
Dagher, Z. R. (1994). 'Does the use of analogies contribute to conceptual change?', *Science Education*, 78, 6, pp. 601–14.
Davis, N. T., McCarty, B. J., Shaw, K. L., and Sidani-Tabbaa, A. (1993). 'Transitions from objectivism to constructivism in science education', *International Journal of Science Education*, 15, 6, pp. 627–35.
Delamont, S. (1989). 'The fingernail on the blackboard? A sociological perspective on science education', *Studies in Science Education*, 16, pp. 25–46.
— S. (1994). 'Accentuating the positive: refocusing the research on girls and science',

Studies in Science Education, 23, pp. 59–74.

Dierking, L. D., and Falk, J. H. (1994). 'Family behaviour and learning in informal science settings', *Science Education*, 78, 1, pp. 57–72.

diSessa, A. (1993). 'Towards an epistemology of physics', *Cognition and Instruction*, 10, 2 and 3, pp. 105–225.

Donnelly, J. (1989). 'The origins of the technical curriculum in England during the 19th and 20th centuries', *Studies in Science Education*, 16, pp. 123–61.

Driver, R. (1989). 'The construction of scientific knowledge in school classrooms', in Millar, R. (ed.), *Doing Science: Images of Science in Science Education*. Lewes: Falmer Press.

— and Oldham, V. (1986). 'A constructivist approach to curriculum development in science', *Studies in Science Education*, 13, pp. 105–22.

— Squires, A., Rushworth, P., and Wood-Robinson, V. (1994). *Making Sense of Secondary Science: Research into Children's Ideas*. London: Routledge.

Driver, R, Leech, J., Millar, R. and Scott, P. (1996). *Young People's Images of Science*. Buckingham: Open University Press.

Duit, R. (1991). 'On the role of analogies and metaphors in learning science', *Science Education*, 75, 6, pp. 649–72.

Dunne, M., and Johnston, J. (1992). 'An awareness of epistemological assumptions: the case of gender studies', *International Journal of Science Education*, 14, 5, pp. 515–26.

Durant, J., Evans, G., and Thomas, G. (1989). 'The public understanding of science', *Nature*, 340, pp. 11–14.

Duschl, R., and Gitomer, D. H. (1991). 'Epistemological perspectives on conceptual change: implications for educational practice', *Journal of Research in Science Teaching*, 28, 9, pp. 839–58.

Feldman, A., and Atkin, J. M. (1993). 'Research in Science Education in the USA', *Journal of Curriculum Studies*, 25, 3, pp. 281–9.

Feyerabend, P. (1975). *Against Method*. London: Verso.

— (1987). *Farewell to Reason*. London: Verso.

Flick, L. (1991). 'Where concepts meet percepts: stimulating analogical thought in children', *Science Education*, 75, 2, pp. 215–30.

Fosnot, C. T. (1993). 'Re-thinking science education: a defense of Piagetian constructivism', *Journal of Research in Science Teaching*, 30, 9, pp. 1189–202.

Gardner, P. (1994). 'Representations of the relationship between science and technology in the curriculum', *Studies in Science Education*, 24, pp. 1–28.

Glasersfeld, E. von (1987). *The Construction of Knowledge*. California: Intersystems Publications.

— (1989). 'Cognition, construction of knowledge, and teaching', *Synthese*, 80, 1, pp. 121–40.

Gleick, J. (1992). *Genius: The Life and Science of Richard Feynman*. New York: Pantheon.

Good, R. (ed.) (1991). Special Issue: 'Students' Models and Epistemologies', *Journal of Research in Science Teaching*, 28, 9.

— (ed.) (1992). Special Issue: Science Curriculum Reform. *Journal of Research in Science Teaching*, 29, 8.

— (ed.) (1993). Special Issue: 'Role of Analogy in Science and Science Teaching', *Journal of Research in Science Teaching*, 30, 10.

Goodman, N. (1978). *Ways of Worldmaking*. New York: Hackett.

Gross, P. R., and Levitt, N. (1994). *Higher Superstition: The Academic Left and its*

Quarrels with Science. Baltimore: The Johns Hopkins University Press.

Guidoni, P. (1985). 'On natural thinking', *European Journal of Science Education*, 7, 2, pp. 133–40.

Gutierrez, R., and Ogborn, J. (1992). 'A causal framework for analysing alternative conceptions', *International Journal of Science Education*, 14,2, pp. 201–20.

Hacker, R. G. (1991). 'Gender differences in science-lesson behaviours', *International Journal of Science Education*, 13,4, pp. 439–46.

—. (1992). 'Gender studies: some methodological and theoretical issues', *International Journal of Science Education*, 14,5, pp. 527–40.

Hacking, I. (1983). *Representing and Intervening*. Cambridge: Cambridge University Press.

Halliday, M. A. K., and Martin, J. R. (1993). *Writing Science: Literary and Discursive Power*. London: Falmer Press.

Hann, K., Brosnan, T., and Ogborn, J. (1992). *CHATTS: Executive Summary Report*. Institute of Education, University of London.

Harding, J. (ed.). (1986). *Perspectives on Gender and Science*. London: Falmer Press.

Harré, R. (1981). *Great Scientific Experiments*. London: Phaidon.

— (1986). *Varieties of Realism*. Oxford: Blackwell.

Head, J. (1985). *The Personal Response to Science*. Cambridge: Cambridge University Press.

— and Ramsden, J. (1990). 'Gender, psychological type and science', *International Journal of Science Education*, 12, 1, pp. 115–21.

Hesse, M. (1963). *Models and Analogies in Science*. London: Sheed & Ward.

Hilton, D. J. (ed.). (1988). *Contemporary Science and Natural Explanation*. Lewes: Harvester Press.

Hodson, D. (1986). 'The role of assessment in the "curriculum cycle": a survey of science department practice', *Research into Science and Technological Education*, 4, 1, pp. 7–17.

Holman, J. (ed.) (1988). Special Issue: 'Science, Technology and Society', *International Journal of Science Education*, 10, 4.

Hunt, A. (1988). 'SATIS approaches to STS', *International Journal of Science Education*, 10, 4, pp. 409–20.

Jenkins, E. W. (1990). 'History of science in British schools: retrospect and prospect', *International Journal of Science Education*, 12, 3, pp. 274–81.

— (1992). 'School science education: towards a reconstruction', *Journal of Curriculum Studies*, 24, 3, pp. 229–46.

— (1994). 'HPS and school science education: remediation or reconstruction?', *International Journal of Science Education*, 16, 6, pp. 613–24.

Jennison, B., and Ogborn, J. (eds). (1994). *Wonder and Delight: Essays in Science Education*. Bristol: Institute of Physics Publishing.

Johnson, M. (1987a). *The Body in the Mind: The Bodily Basis of Meaning, Imagination and Reason*. Chicago: University of Chicago Press.

Johnson, S. (1987b). 'Assessment in science and technology', *Studies in Science Education*, 14, pp. 83–108.

Kelly, A. (ed.). (1981). *The Missing Half*. Manchester: Manchester University Press.

— (ed.) (1987). Special Issue: 'Gender and Science', *International Journal of Science Education*, 9, 3.

Kesidou, S., and Duit, R. (1993). 'Students' conceptions of the second law of thermodynamics', *Journal of Research in Science Teaching*, 30, 1, pp. 85–106.

Klopfer, L. E., and Champagne, A. B. (1991). 'Ghosts of crisis past', *Science Education*, 74, 2, pp. 133–54.

Koballa, T. R. (1992). 'Persuasion and attitude change in science education', *Journal of Research in Science Teaching*, 29, 1, pp. 63–80.

Körner, S. (ed.). (1975). *Explanation*. Oxford: Blackwell.

Koulaidis, V., and Ogborn, J. (1989). 'Philosophy of science: an empirical study of teachers' views', *International Journal of Science Education*, 11, 2, pp. 173–84.

Kuhn, T. (1962). *The Structure of Scientific Revolutions*. Chicago: University of Chicago Press.

Lakin, S., and Wellington, J. (1994). 'Who will teach the "nature of science"?: Teachers' views of science and their implications for science education', *International Journal of Science Education*, 16, 2, pp. 175–90.

Lakoff, G. (1987). *Women, Fire and Dangerous Things*. Chicago: Chicago University Press.

— and Johnson, M. (1980). 'The metaphorical structure of the human conceptual system', *Cognitive Science*, 4, pp. 195–208.

— and Johnson, M. (1981). *Metaphors We Live By*. Chicago: Chicago University Press.

Larochelle, M., and Désautels, J. (1991). 'Of course, it's just obvious': adolescents' ideas of scientific knowledge', *International Journal of Science Education*, 13, 4, pp. 373–90.

Latour, B. (1987). *Science in Action: How to Follow Scientists and Engineers through Society*. Cambridge, MA: Harvard University Press.

Latour, B., and Woolgar, S. (1986). *Laboratory Life: The Construction of Scientific Facts*. Princeton: Princeton University Press.

Law, N. (1988). 'Knowledge structures: where can we find them?', in *Proceedings of the AERA Annual Meeting*, New Orleans, April 1988

— (1990) *Eliciting and Understanding Commonsense Reasoning about Motion*. PhD, University of London.

Layton, D. (1988). 'Revaluing the T in STS', *International Journal of Science Education*, 10, 4, pp. 367–78.

— (1991). 'Science education and praxis: the relation of school science to practical action', *Studies in Science Education*, 19, pp. 43–79.

— Jenkins, E., MacGill, S., and Davey, A. (1993). *Inarticulate Science? Perspectives on the Public Understanding of Science and Some Implications for Science Education*. Driffield: Studies in Education Ltd.

Lemke, J. L. (1990). *Talking Science: Language, Learning and Values*. Norwood New Jersey: Ablex.

Lewis, J. L. (1980). *Science in Society: General Introduction. Teachers' Guide*. London: Association for Science Education and Heinemann.

Lijnse, P. (1991). 'Energy between the life-world of pupils and the world of physics', *Science Education*, 74, 5, pp. 571–83.

Linn, M. C. (1992). 'Science education reform: building on the research base', *Journal of Research in Science Teaching*, 29, 8, pp. 821–40.

Lucas, A. M. (1983). 'Scientific literacy and informal education', *Studies in Science Education*, 10, pp. 1–36.

— (ed.) (1991). Special Issue: Informal Sources for Learning Science, *International Journal of Science Education*, 13, 5.

Mariani, M. C. (1992) 'Some Dimensions of Commonsense Reasoning about the Physical World.' PhD, University of London.

— and Ogborn, J. (1990). 'Commonsense reasoning about conservation: the role of action', *International Journal of Science Education*, 12, 1, pp. 55–66.

— and Ogborn, J. (1991). 'Towards an ontology of commonsense reasoning',

International Journal of Science Education, 13, 1, pp. 69–85.

Martin, B., and Brouwer, W. (1993). 'Exploring personal science', *Science Education*, 77, 4, pp. 441–59.

Marx, G. (1994). 'Shortcut to the future', in Jennison and Ogborn (eds), *Wonder and Delight*, pp. 5–17.

Matthews, M. (ed.) (1990). Special Issue: 'History, Philosophy and Science Teaching', *International Journal of Science Education*, 12, 3.

— (1992). 'Constructivism and empiricism: an incomplete divorce', Manuscript personally communicated.

— (1994). *Science Teaching: The Role of History and Philosophy of Science*. London: Routledge.

— and Winchester, I. (eds) (1989). Special Issue: 'History, Science and Science Teaching', *Interchange*, 20, 2.

— (1990). 'History, philosophy and science teaching: a rapprochement', *Studies in Science Education*, 18, pp. 25–51.

McCulloch, G. (1987). 'School science and technology in 19th and 20th century England: a guide to published sources', *Studies in Science Education*, 14, pp. 1–32.

— Jenkins, E., and Layton, D. (1985). *Technological Revolution? The Politics of School Science and Technology in England and Wales since 1945*. London: Falmer Press.

Medway, P. (1989). 'Issues in the theory and practice of technology education', *Studies in Science Education*, 16, pp. 1–23.

Mellar, H., Bliss, J., Boohan, R., Ogborn, J., and Tompsett, C. (eds) (1994). *Learning with Artificial Worlds*. London: Falmer Press.

Millar, R. (ed.). (1989). *Doing Science: Images of Science in Science Education*. Lewes: Falmer Press.

Nadeau, R., and Desautels, J. (1984). *Epistemology and the Teaching of Science*. Ottawa: Science Council of Canada.

Nicholls, G. (1991) *Case Studies in the Use of Computer Software in the Teaching of Energy*. PhD, University of London.

— and Ogborn, J. (1993). 'Dimensions of children's conceptions of energy', *International Journal of Science Education*, 15, 1, pp. 73–81.

Novak, J. (1988). 'Learning science and science learning', *Studies in Science Education*, 15, pp. 77–101.

Nuffield-Chelsea Curriculum Trust (1990). *Investigating the Nature of Science*. Harlow: Longman.

O'Loughlin, M. (1992). 'Re-thinking science education: Beyond Piagetian constructivism towards a socio-cultural model of teaching and learning', *Journal of Research in Science Teaching*, 29, 8, pp. 791–820.

Ogborn, J. (1985). 'Understanding students' understandings: an example from dynamics', *European Journal of Science Education*, 7, 2, pp. 141–50.

Ogborn, J. (1992). 'Fundamental dimensions of thought about reality: object, action, cause, movement, space and time', in *Teaching about Reference Frames: from Copernicus to Einstein Proceedings of GIREP Conference, August 1991*. Torun, Poland: Nicholas Copernicus University Press.

— (1994a) *Theoretical and Empirical Investigations of the Nature of Scientific and Commonsense Knowledge*. PhD, University of London.

— (1994b). 'A vulgar science curriculum', in Jennison and Ogborn (eds), *Wonder and Delight*, pp. 19–30.

— (forthcoming). 'Constructivist metaphors in science learning', in Tobin (ed.), *Kluwer International Handbook of Science Education*. New York: Kluwer.

— (1995). 'Recovering reality', *Studies in Science Education*, 25, pp. 3–38.
— and Mariani, M. C. (1995). 'The ontology of physical events: a comparison of two groups', *International Journal of Science Education*, 17, 5, pp. 643–61.
— and Martins, I. (1994a). *Metaphorical Reasoning about Genetics* (Commonsense Understandings of Science: Working Paper). Institute of Education: University of London.
— and Martins, I. (1994b). *Metaphorical Understandings of Scientific Ideas* (Commonsense Understandings of Science: Working Paper). Institute of Education: University of London.
Osborne, R., and Freyberg, P. (1985). *Learning in Science: The Implications of Children's Science*. London: Heinemann.
Osborne, R., and Whitrock, M. (1985). 'The generative learning model and its implications for science education', *Studies in Science Education*, 12, pp. 59–87.
Pfundt, H., and Duit, R. (1994). *Bibliography: Student's Alternative Frameworks and Science Education* (IPN Reports). IPN: Kiel.
Piaget, J., and Garcia, R. (1983). *Psychogenèse et Histoire des Sciences*. Paris: Flammarion.
Piaget, J., and Garcia, R. (1987). *Vers une Logique des Significations*. Geneva: Murionde. (translated 1991) *Toward a Logic of Meaning*. New Jersey: Lawrence Erlbaum.
Pickering, A. (1984). Constructing Quarks: *A Sociological History of Particle Physics*. Edinburgh: Edinburgh University Press.
— (ed.). (1992). *Science as Practice and Culture*. Chicago: University of Chicago Press.
Pitt, J. C. (ed.). (1988). *Theories of Explanation*. Oxford: Clarendon Press.
Polanyi, M. (1958). *Personal Knowledge*. London: Routledge.
Popper, K. (1979). *Objective Knowledge*. Oxford: Clarendon Press.
Raizen, S. A. (1991). 'The reform of science education in the USA: Déjà vu or de novo?', *Studies in Science Education*, 19, pp. 1–41.
Ramey-Gassert, L., Walberg, H. J., and Walberg, H. J. (1994). 'Re-examining connections: museums as science learning environments', *Science Education*, 78, 4, 345–63.
Ravetz, J. R. (1971). *Scientific Knowledge and its Social Relations*. New York: Oxford University Press.
Reif, F., and Larkin, J. (1991). 'Cognition in scientific and everyday domains: comparison and learning implication', *Journal of Research in Science Teaching*, 28,9, pp. 733–60.
Rogers, E. (1969). 'Examinations: powerful agents for good or ill in teaching', *American Journal of Physics*, 37, 10, pp. 954–62.
Rorty, R. (1991). *Objectivity, Relativism and Truth*. Cambridge: Cambridge University Press.
Rosier, M. (1990). 'International comparisons in science education', *Studies in Science Education*, 18, pp. 87–104.
Ross, B., and Munby, H. (1991). 'Concept mapping and misconceptions: a study of high-school students' understanding of acids and bases', *International Journal of Science Education*, 13, 1, pp. 11–24.
Roth, W.-M. (1993). 'In the name of constructivism: science education research and the construction of local knowledge', *Journal of Research in Science Teaching*, 30, 7, pp. 799–803.
Rowell, J. A., and Dawson, C. J. (1989). 'Towards an integrated theory and practice for science education', *Studies in Science Education*, 16, pp. 47–73.
Royal Society (1985). *The Public Understanding of Science*. The Royal Society, London.
Ruben, D-H. (1990). *Explaining Explanation*. London: Routledge.
Ryan, A. G., and Aikenhead, G. S. (1992). 'Students' preconceptions about the epistemo-

logy of science', *Science Education*, 76, 6, pp. 559–80.

Ryu, T. (1994). 'Examining inquiring minds?', in Jennison and Ogborn (eds), *Wonder and Delight*, pp. 75-80.

Schank, R. (1986). *Explanation Patterns*. New Jersey: Lawrence Erlbaum.

Schibeci, D. (1984). 'Attitudes to science: an update', *Studies in Science Education*, 11, pp. 26–59.

Sheeran, Y., and Barnes, D. (1991). *School Writing*. Buckingham: Open University Press.

Solomon, J. (1983a). 'Learning about energy: how pupils think in two domains', *European Journal of Science Education*, 5, 1, pp. 49–59.

— (1983b). *SISCON in Schools*. Oxford: Blackwell.

— (1988). 'Science, technology and society courses: tools for thinking about social issues', *International Journal of Science Education*, 10, 4, pp. 379–87.

— (1989). 'Teaching the history of science: Is nothing sacred?', in Shortland, M. and Warwick, A. (eds), *Teaching the History of Science*. Oxford: Blackwell, pp. 42–53.

— (1990). 'The discussion of social issues in the science classroom', *Studies in Science Education*, 18, pp. 105–26.

— (1992). *Getting to Know about Energy in School and Society*. London: Falmer Press.

— (1994). 'Teaching about the nature of science through history', in Jennison and Ogborn (eds), *Wonder and Delight*, pp. 31–44.

— Duveen, J., and Scott, L. (1994). 'Pupils' images of scientific epistemology', *International Journal of Science Education*, 16, 3, pp. 361–73.

Stevenson, J. (1991). 'The long term impact of interactive exhibits', *International Journal of Science Education*, 13, 5, pp. 521–32.

Strike, K., and Posner, G. (1982a). 'Conceptual change and science teaching', *European Journal of Science Education*, 4, pp. 231–40.

Strike, K., and Posner, G. (1982b). 'A revisionist theory of conceptual change', in Duschl, R. and Hamilton, R. (eds), *Philosophy of Science, Cognitive Psychology and Educational Theory and Practice*. Albany New York: State University of New York, pp. 147–76.

Suchting, W. (1992). 'Constructivism deconstructed', *Science and Education*, 1, pp. 223–54.

Sutton, C. (1993a). 'Figuring out a scientific understanding', *Journal of Research in Science Teaching*, 30, 10, pp. 1215–28.

– (1993b). *Words, Science and Learning*. Buckingham: Open University Press.

Sutton, C. R. (ed.). (1991). *Communicating in the Classroom*. London: Hodder & Stoughton.

Thagard, P. (1992). 'Analogy, explanation and education', *Journal of Research in Science Teaching*, 29, 6, pp. 537–45.

Thiele, R. B., and Treagust, D. F. (1994). 'An interpretive examination of high school chemistry teachers' analogical explanations', *Journal of Research in Science Teaching*, 31, 3, pp. 227–42.

Tóth, E. (1994). 'Nuclear literacy', in Jennison and Ogborn (eds), *Wonder and Delight*, pp. 127–33.

Trumper, R. (1990). 'Being constructive: an alternative approach to the teaching of the energy concept – part one', *International Journal of Science Education*, 12, 4, pp. 343–54.

— (1991). 'Being constructive: an alternative approach to the teaching of the energy concept – part two', *International Journal of Science Education*, 13, 1, pp. 1–10.

— (1993). 'Children's energy concepts: a cross-age study', *International Journal of Science Education*, 15, 2, pp. 139–48.

Tukey, J. (1977). *Exploratory Data Analysis*. New York: Addison Wesley.

Viennot, L. (1979a). *Le Raisonnement Spontané en Dynamique Élémentaire*. Paris: Hermann.
— (1979b). 'Spontaneous reasoning in elementary dynamics', *European Journal of Science Education*, 1, 2, pp. 205–21.
Wheatley, G. (1991). 'Constructivist perspectives on science and mathematics education', *Science Education*, 75, 1, pp. 9–22.
Whitelock, D. M. (1990) *Commonsense Understanding of Causes of Motion*. PhD, University of London.
— (1991). 'Investigating a commonsense model of causes of motion with 7 to 16 year old pupils', *International Journal of Science Education*, 13, 3, pp. 321–40.
Wittgenstein, L. (1922). *Tractatus Logico-Philosophicus*. London: Routledge & Kegan Paul.
— (1953). *Philosophical Investigations*. Oxford: Basil Blackwell.
Wynne, B. (1991). 'Knowledges in context', *Science, Technology and Human Values*, 16, 1, pp. 111–21.
Yore, L. D. and Holliday, W. G. (eds) (1994). Special Issue: 'Reading – Writing – Science', *Journal of Research in Science Teaching*, 31, 9.
Ziman, J. (1967). *Public Knowledge*. Cambridge: Cambridge University Press.
— (1976). *The Force of Knowledge: The Scientific Dimension of Society*. Cambridge: Cambridge University Press.
— (1978). *Reliable Knowledge*. Cambridge: Cambridge University Press.
Ziman, J. (1980). *Teaching and Learning about Science and Society*. Cambridge: Cambridge University Press.
— (1994). *Prometheus Bound: Science in a Dynamic Steady State*. Cambridge: Cambridge University Press.

7

TECHNOLOGY

Richard Kimbell

INTRODUCTION

One of the few things about which writers in this field are agreed is that there is a desperate lack of research in technology as a teaching and learning activity in the curriculum:

> Design & Technology lacks a research base in pupils understanding and learning such as is available in the cases of mathematics and science...(DES, 1988).

> Craft Design & Technology stands out as the most under researched area of the curriculum. The literature of the subject barely exists (Penfold, 1988).

The year 1988 was a significant date for technology, since it was in that year that the original National Curriculum Working Group for Design & Technology published its Interim Report. From that report flowed the technology Order (Department of Education and Science [DES],1990) that brought technology to the heart of the National Curriculum (NC) and made it a compulsory study for all pupils between the ages of five and 16. Never before had this been the case.

Twenty-five years earlier, technology did not exist in anything like the form that emerged in the 1990 Order. And 25 years is an astonishingly short germination period for a new curriculum subject, especially given the timeless durability of the vast majority of them. As Williams somewhat acidly observes:

> The fact about our present curriculum is that it was essentially created by the 19th century, following some 18th century models and retaining elements of the mediaeval curriculum near its centre (Williams, 1965).

There are many observers who argue that the new English/Welsh National Curriculum is following precisely in the footsteps laid down in this great tradition. But everyone acknowledges that the exception to the rule is technology. They may not know why it's there – or what it uniquely can contribute to young people's education – but everyone can see it is new. And it is because of this newness – this lack of a stable tradition – that it is vulnerable. The five (or is it six?) versions of NC technology that have done the rounds in the last five years are ample testimony to the uncertainties that surround it. I intend to explore some of these uncertainties in this chapter and in the process we shall see the extent to which research has begun to shed light into some of the darker recesses in our understanding. But there remains more darkness than light and the evil goblin may be just round the corner.

A PRAGMATIC TRADITION

Technology in the school curriculum has grown from *practice* rather than from theory; from teachers in the classroom trying out innovative and often idiosyncratic activities and programmes – rather than from an intellectual analysis of a field of knowledge. And it has been hugely successful. Pupils voted with their feet; courses expanded and proliferated; competitions and prizes led to high-profile public exposure where politicians and others were delighted to shake a few hands for the camera. Eventually, with the growth of Advanced-level work, even the universities caught up with the fact that there was some quite exceptional young talent coming through this route and increasingly they sought it out.

In the hands of a self-selecting group of committed pioneering teachers, its success lay in a heady brew of practicality, intellectual and emotional challenge, and the requirement that pupils think and act autonomously. Whilst it was never articulated in this way, what these teachers were creating was not so much a new subject as a new approach to learning. For at the heart of the challenge of teaching technology lies the conundrum of 'process'.

Nobody, looking at the progressive definitions of NC technology over the last five years, could be in any doubt about the centrality of the *process* of design and development. Technology is the only subject in the NC to be defined exclusively in process terms. The 1990 Order had four Attainment Targets for Design & Technology:

- Identifying needs and opportunities   (…for technological intervention)

- Generating a design proposal   (…to meet the need)

- Planning and making (...the proposed design)
- Appraisal (...of the outcome)
(DES, 1989)

It could hardly have been more procedural, with the specification of knowledge left rather vague and outlined only in the Programmes of Study. Knowledge and skills are not seen as something to be acquired for their own sake – but rather are to be used as resources for action. And it is the process of taking action that remains the cornerstone of the NC definition of technology; the process of identifying needs and responding to them in ways that generate outcomes that can be evaluated. Not surprisingly, the basic mode of teaching is through extended projects that allow pupils to experience and polish this process.

Despite all the upheavals of the last five years this core procedure remains essentially intact – though now defined in only two Attainment Targets ([i] Designing and [ii] Making). It also remains highly contentious and the source of much confusion. It is on this process and the many issues that it raises that I shall focus this chapter. We shall see that it poses some profound questions about the teaching, learning, progression and assessment of pupils in technology and, perhaps not surprisingly, it is consequently an area in which some interesting research studies are now, at long last, being conducted.

In order to set the scene for the debate it might be helpful to outline the reasons for studying technology. What does it contribute to a child's education ?

TECHNOLOGY AS CONCRETE THINKING

We should not perhaps expect too much of NC documents to help elucidate this issue – and indeed the 1989 technology Order describes the 'overall objective' of the subject to be 'to operate effectively and creatively in the made world' (DES/WO, 1990 p.1).

Whilst this might be true, it is also somewhat vague and we have sought to extend and clarify the case for technology:

> The central curriculum claim for technology rests on the uniqueness of its language and consequently the opportunities it presents *for exercising unique ways of thinking about the world and for intervening constructively to change it.* The claim does not rest on the hope that the outcomes of the changes will actually improve anything. It rests rather on the fact that the *process* of trying to do so requires pupils to engage in a challenging, enriching, empowering activity (Kimbell *et al.*,1995).

There is an astonishing closeness between descriptions of the process of Design & Technology and the more general process of thought. At the end of a very long treatise on *Thinking*, Humphreys defines it as 'what happens in experience when an organism, human or animal, meets, recognises, and solves a problem' (Humphreys, 1951).

The process is seen (broadly) as one involving problem clarification, investigation, analysis and exploration, creative attack (action), and subsequent re-evaluation. In fact it is – in generic form – very akin to the descriptions of design processes as outlined in the early (1970s) literature of Design & Technology:

FIGURE 1
(NORTH WESTERN REGIONAL EXAMINATION BOARD [NWREB] 1972)

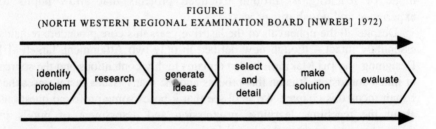

Designing is – in a sense – concrete thinking, and it is no coincidence that in practice designers frequently talk of themselves as 'thinking with a pencil' , a quality that we explicitly encourage in young people in technology programmes.This realisation has been at the centre of the arguments that, since the early days of design education, have carried forward the development of technology in schools in the UK:

> From the simplest problem to the most complex, the design process is concerned with the educational problem of clarifying the thought process or 'reasoning' of the child, indeed it is an attempt to lay bare before the child his [*sic*] own thinking (Kimbell ,1975).

through to:

> The conduct of design activity is made possible by the existence in man of a distinctive capacity of mind...the capacity for cognitive modelling...(the designer) forms images 'in the minds eye' of things and systems as they are, or as they might be. Its strength is that light can be shed on intractable problems by transforming them into terms of all sorts of schemata...such as drawings, diagrams, mock-ups, prototypes and of course, where appropriate, language and notation. These externalisations capture and make communicable the concepts modelled (Archer and Roberts, 1992).

And this is the crux of the matter. The special feature of technology – unlike so much of the curriculum – is that the processes of thought and decision-making are exposed to the light of day. When you go through a design folder you can see the decision-making unfolding before your eyes because the graphics, the models and the prototypes are clear concrete expressions of that thinking. There are several very significant consequences of this:

- you can go back over it with the pupil to examine where critical decisions were made;

- you can look to see the basis of evidence for that decision;

- you can examine points at which alternatives would have been possible;

- and you can use these as jumping off points into new lines of development.

In short, technology not only enhances the thinking and decision making powers of young people, it also enhances their *conscious awareness* of those thought processes.[1] They not only learn to think and make decisions, they also know (and can see) that that is what they are doing.

And the final twist to this tale is that the pupil constituency to which this activity has traditionally appealed is not one that has held intellectual development at the top of its agenda. Before the implementation of the National Curriculum (which made technology a compulsory study for all pupils) there was more than a fair share of difficult and disenchanted pupils in most technology classes. They traditionally found refuge and strength in the practical orientation of the learning environment. For these pupils, technology has often been a transforming experience, not just because it kept them busy and out of trouble (which was a rationale beloved of head teachers) – but because it provided a concrete lever that exposed and got a purchase on their thought processes.

There are of course many other arguments that are advanced for studying technology:

- we live in a technological world – do we not need to help pupils understand it ? (a liberal/educationalist argument)

- pupils will have to find gainful employment – do we not need to help them to acquire the necessary skills of the technological world? (a vocational argument)

- we are, as a species, in danger of so violating our world that we render it uninhabitable – do we not need to help all pupils to become informed about the impacts of technology? (another liberal/educationalist argument)

- the economy of the developed world depends on technology – we need trained personnel to keep it running (an economic policy argument).

But despite sounding familiar and rather grand, these purposes do not get to the heart of the matter. For technology as we have defined it in the NC is neither a liberal arts 'awareness-raising' study, nor a vocational training, nor a tool for macro-economic planning. It might incidentally contribute to these things – but that is not the driving purpose for its being there:

> The case for technology in schools lies in the development of two uniquely human qualities. The first is reflective; and is the ability so to focus our dissatisfactions with the world that we can pinpoint a source in need of change. The second is active; and depends upon that unique capacity of the mind to image and model new ideas and arrangements. These two – working in a tight iterative relationship – are the root-stock from which we can grow the technological capability of our young people. As it grows, they become critical without becoming disenchanted. They become independent and resourceful , empowered not just to identify weakness but to do something about it; to intervene creatively to improve things. It is an immensely satisfying capability that combines practical, intellectual and emotional challenge. It builds confidence and self esteem. And ultimately – as Bronowski[2] points out – it builds civilisations (Kimbell *et al.*,1995).

SOME RESEARCH QUESTIONS AND PROJECTS

In the last 10 years it has become somewhat less exceptional to find genuine research into aspects of technology in schools. I shall outline here the work being done (or recently completed) in three projects that are of significance in the field. They deal with two broad areas of concern:

i)   models of practice – what does/should technology look like in the curriculum ?

ii) problems of assessment – how are we to measure the effectiveness of our efforts ?

Whilst these two issues are necessarily interwoven, the three projects that I shall be drawing on here tend to prioritise towards one or the other. The projects in question are:

1. Understanding Technological Approaches (1992–94), funded by the Economic and Social Research Council and based at the Technology Education Research Unit at Goldsmiths College London.
This project has explored *models of practice* by developing 80 case-

studies of pupils working in technology in 20 schools in the Greater London area. The case studies span all four key stages. The methodology was broadly observational with a data collection system based on trained observers watching literally every minute of the pupil projects and recording what happened in five-minute sessions. The observational data are enriched with discursive data from interviews with the teachers and pupils; and with performance data as a result of assessment of the work. The use of a common observation framework across the key stages enabled the project to compile data and report on progression and continuity issues in ways that have never been possible before. However, with only 80 case-studies over four key stages, the sample is of necessity small and does not claim to be representative. The findings are therefore not necessarily generalisable.

2. *Problem Solving Processes in Technology* (1993–95), funded by the Economic and Social Research Council and based at the Open University (OU), School of Education.

This project explores *models of practice* in technology within key stage three. The basic methodology involves the detailed observation of individual projects in the classroom – and video/audio tape recording them in ways that allow the research team to analyse afterwards what was going on. The observations and recordings are supplemented with detailed and regular discussions with the staff and the pupils involved . The project is concerned with elucidating the models of practice that exist in the minds of the teachers and the pupils and exploring the extent to which these are consistent with the classroom realities. Because of the intensive nature of the case studies and the depth of data in each, the sample size is small and again the findings are not necessarily generalisable.

3. *The Assessment of Performance in Design and Technology* (1985–91), funded by the Department of Education and Science (Assessment of Performance Unit) and based at the Technology Education Research Unit at Goldsmiths College London.

This was a project exploring *problems and approaches to assessment* in technology. The brief was to develop tests of technological ability and (in 1989) to administer them to the nation's 15-year-old cohort. The sample was to be 2 per cent of the whole cohort (approximately 10,000 pupils in 700 schools) throughout England, Wales and Northern Ireland, and was to be largely a random sample. As this survey pre-dated the NC, a significant section of the sample were not taking any technology courses at the time of testing. By virtue of the size of the sample, it provided extremely reliable data that supported generalisable conclusions. However, except for a small sub-sample of the survey, testing was based on short-term, pencil and paper test responses, reducing the ability of the research to comment on the interaction of the tests with practical capability.

ISSUES UNDERLYING MODELS OF PRACTICE

I include on page 178 of this chapter a schematic illustration (Figure 1) of what is supposed to happen as a pupil pursues a technological task from inception to completion. Innumerable variants on this basic process can be found in the literature and one of the most detailed is in the Curriculum Matters series. (DES, 1987), in which there are 15 steps from 'the problem' to 'the solution'. The steps include such things as 'write design brief', 'collect data', 'model ideas' and so on. The models all seek to describe and impose intellectual order on a messy, confusing, creative process. Unfortunately, by trying to describe this order in a comprehensible way, they end up imposing a degree of rigidity and hoop-jumping that runs the risk of destroying the essence of the process. *Description* slides imperceptibly towards *prescription.*

This is the area that has been explored in detail by the Open University research team, and they are less than convinced that the models of the process that teachers claim to follow have any general value. They see two kinds of problem in accepting the notion of a 'generalised' problem-solving procedure.

Descriptions and prescriptions of the process

The first problem is based on the theory of situated cognition, which suggests that learning is socially constructed in real contexts. Learning on this view (see, for example, Rogoff, 1990) is a process of enculturation in which the cognitive processes 'differ according to the domain of thinking and the specifics of the task context'. This leads the OU team to consider the following aspects of pupils' Design and Technology activities:

> First it encourages us to question general problem-solving processes and to seek evidence of how the particular context affects what students do. Secondly it gives us a framework for looking at how students might learn to perform a process such as design, which draws upon models of expert practice in industry and elsewhere (even though the motivation for teaching this process may be quite unrelated to the production of 'expert' designers). Thirdly it focuses our attention on learning as the introduction to aspects of culture, in this case the culture of technological activity ... (McCormick, Murphy and Hennessy, 1994).

In relation to these issues, the OU team conclude – on the basis of their observations of classes in action – that it is difficult to sustain the notion of a generalised process. The 'stages' that the pupils are supposed to progress through are seen as largely unrelated and 'ritualised'. Moreover, these stages were not explicitly taught to the pupils as a set of skills – rather the teachers 'revealed' them implicitly (almost mystically) as they worked through the project:

> The general lack of explicit treatment of the process led to pupils dealing with apparently isolated tasks and caused confusion. For example one pupil was told by the teacher to draw a full-sized version of her kite when she had finished her 3D model, without explanation of its purpose. Neither did this pupil have any sense of an overall process to create meaning in the task for herself (McCormick, Murphy and Hennessy, 1994).

Conceptual knowledge as a resource for the process

The second issue to preoccupy the OU research team is the extent to which it is possible for an abstracted model of problem-solving to accommodate the teaching and learning of conceptual knowledge. The conventional wisdom is that while pursuing technological tasks, knowledge and skills should be *resources for action* rather than ends in themselves. It follows therefore that – as far as possible – knowledge should be acquired on a 'need-to-know' basis rather than being presented in pre-packaged formal lessons. What would normally happen in a project that involved new knowledge is that all pupils would be given some baseline input to allow them to get started – but that thereafter it would be developed more specifically by individual pupils in response to the needs of their projects.

This is not, of course, a straightforward process and the OU team document the issues through some specific projects that they have observed:

> In the first lesson of the electronic badge project the teacher was trying to introduce and develop a whole host of terms and concepts that pupils had existing ideas of and which would be used to differing degrees in the project...In the second lesson the knowledge becomes more exclusively that which is not familiar to pupils...mainly concerned with the symbols and identification of components. Although all this knowledge was the subject of specific teaching, later knowledge was invoked that would not have been available to most pupils. Thus when the teacher did not have enough of the correct value resistor, he gave out two resistors whose combined value (in series) was the same as the one he originally wanted and told pupils to solder them together. This implies that pupils understood the sum of resistors in series. (McCormick and Murphy, 1994).

They document other examples where pupils were led up blind alleys or wasted time on unsuccessful activities by virtue of their conceptual misunderstandings. This is widely recognised to be a very tricky matter indeed,and one which science educators have struggled with for years with very limited success. The science team who ran the Assessment of Performance Unit (APU) surveys in the early 1980s revealed grotesque inadequacies in pupils' understanding. Only 40 per cent of 15-year-olds could satisfactorily connect a battery, bulb and switch into a circuit.[3] This is horrifying evidence of the failure of pupils satisfactorily to internalise what they have been 'taught' in science.

At the time of writing, the OU team have yet to complete their work in this area and it will be interesting to see how they evaluate the strengths and weaknesses of the 'hands on' style of learning that is typical of technology. We should certainly expect that there will be different strengths and weaknesses to those that exist in typical modes of practice in science.

Establishing a basis for progression

The research project 'Understanding Technological Approaches' (UTA) had a different set of priorities – one of which was to trace and document the classroom practices of technology across the four key stages(KS).[4] The idea here was to try to tease out the elements that might make it possible to build a coherent model of progression towards capability. And from among the range of observational measures that have been collected, two in particular have been revealing.

The first, pupil autonomy, registers – on the five minute observation grid – the points at which the teacher is *directing* the pupil to do something in particular or is *supporting* the pupil when they are trying to do something of their own choosing:

> Theoretically, the teacher might be directing or supporting in 100 per cent of the 5 minute time slots, but in reality this never happens. The approximate norm for the projects is that teachers 'direct' activity in 20–25 per cent of the 5 minute time slots and that they 'support' pupils doing what they want to do for 10 per cent of those slots. This leaves (on average) about 65–70 per cent of the slots without any pupil/teacher interaction (Kimbell, Stables and Green, 1995).

These are norms, however, and if we go more deeply into individual cases we can gauge the 'lightness of touch' of the teacher. Some projects show the pupil receiving either direction or support from the teacher in about 50 per cent of the five minute slots throughout the project while others show the total amounting to only 20 per cent. Clearly, in this case the teacher is happy to let the pupil get along on his/her own for much longer periods

It is significant that by far the most intensively 'directed' projects are within Key Stage 3. And it is also significant that projects that tend towards 'support' and away from 'direction' are typically KS1 and 2 projects. This appears to be a consistent trend in the data, and moreover the transition between year 6 and year 7, as pupils move from primary to secondary schools, is particularly stark:

> suffice it here to observe that in terms of the growth towards personal autonomy, this y6–y7 boundary appears to represent a major step backwards. From a condition of relative independence and responsibility in y6, the pupils have reverted to a frightening level of dependency on the teacher. They wait to be told what to do – even when they know perfectly well (and are prepared to tell you) what they might sensibly do next. They seldom do it, preferring to join a queue of other similarly timid souls waiting to ask teacher what they ought to do (Kimbell, Stables and Green 1995).

The second measure of interest here concerns the 'user' of the outcome of the activity. In technological activities there is – or is supposed to be – an outcome which improves something for its user (a better wheelbarrow for the gardener – or a better toothbrush for children). To what extent does the real user make a significant contribution in school technology?

The UTA project set this 'user' data against the project as a whole, and contrasted it with 'manufacturing' data that indicated the points at which the pupil was working out *how to make the product* or is actually *doing the making*:

> The data indicates that these two elements (concern with 'users' or with 'manufacturing') operate reciprocally; when one is high – the other is low. And again a fascinating pattern emerges when these data are plotted across the 11 years of the National Curriculum. Concern with manufacturing issues rises dramatically to a peak in years 6,7 and 8, and falls back towards year 10. By contrast the 'user' data starts high, drops to a low in y7 and rises back to year 10. (Kimbell, Stables and Green 1995)

The principal transition point would appear to be during KS2, within which the data completely cross over. At the start of KS2, projects appear to reflect a high concern with user issues and low concern with manufacturing. By the end of KS2 it is completely reversed. The start of KS3 picks up this dominant concern with manufacturing issues and these data suggest that y7 pupils rarely see the context of the task – or the supposed 'user' of the outcome – as relevant to their project.

Taken as a whole, the data from the UTA project suggest that technology tasks – and hence the projects that flow from them – are seen as very different things in the four key stages. When the observation data are combined with the more discursive and interpretive data derived from conversations with teachers and pupils, the different characters of technology across the key stages begins to emerge:

> *Cultural* technology is characteristic of KS1 ... 'Its all around you and always has been'. Projects here tend to be topic centred across the whole curriculum (eg, Saxons) and technological activity derives from within the topic, involving Saxon forts or transport systems.
>
> *Problem-solving* technology is characteristic of KS2 ... 'Try it for yourself – can you make it work'. Projects often have a fixed starting point – eg a wood strip vehicle chassis – and the challenge is to make it travel as far/fast as possible.
>
> *Disciplinary* technology is typical of KS3 ...'You need to know about this (knowledge/skills)'. Projects are contrived specifically to include a small range of skills/knowledge that the teacher wishes to impart, rather than to tackle tasks that really exist. Pendants (to teach metal fabrication and enamelling), alarms (to teach simple circuits and sensors), rock cakes (to teach ingredient mixes and processing). The product outcome is the motivational sugar on the pill.
>
> *Simulated* technology emerges at the interface of KS3&4... 'This is how real designers work'. A gradual move to individual projects – identified by the pupils themselves and therefore generally having some reality – within which they are expected to be rigorous in the application of an abstracted designerly process and the development of a portfolio that reflects it (Kimbell,1994).

The boundaries of the key stages tend to blur these distinctions and the titles are intended to suggest broadly evolving patterns in the nature of technological tasks. These contrasted models of tasks explain why 'users' are largely seen as irrelevant to pupils in KS3. It is difficult to take a personalised user too seriously when the whole point and focus of the activity is an instructional one common to all pupils in the group. The situation is very different from KS1 where the whole experience (for example, of the Saxons) leads to some awareness of them as living in (and users of) castles or wagons. Similarly, at KS4 where the user re-emerges as significant, it is not infrequently the genuine needs of the user (for example, best mate/grandparent) that prompts the project. The four different models of technology task also explain the contrasted pedagogy of KS2 and 3, with top juniors frequently trying to work things out for themselves and new entrants to the secondary school learning to do (largely) as they are told.

The evidence from this study is clear. Teachers have very different teaching/learning agendas in the four key stages, and these impact so heavily

on the tasks that pupils pursue, that – at present – we can only sensibly talk
about tasks *within* key stages. There is very little common ground between
them that allows us to speak about technological tasks *in general*. We should
not be surprised about this since technology is – as I pointed out at the start
of this chapter – so new in the curriculum. It may be 25 years old in
secondary schools, but it is only five years old in many primary schools.
Developing a progressive pathway towards capability from five to 16 must
be an ambition for the next phase in the development of classroom practices
in technology.

PROBLEMS OF ASSESSMENT

The Assessment of Performance Unit project in Design & Technology
(1985–91) was the first major research project in technology to be
undertaken in the UK since the founding days of the Keele[5] and
Loughborough University[6] projects of the late 1960s and early 1970s. The
project developed three kinds of assessment instrument:

90-minute pencil/paper tests, in which pupils completed structured tasks,
working with restricted resources in a specially designed pupil response
booklet. Because of the degree of external control that was exerted on these
tests, and the fact that large numbers of pupils were involved in them, this
element of the survey provided the most statistically reliable data. However,
because of the short time allowed, each task only examined certain aspects
of capability.

Modelling tests, in which a selection of the 90-minute test tasks were
supplemented with extra time (half a day), a range of soft and rigid
modelling materials and the opportunity for pupils to collaborate in teams.
These tests had strong elements of control within them, and involved pupil
collaboration and discussion. The sample size for these tests was large
enough to provide statistically reliable data, but the tests were run by trained
administrators who could provide additional illuminative assessments. These
tests were therefore seen as a bridge between the 90 minute tests and the third
branch of the survey.

Extended project profiling, in which field-workers monitored pupil
performance on real projects under way in schools over an extended period,
in some cases as long as nine months. The field-workers conducted regular,
individual interviews with pupils, collecting detailed information throughout
the project and building up case records of individual pupil performance. In

this strategy, the emphasis was on collecting illuminative rather than statistically reliable data. Because the *whole project* was scrutinised, all aspect of performance could be monitored and assessed (see Kimbell *et al.,* 1991).

The data from each of these approaches were triangulated by having the 'modelling' and 'project profiling' samples *also* doing selected short tests, and despite the obvious differences in these approaches to testing, they were built around a common concern for the integrity for the designing, making, evaluating activity. The approach was based on *performance* testing, not knowledge and skill testing, and performance testing in technology means finding ways of measuring how well pupils are able to originate ideas, organise their time and resources, conceive of alternative possibilities, model solutions and evaluate them against user needs.

The two major challenges in this project were:

i)   how to build and present test activities in such a way that they would be seen by pupils as being authentic activities – worth engaging in – so that pupils perform to the best of their ability; and

ii)   how to generate an assessment model that could reliably and validly ascribe value to the pupils responses.

Getting activities running

As I pointed out earlier, real technology tasks do not exist *in vacuo.* They exist in real houses or gardens or shops of car parks or hospitals, and the *setting* of the task is a major determinant of the *meaning* of that task. Equally, the success of the outcome can only be determined by examining its operation in the same context. The APU team used a series of videos to capture the range of contexts within which the tasks were embedded. These videos were specifically designed to provides starting-points for action for the pupils.

Once inside a context, however, the nature of *task setting* had a serious impact upon its do-ability and the critical variables here were procedural rather than conceptual. The APU tasks were set at three levels of procedural 'tightness':

1.   Some tasks provided little more than a generalised suggestion that the context was full of potential problems that could usefully be pursued by a designer; for example, 'think about issues of *protection* in this context...' Pupils were then left to identify for themselves the specifics of the tasks they might pursue.

2.   Some tests provided a more comprehensive framework by adding more

precise demands to it; for example,'...think about *the protection of personal possessions from theft'*. Naturally, pupils were getting a better 'steer' in these tests – but still had the opportunity to derive quite disparate tasks within the context.

3. The most tightly specified tasks went yet further and added quite specific design requirements; for example, '....design a travellers' body purse...'. Here was a quite specific starting-point that provided little room either for negotiation or for confusion.

FIGURE 2

A HIERARCHY OF TASKS CONTEXTUAL TASK – FRAMED TASK – SPECIFIC TASK

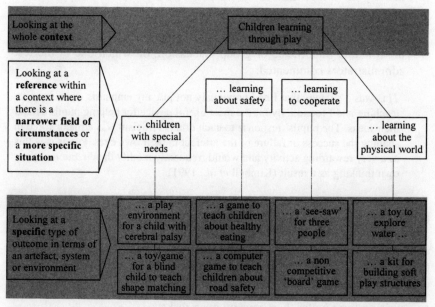

It is easy to understand the differences of demand that exist within these layers of task setting. The contextual level provides plenty of opportunity for pupils to 'take ownership' of the task but there is very little support in it; it is not clear exactly what pupils should get on and do. At the other extreme it is quite obvious what the task is – and hence quite apparent how one might immediately proceed, but it is much more difficult for pupils to generate any personal ownership of the task.

The structuring of the test activities also proved to have a big impact on the ways in which pupils responded. Assuming that 90 minutes are available for the activity, its structure might be very open – with large blocks of time available to the pupils and only limited interventions by the administrator to steer the activity. Alternatively, they might be structured much more heavily – with more interventions and instructions by the administrator. Again the strengths and weaknesses are obvious in retrospect. In tightly structured activities there is plenty of support but less opportunity for pupils just to get on with it. In the more open structure it is much easier to waste time – or lose one's way completely – but those that were on task can get on without interruption.

Two further significant issues in test structuring concern:

- the balance that is struck – in the test demands – between active design activity (drawing, modelling, making etc) and reflective appraisal of where they were going (identifying issues for judgment, identifying strengths and weaknesses in the work etc).

- the role and importance of group discussion, on which one of the test administrators commented:

> This was a strategy that I had previously not put any emphasis on in my own teaching and I found it by far the most useful device for helping pupils extend their ideas. The pupils' response to each others criticism was a major force in shaping the success or failure of the artefact in their own eyes. Pupils saw this as a very rewarding activity and would frequently modify the direction of their own thinking as a result (Kimbell *et al.*, 1991).

As a result of two years of test development, the APU team produced a battery of 28 activities – each of which had a substantial bank of data detailing its effects on the pupils being tested. When they subsequently analysed the performance data in the 1989 survey it became clear that these features of the tests each had a marked impact on the performance of different sub-groups of pupils. Put simply, on average:

- girls perform better than boys on open tasks

- boys perform better than girls on closed tasks

- pupils of lower general ability perform better on more tightly structured activities

- pupils of higher general ability perform better on more loosely structured activities

- boys do better in active test structures and girls in reflective ones

- whilst all pupils benefited from the discussion sessions, high ability girls especially gained.

A further clear finding was that the greater the experience of Design & Technology that pupils had been exposed to in their curriculum, the less marked these tendencies became.

At the conclusion of the project the team reported:

> One is led to the somewhat sinister conclusion that it would be possible – given an understanding of these effects – to design activities deliberately to favour any particular nominated group. More positively, it would also appear to be possible to design activities that largely eliminate bias, or at least balance one sort of bias with another (Kimbell *et al.*,1991).

Making assessments

As a result of the test development programme, the team succeeded in generating tests that drew out from pupils some quite remarkable performance in a very short time. Examples of these pieces of work are detailed in the report (Kimbell *et al.*, 1991). But while the test development phase was interesting, perhaps the most fascinating of all the APU work – in research terms – was the approach developed to assess the quality of pupils work. Faced with 20,000 pieces of work (each pupil completed two tests), where do you start in ascribing quality?

> We felt justified therefore in approaching the assessment function by developing a whole view of capability. Our experience of assessment in Design and Technology (in a variety of forms) led us to the conviction that it is often easier to identify a high quality piece of design work than it is to say in detail *why* it is high quality. Precisely because of the integrated nature of the activity and the complex interactions of the various aspects of it, holistic assessments of excellence – which allow us to take these interactions into account – have been far more commonplace in Design and Technology than in many other, more analytic, areas of the curriculum (Kimbell *et al.*, 1991).

The team recognised, however, that holistic assessment has limitations. It is no good saying, 'This is good, but I don't know why...', especially if one of the purposes of the work is to help teachers to develop their understanding of pupil capability. Accordingly, they devised a means of getting inside the holistic mark to the central traits of good (and poor) performance. But the trick was to do this without defining these traits too rigidly in advance.

The strategy was adapted from a well established technique in experimental psychology:

> It started with us (the research team) in association with a wider group of teachers awarding holistic marks to a range of work from a range of tests in a range of contexts. Our reliability studies gave us confidence in our (and the

teachers) ability to agree on this holistic mark. We then took two scripts – a high scorer (a) and a low scorer (b) – and listed all the things that (a) contained that (b) did not, and all the things that (b) had that (a) did not. This was done by looking for questions ('does this script do/contain....?') to which one could answer *yes* for one script and *no* for the other. *When we found such a question we had identified a discriminator of capability* (Kimbell *et al.*,1991).

With a trained group of markers, this technique was pursued with countless pieces of work, resulting in a very long lists of discriminating questions. It then became necessary to see to what extent they could be grouped and prioritised:

> We coined the expression 'fingerprinting' the scripts because, like a fingerprint, each script was unique, but by building up a list of discriminating yes's and no's it became possible to describe the uniqueness in any particular script. Moreover, as computers are adept at handling such simple (binary) data, it became possible to ask the computer to generalise these descriptors by selecting all high scorers and printing out the discriminating characteristics that they did contain and those that they did not contain.

Whilst the holistic mark enabled the team to *value* a piece of work, the yes/no responses provided a composite *description* of it and the outcome of this experimental work was a three-stage assessment regime.

The order of events is critical here, moving from broad judgement down to progressively finer detail. The approach combined reliable judgement with informative detail, and it is one that the team strongly recommended

FIGURE 3

START WITH THE 'BIG PICTURE'

| holistic judgment on a sliding scale (1-5) | broad categories of performance judged on a sliding scale (1-5) | individual discriminators (yes/no) |

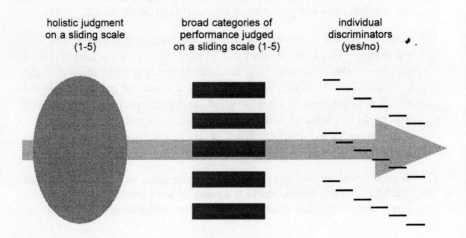

both to School Examination and Assessment Council (SEAC) and to the National Curriculum Council (NCC) when it became clear that NC assessment was to include Subject scores, Attainment Target scores and Statements of Attainment on a yes/no basis. The parallel was obvious.

It is greatly to be regretted that it took five years of pain and suffering and ultimate revolution in the classroom to persuade these bodies – and the responsible Minister – that working in the opposite direction (from minuscule Statements up to broad Levels) is neither practicable nor informative. It is like wading uphill through treacle in an attempt to discover some Ultimate Truth, only to find when you eventually (exhausted) get there, that you knew it all along. What made this procedure even more idiotic was that on the occasions that teachers were surprised by the Ultimate Truth – because it did not conform to their intuitive professional understanding – they would typically go back and rearrange the detail in order to get the result they knew to be right.[7]

CONCLUSION

The sad story of NC assessment and the heartache that it created for teachers has one other interesting dimension that provides an important postscript to this chapter. And it is one that demonstrates the interconnectedness of the two strands I have sought to draw out. *Models of practice* in the classroom are tightly related to the kinds of *assessment* that are being applied, and, in technology, the uncertainties that have surrounded the former have not been helped by the more general turmoil surrounding the latter.

It is important to remember, however, that it need not have been like this. Indeed the postscript for this chapter is not about technology – but about research and its importance to the educational endeavour. But technology does provide a useful example. The 1990 technology Order contained 119 Statements of Attainment (SoA). In a draft 1992 revision this was simplified to 74, and it now currently stands (after the fifth revision) at 16 SoA (one per Attainment Target per level). This demonstrates a slow, grudging acceptance of the facts of life in the classroom. The minutely atomised assessments that were required under the 1990 Order were not only far too time consuming, they were ultimately self-defeating since they prevented teachers from exercising professional judgement at a level at which they were used to operating.

The assessment policy was simply wrong. It was neither helpful nor practicable to organise a curriculum and assess pupil performance through such small units. And quite apart from the cost in human misery and the countless wasted hours of professional teachers, the policy also precipitated an absolutely prodigious waste of money that was desperately needed for real purposes in schools.

The whole destructive fiasco might have been excusable if we were breaking new ground and venturing into territory that was unresearched. But we were not. The APU research had unequivocally demonstrated the practicability and the reliability of working from the holistic towards more atomised assessment *and the inappropriateness of working the other way.* Subsequently, the first report of the CATS (Consortium for Assessment and Testing in Schools) agency – responsible for developing the first round of NC Standard Assessment Tasks – reported on its trial materials as early as 1990:

> Our recent trials of this material – in which we asked teachers to re-mark a selection of work – give us confidence that making this holistic judgment is a helpful way of initiating the assessment exercise.

> There are several reasons for using this professional Profile Component (PC) judgment as an entry point into the ATs and SoA;

> i) At a practical level, the sheer labour of tracking up through dozens of SoA in order to arrive at a level that you 'know' to be about right for a pupil, represents a serious waste of time and energy for teachers.

> ii) The small and (to advanced pupils) insignificant steps that are represented in lower level SoA have often been fully internalised at higher levels – so do not exist as recordable performances. Accordingly, success at level 8 in a quality does not imply that pupils can now score all of levels 1–7, so starting at the bottom and working up the levels as a marking mechanism may seriously disadvantage some pupils.

> iii) But, fundamentally, because of the variables that arise through the interaction of the procedural SoA with the conceptual PoS, the individual SoA is not the most appropriate first line of assessment. Calibrating the overall level is far more simply (and more reliably) tackled, and the fine detail of the SoA can then be charted. Unless we have a view about the overall level, it is not possible to key into the appropriate conceptual demands at that level (CATS: *Technology,* 1990).

The message was ignored – and the messenger was shot. New contracts for SAT development went to new agencies who might produce more acceptable 'findings'.

I recall a poster that used to hang in the office of a friend of mine at Goldsmiths. It depicted a friendly-looking giant of a gorilla – and the message at the bottom declared 'If you think education is expensive – try ignorance'. It should perhaps have read 'If you think research is expensive – try ignoring it'.

NOTES

1. The term 'meta-cognition' has been applied to this phenomenon.
2. Bronowski (1971) makes the case that it is man's ability to imagine other ways of being – and then to bring them about – that sets us apart from the rest of the animal kingdom:

> Among the multitude of animals which scamper, fly, burrow, and swim around us, man is the only one who is not locked into his environment. His imagination, his reason, his emotional subtlety and toughness, make it possible for him not to accept the environment but to change it. And that series of inventions, by which man from age to age has remade his environment...I call...*The Ascent of Man.*

3. See 'Electricity at age 15' (APU 1984).
4. The four key stages of the UK NC are divided as follows: 5–7 yrs (KS1); 7–11 yrs (KS2); 11–14 yrs (KS3); 14–16 yrs (KS4).
5. 'Education through the Use of Materials', directed by Professor John Eggleston.
6. 'Project Technology', directed by Professor Geoff Harrison.
7. For a full analysis of the problems associated with this model of NC assessment, see Kimbell, 1994a.

REFERENCES

Archer, B. and Roberts, P. (1992).'Design and Technological Awareness in Education', in *Modelling: The Language of Designing. Occasional Paper No. 1.* Loughborough University of Technology.

Baynes, K. (1992). 'The role of modelling in the Industrial Revolution', in *Modelling: The Language of Designing.* Occasional Paper No 1. Loughborough University of Technology.

Bronowski, J. (1973). *The Ascent of Man.* London: British Broadcasting Corporation

Consortium for Assessment & Testing in Schools (CATS) (1990). *Standard Assessment Tasks in Technology: Pilot Report.* London: Hodder & Stoughton.

Department of Education and Science/Welsh Office (1987). *Craft Design & Technology from 5–16: Curriculum Matters 9.* London: HMSO.

— (1988). *National Curriculum Design & Technology Working Group – Interim Report.* DES.

— (1989). *Design & Technology for Ages 5–16.* London: HMSO.

— (1994). *National Curriculum Design & Technology Statutory Order.* London: HMSO.

Humphreys, G. (1951). *Thinking.* London: Methuen.

Kelly, V., Kimbell. R. A, Patterson. V., Saxton, J., and Stables, K. (1987). *Design and Technological Activity; A Framework for Assessment.* London: HMSO.

Kimbell, R. A .(1975), *Design Education: The Foundation Years.* London: Routledge & Kegan Paul.

— (1994). 'Tasks in Technology: An analysis of their purposes and effects', *The International Journal of Technology and Design Education* 1, 1–15, Kluwer Academic Publishers.

— (1994a). 'Progression in Learning and the Assessment of Pupil Attainment', in Layton, D. (ed.), *Innovations in Science and Technology Education Vol. 5.* Paris: UNESCO.

Kimbell, R. A., Stables, K., Wheeler, T., Wozniak, A., Kelly, V. (1991). *The Assessment of Performance in Design and Technology: The final report of the Design & Technology APU Project.* Schools Examination and Assessment Authority (SEAC/HMSO).

Kimbell, R. A., Stables, K., Green, R. (1995). *Understanding Technological Activities.* Milton Keynes: Open University Press.

McCormick, R., Murphy, P. and Hennessy, S. (1994). 'Problem solving in design & technology: a case of situated learning'. Paper presented at the American Educational Research Association. New Orleans, USA. April 1994.

—, and Murphy P. (1994). 'Learning the process of technology'. Paper presented to the British Education Research Association annual conference. Oxford. Sept. 1994.

NWREB (North Western Regional Examination Board) (1972). *Certificate of Secondary Education: Studies in Design.* NWREB.

Penfold, J. (1988). *Craft Design & Technology; Past Present and Future.* Stoke on Trent: Trentham Books.

Rogoff, B. (1990). *Apprenticeship in Thinking: Cognitive Development in a Social Context.* Oxford: Oxford University Press.

Secondary Examinations Council (SEC) (1986). *Craft Design & Technology GCSE: A Guide for Teachers.* Milton Keynes: Open University Press.

Thompson, R. (1959). *The Psychology of Thinking.* Harmondsworth: Penguin.

Williams, R. (1965). *The Long Revolution.* Harmondsworth: Penguin.

8

ECONOMICS AND BUSINESS EDUCATION

David J. Whitehead

INTRODUCTION

This chapter is written specifically for those scholars who are planning to undertake research in the field of economics and business education. Interested readers will already be reasonably well acquainted with the nature of the curriculum in these subjects, so very little space is devoted to the historical development of economics and business education.The primary purpose of the chapter is to give as much guidance as possible to potential researchers.

After a brief résumé of the growth of these subjects in the UK,attention is focused on the parallel development of research in cognate areas, both in the UK and abroad, particularly in the USA. An annotated bibliography of publications is then provided.

The following section divides the field into areas of study in which research has already been done. Suggestions are given for fertile lines of enquiry, and lists are appended of articles, dissertations and chapters in books in each area.

THE GROWTH OF ECONOMICS AND BUSINESS EDUCATION

Economics as a school subject at Advanced Level began to be taught in the 1950s, and experienced rapid growth in the 1960s and 1970s. By the 1980s, it had become one of the most frequently chosen subjects at this level. Business studies was introduced rather later, in the late 1960s, again at Advanced Level, and also experienced a rapid growth in the 1980s. By the mid-1990s, business studies was overtaking economics in terms of subject entries at Advanced Level.

Both subjects eventually came to be offered at Ordinary Level (subsequently GCSE) for the 14–16 age range, partly because of pressure from established Advanced Level teachers of the subject. Economics never grew beyond a minor subject at this level, but there was a very fast expansion in pupils electing to study business studies.

The introduction of the National Curriculum was a serious setback for both subjects, since neither featured in the list of core and foundation subjects to be taught to pupils up to the age of 16. Apart from some reference to business studies topics in the Technology guidelines for the National Curriculum, the subjects were only included as a cross-curricular theme, entitled Economic and Industrial Understanding. This was inconsistent with the government's hitherto strong support in particular for economic literacy. The development of 'economic awareness' enabled the authorities to argue that the infusion approach to economics and business education was a solution to the problem of scarce curricular time. While some schools took the cross-curricular themes seriously, many did not, and by 1995 few considered them a high priority. Nevertheless, economics and particularly business studies continued to enjoy popularity at Key Stage 4, especially once the government relaxed the number of subjects that had to be studied at this level.

Somewhat belatedly, teachers began to be trained specifically to teach these subjects: in 1972, the first full-time postgraduate teacher-training course in economics education was established, followed in 1975 by a similar course in business education (both at the University of London Institute of Education). In 1980, the first masters' degree in Economics Education was launched at the London University Institute of Education, and this led to a number of small-scale research projects presented as dissertations. Some of these were condensed into Research Papers, published by the Department of Economics and Business Education. By the late 1980s, additional masters' degree courses in Economics and Business Education at Manchester and London Universities added to the flow of small-scale enquiries in the field.

RESEARCH IN ECONOMICS AND BUSINESS EDUCATION

Research began in the 1960s, in both the UK and the USA. In the late 1960s, Professor Keith Lumsden established a centre for research in economics education at Heriot-Watt University in Edinburgh, and initiated a programme that mirrored similar developments in the USA. As more lecturers came to be appointed to teacher-training positions, so the opportunities for research grew. By 1975, 791 studies relating to economics education in schools had been published, all of them in the United States. (Whitehead, 1982, p. 306). While hundreds of doctoral theses have been written on economics education issues in America, only two have so far been awarded in the United Kingdom. In order to bring together scholars with a common interest in economics education, a research seminar was held in Manchester in 1973, which precipitated a first attempt at producing a research agenda for economics educators, published in *Curriculum Development in Economics* (Whitehead, 1974).

A second research seminar was organised in 1985, which resulted in the publication *Economics Education Research and Development Issues* (Hodkinson and Whitehead, 1986). This conference was more ambitious than that held in 1973, and represented the first attempt to bring together scholars from all over the world involved in research in the field (though, admittedly, the annual conferences of the Joint Council on Economic Education in the USA also attracted a few non-American academics).

Continuing the trend of holding such academic seminars approximately once every decade, the next International Research Seminar was held in Liverpool in April 1995. Significantly, this conference focused as much on curriculum development as on research. Area studies also featured strongly, with reports on economics education in Japan, Bulgaria, Poland, Russia and Australia.

Research in economics and business education in the UK has always been informed by progress made elsewhere, and especially in the USA. There are probably 50 research articles published in this field in the USA for every one in the rest of the world. This chapter would therefore be quite unbalanced were it not to summarise the major strands of American research. However, because it is so well documented, and articles reviewing relevant research there are so readily available, less space will be devoted to it than its importance warrants. In contrast, British and other research is not discussed at the same depth in research synopses, and it is largely ignored in the American literature reviews.

One way of classifying research is by the *phase* to which it applies. Thus, in the USA, synoptic reviews normally group studies into those concerned with primary, secondary and tertiary education. In the UK, various research studies have concentrated on specific age groups, from primary upwards (Whitehead, 1978).

In the USA, centres of economics education were established, normally located in university economics faculties, and affiliated to the National Council on Economic Education (NCEE). Thus the centre leader was typically an economist who had some interest in educational issues. As a result, most early research focused on the university sector, especially on the first year 'Principles of Economics' course. By the late 1970s, more interest began to be taken in the secondary and, to some extent, primary curricula. A strong motivation here was the desire to promote economics in the secondary school curriculum.

Another method of classification is by *topic*, and this type of analysis is used below for the benefit of potential researchers in the field. Judgements have had to be made about how to fit some research studies into the procrustean bed of such a list, for example, an investigation of assessment in South Africa could sit equally well under 'Assessment' or 'Area Studies'.

An alternative way of sorting research is by its *design and methodology*. The bulk of American research might be described as empirical, and a brief perusal of the *Journal of Economic Education* will confirm this. In contrast, much research work in the UK is more philosophical in character, or verging on curriculum development. One explanation for this difference may be that most of the American research is carried out by economists well-versed in econometric techniques, and anxious to apply them to educational contexts, whereas in the UK, enquiries are normally carried out by educators. Such scholars usually have a background as schoolteachers, and the kind of issues that concern them do not yield easily to numerical analysis. Another possible reason for the predominance of empirical studies may be that research grants are more easily obtainable for such work in the social sciences.

In the first flurries of research into cognitive gain in economics, it was confidently hoped and predicted that once the full complement of independent variables had been entered into the multiple regression equation, educators would be able to pronounce judgement about the relative importance of, for example, teacher qualifications, student ability, methods of teaching used and so forth. Studies such as Lumsden (1980) and those reported in the *Journal of Economic Education* show that such methods can take us only a certain distance down the road to a 'scientific' approach to economics education. Indeed, it can confidently be asserted that the massive empirical assault on the efficacy of alternative teaching and learning strategies has had a negligible impact on classroom teachers and the methods they employ. Much more striking has been the evolution of modes of examination that require a more inductive and skills-based approach by students, though whether these changes were precipitated by the empirical findings of American research or the philosophical debates in the English literature is debatable.

Over 20 years ago, such reservations were voiced at the first research seminar referred to above (Ryba, 1974, p. 247). Ryba proposed the encouragement of specific in-depth studies of particular classrooms and of action research. Such research is easier to mount than large scale empirical studies, and in recent years journals such as *Economic Awareness* (University of Manchester School of Education) have published much work of this kind.

In the same article, Ryba published a checklist of major research needs related to curriculum development in economics. He was right in predicting that many of the suggestions listed there would take a very long time to implement. Given the paucity of research work in the UK in this field, it is not surprising that most of those research proposals still remain virgin territory. The broad areas which emerged then were: aims and objectives; methods and materials; the structure of economics in relation to the curriculum; examinations and evaluation; pupil and student attitudes; perceptions and capabilities; and the role of economics in further and teacher education.

This chapter concentrates principally on research studies on the secondary school economics and business studies curriculum. For researchers interested in pursuing their studies at the tertiary level, the most important text is *The Principles of Economics Course* (Saunders and Walstad, 1990). The three sections of this overview deal with goals and objectives of the principles course (the first-semester economics course in American universities), instructional methods, and evaluation of instruction. Researchers wishing to obtain an overview of research at the college level should turn to Chapter 20, in which Siegfried and Walstad provide an historical background, and then consider the following areas of research: the measurement of educational outputs; student characteristics and economics teaching (evaluation of teaching, attitudes and achievement, effort and study time, learning technology, gender); and course format and student learning (innovative pedagogies, textbook, class size, course sequence, graduate student instructors). Sixty-three references enrich this chapter.

Several attempts have been made to review the state of the art in research in economics education at the school level. A major study in 1977 resulted in the following findings (Dawson, 1977, pp. 85–103):

Elementary School

1. Pupils can learn some basic economic facts and concepts.

2. Older pupils learn more than younger pupils.

3. Teachers trained in economics education are more effective than untrained teachers.

4. There is a relationship between pupils' socio-economic background and their economic understanding.

5. Gender is not significant in pupils' learning of economics.

7. Academic and reading abilities are important factors.

8. Pupils' retain some of their learning, at least for a year.

9. Maturation may be a factor in economic knowledge.

10. Relating economics to pupils' needs and interests yields positive results.

11. Elementary schoolteachers learn economics just as well when economics instruction is combined with pedagogy as they do in 'pure' economics courses.

12. Economics is inadequately treated in most elementary school social studies textbooks, and the reading level in most books is too high.

Secondary School

1. High school economics courses are effective in increasing economic understanding.

2. Tertiary economics students who study economics in high school may have an advantage over those who do not.

3. High school economics does have a lasting impact, at least for many pupils and for certain types of economic knowledge.

4. Pupils learn more economics when it is related to their interests.

5. Using good materials, pupils can learn some economics, but they will learn even more if their teachers have been specially trained in the use of such materials.

6. Economics can be taught successfully by integrating it with other subjects in the high school curriculum.

7. A variety of methods can be used to teach high school economics.

8. Pupil' attitudes and opinions can be affected by economics instruction.

9. Teachers who have received in-service training in economics education are more effective than untrained teachers.

10. Gender may or may not be significant in economic learning at the high school level.

11. There is a relationship between pupil age and ability to learn.

12. Class and school size may be factors in pupil learning of economics.

13. Scholastic ability, grade point average, socio-economic level, and enrolment in an academic as compared with a vocational course may affect pupil learning of economics.

14. High school social studies textbooks have improved but are still deficient in economics coverage.

While these typical findings from American research may seem trite and banal, it is important to stress that they are not just hunches, but empirically determined. Many could be treated as hypotheses for future studies.

An authoritative survey of the position of economics education at the secondary level in the USA may be found in *Economics Instruction in High Schools*. (Walstad, 1992, pp. 209–51). A more recent analysis of research on high school economics in the United States (Becker, Greene and Rosen, 1994, pp. 89–108) identified four aspects of research findings:

1 measurement of knowledge;

2. research design, modelling and findings (special projects, pupils' ability, teacher ability, course work, technology, gender and race, age and time usage, and lasting effects);

3. test score changes as value added;

4. problems of data loss.

In order to provide more detailed, specific guidance to researchers, the classification of studies used here is more complex than that usually employed. Potential researchers are also advised to consult the publications listed below to obtain an overview of past and current preoccupations of scholars in this field.

SIGNIFICANT BOOKS FOR ECONOMICS AND BUSINESS EDUCATION RESEARCH

1. Hodkinson, S. and Whitehead, D. J. (eds), *Economics Education: Research and Development Issues* . Harlow: Longman, 1986.

2. Saunders, P. and Walstad, W. B. (eds), *The Principles of Economics Course*. New York: McGraw-Hill, 1990.

3. Walstad, W. B. (ed.) *An International Perspective on Economic Education*. Norwell, MA: Kluwer Academic Publishers, 1994.

4. Walstad, W. B. and Soper, J. C. (eds), *Effective Economic Education in*

the Schools. New York: Joint Council on Economic Education, 1991.

5. Wentworth, D. R. , Hansen, W. L. and Hawke, S. H. (eds), *Perspectives on Economic Education.* New York: Joint Council on Economic Education, 1977.

6. Whitehead, D. J. (ed.), *Curriculum Development in Economics.* London: Heinemann Educational, 1974.

(NB: These publications are referred to by number in the bibliographies below.)

MAJOR ARTICLES REVIEWING RESEARCH IN ECONOMICS EDUCATION

Becker, W. , Greene, W. and Rosen, S. 'Research on high school economics in the United States: further considerations' in (3).

Dawson, G, G. 'Research in economic education at the precollege level' in (5).

Highsmith, R. 'The Research Core of Economic Education', in *Theory into Practice,* Vol. 26, No. 3 , Summer 1987, pp. 216–23.

Schug, M. C. and Walstad, W. B. 'Teaching and Learning Economics', in J. P. Shaver (ed.), *Handbook of Research on Social Studies Teaching and Learning.* New York: Macmillan, 1991, pp. 411–19.

Walstad, W. B. 'Research on economics education in the USA: some implications for Europe', in *Economia,* Vol. 2, Part 1, Summer 1992, pp. 18–25.

IMPORTANT JOURNALS TO CONSULT

A. *The Journal of Economic Education.* Quarterly. Sponsored by the National Council on Economic Education, New York, and published by Heldref Publications, 1319 Eighteenth Street, NW, Washington, DC 20036-1802, USA. Four sections include: research in economic education; economic instruction; content articles in economics information and features. The *JEE* ranks 27th out of 130 economic journals in terms of impact-adjusted citations in 1990 to 1985–89 articles. It is the most scholarly academic journal in the world in the field, and its particular strength is in the quantitative kind of empirical research. Many articles deal with research methodology. In recent years, it has focused less on college-level economics and more on research at the secondary level. The Summer 1990 issue is devoted entirely to research in economics education.

B. *Economics and Business Education*. Quarterly. Published by the Economics and Business Education Association; 1a Keymer Road, Hassocks, West Sussex BN6 8AD. Unlike the *JEE*, this journal is aimed at practising teachers, and its main sections are: economics and business (content articles); economics education; business education; resources review. However, the education sections do sometimes contain a research article.

C. *Economia*. Twice per annum. Published by the Association of European Economics Education, c/o S. Hurd, Staffordshire University, Stoke-on-Trent ST4 2DF. This journal has articles by economics and business educators throughout Europe, as well as occasional review articles from elsewhere. It has a section on research in economics education, as well as others on economic and business curriculum and pedagogy, reviews, database articles and AEEE and national news.

D. *The American Economic Review*. The Papers and Proceedings of the *AER* has a section on economics education in each May issue, which is sponsored by the Committee on Economic Education of the American Economic Association. Most of the articles in this highly reputable journal concern college economics, but some focus on the high school.

Theses refer either to London University Institute of Education MA dissertations (LUIE) or Manchester University Department of Education MA theses (MU).

TOPICS IN ECONOMICS AND BUSINESS EDUCATION RESEARCH

The next section provides a researchers' guide to particular fields of enquiry in economics and business education. Sixteen fields have been demarcated. Each begins with a summary of the research in that field. This is extremely condensed and eclectic: readers who want to delve further may consult the research review articles listed on pages 215–16, and the preliminary reading suggested under each topic. After the research summary, possible questions for investigation are listed, followed by the preliminary reading. Each brief bibliography reflects the judgement of the writer about the value of particular research articles. Once researchers have begun to consult the articles proposed, they will soon encounter a plethora of further references.

1. PEDAGOGY

Despite a multitude of research studies investigating the relative effectiveness of alternative pedagogical practices, very little evidence has been obtained about which methods should be used in classrooms. Some research shows the relative effectiveness of programmed learning, but it is symptomatic of the irrelevance of much educational research that this finding has had no discernible effect on how economics is taught. In the US, there is some evidence that the use of particular television series enhances student understanding. One of the problems of such research is the ethical one of using different techniques or resources with different classes, in order to try to measure relative changes in economic understanding. Should the teacher effectively deny one class exposure to a hypothesised superior resource or strategy in order that he may make comparisons between two classes?

Computer-assisted learning appears to have a comparative advantage in teaching which uses databases and simulations. But, despite the grandiose research designs of some projects, such as that of Professor Lumsden in the 1960s and 1970s, and the Economics Association 14–16 Project in the late 1970s and early 1980s, it is still not possible to pronounce authoritatively on the relative merits of, for example, didactic teaching compared with individualised learning. Such large-scale projects are emasculated by their lack of detailed investigation and description of what actually takes place in economics lessons. Surveys of classroom practice may not accurately reflect teachers' actual behaviour. One problem with asking teachers what form of instruction they use with their pupils is that what teachers say they do and what they actually do may be rather different. A natural tendency exists to stress those activities which the teacher thinks are approved by the researcher. 'Dictating notes' rarely features in such responses, though it is a common teacher activity. Responses provide no information about how effectively the teacher organises each type of activity. However, small-scale case studies may uncover aspects of teaching and learning which are masked by anonymous questionnaires. In particular, while studies indicate that teachers *per se* have negligible effects on student learning, relative to other factors, it is possible that such small observed effects are the consequence of averaging large but offsetting factors. By carefully investigating selected representative schools on the basis of survey responses, it might be possible to link 'successful' departments or teachers with particular teaching styles, resources or other factors. Recent studies of 'value added' or cognitive gain may suggest procedures for application to economics and business education.

Research Questions

How do teachers justify their teaching methods?
Can the educational value of alternative teaching methods be assessed experimentally?
Do different parts of the curriculum lend themselves to specific teaching and learning activities?
What parts of the syllabus do pupils find particularly difficult?
What resources and strategies might be developed to overcome learning difficulties?
Why do teachers use particular resources with their classes?
What is the scope for individualised learning in economics or business education?
How effectively is knowledge about curriculum materials disseminated?
What is the current context and practice in economics and business studies lessons?
What is the relationship between how these subjects are taught and the expressed aims of economics educators?

Preliminary Reading

Ajello, A. M. *et al.* 'Teaching economics in the primary school: content and methods', in (1).
LUIE: Carr, N. J. 'An evaluation of the use of case studies in Economics at Advanced Level Economics in Schools'. 1982.
LUIE: Charles, M. G. 'The use of a computer package to assist with the data response paper in Advanced Level Economics'. 1986.
LUIE: Minogue, C. 'An investigation into the value of computer assisted learning in economics education: a case study with special reference to computer simulations'. 1988.
LUIE: Monk, D. 'Recent developments in computer aided learning: a case study'. 1988.
LUIE: Riley, C. 'An investigation into the value of educational drama in the development of economic understanding'. 1987.
LUIE: Stonhold, B. 'An investigation into the use of flexible learning programmes in GCE A Level Economics'. 1993.
LUIE: Tribe, J. 'Whither common skills? A critical examination of the common skills movement with particular reference to business education'. 1992.
LUIE: Wilson, D. 'Infusion of critical thinking into the teaching/learning of GCE A Level Economics'. 1994.
LUIE: Wood, K. R. J. 'An analysis and evaluation of computer materials

developed for use in the economics curriculum'. 1982.
MU: Acharya, J. P. 'Introducing computer assisted learning in economics education: implications for Nepal'. 1992.
Gregory, A. 'Using the media in developing economics curricula', in (1).
Hurd, S: 'Report on the 1989 National Survey of Computer Use in Economic and Business Education' in *Economics*, Vol. 26, Part 3, pp. 134–40.
Lumsden, K. G. and Scott, A. 'The comparative advantage of microcomputers in economics teaching', in *Economics*, Vol. 19, Part 3, pp. 87–9.

2. PHILOSOPHICAL ISSUES: THE NATURE OF THE SUBJECTS

In the early literature, writers agonised over the nature and objectives of economics education. In economics, writers sought to state and justify a core of concepts and an analytical framework. In business studies, the single-subject approach was superseded by an approach which centred on the core concept of decision-making in organisations. In recent years, the focus has shifted to an analysis of why little attention is devoted to alternative paradigms, and comparative treatments. In the 1970s, work on taxonomies of educational objectives was applied to economics education. At that time, it appeared that economic analysis in schools rarely reached the higher levels of the cognitive domain, and completely ignored the affective domain. Both these observations had some impact in terms of expanding the range of assessment instruments in order to make tests more demanding, and in encouraging a debate about the extent to which economics could or should be taught as a value-free science.

Research Questions

What are the goals of economics and business education?
What educational objectives are implicit in the nature of the subjects?
What societal goals might be achieved through economics and business education?
What objectives do teachers have in economics and business education?

Preliminary Reading

LUIE: Jeffreys, D. 'Towards a theory of economics education'. 1983.
LUIE: Lines, D. R.'Business Studies: the search for a paradigm'. 1987.
Dawson, G. 'Is economic science scientific – or is it better than that?' in (1).
Helburn, S. W. 'Economics and economics education: the selective use of

discipline structures in economics curricula' in (1).
Saunders, P. *et al. A Framework for Teaching the Basic Concepts* (2nd edn).
New York: Joint Council on Economic Education, 1984.
Wilkes, R. 'Towards a new paradigm for the teaching of economics' in (1).

3. COGNITIVE GAIN RESEARCH

In order to measure the change in economic understanding resulting from particular courses, methods and other independent variables, it was necessary to develop instruments that measured such cognitive gain. From the 1960s, an array of such tests have been developed in the United States. Principal among extant versions are the *Test of Economic Knowledge*, for use with 14–15-year-old students, the *Test of Economic Literacy*, for use with year 12–13-year-old students, the *Test of Understanding in College Economics* (all available from the National Council on Economic Education). There are also other instruments available, for example for use with younger pupils. Despite the criticisms levelled by radical economics educators at such tests, they continue to be widely used, and are also becoming a frequently used tool for measuring economic literacy in other countries, such as the UK, Greece, Germany and Austria, and in Eastern Europe. Apart from changes to terminology, few alterations typically need to be made to match curricula elsewhere, since the tests focus on fundamental economic concepts. A greater problem is that when they are used as both pre- and post-test, it is not clear whether the questions are couched in language appropriate for someone who has not begun formally to study the subject. Moreover, their use in international comparisons of economic literacy is fraught with difficulties, because the intellectual characteristics of the populations sampled may not be identical. A typical example is the United Kingdom, where Advanced Level students are academically selected, compared with the USA, where students of a similar age show a much wider spread of ability.

Since the late 1960s, Professors Lumsden and Scott have grappled tenaciously with a variety of research questions. They aimed to form a complete and accurate picture of the state of economics education in the UK, with reference to, for example, teacher and pupil characteristics, materials, teacher aims, course content, examination types, class size, hours spent studying, and teaching methods. Second, they attempted to establish what kind of economic understanding was needed for effective participation in society, and to prescribe what was required to increase the level of economic understanding obtained by formal education. A third aim was to prepare, test and publish a comprehensive objective test to facilitate course evaluation and teaching experimentation at the local level. Finally, they hoped to publish a manual of new teaching methods and materials, so that innovating teachers might experiment with and adopt those techniques which were most suited to their students' capabilities and needs. This intention proved over-optimistic, but the remaining research activity was completed and published (Lumsden, 1980). The research team proceeded to conduct various studies in the university and other sectors, and to develop and market the very popular computerised macroeconomic simulation *Running the British Economy*. But the bulk of the research findings, however their intrinsic interest and value is judged, had minimal impact on the practice of economics teaching in Britain.

Research Questions

To what extent are instruments for measuring economic understanding transferable to other cultural contexts?

Do appropriate tests exist for measuring economics and business studies understanding?

Is it possible to devise tests for business studies similar to those developed for measuring economic understanding?

Preliminary Reading

Beck, K. and Krumm, V. 'Economic literacy in German-speaking countries and the United States: methods and first results of a comparative study', in (3).

Lumsden, K. G. 'Economics Education in Britain. An Economics Education Project', in *Economics* Vol. 8, Part 1, pp. 35–7.

Lumsden, K. G. 'Economics Education Project – report on preliminary university study', in *Economics,* Vol. 8, Part 5, pp. 260–73.

Lumsden, K. G. and Attiyeh, R. 'The core of basic economics', in *Economics,* Vol. 9, Part 1, pp. 33–40.

Lumsden, K. G., Attiyeh, R. and Scott, A. *Economics Education in the United Kingdom,* London: Heinemann Educational, 1980, *passim.*

Makridou-Boussiou, D. and Papanastassiou, D. 'The Test of Economic Literacy and the economic understanding of Greek grammar school students', in *Economia,* Vol. 4, Part 1, pp. 28–31.

Scott, A. 'Economics teachers', in *Economics,* Vol. 10, Part 5, pp. 311–22.

Scott, A. 'Economics pupils', in *Economics,* Vol. 12, Part 1, pp. 25–30.

Scott, A. 'Research into economics efficiency in the teaching of economics: some fundamental problems', in (6).

Soper, J. C. and Walstad, W. B. 'Economic knowledge in junior high and elementary schools', in (4).

Whitehead, D. J. and Halil, T. 'The Test of Economic Knowledge: standardisation in the UK', in *Economia,* Vol. 4, Part 2, Winter 1994, pp. 59–65.

Whitehead, D. J. 'Research in economics education in the present curriculum and political climate' in *Journal of Curriculum Studies,* Vol. 13, Part 3, July–Sept., 1982.

Whitehead, D. J. and Halil, T. 'Economic literacy in the UK and the USA: an empirical analysis', in *Economics,* Vol. 26, Part 1, pp. 33–8.

4. ECONOMIC LITERACY: POLITICS OF THE CURRICULUM

In the United States, the National Council on Economic Education has long struggled to find *Lebensraum* for economics education in the school curriculum. There, economics is typically taught through a social studies or history course, rather than as a discrete subject, although the Advanced Placement Program is a significant provision for pre-university students. The Developmental Economic Education Program, launched over 30 years ago as an in-service teacher-training programme, was avidly taken up by school districts, but its effect on the economic understanding of students was less startling. It is ironic that the generously funded organisation NCEE has had so little impact on the extent of economics education in schools in the USA. Findings on the cross-curricular or infusion approach to economics education demonstrate its futility, given the priorities of teachers of other subjects. Single-subject delivery of either economics or business studies is much more likely to result in significant cognitive gain.

In the United Kingdom, while members of the government were happy to lend support to economics as long as it demonstrated the important of wealth creation and the virtues of the market economy, they were less enthusiastic about proposals to develop a more critical approach. Business studies seemed more in tune with the *Zeitgeist,* and students in a time of unnecessarily high unemployment began to choose this subject for its supposedly more vocational qualities. However, no recent research studies have investigated why students opt for particular subjects, whether at the age of 15 or 17.

Research Questions

How is economic literacy to be defined?
What economics and business studies are taught in primary and secondary schools in the UK?
What syllabuses are used, and why are they chosen?

To what extent is Economic and Industrial Understanding part of the curriculum of secondary schools?

How effective is the infusion approach to economics education?

How far are economics and business concepts taught in vocational courses in schools?

What is the relationship between economics and business studies, and the other social sciences that are taught in secondary schools?

To what extent can and should economics and business education feature in Key Stages 1 to 3?

What are the consequences of studying both economics and business studies to A Level?

What economics and business ideas do teachers think are most valuable?

What attitudes do teachers display towards current syllabuses?

Preliminary Reading

LUIE: Hopkins, J. 'An account of an investigation into the development of economic and industrial understanding in primary schools in England'. 1991.

LUIE: Wall, S. E. 'Implementing a course in economic awareness for 11 to 14 year olds: a case study'. 1987.

LUIE: Wilkinson, S. K. 'Education for economic and industrial awareness: what do trade unions think?' 1987.

LUIE: Wilson, A. 'What we know about young people's understanding of key concepts in citizenship and economic and industrial understanding'. 1994.

MU: Arden, Y. 'EIU and careers education and guidance in the whole school curriculum'. 1993.

MU: Burleton, S.'Across the great divide: primary/secondary links through economic awareness'. 1990.

MU: Clarke, P. 'The development of economic awareness as a cross curricular theme in one school: an evaluation of the work of the coordinator'. 1992.

MU: Davis, P. (M. Phil. thesis). 'Geographical education and economic awareness: a study of a secondary school department'. 1991.

MU: Harold, P. 'Cross-curricularity and EIU in an urban 11–16 school'. 1993.

MU: Yuen, C. 'The management of the whole school curriculum with particular reference to economic awareness'. 1992.

Craft, A. 'World trends in economic literacy', in *Economia* Vol. 1, Part 2, Winter 1991, pp. 54–8.

Hansen, W. L. 'The state of economic literacy', in (5).

Walstad, W. B. and Soper, J. C. 'Economic literacy in senior high schools', in (4).

Watts, M. 'Research on DEEP: the first 25 years', in (4).

5. PUPILS' UNDERSTANDING OF ECONOMICS CONCEPTS

Some research studies are sceptical about the value of a small input of teaching to achieve any reasonable level of economic literacy. There may well be some time allocation below which such provision is nugatory, especially in the light of research which shows the (lack of) lasting effects of teaching economics. Much research interprets the statistics from multiple-choice tests, but more enlightening might be an analysis of the commonest errors made, the distractors which are most frequently chosen. We know very little about the specific concepts that students find difficult, and why. We need to know more about the common misconceptions held by the general adult population that has never been exposed to a formal course in the subject. Perhaps we need to spend our time 'unteaching uneconomics'. As Mark Twain said, 'It's not what they *don't* know that's the problem, it's what they *do* know that ain't so'. A number of recent studies have sought to demonstrate that young people often have an inaccurate idea of concepts such as 'price' and 'cost', though the extent to which such distinctions are semantic is largely ignored. Children may have a sound understanding of a concept without knowing what is the correct technical word for describing it. In this field, linguistic analysis may be less revealing than behavioural.

Research Questions

Do pupils display different attitudes to alternative ways of teaching the subjects?
What attitudes do pupils have to different parts of the syllabus they learn?
How do pupils acquire understanding of economics and business studies concepts?
What is the significance of the combinations of other subjects pupils study with economics or business education?
What are the most common errors and misunderstandings in learning economics and business studies?
Why are conceptual errors made?
What concepts do students find most difficult to comprehend?

Preliminary Reading

LUIE: Thomas, L. M. 'An investigation of economics understanding among pupils aged 12–16 years'. Ph.D. thesis, University of London, 1983.

LUIE: Brown, D. J. 'The meanings assigned to some economic terms: a case study of some 13–14 year old pupils'. 1984.

MU: Cribb, B. 'Insights into perspectives on effective learning in Business Education 16–19'. 1993.

LUIE: Douglass, M. A. 'Phenomenographic investigation into students' economic learning in a mini-enterprise context'. 1991.

Dahlgren, L. O. and Marton, F. 'A research project on higher education: investigation into the learning and teaching of basic concepts in economics', in *European Association for Research and Development in Higher Education*, 1976.

Danziger, K 'Children's earliest conceptions of economic relationships', in *Journal of Social Psychology*, 47, pp. 231–40.

Fox, K. F. A. 'What children bring to school: the beginnings of economics education', in *Social Education*, 42 (6), pp. 478–81.

Furnham, A. 'Children's understanding of the economic world', in *Australian Journal of Education*, Vol. 30, No. 3, 1976, pp.219–40.

Gilliard, J. V. *et al. Economics, What and when: scope and sequence guidelines K-12.* New York: Joint Council on Economic Education, 1988.

Schug, M. C. 'The development of students' economic thought: implications for instruction', in (4).

6. ECONOMICS, BUSINESS STUDIES AND EDUCATIONAL THEORY

Some of the earliest articles in *Economics* discuss the impact that educational theories might have on the way in which economics should be taught. In brief, economics was traditionally taught in an extremely didactic fashion, but educational theorists took the view that such a strategy could only succeed if teachers had very limited objectives. Any intention to develop students' thinking, communication and problem-solving skills required a much more extensive menu of teaching and learning activities. Gestalt theory showed how important it was to provide students with an overview of the syllabus, theory, topic or concept both before and after proceeding. Theories of motivation highlighted the need for positive reinforcement and giving students more responsibility for their own learning. Research on learning and memory stressed the importance of the connectivity of concepts, and the need to link both forwards and backwards, as well as the significance of mnemonic devices. Research on educational assessment showed the importance of a varied collection of testing strategies in order to neutralise gender, class and other forms of bias, and to ensure that students could understand the scope for applying general economics/business studies principles even when the questions were disguised in normal English.

Research Questions

What teaching, learning and curriculum models are appropriate for economics and business education?

What is the relative importance of verbal information, intellectual skills, cognitive strategies and attitudes in learning economics and business studies?

Are taxonomies of educational objectives helpful in specifying the economics/business studies curriculum?

To what extent do problem-solving strategies cut across conventional classifications of learning theory?

What teaching strategies are appropriate to achieve different types of learning?

Is the mastery learning approach appropriate for economics/business education?

What are the appropriate pedagogies for teaching affective aspects of economics/business studies?

Preliminary Reading

Allen, D. I. 'Learning Models and teaching strategies in commercial and economic education' in A. Gregory (ed.), *Directions in Commercial, Economic and Legal Education in Australia.* Melbourne, Australia: VCTA, 1979, pp. 187–234.

Dunning, K. 'What economics should we teach?' in *Economics,* Vol. 8 , Part 4, pp. 199–206.

Dunning, K. 'To know economics' in *Economics,* Vol. 9, Part 4, pp. 225–32.

Lucas, J. 'Models in Economics', in *Economics,* Vol. 15, Part 4, pp.118–20.

Entwistle, H . 'Educational theory and the teaching of economics', in *Economics* Vol. 6, Part 4, pp. 203–9.

Harbury, C. D. 'Economic policy and the citizen', in *Economics,* Vol. 8, Part 5, pp. 237–47.

Pearmain, K. C. 'Teaching and methodology', in *Economics,* Vol. 7, Part 6, pp. 283–5.

Ryba, R. and Drake, K. 'Towards a taxonomy of educational objectives for economics?' in (6).

Saunders, P. 'Learning theory and instructional objectives', in (2).

Thomas, L. M. 'A New Perspective on Learning – What does it mean for Economics?', in *Economics,* Vol. 27, Part 2, pp. 79–83.

Whitehead, D. J. 'Learning Processes and Teaching Strategies in Economics Education', in *Economics*, Vol. 19, Part 4, pp. 141–8.

7. SCHOOLS/INDUSTRY LINKS

Most studies in this area investigate the value of particular strategies for linking the teaching of economics/business studies to the world of work. Some of the earliest articles in *Economics* describe the value of activities such as touring the Covent Garden fruit market at 5a.m.! An unsurprising finding of such studies is that extra-curricular activities increase student motivation. Their impact on cognitive development is less certain, though it is unlikely to be adverse. While work in the community was originally seen as a time-consuming addition to the teacher's workload (by those who would rather not do it), current syllabuses (such as General Certificate of Secondary Education and General National Vocational Qualification) often require students to prepare assignments based on local research. More studies are now needed to gauge the effectiveness of a variety of strategies to achieve strong, worthwhile links. Also, very little empirical investigation has been made into the value of mini-enterprise activities, which are currently in vogue.

Research Questions

What strategies might teachers adopt in developing links with their local community?
What educational outcomes result from extra-curricular visits?
How may links be nurtured when organisations feel overused and 'linkwilt' develops?
What is the best way of employing adults other than teachers in the classroom?
What are the cognitive benefits of mini-enterprise activities?
Does work experience have a comparative advantage for economics/business studies students?

Preliminary Reading

LUIE: Allen, P. 'An investigation into the use made in economics and allied subjects of material supplied by industry'. 1987.
LUIE: Carr, B. 'An investigation into the role of the work related curriculum with particular reference to two secondary schools in the London Borough of Redbridge'.1994.
LUIE: Hollinghum, P. 'The effect of school/industry liaison on economics education with special reference to BP's "Learning for a Changing World" in Essex'. 1987.

LUIE: Lawrence, B. 'Mini-enterprise activities-outcomes for teachers and students'.1988.
LUIE: Levett, L. 'An investigation to discover whether experiential learning in the form of industry days constitutes a valid educational experience'.1994.
LUIE: Smith, P. 'Economics field courses: an evaluation'. 1984.
LUIE: Thomas, M. 'An industry-education partnership. An investigation of the gains made by a group working towards AS Business Studies'.1994.
MU: Rudder, J. 'Work shadowing at Loxley College: an exploration of the process of development of the scheme'. 1993.
Cook, R. *Education-industry links: an overview of evaluation findings.* 1989. Sheffield Training Agency. TVEI Evaluation Working Paper No. 3.
Livesey, F. 'The relevance of GCE Economics to industry and the professions', in *Economics,* Vol. 15, Part 4, Winter 1979, pp. 110–17.

8. VALUES, ATTITUDES AND BIAS

In the United States, research on attitudes has focused on two questions. What are the attitudes of students towards the subject itself? This significant issue has been largely ignored elsewhere, though Lumsden (1980) did ask pupils why they had decided to study economics. In business studies, there was an unpublished study in the late 1970s which followed up people who had studied Advanced Level Business Studies in schools, to see how much they valued studying the subject five years after leaving school. The other main thrust of American research on attitudes investigates the extent to which students' view on economic issues conforms to that of professional economists. Such scales are supposed to measure the economic sophistication of students. As might be expected, increased exposure to economics education increases students' attitude sophistication. In the UK, research has centred on attempting to measure how students' attitudes to economic issues change as a result of studying Advanced Level Economics. The difficulty is that most attitude scales are multidimensional, thus rendering measurement of change extremely hazardous. Other studies have exposed various kinds of bias in teaching materials, in the pedagogical approaches of teachers of these subjects, and in the syllabuses which are studied in schools. Attempts to reveal the latent or explicit bias of teachers have proved largely unsuccessful, since the methodological problems are intractable. More modest investigations of classroom practice are likely to illuminate more brightly this presently impenetrable field of study.

Research Questions

To what extent are value judgements overt or concealed in economics and business education?

Does bias exist in teaching resources, syllabuses, teaching methods and extra-curricular activities?

Do students have an opportunity to consider the ends of economic systems?

Is the teaching of economics and business studies biassed?

Do suitable instruments exist for measuring pupils' atititudes?

Why do students decide to study economics or business studies?

What are the attitudes of teachers to economics and business issues?

Preliminary Reading

LUIE: Carr, A. 'A study of the attitudes of UK Jewish teenagers concerning Third World economic development'.1994.

LUIE: Lee, M. 'A survey of the economic attitudes of Hong Kong secondary school teachers'. 1994.

LUIE: Munday, S. 'An investigation into the effects of a PSE module on development issues upon the attitudes of Year Ten students'. 1993.

LUIE: Radford, A. 'Bias in 'A' Level Economics textbooks: a case study'. 1989.

LUIE: Whitehead, D. J. (Ph.D. thesis). 'A study of the effects of an Advanced Level Economics course on attitudes to economics issues'. 1984.

Becker, W., Walstad, W. B. and Watts, M. 'A comparison of the views of economists, economic educators, teachers, and journalists on economic issues', in (3).

Brittan, S. *Is there an economic consensus?* London: Macmillan, 1973.

Dawson, G. 'The objectivity of economics', in *Economics,* Vol. 16, Part 1, pp. 24–7.

Helm, R. 'Values in Economics', in *Economics* Vol. 15, Part 1, pp. 11–15.

Lawson, C. W. 'The conservatism of economics', in *Economics,* Vol. 10, Part 2, pp. 71–8.

Lee, N. 'A note on bias in economics education', in *Economics,* Vol. 15, Part 1, pp. 16–17.

Lee, N. 'Putting the heart back into economic man', in *Economics,* Vol. 22, Part 3, pp. 22–3, 92–5.

Luker, W. A. *et al.* 'The effect of instruction in basic microeconomics on interventionist/non-interventionist attitudes', in (1).

O'Brien, M. U. and Ingels, S. J. 'The Economics Values Inventory', in *Journal of Economic Education,* Vol. 18, No. 1 (Winter 1987), pp. 7–18.

Robinson, T. K. 'Values in Economics Education', in *Economics,* Vol. 26, Part 4, pp. 165–9.

Soper, J. C. and Walstad, W. B. 'On Measuring Economic Attitudes', in *Journal of Economic Education,* Vol. 14, Pt 4 (Fall 1983), pp. 4–17.

Szreter, R. 'The teacher of economics and the problem of political bias', in *Economics,* Vol. 9, Part 6, pp. 353–7.

Webster, A. 'Ideology and 'A' level economics textbooks', in *Economics,* Vol. 14, Part 3, pp. 85–7.

Whitehead, D. J. 'Students' attitudes to economics issues', in *Economics,* Vol. 22, Part 1, pp. 24–32.

Whitehead, D. J. 'Values in Economics Teaching' in G. B. J. Atkinson (ed.), *Teaching Economics.* London: Heinemann Educational, 1985.

Whitehead, D. J. 'The measurement of attitudes to economics issues: some problems', in (1).

9. GENDER AND RACE ISSUES

A large number of studies have pointed up the significant difference in test scores of males and females. At any rate, males perform better than females at the start of a course of instruction, but if measurement is in terms of cognitive gain, taking into account the initial stock of knowledge, then there appears to be no significant difference in performance. In other words, for whatever reason, males come to the subject with more knowledge, but females learn economics as effectively as males. Some researchers have attributed score differences to the way in which economic understanding is assessed. If females write better essays than males, but find multiple choice tests more difficult, then the kind of test used will bias the outcome.

Research Questions

Do resources for teaching accurately portray the roles of ethnic minorities and women in the economic system?

To what extent does the teaching of economics and business studies reflect multicultural society?

Are teachers and resources used in teaching balanced from the viewpoint of gender perspectives?

Preliminary Reading

LUIE: Gavin, M. 'Anti-racist education and the economics curriculum'. 1989.

LUIE: Goddard, B. 'The contribution of economics to multicultural and anti-racist education'. 1985.

LUIE: Loewenstein, C. 'The economics education of girls'. 1983.

Bolton, C. 'Gender equality and business education', in *Economics and*

Business Education, Vol. 11, Part 2, Summer 1994, pp. 87–90.

Ferber, M. A. 'Gender and the study of economics', in (2).

Ladd, H. F. 'Male-female differences in precollege economic education', in (5).

Lumsden, K. G. and Scott, A. 'The economics student reexamined: male-female differences in comprehension', in *Journal of Economic Education,* Vol. 18, Part 4 (Fall, 1987), pp. 365–75.

10. AREA AND COMPARATIVE STUDIES

Studies in this area have little theoretical interest, tending to describe syllabuses, the status of economics and business studies in the curriculum, and issues of direct concern to the country concerned but not necessarily elsewhere. However, in the 1990s, two significant fields of enquiry have been opened up. One concerns research in cognitive gain (see above, p.209). Most studies involve using one of the American standardised tests of economic understanding to assess the extent of economic literacy amongst particular groups of the school population. The other strand of comparative research focuses on the emerging capitalist economies, particularly in Eastern Europe. These reports describe the pre-existent menu of Marxist economics, and the school system's needs for new curricula, resources, and above all, teachers knowledgeable about market economics, the mixed economy, and pedagogical strategies that are less didactic than was deemed appropriate when dissent was anti-social.

Research Questions

To what extent are Western models of economics and business education appropriate for Eastern European countries?

Do economics graduates in different countries have similar understanding of basic economic concepts?

Does the provision of economics and business education vary significantly in different parts of the country?

What the the main differences between business education in schools in different countries in Western Europe?

Preliminary Reading

LUIE: Cressey, B. D. 'The provision of economics education in the UK with special reference to the London Borough of Barking'. 1982.

LUIE: Curtis, P. J. D. 'A cognitive skills evaluation of selected British and South African A Level and matriculation Economics examinations'. 1988.

LUIE: Pennant, T. 'Aspects of economics and business studies in upper secondary education in Germany and England'. 1994.

Walstad, W. B. 'An assessment of economics instruction in American high schools', in (3).

Whitehead, D. J. 'The Market for Economics Teachers' in *Economics* Vol. 24, Part 1, pp. 13–17.

Whitehead, D. J. 'Economic understanding in the United Kingdom', in (3).

11. ASSESSMENT AND EXAMINATIONS

Thirty years ago, articles were already being written comparing the results of various cohorts of students in relation to different modes of examination. Other studies used Bloom's taxonomy of educational objectives to analyse essay papers of different examination boards, revealing that some boards asked much more searching questions than others. Over the next 20 years, product differentiation in terms of the syllabus and examination modes narrowed, partly as the result of the introduction of a common core syllabus used by all the boards. Other studies have highlighted the gender differences in performance on different types of examination (see above, p.220). Vagaries and unreliability in marking are sometimes exposed when teachers publish details of the divergent results achieved by their students when taking the examinations of more than one examination board.

Research Questions

Are syllabuses comparable between examination boards?

What variety is available in modes of examining economics and business studies?

Do different syllabuses require pupils to reach different levels of the cognitive domain?

Do different examinations require pupils to show competence in different levels of skills?

To what extent do examinations achieve their goal of assessing economic and business understanding?

Should techniques of oral examining be developed?

How useful is the *viva voce* as a constituent of an examination?

What kind of diagnostic tests might be developed to reveal pupils' misunderstandings?

Preliminary Reading

LUIE: Jones, R. D. 'The development of criteria to assess 'A' Level Economics syllabuses'. 1987.
LUIE: Lawrence, J. A. 'An investigation of the possibilities and advantages of oral testing at GCSE'. 1988.
LUIE: Lyons, A. 'Oral assessment in A Level Economics'. 1991.
LUIE: Martin, J. 'An investigation of the value of coursework as an assessed component in business studies courses'. 1994.
LUIE: Moon, R. D. 'Oral assessment in GCSE Economics'. 1988.
LUIE: Pang, S. 'Assessment of economics in the context of a business studies diploma programme'. 1988.
LUIE: Preece, C. B. 'An examination of some of the problems created for teachers of economics by the coursework requirement of GCSE'. 1989.
MU: Andrews, S. 'GCSE Business Studies in three educational institutions'. 1994.

12. VOCATIONAL COURSES

Researchers have so far paid little attention to vocational issues. This may be partly due to the stress put by economics and business educators on the non-vocational character of their subjects (in the crude utilitarian sense). Studies have often attempted to link syllabuses which claim to be vocational with the requirements of the world of work, as determined by either the course providers or the market for their trainees. With the advent of general vocational courses in schools, many research questions remain to be answered.

Research Questions

Should the economics component of a vocational course differ from that provided as part of general education?
Do the skills and knowledge required by potential employers match those provided by vocational economics and business courses?
What is the level of business understanding of GNVQ Advanced students compared with Advanced Level Business Studies students?

Preliminary Reading

LUIE: Duncan, J. R. 'The role of economics on courses leading to professional qualifications in accountancy or banking'. 1985.

LUIE: Hayes, C. A. 'The assessment of economics understanding of BTEC National students in a group work situation'. 1988.
LUIE: King, B. 'Economic understanding and BEC National Level students'. 1982.
LUIE: Pittwood, A. 'The provision of economics in the BEC National Awards curriculum, and the demand for economics understanding by industry'. 1983.
LUIE: Powell, R. 'Economics education in TVEI'. 1986.

13. SCHOOL–UNIVERSITY LINKS AND TERTIARY EDUCATION

Apart from a a few studies in the 1970s, and a couple of recent vintage, little work has been done on investigating the relationship between secondary and tertiary provision of economics and business studies. Whereas many academic subjects flow on quite easily from school to college, economics in particular has never benefited from such coherence, mainly because it has always been possible (and historically preferred) for students to begin their study of the subject in higher education. No one has yet grappled with the question of how to present appropriate challenges to business studies undergraduates who have already taken the subject to quite a high level in their Advanced Level studies at school.

Research Questions

What provision do universities make for students who have already studied economics or business studies at school?
Should the school curriculum suit those who intend to proceed with their specialism at university?
How could university scholars in economics and business studies be encouraged to become more involved in education, as in the NCEE centres in the USA?
What is the influence of universities on the examination boards and their syllabus committees?

Preliminary Reading

LUIE: Curran, J. G. M. 'Economics degree education at seven English polytechnics: an enquiry'. 1989.
Hadjimatheou, G. and Rendall, R. 'Students' characteristics and economics degree performance', in *Economics*, Vol. 22, Part 4, pp. 157–61.
Siegfried, J. J. and Walstad, W. B. 'Research on teaching college economics', in (2).

Wall, N. 'University economics and school economics: the chasms and bridges', in *Economics,* Vol. 18, Part 3, pp. 104–7.

Wall, N. 'University economics and school economics: a follow-up survey', in *Economics,* Vol. 19, Part 2, pp. 54–7.

14. TEACHER TRAINING

The main finding of American research is that teachers who have taken more economics courses at college teach the subject better than those who took fewer. Such findings are of little relevance in the UK, where most teachers are honours graduates in economics or business studies. In Britain, little research has been conducted into teacher education, for example by comparing one course with another, or with those adopted in the rest of Europe. In Britain, the shift to an almost entirely school-based training course was carried out despite the opposition of many professional teacher trainers and the overwhelming number of student teachers, most of whom valued the rigorous university-based part of their course and the overarching perspective of their tutors. While descriptive surveys of particular teacher-training courses have been published, comparative reviews are rare in economics and business education. Policy changes rarely reflect experience and research elsewhere. For example, France is moving back from a too heavily school-based approach to a challenging university-based course for teacher training, while the UK is galloping in the opposite direction.

Research Questions

What is the content of teacher education courses in economics and business education?

What are the objectives of teacher-training courses?

What skills are developed by teacher-training courses?

What are the qualifications and working background of beginning teachers?

What are the attitudes of beginning teachers to alternative teaching and learning activities?

What kind of in-service provision is required by teachers of economics and business studies?

What is the role of professional subject teacher associations in the provision of in-service training?

How useful are professional journals to teachers of economics and business studies?

Do the aims of teacher educators in economics and business education reflect the requirements of practising teachers?

What teacher qualities influence the economics learning of students?

Preliminary Reading

LUIE: Evans, E. L. 'A study into the operation of the PGCE at two university departments of education preparing teachers of economics and business studies'. 1990.

MU: Butroyd, R. 'Subject knowledge and subject applications in a new PGCE Business Studies course – a review'. 1994.

Achtenhagen, F. and Weber, S. 'Training Teachers of Commerce and Business at Georg August University, Göttingen, Germany', in *Economia*, Vol. 4, Part 1, pp. 22–7.

Mackey, J. A. , Glenn, A. D. and Lewis, D. R. 'Current and future needs for teacher training in economic education' , in (5).

Salemi, M. K. 'Using videotape for teacher development and self-evaluation', in (2).

Wilson, M. 'An integrated economics education training model for teachers', in (1).

15. ADULT EDUCATION

Few researchers have any experience of adult education, which is probably why there has been little attempt to explore this field.

Research Questions

What is the curriculum of economics and business classes in adult education institutes?
What are the objectives of adult students of economics and business studies?
What pedagogical strategies are appropriate for adult learners of economics and business studies?

Preliminary Reading

LUIE: Freedman, T. 'The provision of economics education for adults in the UK, with special reference to the London area'. 1986.

LUIE: Masters, R. 'Adult economic understanding of party election broadcasts'. 1988.

Whitehead, D. J. *Assessing the economic understanding of adults.* Proceedings of Conference held at Manchester University, 1987. Economics Association.

16. RESEARCH METHODOLOGY AND NEEDS

Most of the major works dealing with the state of economics education conclude with a catalogue of research needs, few of which have ever attracted more than a minute number of activists in this field. In the United States, recondite arguments about research methodology prevail, with considerable space devoted in the *Journal of Economic Education* to virtuosic displays of sophisticated demolition of other scholars' research designs. British preoccupations, by contrast, seem very prosaic, pragmatic and, from the American perspective, unscientific.

Research Questions

What would constitute an effective training in research techniques for scholars in economics and business education?
How could placing research needs in an order of priority be justified?
What research instruments apart from standardised tests of economic literacy might be developed to help investigation in this field?

Preliminary Reading

Atkinson, B. 'Classroom research in economics education', in *Economics*, Vol. 10, Part 5, pp. 322–9.
Atkinson, B. 'Classroom curriculum development in economics', in *Economics,* Vol. 10, Part 6, pp. 375–82.
Atkinson, B. 'Surveys and questionnaires in economics education research', in *Economics,* Vol. 11, Part 3, pp. 157–64.
Atkinson, B. 'Interaction analysis and the economics teacher', in *Economics,* Vol.11, Part 4, pp. 227–32.
Baumol, W. J. 'Research on High School Economic Education: Discussion', in *Journal of Economic Education,* Vol. 21, Pt 3 (Summer, 1990), pp. 246–7.
Becker, W. E. , Greene, W. and Rosen, S. 'Research on High School Economic Education' in *Journal of Economic Education,* Vol. 21, Pt 3, (Summer, 1990), pp. 231–45.
Becker, W. E. and Walstad, W. B. *Econometric Modelling in Economic Education Research.* The Hague: Kluwer-Nijhoff, 1987.
Lumsden, K. G. *et al.* 'A comparison between multiple regression and log-linear analyses as applied to educational data', in (1).
Powell, R. A. 'Economics education: research and development issues', in *Economics,* Vol. 22, Part 1, pp. 21–3.
Ryba, R. H. 'The economics curriculum: looking to the future, checklist of

major research needs', in (6).

Soper, J. C. 'Needs for evaluation in economic education', in (5).

Walstad, W. B. 'Research on High School Economic Education: Comment', in *Journal of Economic Education*, Vol. 21, Part 3 (Summer, 1990), pp. 248–54.

CONCLUSION

It is prudent finally to take a modest view of the value of educational research. According to Walker, 'most educational research simply does not directly connect with the world it purports to study' (Walker, 1986, p. 204). A frequent criticism of the typical economics research project is that it is based on unrealistic assumptions, and the mathematical model propounded has tenuous or intentionally few relations with the real world. Unfortunately, this stricture might also be applied to research in education, not only in the field of economic and business education. It is not possible to provide one instance of how economics and business studies lessons have been changed as a result of research. If this is the case, it is hard to justify the resources that are devoted to such studies (apart from career advancement for the researchers concerned). Teachers and teaching are influenced principally by the syllabus they choose (or are required) to teach, the examination modes dictated by the accrediting agency, the nature of their students, and the availability of suitable resources. Textbook writers and examination boards could make a much stronger claim to be the catalysts of change than could educational researchers, however well-intentioned their studies. Even teacher trainers may claim a scintilla of influence on the strategies of novitiate teachers. It is hard then to resist the temptation to view educational researchers and teachers as discrete groups that hardly impinge on one another. Research articles are published in academic journals, unread by teachers, while magazines aimed at the teacher market rarely publish reports of cognate research.

However, since it is presumably the ultimate objective of research to improve further the practice of economics and business studies teaching, it is important that research should be orientated to that end.

REFERENCES

Becker, W. , Greene, W. and Rosen, S. (1994). 'Research on High School Economics in the United States: Further Considerations', in Walstad, W. B. (ed.), *An International Perspective on Economic Education*. Norwell, MA. USA: Kluwer Academic Publishers.

Dawson, G. G. (1977). 'Research in Economic Education at the Precollege Level', in Wentworth, Hansen and Hawke (eds), *Perspectives on Economic Education.* New York: Joint Council on Economic Education.

Lumsden, K. G. *et al.* (1980). *Economics Education in the United Kingdom.* London: Heinemann Educational.

Ryba, R. (1974). 'The economics curriculum: looking to the future', in Whitehead, D. J. (ed.), *Curriculum Development in Economics.* London: Heinemann Educational.

Saunders, P. and Walstad, W. B. (1990). *The Principles of Economics Course.* New York: McGraw-Hill.

Walker, R. (1986) in Hammersley, M. (ed.) *Controversies in Classroom Research.* Milton Keynes: Open University Press.

Walstad, W. B. (1992). 'Economics Instruction in High Schools', in *Journal of Economic Literature,* Vol. XXX (December, 1992).

Whitehead, D. J. (1978). 'An analysis of dissemination strategies for curriculum projects with particular reference to the Schools Council History, Geography and Social Science 8–13 Project', M. Phil. thesis, University of London.

— (1982). 'Research in Economics Education in the present curriculum and political climate', in *Journal of Curriculum Studies,* Vol. 14, Part 3 (July–Sept. 1982), pp. 306–10.

9

MODERN FOREIGN LANGUAGES

Colin Wringe

INTRODUCTION

The dominant, indeed all but universally accepted paradigm in Modern Foreign Language teaching is currently provided by the notion of so-called communicative competence. Writers attempting to present this concept are inclined to refer to Hymes's (1972) article, itself entitled 'On Communicative Competence', in which the character of language used as a social rather than a purely intellectual ability is emphasised. The more erudite among such writers may also refer to such linguistic philosophers as Wittgenstein (1953) who draws attention to the way meaning is defined by use and Austin (1962) and Searle (1969), the titles of whose relevant works (*How to do Things with Words* and *Speech Acts*) provide useful slogans to emphasise the main thrust of the language teaching and learning process based on the communicative idea.

The notion of communicative competence first finds application to the practical business of foreign teaching and learning in the field of research on language syllabus design. Traditionally, language syllabuses have been spelled out in terms of grammar, lexis and 'idioms', that is, individual items that cannot be directly mapped on to the mother tongue using the rules of grammar. The fact that many who had followed such syllabuses with apparent success were unimpressive language users in practice seemed to indicate that language learning involved something more. The notion of language as a holistic social competence seemed to offer an alternative way of planning language study. Henceforth the goal becomes not to acquire the exhaustive competence of Chomsky's (1965) 'ideal speaker-listener, in a completely homogeneous speech community, who knows the language perfectly', or the mastery of Saussure's (1949) idealised 'langue' (as opposed to the idiosyncratic 'parole' of the individual speaker), but to meet the communication needs of particular learners. What the learner needs to know may then be broken down into a range of functions (seeking information, getting things done, socialising etc.), general notions (time, space, relationships, etc.), language skills (usually identified as listening, speaking, reading and writing), as well as lists of topics the learner may need to speak about and situations in which he/she may need to do so. Once this has been done it becomes possible to write in the particular 'exponents' or actual items in the target language which the learner needs to acquire.

The theoretical framework for such an analysis is worked out in considerable detail by Munby (1978) among others. Before making any impact on the consciousness of Modern Language teachers in schools, the implications of this work were enthusiastically exploited by those involved in the teaching of English as a Second Language, especially in the development of language courses in English for often highly specific, including academic, purposes.

During the 1960s and 1970s Modern Language teaching in Britain and elsewhere had been beset by a period of frenetic, and now regarded by general consent as relatively unsuccessful, experimentation based on behavioural notions of repetition and reinforcement involving the use of audio-visual systems and the language laboratory which were mainly used for intensive and often decontextualised drilling. In the then newly introduced comprehensive schools, supposedly less able children, with whom both traditional and audio-visual approaches were manifestly unsuccessful, were offered the compromise alternative of so-called European Studies, describing life and institutions in other European countries, usually France, with the addition of 'survival language', that is, communicative language teaching in an elementary form. This, however, was perceived as a retreat from language teaching for a substantial proportion of the school population and was superseded by the graded objectives movement building upon the notion of survival language for pupils in the younger forms and lower bands. The theoretical underpinnings of this movement are to be found notably in Harding and Page (1974), and Harding and Naylor (1979), and the movement's success is documented in Harding, Page and Rowell (1980) and Buckby (1981).

Historically, the communicative paradigm appears to have reached the British Modern Languages world via the so-called Strasbourg Studies of the early 1970s. These were intended to lay the foundations for a European unit credit system for language studies for vocational purposes (Van Ek and others 1973) and sought to identify, among other things, the lowest or 'Threshold' Level at which useful linguistic achievement could be identified and accredited. The influence of the above-mentioned studies, and possibly also Peck's (1976) and Page's (1979) accounts of their findings is manifest in the first set of National Criteria for GCSE French and subsequent GCSE language syllabuses and, therefore, indirectly in the current National Curriculum Order for Modern Foreign Languages. Effective communication based on the four skills, language functions, topics and settings (described in the National Curriculum document as 'areas of experience') are clearly established as the central and, in the minds of many, the only goal of Modern Language teaching.

IN THE SHADOW OF COMMUNICATIVE COMPETENCE

Following the overwhelming success among language teachers of the communicative paradigm which, despite gloomy predictions, is not turning out to be just another disappointing bandwagon, a number of other lines of empirical research which previously seemed likely to produce such steady improvement as was likely to be possible in foreign language learning, appear to have dried up, or at least gone relatively quiet.

The discrediting of a Skinnerian model of language acquisition has meant that the previously much discussed topic of motivation in language teaching has recently received little attention. Audio-visual methods have been abandoned and evaluations of the language laboratory (Green, 1975; Winter, 1982) indicate that its use for its original purpose of intensive drilling has little or no beneficial effect. Memory, previously regarded as important to the learning of grammar and lexis (see, for example, McDonough, 1981, pp. 59–76) has received little recent attention from modern linguists, though the learning of words and phrases by heart appears in the National Curriculum Modern Languages Programmes of Study. Work by Gruneberg and his associates (Gruneberg and Jacobs, 1991; Gruneberg and Sykes, 1991) relying upon word association which forms the basis of a number of commercially successful language-learning courses, would probably be regarded as idiosyncratic by many modern linguists. Opinion regarding optimal ages for foreign language learning has been in a state of undisturbed equilibrium for some time. If the young and very young have certain advantages of ease and facility of acquisition, language learned in the early years may be quickly and completely forgotten and the advantage of the young may be equalised or outweighed by the strategic learning skills of older students (Hamers and Blanc, 1989, pp. 222–4). Either way, the issue of optimal learning ages is unlikely to exert significant influence on mainstream language teaching policy in the near future. The psychological and social conditions of successful language learning and the effect of personality and similar factors on language learning (Gardner and Lambert, 1972) may remain of interest to researchers in the psychological and social science disciplines but do not substantially feed into language teaching practice.

The theoretical work of Chomsky (1965) positing linguistic universals and a deep structure of universal grammar underlying the surface structure of actual languages once seemed to hold promise for language teachers seeking a panacea for what then seemed insuperable problems in the selection and ordering of material. In fact, Chomsky's own warning that his work probably had few direct implications for the practical business of language teaching appears to date to have been correct.

The once popular activity of simple linguistic comparison and error analysis is continued by some researchers (Fakuade, 1991; Ajiboye, 1992) and may be helpful to those seeking phonetic and grammatical accuracy rather than communicative success. Related but more theoretically sophisticated work on interlanguage (Selinker, 1992; Corder, 1981) is more fertile in encouraging teachers to take a less censorious view of so-called 'errors' than has traditionally been the case. The prime practical implication of interlanguage theory is that the learner's imperfect utterances represent a stage on the way to proper mastery of the target language, and that many errors are simply incorrect hypotheses which the learner will eventually discard without teacher intervention. Freed from the behaviourist assumption that uncorrected errors may become ingrained, the teacher may therefore allow less than perfectly expressed communicative activity in the language to continue largely without interruption, concentrating on certain key errors. which by virtue of their frequency or failure to actually impede communication, threaten to become fossilised in the learner's repertoire.

Almost certainly the most significant body of recent and current work for the immediate development of language teaching practice in Britain and elsewhere has been that of Krashen which, despite criticism on matters of detail (McLaughlin, 1987), offers insights which both confirm the validity of communicative approaches to language learning and points to ways in which its implementation may be rendered more effective. It may therefore be appropriate to set out explicitly what Krashen (1987) describes as his five principal hypotheses. These are:

1. The distinction between language 'learning' by means of prescription and more or less formal 'language practice' in an academic situation and language 'acqusition' which occurs when language is used for genuine communicative purposes. It is held that the process of 'acquisition' rather than 'learning' is responsible for our increasing competence in the use of the language.

2. The natural order hypothesis that the structures of a language tend to be acquired in a particular order.

3. The monitor hypothesis that formal learning does not contribute to fluency but may enable the learner to check utterances and especially written use of the language for correctness.

4. The input hypothesis, that our progress in the language depends on our encountering a good volume of 'comprehensible input' just beyond our current level of competence. The use of contextual clues to support comprehension plays an important part in this process.

5. The affective filter hypothesis that low anxiety and a good self-image are favourable to language acquisition.

It is not clear how widely Krashen's actual work is known to British teachers, textbook writers and curriculum designers or, indeed, how far developments consistent with his ideas may be attributed to his influence. His work is very much a scholarly synthesis of the insights and empirical contributions of a number of researchers. Nevertheless, the favouring of genuinely communicative classroom activity, including recent strongly pronounced moves to encourage active use of the target language for classroom business by pupils themselves, is well in line with his insistence on the value of 'acquisition' as the means of developing learners' communicative use of the language. It must be said that the natural order hypothesis appears as yet to exert little influence on the order in which material is presented in the most widely-used language courses. Here, more general psychological considerations such as starting from the child and his/her immediate experience and working out to the wider world play a much more prominent role. Teachers' ambivalent attitudes towards correction likewise appear to owe more to general psychological considerations than specifically to Krashen's monitor hypothesis. If it is felt that one should not inhibit or undermine the confidence of learners, the explanation is often given in Skinnerian terms: by rebuking the learner for making a mistake one is negatively reinforcing the act of attempting to use the foreign language itself. By contrast, the implications of both the input hypothesis and the affective filter hypothesis appear to be widely appreciated by both teachers and others. The most recent National Curriculum Modern Languages document stresses at a number of points that pupils should be presented with language, some of which is unfamiliar, and both teachers and textbook writers are often at pains to provide contextual, especially visual, support for the comprehension of meaning. Textbook writers also go to considerable lengths to devise what they at least consider to be fun activities and foster good self-images on the part of pupils.

THE CURRENT PICTURE IN BRITAIN

Most, if not all of the theoretical work currently taking place into the nature of language and language learning and acquisition is located in departments of Applied Linguistics rather than in institutions directly concerned with the practical business of initial or in-service training of language teachers. The most productive writers are based in the United States and, insofar as they are concerned with actual teaching at all, their focus is upon the task of teaching the world's population to speak English. Though certain controversies continue at a theoretical and empirical level these are, for the most part, well within the framework of what has been described as the dominant paradigm and concern the finer details of how the acquisition of language, including a second language, takes place in a real or contrived situation.

It must be acknowledged that the findings, indeed the very existence, of such work are largely unknown and widely regarded as being of little relevance to the great majority of those concerned with the teaching of foreign languages in Britain. This has become particularly marked in the wake of government imposed changes in initial teacher training – requiring that such training should be more or less exclusively practical and competence based, and the institution of accreditation and inspection procedures ensuring that this requirement is complied with. For classroom teachers, and to an increasing extent for those who train them, the nature and goals of language teaching are no longer felt to be matters of speculation and enquiry but are quite tightly determined not only by National Curriculum Level Descriptions and implied assessment procedures but by actual Programmes of Study, which specify a number of teaching procedures which not only receive little support from research but may be regarded as inappropriate by many reflective classroom practitioners.

This is not to deny that a good deal of thought and creativity may currently go into the business of Modern Language teaching in Britain, though at the level of developmental rather than fundamental research. In particular, those who under other circumstances might have carried out more rigorous research in the field have devoted themselves to the creation of imaginative and stimulating multi-media teaching materials in line with National Curriculum requirements. These may involve the accumulation of extensive authentic printed and recorded materials and computer based activities embodying the general principles of a communicative approach and its development by Krashen and others. Widely used materials produced by Taylor and Edwards (1982), Buckby and others (1992 and 1993), Jenkins and Jones (1991), and Goodman-Stevens, Rogers and Briggs (1989) are cases in point.

The new requirements placed, or apparently placed, on pupils and their Modern Language teachers by the National Curriculum and the prospects of inspection and appraisal have led to the production of short, readable guides on highly specific aspects of Modern Language teaching regarded by teachers themselves as problematic, or identified as such in government documentation. The CILT (Centre for Information on Language Teaching and Research) 'Pathfinder' series of such works contains some 15 guides on such aspects as planning Modern Language schemes of work, progressing through the Modern Foreign Languages attainment targets, continuous assessment and recording and equal opportunities in Modern Languages. A similar series published by the Association for Language Learning (ALL) comprises six short guides on such topics as using the target language, teaching and learning grammar and classroom management in Modern Languages lessons. In the main, these are either inspirational or are based on common sense and the recognised experience or competence of their authors, normally making little, if any, direct or indirect reference to research. Currently, the overriding preoccupation of classroom practitioners is with survival and reassurance, and the search for 'good ideas' for stimulating and National Curriculum conforming lessons, rather than with a deeper understanding of the language learning process.

Such large-scale research as has taken place in the field of Modern Language Teaching in Britain recently has been concerned not with the nature of the language learning process itself and how it can best be promoted, but tends rather to consist of survey-based monitoring of implementation, practice and performance in the foreign language classroom and of the responses and attitudes of foreign language teachers and their pupils. Particularly in larger, funded projects, this has usually been policy-driven and has arisen from DES concern with what was seen, as far back as 1977 (HMI, 1977), as the parlous state of Modern Languages in Britain, as well as from government concern with educational standards generally. In many respects, the HMI 1977 survey of Modern Language teaching in 83 comprehensive schools may still be seen as seminal for many Modern Language developments and the surveys and enquiries related to them.

Starting from the assumptions of the communicative paradigm, that achievement in foreign languages was to be defined in terms of the ability to aurally comprehend, speak, read and write the language, the Assessment of Performance unit (APU, 1987) devised and applied a battery of tests of these skills for their survey of Modern Language performance in schools. Together with the successful experience of the graded objectives movement, these tests have served as models both for many of the GCSE tests and for subsequent National Curriculum Levels of Attainment and Level Descriptions.

A particular concern expressed in the 1977 HMI document was the vulnerable position of languages other than French as grammar schools gave way to comprehensives and second foreign languages were dropped in favour of other priorities. That languages other than French were indeed under threat was confirmed by a Schools Council survey undertaken by Hadley (1981). Though staffing problems were seen as a probable obstacle to the diversification of first foreign languages (an option preferred to simply supporting the teaching of second foreign languages), it was decided to investigate the availability of 'unused teaching capacity', that is, the existence of teachers qualified to teach languages other than French but not actually doing so. An NFER survey with a small number of follow-up interviews was carried out in 1987–88 (Rees, 1989). The survey considered the qualifications and experience of such teachers as well as the degree to which they had maintained their language skills, and their views as to the training necessary to enable them to teach their 'dormant' language at secondary level. Though containing a number of caveats, the report concluded that there was within the existing teaching force some scope for the expansion of languages other than French as the first foreign language.

The potential for a policy of first foreign language diversification was also investigated by a five-year (1987–92) project funded by the Leverhulme Trust. This project, the Oxford First Foreign Language Diversification Project (OXPROD), investigated pupils' responses to the teaching of languages other than French as the first foreign language, as well as certain administrative considerations that might stand in the way of such a policy. Questionnaire surveys and follow-up interviews were carried out in six main project schools and some 35 associated schools, leading to the conclusion that there was nothing in the nature of German and Spanish as curriculum subjects to make them inherently unsuitable for first foreign language provision, though a number of potential administrative problems were identified. (Phillips and Filmer-Sankey, 1993; Filmer-Sankey, 1993). Concurrently with these two investigations, a number of local initiatives were taken to implement the policy of first foreign language diversification, with the assistance of Educational Support Grants.

Examples of policy implementation studies are provided by Johnstone and Mitchell's project entitled Communicative Interaction in Elementary Foreign Language Teaching, funded by the Scottish Education Department in the early 1980s (Mitchell, 1988), and Mellor and Stafford's recent and much more limited study of the first year of implementation of the National Curriculum in Modern Foreign languages (Mellor and Stafford, 1994) sponsored by the Association for Language Learning. As well as providing the basis for Johnstone's (1989) handbook on communicative language teaching, the research of Johnstone and Mitchell demonstrates the extent to which the procedures indicated by an ideal communicative approach are modified in practice by conditions in the real life classroom during the first two years of foreign language learning in Scottish secondary schools.

The survey of Mellor and Stafford is valuable in providing an independent and alternative perspective to that of HMI upon the early implementation of the National Curriculum. The authors note the benefits flowing from the National Curriculum's insistence on the use of the target language for classroom business and the progress of first foreign language diversification, but draw attention to many anxieties and difficulties experienced by teachers, as well as the limitations upon implementation necessarily imposed by financial stringency.

Whether consciously so intended or not, one possible justification for the policy of including a foreign language in the curriculum of all secondary pupils is provided by the aim of offering insights into the culture and civilisation of other countries and encouraging positive attitudes to the speakers of other languages. This aim is identified by HMI (1981) and persistently reappears in the first set of National Criteria for 'French' (explicitly intended to apply to all foreign language syllabuses) and subsequently in the various successive Draft and Parliamentary Orders for Modern Foreign Languages.

Some doubt was cast on whether this aim was achieved by the teaching of a foreign language, at least in the primary school, by the research of Burstall in the early 1970s (Burstall, 1973). The thoughtful and perceptive ethnographic study of Byram, Esarte-Sarries and Taylor (Byram, 1989; Byram and Esarte-Sarries, 1990; Byram, Esarte-Sarries and Taylor, 1991), funded by the ESRC, is not specifically designed to answer the question of whether such attitudes are promoted by foreign language learning or not. Instead, the study investigates the attitudes and degree of ethnocentrism of older primary and younger secondary school pupils and the ways in which language textbooks and the work of foreign language teachers may impact upon these attitudes. This research has given rise to four books written or edited by the researchers, to symposia in Durham and Manchester and to a number of papers on related subjects by colleagues in France and Germany (for example, Klippel, 1990; Buttjes, 1990; Cain, 1990; Kramer, 1990). It is not yet clear how far current foreign language teaching and the new post-National Curriculum generation of language course materials respond to Byram, Esarte-Sarries and Taylor's strictures regarding the unstructured and fragmentary nature of the cultural content of language courses; the issue is nevertheless clearly in the consciousness of many language teachers and teacher trainers, while the copious use of authentic materials together with the prevailing mood of political correctness with regard to cultural differences may be helpful in reducing the high degree of ethnocentrism reported by the researchers.

As well as at secondary school level, large-scale systematic language learning surveys have also been carried out in higher education and into the language needs of industry and commerce. In 1985, the Nuffield Modern Languages Enquiry attempted to gain a picture of then current Modern Language teaching practice in higher education by means of a 24-page questionnaire administered to some 600 students. On the basis of replies to this questionnaire, Meara (1993, 1994a, 1994b) profiles the model Modern Language student as typically female, spending some three hours a week attending language classes (largely translation), four hours a week attending lectures given in English, two hours each in reading and writing the foreign language and in talking in the foreign language with a native speaker. Disturbing discrepancies were found between the views of students and their teachers as to what were the most important skills to be acquired in a Modern Languages degree course and students appeared to be somewhat complacent with regard to their own abilities in comparison with what they regarded as the ideal. The Enquiry's findings with regard to the 'year abroad' supplements those of Willis *et al.* (1977) and Dyson (1988), suggesting that the listening and speaking skills of students improve more markedly than those of reading and writing, that many students were left largely to their own devices during the period of residence abroad and that students regarded work placements as more profitable than study placements.

Other studies of Modern Language teaching in higher education include those of Evans (1988), of Nott (1990) who reports the changing nature of Modern Language degree courses and the employment destinations of language graduates, of Bayley (1994) who produces a comprehensive account of changing approaches to the teaching of Literature in Modern Language courses at British universities, and Barro and Grimm (1993) who describe an interesting three-year development project at Thames Valley University to integrate language learning and cultural studies in higher education. Most recently, Coleman (1994) has undertaken large-scale student surveys which reveal disturbing differences of attainment between students at different universities and, perhaps even more disturbing, the fact that language students returning from a year's residence abroad are less well disposed towards the inhabitants of the country visited than they were before their departure.

The language needs of industry and commerce have also been subject to funded surveys and a range of other investigations. An early study by Emmans, Hawkins and Westoby (1974) established the relatively greater importance in an employment situation of the skills of listening, speaking and reading rather than writing, as well as the low priority attached to language skills by British employers when making senior appointments.

More recently, Hagen (1988) reports 13 regional surveys of language use in some 5,000 British companies establishing the clear link between language skills and export performance, as well as demonstrating the particularly acute need for employees capable of operating in German and Japanese. Hagen (1992) also reports the findings of studies of Dutch and German firms, pointing to the increasing internationalisation of the everyday working environment both abroad and in Britain, and the extent to which British firms and British employees are losing out because of their lack of language skills. Following a small interview-based study of firms in the Sheffield area, Clowes (1994) notes an encouraging level of awareness of the increasing need for language skills in the future combined (or so it would seem from his conclusions) with a remarkable failure to understand what schools can reasonably be asked to deliver.

ROLES OF THE CENTRE FOR INFORMATION ON LANGUAGE TEACHING AND RESEARCH (CILT) AND THE ASSOCIATION FOR LANGUAGE LEARNING (ALL)

For many years CILT has supported research in Modern Language teaching by maintaining an extensive library of language teaching materials, journals and other publications. While continuing to support research, however, the Centre's major activity currently lies in the direction of disseminating the outcomes of research and producing other publications supportive of good practice. In the 1970s, the Centre collaborated with the BBC in the production of four television programmes, which were widely recorded and used in initial and in-service training, explaining the rationale and techniques of the graded objectives movement. More recently its video *In Focus* (Bromidge and Burch, 1993) is proving valuable in disseminating techniques for increasing the use of the target language in the classroom. In addition to publishing the Pathfinder guides to good practice in the secondary language classroom, CILT publishes language teaching information compendia, works on technology in language learning, on English as a Second Language and on the Community Languages. CILT also publishes a series of books on Applied Linguistics with the British Association of Applied Linguistics.

The ALL, in addition to its role in speaking for language teachers on matters of national policy, supporting a network of local branches, providing in-service training and undertaking a number of Modern Language publishing ventures, also organises an annual conference and publishes the *Language Learning Journal* and a range of other journals which are language specific. Both conference and journals provide outlets for views, information and reports of language teaching research. The Association's annual conference may attract upwards of 1,500 participants and the *Language Learning Journal* is received by all 6,000 of the Association's members as well as university libraries and many other readers world-wide. The Association is, therefore, the channel by means of which the results of much highly practical, often small-scale, classroom-based language teaching research is communicated to teachers.

As a matter of editorial policy the *Language Learning Journal* encourages classroom practitioners' own reports of innovative teaching approaches as well as reports of research of more rigorous kinds. In fact, however, articles which at first sight may appear to be simple narratives of an individual teacher's personal practice often merit the status of serious, if small-scale, developmental studies. Frequently, these will arise from careful, thoughtful and theoretically well-conceived efforts to overcome a particular long-standing problem or to incorporate a new development into on-going practice. In certain cases the developments described may have received material support from the institutions in which they have taken place or be the result of sustained co-operation between secondary schools and departments of education.

Well-represented topics for such small-scale research have been the teaching of the four language skills of listening (McColl, 1992a), speaking (Chambers and Richards, 1992; McColl, 1992b; Ducroquet, 1991), reading (Grenfell, 1992; Klapper, 1992a, 1992b, 1993) and writing (Atkinson, 1992; Morgan, 1994), the development and use of computer-assisted language learning (White and Wacha, 1992; Higham and Morris 1993; Bourne 1993), the teaching of foreign languages to the less able and those with special needs (Chambers, 1993; Chambers and Cawthorn, 1993; McKenna,1994) and initiatives in teacher training and retraining (B. Jones, 1993; M. G. Jones, 1994a).

Rigorous and scholarly desk studies have included contributions to topical language learning debates such as the use of the target language in teaching (Atkinson, 1993; M.G. Jones, 1994 and Hamilton, 1994) and testing (Page, 1993; Woods and Neather, 1994), the teaching of literature in Modern Language courses (Chambers, 1991; Hambrook, 1993) and the teaching of grammar (Adamson, 1990; Heafford, 1993; Hood, 1994). Studies of developments abroad have been produced by Khruslov (1993), Yao (1993) and Cunningham (1994), and detailed research in less widely taught languages by Plascencia (1992), Ajiboye (1992) and Cook (1994). In addition to studies mentioned earlier, notable experimental and questionnaire research is reported by Aplin (1991) on the reasons given by sixth formers for not continuing with the study of Languages, Adamson (1993) on the use of the target language in the primary classroom and Ollerenshaw (1994) on the teaching of Hindi and its effects on learner attitudes. Ducroquet (1994) has produced a devastating analysis of the shortcomings of a number of standard bilingual dictionaries.

In addition to supporting language teaching journals and national and regional conferences the ALL is also participating along with 11 other national language associations in a major European Union project in the field of in-service teacher education. This three-year project ('Formation Autonome des Professeurs des Langues Vivantes lors de Séjours dans des Institutions Scolaires à l'Etranger') will develop procedures and learning support materials to enable teachers to benefit in a rigorous and structured way from individual visits to colleagues in other European countries. Draft learning materials developed and tried out to date concern general matters of language pedagogy, differences of classroom discourse between the teacher's own country and the country visited, differences of school culture and the cultural content of language courses. It is expected that some 150 language teachers will visit educational institutions in other European countries during 1994–96. The project, directed by Michel Candélier of the Université René Descartes in Paris, has received some 100,000 ECU for the first two years. Publication of the project's findings and a dissemination conference are envisaged for autumn 1996.

CONCLUSION

We have discussed the theoretical roots of the prevailing paradigm of language teaching, and the processes by which the results of fundamental research in linguistics and language acquisition theory have impinged upon practising teachers of Modern Foreign Languages. We have also seen how other, potentially fertile lines of enquiry have been temporarily eclipsed by emphasis on so-called communicative approaches. Currently, much of the work on foreign language teaching being read by language teachers is of a prescriptive or directly guiding nature, aimed at supporting teachers in meeting the requirements of the National Curriculum and reflecting, in the main, the inspiration and practical experience of its writers rather than rigorous research. With the partial exception of work by Byram and his associates in the field of languages and cultural studies, funded research in foreign language teaching in Britain has tended to be survey-based and policy-driven, relating to such matters as language diversification, policy implementation, developments, student experience and achievement in higher education and the language needs of industry. We have also discussed the role of CILT and that of the ALL in disseminating and supporting development and research.

As regards the future, it is cautiously predicted that at least as far as those closely connected with the practical business of language teaching in Britain are concerned, we are in for a sustained period of normal science. It is unlikely that the utilitarian goal of effective communication will be dislodged from its central position in the immediate future and there are ample opportunities for detailed investigation into how this may most successfully be achieved. It is hoped, however, that we shall see a move away from emphasis on large-scale survey investigations which, though undoubtedly attractive to policy-makers and sponsoring bodies, offer teachers little in the way of imaginative or intellectual stimulation. Once teachers, teacher-trainers and others concerned with language teaching have overcome the intellectual paralysis induced by the perceived threatening nature of current educational and curriculum policies, it is to be hoped that researchers, including teachers-as-researchers, will turn their attention to more fundamental aspects of the language learning process or, indeed, of human communication itself. In this, as always, we may have much to learn from those concerned with second language teaching, including the teaching of English as a second language, world-wide.

REFERENCES

Adamson, R. (1990). 'Is there such a thing as communicative grammar?', *Language Learning Journal*, 2, pp. 25–7.
Adamson, R.(1993). 'What teachers say: language use in the primary classroom', *Language Learning Journal*, 8, pp. 8–11.
Ajiboye, T. (1994) 'Politeness marking in Yoruba and Yoruba learners of French', *Language Learning Journal*, 6, pp. 83–6.
Aplin, R. (1991). 'The ones who got away: the views of those who opt out of languages', *Language Learning Journal*, 4, pp. 2–4.
APU (1987). *Foreign Language Performance in Schools: Report on the 1985 Survey of French, German and Spanish*. London: Department of Education and Science.
Atkinson, D. (1993). 'Teaching in the target language: a problem in the current orthodoxy', *Language Learning Journal*, 8, pp. 2–5.
Atkinson, M. M. (1992) 'Formality and informality in the communicative classroom', *Language Learning Journal*, 5, pp. 6–7.
Austin, J. L. (1962). *How to do Things with Words*. Oxford: Oxford University Press.
Barro, A. and Grimm, H. (1993). 'Integrating language learning and Cultural Studies: an ethnographic approach to the year abroad', in Coleman, J. and Rouxville, A. (eds), *Integrating New Approaches*. London: CILT.
Bayley, S. (1994). 'Literature in the modern languages curriculum of British universities', *Language Learning Journal*, 9, pp. 41–5.
Bourne, R. (1993). 'Developing IT in Modern Languages', *Language Learning Journal*, 8, pp. 51–3.
Bromidge, W. and Burch, J. (1993). *In Focus* (Video and Teacher's Notes). London: CILT.
Buckby, M. and others (1981). *Graded Objectives and Tests for Modern Languages; an evaluation*. London: Schools Council.

— and others (1992). *Auto*. London: HarperCollins.

— and others (1993) *Solo*. London: HarperCollins.

Burstall, C. and others (1973). *Primary French in the Balance*. Windsor: NFER.

Buttjes, D. (1990). 'Teaching foreign languages and culture: social impact and political significance', *Language Learning Journal*, 2, pp. 53–7.

Byram, M. (1989). *Cultural Studies in Foreign Language Education*. Clevedon, PA: Multilingual Matters.

— and Esarte-Sarries, V. (1990). *Investigating Cultural Studies in Language Teaching*. Clevedon, PA: Multilingual Matters.

—, Esarte-Sarries, V. and Taylor, S. (1991). *Cultural Studies and Language Learning*. Clevedon, PA: Multilingual Matters.

Cain, A. (1990) 'French secondary school students' perceptions of foreign cultures', *Language Learning Journal*, 2, pp. 48–52.

Cawthorn, I. and Chambers, G. (1993). 'The special needs of the deaf foreign language learner', *Language Learning Journal*, 7, pp. 47–9.

Chambers, F. and Richards, B. (1992). 'Criteria for oral assessment', *Language Learning Journal*, 6, pp. 5–9.

Chambers, G. (1991). 'Suggested approaches to A level Literature', *Language Learning Journal*, 4, 5–9.

— (1993) 'Taking the "de" out of demotivation', *Language Learning Journal*, 7, pp. 13–16.

Chomsky, N. (1965). *Aspects of a Theory of Syntax*. Cambridge, MA: MIT Press.

Clowes, P. (1994) 'What *are* the language needs of industry?' *Language Learning Journal*, 9, pp. 22–5.

Coleman, J. (1994). 'Degrees of proficiency: assessing the progress and achievement of university language learners', *French Studies Bulletin*, 50, pp. 11–15.

Cook, M. (1994). 'Pitfalls in the teaching of a lesser taught language', *Language Learning Journal*, 9, pp. 66–7.

Corder, S. P. (1981). *Error Analysis and Interlanguage*. Oxford: Oxford University Press.

Cunningham, D. (1994). 'Continuity in LOTE curriculum and methodology', *Language Learning Journal*, 10, pp. 69–74.

Ducroquet, L. (1991). 'Role-play: an assessment', *Language Learning Journal*, 3, pp. 49–50.

— (1994) 'Are bilingual dictionaries useful tools?', *Language Learning Journal*, 9, pp. 48–51.

Dyson, P. (1988). *The Year Abroad*. London: Central Bureau for Educational Visits and Exchanges.

Emmans, K., Hawkins, E. and Westoby, A. (1974). *The Use of Foreign Languages in the Private Sector of Industry and Commerce*. York: University Language Centre.

Evans, C. H. (1988). *Language People: the Experience of Teaching and Learning Modern Languages in British Universities*. Milton Keynes: Open University Press.

Fakuade,G. (1991). 'Stress and intonation in Jukun and English: implications for English as a second language', *Language Learning Journal*, 3, pp. 81–3.

Filmer-Sankey, C, (1993) 'OXPROD: a summative account', *Language Learning Journal*, 7, pp. 5–8.

Gardner, R. C. and Lambert, W. E. (1972). *Attitudes and Motivation in Second Language Learning*. Rowley, MA: Newbury House.

Goodman-Stevens, B. Rogers, P. and Briggs, L. (1989). *Zickzack*, Walton-on-Thames: Nelson.

Green, P. S. (ed.) (1975). *The Language Laboratory in School*. London: Oliver & Boyd.

Grenfell, M. (1992). 'Process reading in the communicative classroom', *Language Learning Journal*, 6, pp. 48–52.

Gruneberg, M. and Jacobs, G. C. (1991). 'In defense of Linkword', *Language Learning Journal*, 3, pp. 25–9.

Gruneberg, M. and Sykes, R. (1991) 'Individual differences and attitudes to the Keyword method of foreign language learning', *Language Learning Journal*, 4, pp. 60–2.

Hadley, C. G. (ed.) (1981). *Languages Other than French in the Secondary School*. London: Schools Council.

Hagen, S. (1992). 'Language policy and strategy issues in the new Europe', *Language Learning Journal*, 5, pp. 31–4.

— (ed.) (1988). *Languages in British Business*. Newcastle-upon-Tyne and London: Newcastle-upon-Tyne Polytechnic and CILT.

Hambrook, G. (1994). 'Language learning and literary studies', *Language Learning Journal*, 9, pp. 46–7.

Hamers, J. F. and Blanc, M. H. A. (1989). *Bilinguality and Bilingualism*. Cambridge: Cambridge University Press.

Hamilton, J. (1994). 'Using the target language: from Pilton to Tokyo; a journey through the earth's crust', *Language Learning Journal*, 10, pp. 16–18.

Harding, A. and Naylor, J.-A. (1979). 'Graded objectives in second language learning: a way ahead', *Audio-Visual Language Journal*, 17/3, pp. 169–74.

Harding, A. and Page, B. (1974). 'An alternative model of Modern Language language examinations', *Audio-Visual Language Journal*, 12/3, pp. 237–41.

Harding, A., Page, B., and Rowell, S. (1980). *Graded Objectives in Modern Languages*. London: CILT.

Heafford, M. (1993). 'What is grammar/ Who is she?' *Language Learning Journal*, 7, pp. 55–8.

Higham, J. and Morris, D. (1993). 'Developing information technology through in-service and initial teacher education: a hypercard project', *Language Learning Journal*, 7, pp. 31–5.

HMI (1977). *Modern Languages in Comprehensive Schools*. London: HMSO.

HMI (1987). *Modern Foreign Languages*. London: HMSO.

Hymes, D. (1972).'On communicative competence', in Pride, J. B. and Holmes, J. (eds), *Sociolinguistics: selected readings*. Harmondsworth: Penguin.

Jenkins, J. and Jones, B. (1991). *Spirale*. London: Hodder & Stoughton

Johnstone, R. (1989). *Communicative Interaction: a Guide for Language Teachers*. London: CILT.

Jones, B. (1993). 'Return to Modern Language teaching?: a returners' course', *Language Learning Journal*, 8, pp. 74–6.

Jones, M. G. (1994b). 'Tower of Babel or English unlimited?' *Language Learning Journal*, 10, pp. 28–31.

Jones, M.G. (1994a). Retraining French teachers: a North Wales case study', *Language Learning Journal*, 9, pp. 57–9.

Klapper, J. (1992a). 'Reading in a foreign language: theoretical issues', *Language Learning Journal*, 5, pp. 27–30.

— (1992b). 'Preliminary considerations for the teaching of foreign language reading', *Language Learning Journal*, 6, pp. 53–6.

— (1993). 'Practicable skills and practical constraints in foreign language reading', *Language Learning Journal*, 7, pp. 50–4.

Klippel, F. (1990). 'From nursery rhymes to TV documentaries', *Language Learning Journal*, 1, pp. 58–62.

Kramer, J. (1990). 'Teaching the cultural, historical and intercultural to advanced language learners', *Language Learning Journal*, 2, pp. 58–61.

Krashen, S. D. (1987). *Principles and Practice in Second Language Acquisition*. Englewood Cliffs NJ: Prentice Hall.

McColl, H. (1992a). 'Listening skills and the hearing impaired child', *Language Learning Journal*, 6, pp. 41–2.

— (1992b). 'Achieving student autonomy in speaking through the use of video', *Language Learning Journal* 5, pp. 25–6.

McDonough, S. H. (1981). *Psychology in Foreign Language Teaching*. London: Allen & Unwin.

McKenna, N. (1994). 'Setting off: holiday French in a school for pupils with special needs', *Language Learning Journal*, 10, pp. 42–42.

McLaughlin, B. (1987). *Theories of Second Learning*. London: Hodder & Stoughton.

Meara, P. (1993). 'What do students do on a language course?' *Language Learning Journal*, 8, pp. 26–31.

— (1994a). 'What should language students be able to do?' *Language Learning Journal*, 9, pp. 36–40.

— (1994b). 'The year abroad and its effects', *Language Learning Journal*, 10, pp. 32–8.

Mellor, J. and Stafford, J. (1994). 'National curriculum in modern foreign languages – the first year of implementation: the ALL survey', *Language Learning Journal*, 10, pp. 2–5.

Mitchell, R. (1988). *Communicative Language Teaching in Practice*, London: CILT.

Morgan, C. (1994). 'Creative writing in foreign language teaching', *Language Learning Journal*, 10, pp. 44–7.

Munby, J. (1978). *Communicative Syllabus Design*. Cambridge: Cambridge University Press.

Nott, D. (1990). 'Modern languages in higher education', *Language Learning Journal*, 1, pp. 44–7.

Ollerenshaw, J. L. (1994). 'Learning Hindi as a taster language: a study of pupils' change in attitudes', *Language Learning Journal*, 10, pp. 58–63.

Page, B. (1979) 'Notions, functions and threshold levels: a review of the significance for language teachers of the work of the Council of Europe', *Audio-Visual Language Journal*, 17, 2, pp. 115–22.

— (1993). 'The target language and examinations', *Language Learning Journal*, 8, pp. 6–7.

Peck, A. (1976). 'Functional-notional syllabuses and their importance for defining levels of linguistic proficiency', *Audio-Visual Language Journal*, 14/2, pp. 95–106

Phillips, D. and Filmer-Sankey, C. (1993). *Diversification in Modern Language Teaching*. London: Routledge.

Plascencia, M. (1992). 'Politeness in mediated telpephone conversations in Ecuadorian Spanish and British English', *Language Learning Journal*, 6, pp. 80–2.

Rees, F. (1989). *Languages for a Change*. Windsor: NFER-Nelson.

Saussure, F. de (1949). *Cours de Linguistique Générale*. Paris: Payot.

Searle, J. R. (1969). *Speech Acts: An Essay in the Philosophy of Language*. Cambridge: Cambridge University Press.

Selinker, L. (1992). *Rediscovering Interlanguage*. Harlow: Longman.

Taylor, G. and Edwards, D. (1992). *Etoiles*. London and Harlow: BBC Enterprises and Longman.

Van Ek, J. A. and others (1973). *Systems Development in Adult Language Learning*. Strasbourg: Council of Europe.

White, C. and Wacha, H. (1992). 'Information technology and Modern Languages', *Language Learning Journal*, 5, pp. 40–3.

Willis, F. and others (1977). *Residence Abroad and the Student of Modern Languages*, Bradford, University Language Centre.

Winter, R. (1982). 'The Effectiveness of the Language Laboratory in Mixed Ability Teaching in Schools', University of Sheffield, unpublished PhD. thesis.

Wittgenstein, L. (1953). *Philosophical Investigations*. Oxford: Blackwell.

Woods, C. and Neather, T. (1994). 'Target language testing in KS4 examinations', *Language Learning Journal*, 10, pp. 19–21.

Yao, X. (1993). 'Foreign languages in Chinese education', *Language Learning Journal*, 7, pp. 74–7.

10

EDUCATION POLICY

Stewart Ranson

INTRODUCTION

The Conservative government's radical reconstruction of education since the late 1980s has been designed not only to improve 'a service' but also to play a central role in the wider reform of the polity. The post-war world constituted a political order of *social democracy* based upon the principles of justice and equality of opportunity and designed to ameliorate class disadvantage and class division. Public goods were conceived as requiring collective choice and action. Thus the significance of *systems* of administrative planning (the LEA) and institutional organisation (the comprehensive school). Now these beliefs are called into question. A new political order of *neo-liberal consumer democracy* is being constituted, based upon different principles of rights and *choice* designed to enhance the agency of the individual. The public (as consumer) is being empowered at the expense of the (professional) provider. Public goods are conceived as aggregated private choices. Individual (negative) freedom will, it is purported, better deliver the goals of opportunity and social change. These political purposes have been invested in a programme of policy formation and legislative implementation as extensive as anything seen for a generation.The policy agenda has embraced the creation of markets and the differentiation of governance, consumer choice and participation, devolved institutional management, and a national curriculum.

This reform agenda created an extraordinary opportunity for the education research community to study changes to the service over time. Researchers could investigate theoretical perspectives and explore a variety of methodological approaches to empirical work and data analysis. This opportunity has been seized and by the mid-1990s a vast literature now exists on the impact of the ERA (Education Reform Act, 1988) agenda on education. A number of volumes have begun to appear on how education researchers approached the theoretical, methodological and ethical issues involved in studying the ERA (Finch, 1986; Burgess, 1989; Walford, 1991, 1994; Halpin and Troyna, 1994).

This chapter focuses upon one significant debate which has preoccupied education researchers: theorising the nature of education policy. The debate has increasingly become a dispute between pluralists and Marxists and their different theoretical analyses of the role of the state in education policy and its reform. This chapter charts the main lineages of the discourse within this field since the 1970s; argues for a framework of analysis that seeks to dissolve some of the differences between pluralism and Marxism; and concludes by arguing for a radical redirection of the field, encouraging theorists to draw upon political theory as well as political sociology in order to focus upon the role of public policy in establishing the purposes and conditions of democracy in the learning society.

THE CHANGING TRADITIONS OF EDUCATION POLICY ANALYSIS

There have been two cycles of the debate between pluralism and Marxism over the theoretical direction of education policy analysis. The first took place in the 1980s with neo-Marxists questioning the taken-for-granted assumptions of 'partnership' in the governance of education and criticising the inadequacies of the dominant pluralist framework; and the second occurs in the 1990s with a new phase of theoretical and critical pluralism contesting the limitations of a narrow state control model for theorising the complexities of New Right education policies. The discussion begins by establishing the characteristics of the pluralist tradition which dominated the field for much of the post-war period until the mid-1970s.

1. Post-War Partnership, Pluralism and Public Administration

Education became the key-stone of public policy making during the post-war period. A broad social and political consensus supported the role of education in enabling economic growth, equality of opportunity and social justice. A rising birth rate, economic growth and, most importantly, political will for social reform, coalesced in the expansion of education. During the 1960s and early 1970s the service enjoyed a period of unrivalled growth and privilege. Education policy focused upon the fundamental change of introducing comprehensive schools in place of a tripartite school system which selected and excluded the majority of young people.

The system of education governance constituted by the 1944 Education

Act provided an appropriate framework to support the growth of a service committed to the expansion of opportunity. The 1944 Act was not without its contradictions and ambiguities. Such creative ambivalence was intrinsic to a settlement which sought to systematise yet divide powers and responsibilities between partners to the service. The Act sought to establish a national education service, led by strong central government, and therefore created for the first time a Minister of Education ostensibly with absolute powers. The previous President of the Board of Education merely had 'superintendence of matters relating to education', but the 1944 Act installed a Minister who was: 'to promote the education of the people of England and Wales and the progressive development of institutions devoted to that purpose and to secure the effective executive by local authorities *under his control and direction* of the national policy...' (Section 1, 1944 Act: my italics). Nevertheless, despite the manifest policy of strengthening the central authority, the 1944 Act provided the Minister with only limited and specific powers. The newly constituted Local Education Authority had wide-ranging responsibilities and powers to provide education in order to develop their local schools and communities. But just as the Minister of Education was not provided with direct control of the LEA, so they in turn were deprived of absolute direction of their schools and colleges. Institutions were given a quasi-autonomous status under the general guidance of a governing or managing body.

By creating two strong authorities – central and local government – responsible for the provision of education and by leaving it unclear as to the nature of the relationship between them, the Act was implying that they would have to work together: and both with a third interest – the teachers. The key tasks, therefore, of winning resources, of planning and providing institutions, and of developing curriculum and teaching methods came to be divided between three of the critical partners to the service: the centre, locality and institutions; between ministers, councillors and teachers. The 1944 Act thus created a 'complex web of interdependent relationships among the manifold participants' (Weaver, 1976). Whitehall was to promote education, town and county hall were to plan and provide, and teachers were to nurture the learning process so as to meet the needs of children and the wishes of parents. The constitutive system of the government of education formed a complex, 'polycentred' division of power and responsibility appropriate to differentiated tasks. Power was diffused between the partners. The upshot is what Briault (1976) has called a 'distributed' system of decision taking and responsibility, so as to form a 'triangle of tension' of checks and balances. Emphasis was given to the value and spirit of partnership. Celebrating a jubilee of the creation of a centralised department, the Ministry stressed the importance of 'the progressive partnership between the central department, the local education authorities and the teachers'. The Secretary to the Association of Education Committees, Sir William Alexander, affirmed the significance of smooth and flexible partnership in education.

This account of the distribution of power between centres of decision-making, each of which experienced significant autonomy and control of resources, illustrates a *pluralist* perspective on governance and the state. As Alford and Friedland (1985) describe, the pluralist state is a highly differentiated mosaic accessible to influence of voters and diverse groups which compete for influence governmental decisions. At the level of society, a consensual value system defines the boundaries of state action.

The Dominance of Public Administration

The work of educational policy analysts focused in the main upon careful description and discussion of the emerging framework of education government and policy formation. The roles and responsibilities within the structure of education government were carefully described (Kogan, 1971, on the system of government; Weaver, 1979, on the Central Department; Regan, 1974 and Jennings, 1977, on local government; Weaver, 1976, Briault, 1976, Griffith, 1966, Fowler *et al.*, 1973 and Bogdanor, 1979, on the relations between central and local government; Baron and Howell, 1974, on school governance). The implementation of comprehensive reorganisation was closely monitored (Fenwick, 1976; Fenwick and McBride; Ribbins and Brown, 1979; Pattison, 1980; James, 1980), and the relations between teachers, local authorities and central government (Coates, 1972; Saran, 1973).

The best work in the public administration tradition has never been merely descriptive. Studies would seek to analyse the effectiveness of public policy by examining the internal consistency of public policy, or the rationality of the way legal rules were administered, or the appropriateness of the means chosen to implement the determining values of the polity. The potential tensions within public policy-making would become the focus of analysis. Thus for Kogan (1971) the values and chosen purposes decide the nature of the educational task, as well as the appropriate allocation of responsibility and distribution of authority: 'The ways in which different countries govern their education thus relate to the philosophies and practices predominant in their schools. Organisation relates to the tasks to be performed and to concepts of how the tasks can best be performed' (p. 12). Choice about the purposes and institutional arrangements of education will express the values and political culture of a society in its historical setting. Public administration was typically sensitive to values and the normative order which shaped government and public policy.

Kogan's work (1975, 1978, 1979, 1985) has always had a conceptual and analytical rigour which made him the leading authority on the government and politics of education policy within the public administration tradition. He eschews theoretical model building yet his work is informed by the literatures of policy analysis and decision-making. His approach to understanding education policy is to chart the historical development of policy, grasp the context of changing values, to map the 'interest groups' and their relationship to policy formation. Institutions have a distinctive place in according continuity and legitimacy to policy development. The system of education is regarded as pluralistic 'inasmuch as authority and power are distributed among well defined institutions at different levels such as the DES, local authorities and schools and colleges' (1975, p. 231). Furthermore, 'any single policy takes on multiple guises and is viewed differently at many points of a complex system' (p. 238). To this complexity is added a sophisticated grasp of the way 'non-decision making' and 'disjointed incrementalism' erode the formal rationality of policy formation.

This framework, when applied to the unfolding system of post war education, produced an analysis of a strong institutional fabric that encouraged the interaction of levels of government and which worked according to consensual assumptions. The framework implied mutual orientation to negotiate different interests within a shared national system of education. The policy process 'sanctioned changes....not so much through a rational process in which all needs were pursued consistently and needs clarified but were, instead, caused by a few political leaders and permanent officials reacting at the centre and within local authorities to a wider system of interest and pressure and imposing rationality later' (1975, p. 24). Kogan concluded his study of policy-making by emphasising the untidiness of the policy system: 'pluralistic, incremental, unsystematic, reactive'. While such a pluralistic system had produced excellent innovations Kogan believed it could be vulnerable to poor decision-making:

> It is difficult to see where in the system where in the system any policy maker can ever be challenged effectively. It is not clear how aggregation of practice takes place. Local examples of good practice ... are not well mediated. The DES denies it has power to aggregate or lead, yet it plainly does so. So we have a situation in which power is not explicit, in which criticism and discontent have no clear outlet and in which parental opinion still has no way into the system. Effective public review is non-existent (Kogan, 1975, p. 238).

While Kogan stressed the pluralism of education he resisted attributing the idea of 'partnership' to the system of governance because that implied there was equality between the different interests. Power is distributed but enevenly. Kogan's anxiety was that within such a fragmented system the

DES wielded 'determinant authority and great power', but that the ideals of democratic and pluralistic governance required more than that. If the systems guiding values of pluralism were to be realised then further change and reform would be necessary.

Pluralist Explanations of Governance and Policy
The best tradition of public administration contributed sophisticated conceptual analysis of the institutional forms of government and policy-making. Yet a younger generation became more critical. Dunleavy (1982) believed the tradition of public administration focused pre-eminently on

> the institutions, organizational structures and decision/implementation processes of government. It is largely a 'formal' field, concerned with arrangements and procedures for making decisions, rather than with the substance or impacts of these decisions. It is also a relatively micro-level subject, often concerned with description rather than with macro-themes or large-scale theorising. Finally it is an area of study which is largely 'applied' and closely linked with practical problems and practical solutions; it is or should be concerned with 'administration in the sense which is synonymous with organising, managing or just 'getting things done' (Dunleavy, 1982, p. 215).

Public administration typically lacked theoretical analysis that would enable explanation rather than description of the way government was organised and decisions taken. Some researchers within this tradition sought to fill this vacuum and began to draw upon theoretical models that were appropriate to the prevailing understandings of a devolved and distributed system of governance. The theoretical model of exchange and power (known as the resource dependency theory) had acquired much analytical status and leverage in the study of organisations and inter-organisational relations (cf. Aldrich, 1976, 1979; Benson, 1975; Aiken and Hage, 1978; Pfeffer and Salancik, 1978). It derived primarily from American studies into the problems of achieving co-ordination among social welfare organisations, employment service agencies, community organisations, etc. But the theoretical developments in the model allowed greater empirical range, particularly into inter-governmental relations (cf. Crozier and Thoenig, 1976; Hanf and Scharpf, 1978). The resource dependency model was adopted by the Social Science Research Council (as the Economic and Social Research Council was then known) to form a framework for a series of studies they have commissioned to examine relations between central and local government (cf. Rhodes, 1981, 1988; Jones, 1980). A number of applications of the model were made to education including Ranson (1980; 1990), Salter and Tapper (1981), McPherson and Raab (1988); Loughlin

(1986) and Rhodes (1988). The outstanding application of the model was developed by Archer (1979; 1981).

The theory, based on concepts of interest exchange and power, conceives the relations between levels of government as forming a complex network of organisations, agencies and interest groups. These 'actors' live in an environment of uncertainty produced by the scarcity of resources necessary to ensure survival. They can pursue their interests and acquire the strategic resources necessary for managing uncertainty only by escaping or creating dependencies amongst the other actors. Autonomy and power provide the critical bargaining levers to manipulate exchange relationships in the network. The operation of the network is shaped by the pattern of resource ownership and the structure of dependencies. The powerful actor can win more resources and so ensure the delivery of its services, implement its policies as well as protect and extend the boundaries of its influence and domination. Resources are defined broadly, for example, as finance or authority or information. To monopolise the ownership of such critical resources is to create dependencies, exact compliance and accrue power. Blau (1964) sought to articulate the conditions which actors must meet if they are to maximise autonomy and bargaining power in an exchange relationship. First, possess strategic resources which others may desire; second, ensure that these resources are scarce and unavailable elsewhere; third, have the capacity to use coercive sanctions if necessary; and, lastly, be indifferent to the resources possessed by other actors.

Here is a plausible theoretical framework which can account for the changes in the governance of post-war education. Actors who monopolise resources that are critical to the network accrue power, ensure the compliance of others and survive. It specifies an abstract comparative model and, in the hands of a few (notably Archer), possesses an historical dimension. An underlying social mechanism of competitive self-interest constrained by power relations has been exposed in a way which lends order to, and makes causal sense of, complex everyday experience. Yet, there are deficiencies in such a theoretical framework; a number of its assumptions are problematic. The first is the *assumption about the nature of the actors*. The framework is shaped by its cultural source: American studies of co-ordination problems among competing welfare agencies, etc. The organisations being studied were relatively equal. Such assumptions are inappropriate when the focus becomes the relationships between the state and other organisations: the relationship is different in kind. Second, a different understanding of the actors involved would undermine the *assumptions of exchange*. All actors, it is supposed, have the possibility of renegotiating their position with a little shrewd politicking. Such assumptions will not do. Transactions with the state are by definition likely to be unequal and as a last resort it will usually find the powers and resources to win most games. Third, the *assumptions about the notion of meaning* are arguable. The orientations of actors as defined solely by sectional interests and the purposive pursuit of resources and autonomy is too limiting. Values and beliefs (cf. Evetts, 1973; Taylor, 1978; Kogan and Becher, 1980) are not subordinate epiphenomena and may tie the network of actors together in a domain consensus, thus undermining the basic assumption in this model of competitive, instrumental, rationality. Finally, the *assumptions about the environment* are equally limiting theoretically. The significant environment, so the argument goes, is only made up of other 'organised' actors but this may be begging the question as to what are the significant features of the environment: what of deeper seated functional dilemmas surrounding, for example, the economy, or what of the significance of more amorphous interests (of social class) that lie behind 'the actors' typically considered?

The resource dependency theory is a plausible theoretical framework. But the social mechanisms it unearths are situated quite close to the surface. The analysis it reveals of purposively interested actors is close to our experience. The explanation is close to being a good story. This theoretical account may require supplementing and rounding out, if not recasting.

2. Steering Crises, the State and Neo-Marxist Theory

With the deepening economic crises of the 1970s the state, increasingly preoccupied with the 'steering problems' created, has progressively extended its boundaries of political leverage to control economic and social subsystems. The extension of steering capacity, however, presupposed the emergence of new modes of rationality, 'new technically utilisable knowledge about subsystems' and their operation (Blau and Schoenherr, 1971; Offe, 1975; Habermas, 1976) to ensure detailed planning and control of public service. Education was at the centre of strategies of control and reproduction of the skills and dispositions which the system requires. Bourdieu and Passeron (1977) argued that education, though possessing relative independence from the economy, played a critical role in reproducing the 'cultural capital' necessary for maintaining the structure and relations of the economic system. Bernstein (1975) equally suggested that the mode of production was anterior to the mode of education and that the stronger the systemic relations between the two the stronger the grip of the modes of production on the codes of education.

The Neo-Marxist Critique of Pluralism
The accelerating centralisation of the state from the mid 1970s led a number of education policy analysts (particularly Dale and Ozga) to attack not only

the appropriateness of pluralism for an understanding of this restructuring but, building on the work of CCCS (1981) and Simon (1965; 1974), its inherent limitations for any adequate analysis of education because of its neglect of state power in policy making and implementation.

Ozga (1987; 1990) and then in collaboration with Gewirtz (Gewirtz and Ozga, 1990; Ozga and Gewirtz, 1994) have developed a critical analysis of those studies which have developed a pluralist interpretation of the historical origins and legal construction of the post-war government of education as a partnership. Such studies have typically sought to contrast the emerging *dirigiste* style of Thatcherite education policy-making with the earlier commitment to 'negotiation, bargaining and consensus'. This position, Gewirtz and Ozga argue, exaggerates the differences between past and present so as to reinforce 'concentration on short-term and superficial explanations of change in education policy-making':

> Our argument is that we need to re-examine partnership and pluralism, not simply with the intention of achieving a better understanding of the past, but in order to arrive at a clearer assessment of what has, and has not changed fundamentally in education policy-making in more recent years (Gewirtz and Ozga, 1990, p. 37).

Their intention is to replace 'pluralism as the dominant theoretical approach to the study of education policy-making in the UK and to argue the case for a more state-centred, historically-grounded approach' (1990, p. 37). They have built upon the work of Dale (1982; 1983; 1986; 1989; 1992a/b; 1994) who, like them, attacked the study of 'education politics' as well as the major approaches to the sociology of education ('structural functionalist', 'the new sociology of education', and 'the political economy of education') for marginalising the role of the state in the system of education. A focus upon the state will provide neglected *explanations* both of patterns of provision and the sources of change. The state, Dale argues, addresses three core problems of capitalist societies: 'support of the capital accumulation process; guaranteeing a context for its continued expansion; and the legitimation of the capitalist mode of production, including the State's own part in it' (1982 p. 133). Essential to an understanding of the working of the state is a recognition of the chronic internal contradictions between these core problems, in particular, the tension between the demand to use 'surplus value' to enhance accumulation or to increase spending on 'non-commodity' welfare services such as education. How the state specifies the problems or chooses the means to resolve the contradictions it faces together with its imperfect knowledge to realise its objectives, reveal 'the relative autonomy of the education state apparatus'. What can be achieved through education, however, 'is constrained not only by the problems confronting it but also by the nature of the apparatus for tackling them' (p. 140). Traditions of organisation operate to select particular issues and styles of decision making. Gewirtz and Ozga (1990) argue that the kind of modifications of the traditional Marxist approach, made by McLennan (1984) are relevant to the development of a more complex education policy analysis:

- the state does possess a degree of autonomy (relative autonomy) from the economy

- it may be capable of acting in its own interest (and not only as 'the executive of the bourgeoisie')

- the activities of the state are not limited to the furtherance of capitalism, these other activities may, indeed, temporarily interfere with its 'pro-capitalist' functions.

- the state has to address contradictory problems, and its solutions therefore generate further tensions and problems

- state policy is not simply imposed on a duped and quiescent population, but is resisted and sometimes modified in significant ways.

The work of Bourdieu (1977) and some of the work of Althusser (1971) are approved for their emphasis upon 'the mediated relationship between education and production' and the recognition of education 'as an autonomous region with its own distinct qualities, its own history, its particular ideological and political practices'.

Dale and Ozga (1991) have preferred to term their work neo-Marxist, distinguishing it from its classical form which, they argue, tends 'to reduce a very complicated process to a single dimension' (p.12) by treating politics as a mere effect of changes in the economic base. Rather 'state policy is not uncontestedly imposed on a duped and quiescent population, but is continually and sometimes successfully, resisted in various ways' (Gewirtz and Ozga, p. 40). Gewirtz and Ozga illustrate these complexities through recent work on teacher–state relations (Lawn, 1987; Lawn and Ozga, 1986; Ozga, 1989) which emphasises the strategic role of the state in managing the teaching force yet acknowledges the significance of teacher's action in causing the state, within specific political contexts, to adjust its policies. Thus, in response to the economic crisis of the 1860s and concern of teachers that working-class children should receive more than mere training, the state imposed 'direct rule'. Yet 'that period ended with the introduction of indirect rule when the colonial practice of allowing limited autonomy in exchange for good behaviour was translated into the education system through the appearance of decentralisation, the cultivation of local 'chiefs' and the fostering of 'licensed' teacher professionalism' (p. 40). This structure of power, they argue, was the 'progenitor of partnership' and serves to illustrate the 'unmanageable contradictions faced by the state in managing the education system'. Whereas 'direct rule' provokes opposition and inefficiency, indirect rule increases local autonomy which can generate alternative policies that counter the state's function of capital accumulation. In this analysis

> The 1944 Education Act is not...the cornerstone of partnership, but an attempt to win back control over the system which was politically problematic because of the raised level of post-war expectation. The '44 Act is centrist in character, but the previous period of indirect rule, together with the characteristics of the post-war period which favoured local resistance to control and placed the Ministry at a disadvantage, circumstances such as the need for a major building programme, allowed LEAs, and, to a certain extent teachers, to extend partnership beyond its co-optive, limited meanings (Gewirtz and Ozga, 1990, p. 41).

McPherson and Raab (1987) approve of this willingness to 'relax holistic, monocausal assumptions about the nature of social relations in the short and medium term, and to allow considerable explanatory autonomy to individual agency' (p. 12). However, they argue, that 'at the empirical level it is difficult to see how the resultant explanations differ from those that pluralism might offer'. Gewirtz and Ozga (1990, p. 41) retort that this is 'a significant and misleading elision of evidence and explanation. We may, indeed, be looking at similar, or even the same, evidence, our explanations remain very different.' The issue of the potential overlap between different perspectives will be returned to in the final section.

3. Neo-Pluralist Theorising of the New Right Restructuring of Education

Seeking to analyse the period from the 1970s to the late 1980s, focusing in particular upon the origins, construction and implementation of the 1988 Education Reform Act, Ball (1990) describes his approach as an exercise in 'contemporary history' and 'policy sociology'. Ball's recurring emphasis upon 'the complexity of recent education policy making' establishes the underlying presuppositions of his work. Reflecting his ethnographic background, the world he seeks to understand is messy and complex:

> policy-making in a modern, complex, plural society like Britain is unwieldy and complex. It is often unscientific and irrational, whatever the claims of the policy makers to the contrary. In particular, the 1988 Education Reform Act contains a number of shots in the dark, policies without pedigree (Ball, 1990, p. 3).

The challenge for the policy analyst is to 'retain (this) messiness and complexity and still be penetrating' (1990, p.9). Education policy studies can only realise this end by moving beyond both the traditional approach of 'commentary and critique', 'micro' ethnographies of policy implementation and, in particular, the simplicities of the classical Marxist model of the state with its assumptions of top-down, linear control in which 'policy... "gets done" to people by a chain of implementers whose roles are clearly defined by legislation' (Bowe and Ball with Gold, 1992, p. 7). This state control model of policy, it is argued, is hardly the best place to start to understand the complexities of the 1988 ERA. Ball prefers to develop theoretical and conceptual analysis that is 'best described as eclectic or pragmatic' (1990, p. 2):

> Abstract accounts tend towards tidy generalities and often fail to capture the messy realities of influence, pressure, dogma, expediency, conflict, compromise, intransigency, resistance, error, opposition and pragmatism in the policy process (1990, p.9).

Ball accomplishes this by developing what he is willing to term a 'Weberian neo pluralist' approach which faces up to the complexity of social forms: 'education is not simply a direct response to dominant interests' and is better understood with Shapiro (1980) '... not as reflecting the interests of one social class (commonly the industrial middle class), but as responding to a complex and heterogeneous configuration of elements (including ideologies that are residual or emergent, as well as currently dominant' (p. 328). Like Weber, Ball believes that any explanation of social forms must be adequate at the level of meaning and of cause. Thus Ball's theory embraces 'agency and the ideological category of the individual' (p.9) so that any explanation of education policy must involve analysing what 'individuals and groups actually do and say in the arenas of influence in which they move' (p.9). Yet Ball is willing to identify, beneath the complexity, underlying structural continuities:

> the role of representative institutions in social democratic politics is constrained and distorted by the obvious inequalities of power inherent in capitalism. We have a 'deformed polyarchy' (Dunleavy and O'Leary, 1987, p.287) wherein behind the facade of public politics, the state also responds, directly, immediately and sensitively to economic pressures from business, both those expressed in overt and latent use of economic muscle and the considerable presence of business influence inside the various input politics channels. (Ball, 1990, p. 2).

Ball seeks to deploy different theoretical strategies to make sense of the complex policy world he is studying, 'alternative interpretations and analyses of "the process" and "the case" are tried out for their adequacy' (p.2). Ball's different theoretical strategies are accommodated within an Althusserian framework which defines social systems in terms of their ideological, political and economic levels. Each level requires its own appropriate theoretical strategy. Thus the economic level requires a 'structural analysis' that will examine the contribution which education makes to productivity and therefore the relation of education to capital. The theoretical strategy appropriate to investigate the political level is 'realist/interactionist', involving analysis of the politics and governance of education and the changing interventions of influential groups and constituencies in the policy process. The ideological level of the appropriate form of investigation is a 'discursive' analysis of the ways in which education policy is conceived and discussed, and thus the way it is involved in the transmission of a dominant culture. Theory needs to analyse each level in its own terms as well as the nature of their interrelationships: 'Each level is a source and resource for education policy making: that is, each levels has effects in its own terms on the nature and possibility of policy' (p. 11). Change in education policy derives from the contradictions within and between the three levels.

Investigating the nature of the relationship between the three levels within education systems leads Ball into one of the frequently visited territories of social theory: the issue of autonomy and determination between parts of a social system, in particular the degree of economic determination of social forms. What is at stake, however, in this issue is the debate between pluralism and Marxism. Ball believes that the way of 'resolving (but not dissolving) the theoretical gap between pluralism and those of neo-Marxism which gives central place to the role of the state' (p. 13) lie, following Hargreaves (1983), Williams (1978) and Wright (1979), in understanding the issue of *relative autonomy* in terms of 'delimitation, as opposed to determination' (p.13). While economic structures set boundaries to ideological and political forms they constrain rather than pre-determine in any mechanistic manner how those forms develop. Thus education 'is not immediately and directly produced by these constraints (p. 14). There is, therefore, 'an important difference between recognising that there are boundaries to the possibility of structure and arguing that those possibilities are structurally pre-ordained' (p. 13). Ball believes that this distinction – between 'that which is possible' (what actually occurs), and 'the limits of the possible' (what is in effect impossible) – can be grounded empirically and thus provide the debate between the protagonists on education policy with some analytical weight. This analysis reaffirms Ball's neo-pluralism:

> Once one takes on board the ideas of autonomy, delimitation and agency then much of the tidiness offered by cruder versions of state theory is inevitably

lost. We must accept, again as Hargreaves (1983, p. 49) points out, 'Multicausal(ity), pluralistic conflict, administrative complexity and historical inertia' as having equal theoretical and conceptual relevance in understanding actual policy-making processes as does the logic and development of the capitalistic mode of production'. Conflicts and struggles about education may very well be based on or organised around all kinds of non-economic considerations – those of race, gender, religion and professional status, for instance. (Ball, 1990, pp. 14–15).

While this analysis establishes the prerequisite of theoretical complexity Ball is still left needing to explain change in education policy. The framework of structural limitation provides, he believes, only 'a weak version of change': 'it seemingly cannot tell us where change comes from, that is how the notion of what is appropriate, rather than possible, is established' (p.15). Change is theorised as deriving from the working of agency (the struggle and conflict between the projects and strategies of different interest groups to dominate the state) within 'the cracks, fissures, contradictions (p. 16) that appear within structural limits of social reproduction. The concepts of 'relative autonomy, agency, and delimitation' thus form the core framework for theorising education policy and its patterns of change.

This rather obscure theoretical formulation of change is helpfully remedied in analysis of the policy process. Ball's study with Bowe and Gold, *Reforming Education and Changing Schools: Case Studies in Policy Sociology* (1992), develops a thesis of a policy cycle that belies any simplistic, linear model of policy formulation and implementation and argues instead for an understanding of the complex mediation of policy. In three contexts – of influence, of policy text production, and of practice – it is proposed that at each stage of the cycle of formulation to practice policy is subject to complex determinations such that policy writers may be unable to control the meaning and implementation of their texts. Because of the gaps and contradictions within, the policy process allows the micro-political processes of struggle and influence at each stage 'to recontextualise' the meaning, implementation and practice of policy. The Technical and Vocational Education Initiative (TVEI) is the exemplar of this idea in which a top-down imposed policy 'was appropriated by the teaching profession for very different purposes to those intended by the policy' (Bowe and Ball, 1992, p. 9). Likewise for Ball and his colleagues, not only does the extent of state control of policy following the 1988 ERA 'remain an empirical question', for them, it is clear that the state having legislated for the restructuring of education through ERA has actually been unable to control its implementation, because schools are able to reinterpret and re-create their understanding of the legislation, thus producing something very different from the legislators' intentions.

The work of Barthes (quoted in Hawkes, 1977) and, in particular, the distinction between 'readerly' and 'writerly' texts provides Ball and his colleagues with a means of theorising the way in which the context of practice is amenable to continual interpretation and recreation. Writerly texts 'self-consciously invite the reader to "join-in", to co-operate and co-author' (p. 11) so that the reader is encouraged to feel a sense of creative 'ownership' (TVEI texts are cited here as illustrations). In readerly texts, however, there is the minimum of opportunity for creative interpretation by the reader: uniform and non-negotiable meanings are imposed on the reader (for example, the National Curriculum, with its technical language of levels and attainment targets etc.). The authors believe that although there are constraints on interpretation, the 1988 ERA is essentially a 'writerly text' in which 'local' initiatives intervene in 'national' policies to create new possibilities: 'in effect the ERA is being constantly rewritten as different kinds of "official" texts and utterances are produced by key actors or agencies of government ... Thus a whole variety and criss-cross of meanings and interpretations are put into circulation' (Bowe and Ball, 1992, p. 12). The complexity of writers is matched by the plurality of readers and within the interstices created considerable opportunities exist for reinterpreting and re-forming the disputed uncertainties of the 'official' texts:

> our concern has been to explore policy-making, in terms of the processes of value dispute and material influence which underlie and invest the formation of policy discourses, as well as to portray and analyse the processes of active interpretation and meaning-making which relate policy texts to practice. In part this involves the identification of resistance, accommodation, subterfuge and conformity within and between arenas of practice and plotting of clashes and mismatches between contending discourses at work in these arenas, e.g., professionalism vs conformity, autonomy vs. latitude...Furthermore it is important to acknowledge that policy intentions may contain ambiguities, contradictions and ommissions that provide particular opportunities for parties to the 'implementation' process, what we term 'space' for manoeuvre (Bowe and Ball with Gold, 1992 p. 13–14).

The formal power of the state is thus strongly circumscribed by the struggles to influence interpetation and action at each stage of the policy cycle. A 'state control model' of education policy, with its top-down linearity, is thus inapposite for education policy analysis. The authors 'want to approach legislation as but one aspect of a *continual* process in which the loci of power are constantly shifting as the various resources implicit and explicit in texts are recontextualised and employed in the struggle to maintain or change views of schooling' (1992, p. 13). The policy process, they conclude, therefore, though constrained, 'is one of complexity, it is one of policy making and remaking. It is often difficult, if not impossible to control or predict the effects of policy' (p. 23).

4. The Marxist Critique of Neo-Pluralism

In his editorial role on *The Journal of Education Policy* Stephen Ball, in 1992, called for papers to develop a theoretical dialogue on education policy analysis. One response formed a sustained critique of his own position and produced a reply (Ball, 1994). Hatcher and Troyna (1994) challenge 'the efficacy of his theoretical eclecticism' which, they argue, lead him into contradiction, a distorted understanding of the distribution of power within the education policy cycle, empirical data which leaves his theoretical positions unsupported and his agenda of reconciling pluralist and Marxist approaches unfulfilled:

> We will argue for an understanding of the policy process that, while acknowledging processes of institutional reinterpretation, gives much greater weight to the ability of the state to control outcomes than Ball and his colleagues do (p.162).

Hatcher and Troyna develop a very different interpretive analysis of the ERA policy process. They believe that Barthes' distinction is not particularly helpful obscuring more than it illuminates. First, the ERA was clearly not '*intended* to be a writerly text' which invited creative reinterpretation. Rather it was intended to impose a considerable degree of non-negotiable structure upon the service. The dissolution of the Inner London Education Authority is perhaps the starkest illustration: 'No negotiation, no room for manoeuvre, no receptivity to the views of local residents and voters' (p. 164). The National Curriculum (NC) and Local Management of Schools (LMS) form other examples. The evidence of Ball's own research reinforces, Hatcher and Troyna argue, a view that the NC subject divisions impose more constraint than scope for discretion, while even *within* subject areas despite the incoherence and resistance which Ball illuminate, their own research once more supports a view that 'State control has the upper hand'. The standard attainment targets (SATs), which are much more like readerly than writerly policy texts, cement the constraints: 'The imposition of national testing locks the National Curriculum in place as the dominant framework of teachers' work whatever opportunities teachers may continue to take to evade or reshape it' (p. 165). The constraints of policy are even more apparent in LMS where 'the quasi-market mechanism of per capita funding is a classic example of the state's ability to impose its policies regardless...formula funding is not a 'writerly text' (p. 164). Hatcher and Troyna conclude this point with a telling general critique. It is not enough, they stress, to indicate that the world is complex and various. The purpose of analysis is to discriminate degrees of influence in the world, to evaluate the totality of the many factors which interplay. Thus, although in the NC there is clearly a complex interplay of influences, nevertheless 'state control has the upper hand'.

LMS provides support for the authors' second critique of the Barthes image. They argue that 'the analogy between literary texts and state policy tends to obscure the difference between the discursive and the non-discursive' (p. 163). While policies, like texts, cannot be controlled at the level of discourse they can, unlike texts, be regulated at the operational level of practice. Although age-weighted pupil formulas may have allowed much interpretation at the level of discourse, in practice their implementation is tightly regulated at the level of local discretion.

Hatcher and Troyna argue that Ball's policy cycle, with its emphasis upon micro-political recontextualising of policy especially within schools, neglects the prior structuring of the cycle and thus distorts the relative power of those involved, especially the state. Ball's ethnographic reading of the policy cycle, it is argued, drawing upon Dale (1992), depends upon a flawed notion of the functional separation of policy formulation from implementation. With Dale they agree that there can be no doubt that 'a focus on the state is not only necessary, but the most important component of any adequate understanding of education policy' (Dale, 1992, p. 388).

Hatcher and Troyna concur that the state must be centre stage in analysis of the policy process and though they begin from Dale and Ozga's (1991) formulation of the functions of the capitalist state (set out above), they want to 'stress how that entails the state intervening in and striving to regulate *all* social relations, including those of gender and family, "race" and nation, in the interests of capital' (p. 158). They also reject Dale and Ozga's insistence upon the notion of *neo* Marxism arguing, with Miliband (1983, p. 58), that the idea of the state acting at the behest of, rather than on behalf of the ruling class, is 'a vulgar deformation of the thought of Marx and Engels'. It is because, Hatcher and Troyna argue, that economic power is fragmented 'that state power has to be relatively autonomous, precisely in order to pursue the *general* interests of capital' (p. 159). Thus the state has interests of its own though

> not ... *independent* to those of capital. On the contrary the distinguishing feature of the Thatcher governments was the radical detemination with which they were prepared to overturn the entire post-war settlement in order to construct a new hegemony, in conformity with what they saw as the *general and strategic* needs of capital, in terms of accumulation, contextual

reproduction and legitimation. Whether they were successful is another question, but the class commitment is surely not in doubt (p. 160).

Ball (1990) (paradoxically, given his general pluralist stance) supports such an analysis: 'I want to argue that social welfare has been significantly *restructured* and *repositioned* in response to the crisis of capital accumulation' (1990, p. 79). Hatcher and Troyna argue that the theoretical conclusion of their analysis implies: first, that 'the level of the economic does not merely provide a context, a set of limits; it actively intervenes in and shapes the political, the social, the cultural, the ideological; and second, that an acknowledgement of the primacy of the relationship between economic power and state power does not compel a rigid and mechanistic reading off from the economic' (p. 159). With Geras (1990), they propose that different types of polity and state are possible within capitalist society.

The different interpretations of Althusser reveal the opposed theoretical positions. Hatcher and Troyna criticise Ball's selective reading, which appropriates the rejection of economic reductionism and the theorising of social formations in terms of relatively autonomous levels but ignores the structuralist denial of agency so as to create a distored 'pluralist' Althusser. What is lost in this reading is precisely the sense of social formation. Althusser's insistence that the task of historical materialism is, as Geras (1972, p. 62) put it, to 'study the different practices in their specificity, and their relations to one another in the complex unity of social practice which is the social formation'. Hatcher and Troyna reinforce the point: what is omitted is the 'emphasis on the complexly structured and determined unity of the social structure which Althusser emphasises when he calls the social formation *a structure in dominance*. Only at the level of the social totality do the combined effects of mutliple determinations and contradictions work themselves out. Without this analytic category, Althusser's theorization of complexity is reduced to mere plurality' (p. 161).

TOWARDS A FRAMEWORK FOR EDUCATIONAL POLICY ANALYSIS

Researchers on education policy have generated, over the past decade, a burgeoning literature on the issue of how policy should be theorised. Very different perspectives have developed with protagonists often aligned around a debate between pluralist and Marxist analyses of education policy. The theoretical quality of the discourse has increased to an impressive level yet there are, I propose, three areas of neglect which need remedying if an adequate theoretical framework of the role of policy in the public domain is to be developed. First, and paradoxically, the idea of policy itself, especially policy-as-public-policy, remains under-conceptualised; second, an adequate theorising of public policy in the polity will require more integration and less division between the perspectives if Ozga's (1987) call for a policy analysis that is 'rooted in the social science tradition, historically informed and drawing on qualitative and illuminative techniques' (p. 144) is to be realised; and third, the theorising is over-determined by presenting issues and paradigms of the historical moment, and if analysis is to make its distinctive contribution to public policy then political philosophy needs to complement political sociology so that a theory of democracy for the learning society can emerge. These issues will be discussed in turn.

1. Conceptualising Policy

'Policies', Kogan (1975, p. 55) proposed, 'are the operational statements of values – statements of prescriptive intent, the authoritative allocation of values', 'programmatic utterances'. Since Kogan's seminal work there has been an odd silence in much education policy studies: that analysis has routinely neglected to conceptualise what was ostensibly the focus of study – policy – and neglected an accessible literature on policy studies which made available appropriate understandings of the policy process. The work of Raab (1990; 1992 a/b; 1994) and Bowe and Ball with Gold (1992) has begun to redress this neglect.

Policies are statements which are typically expressed both in utterance and in textual form. They have a distinctive and formal purpose for organisations and governments in codifying and publicising the values that are to inform future practice and thus encapsulate prescriptions for reform. Policies, as Ball (1990) emphasises, project images of the ideal. Policies are thus orientated to change and action, providing public intent of transforming practice according to ideal values. Policies, therefore, systematically challenge the taken-for-granted assumptions and practices in organisation or state in a number of ways:

– future orientation rather than inherited routine and tradition

– systematic rather than incremental and ad hoc

– explicit analysis rather than the implicit and unexamined

– the thought through rather than muddling through

– the dynamism of change rather than stability

– the proactive rather than reactive.

Thus the form (orientation to change) and substance (the value orientation)

of policy challenge the practice and traditions of organisational working in ways that can generate conflict. Agreement about change and values are not given and are likely to be 'essentially contested' within organisations as much as the polity as a whole, as different interest groups struggle to acquire influence over purposes and resources.

Policy is, therefore, necessarily a temporal process involving issues of task (how policy is to be formulated and carried into practice) and of people (who is to be involved in the process), which stretch over time in the pursuit of change. When the debate between pluralism and Marxism did engage with conceptions of the policy process the oppositions were typically cast in terms of binary absolutes rather the possibilities on dimensions that form continua. A number of such dimensions need to be clarified to form a framework for the investigation of policy development, the outcomes of which are determined empirically (cf. Hogwood and Gunn, 1984; Stewart, 1980 a/b; 1984; 1986; Skelcher, 1980; Leach and Stewart, 1982; Ham and Hill, 1993):

i   *The scope of policy*
     Whether the policy process focuses upon a particular issue or encompasses the whole of organisational or state activity is an empirical matter.

ii   *The moments of policy*
     Thus, for example, whether policy formulation is necessarily or contingently related to implementation appears as a definitional rather than an empirical question. Understanding the policy process, rather, requires analytical abstraction of the 'moments' of policy – its generation, formulation, implementation and evaluation – and a recognition of which of these stages actually occurs and whether those that do form interdependent or discrete processes are questions that can only be tested empirically.

iii *The organisation of policy*
     Is the generation of a policy process an ad hoc affair triggered by some contingent event, or is it part of a 'policy cycle' which is integral to the decision processes of an organisation or the state? Are functions and roles clarified within an organisation or the state to control and manage the policy process, and what degree of formal or hierarchical authority is invested in them? What structures of control and regulation exist?

iv   *The planning of policy*
     How the stages and moments of policy are related to each other and the degree of rational analysis invested in planning their interrelationship is an empirical question. Policy analysis seeks to expose and critically examine the policy choices and practices of planning policy. The more pieces of information are brought together in the process, then the

greater the rationality of policy planning. Information about: the changing context and the issues faced; existing activities and policies; values and aspirations; needs; and available resources.

v   *The involvement in policy*
Who participates in the policy process? Is policy generated and controlled 'top-down', or is involvement a democratic process in which representatives take part in all or some stages of policy, or is involvement a political process dependent upon power and ownership of 'resources'?

For the educational theorist, however, the task is to illuminate the public dimensions of such a conceptual framework. The debate has lacked an understanding of the function of *public* policy in encapsulating ideal values and defining practice for the purpose and organisation of the public domain. The distinctiveness of public policy lies in the purposes and policies it clarifies for the members of a society as a whole, the values and interests they may hold in common and the activities they undertake together, that is, in their role as citizens. Publicness clarifies the boundary between the 'I' and 'we' in civil society. Public purpose thus lies in reconciling the complex plurality of citizens and their necessary shared membership of and responsibility towards the community as a whole. Forming judgements about need and the rationing of scarce resources so as to balance competing values thus becomes a distinctive public task, and upon the quality of such judgements, services and accountability will depend the degree of consent and legitimacy the public accord the polity.

Public policy is thus intrinsically political (Beetham, 1987) and this characterises its defining processes and institutional forms. Public policies, by projecting images of an ideal society, codify the values which express prescriptions for social change. The orientation is to challenge and change social practice. Because agreement is likely to be 'essentially contested', as different interest groups struggle to acquire influence over purposes and resources, the task of public management is to enable the participation, discourse and choice that can balance competing priorities.

Public policy and management are driven, therefore, by distinctively different purposes, conditions and tasks. How the dominant values and agendas for the political constitution of the public domain are to be understood and explained is a task both for theoretical analysis and for political philosophy.

2. Theorising Public Policy

The fissiparous tendencies of theorists, striving to emphasise the virtues of a particular perspective, can fragment the task of explanation which requires some critical interrelating of those different approaches. An adequate understanding of public policy demands a multi-theoretic and multi-disciplinary analysis. A number of theoretical and methodological presuppositions can form the basis, it is argued, for a more integrated approach to explanatory analysis. Theoretical analysis of public policy should accommodate:

(i) Historical location: Only an interpretive analysis of the transformations of our time can make sense of the temporal and structural context of public policy development. Barraclough (1967) believed that if contemporary history was to become a heavyweight discipline, able to offer more than a superficial discussion of events, then it had 'to clarify the basic structural changes which have shaped the modern world. These changes are fundamental because they fix the skeleton or framework within which political action takes place' (1967, p. 16, in Ball, 1990, p. 1).

What Barraclough takes to be the prerequisite for history, reinforced by Hobsbawn (1994), Gellner (1964;1988) conceives as the subject matter for the contemporary social sciences – to interpret the structural transformation of our time, though this injunction was typically to study the impact of the industrial revolution rather than the contemporary post-industrial revolution. The economic, social and political transformations of our time (Ranson, 1992) are altering fundamentally the structure of experience: the capacities each person needs to flourish, what it is to live in society, the nature of work and the form taken by polity. The changes raise deep questions for the government of education and for the polity in general about: *what is it to be a person*? Is a person a passive being or possessed of powers that define his or her essential agency? *Is there any such thing as a society* and what is it? An aggregation of individuals or some form of social and linguistic community? *What should be the nature of the polity*? What is it to be a member and with what rights and duties? What distribution of power and wealth is consistent with justice and freedom? Who should take decisions and how? What forms of accountability and representation define our democracy?

(ii) Theorising action and structure: Much theoretical writing has created a mistaken opposition between the agency and structure in explaining change when arguably only a theorising of their necessary interrelationship can make sense of social and political reality. Turner (1981) has emphasised the considerable overlap in the work of Weber and Marx in their analysis of capital formation and accumulation. The characterisation of Weber's work as 'subjectivist', in some phenomenological and Marxist perspectives, neglects his emphasis upon the dual interplay of agency and structure in the creation

of historical periods such as the increasing rationalisation of social forms in the modern world.

> The type of social science in which we are interested is an *empirical science* of concrete reality (*Wirklichkeitswissenschaft*). Our aim is the understanding of the characteristic uniqueness of the reality in which we move. We wish to understand on the one hand the relationships and cultural significance of individual events in their contemporary manifestations and on the other the causes of their being *so* and not *otherwise* (Weber, *The Methodology of the Social Sciences*, 1949, p. 72).

The work of Giddens (1976; 1984) and Archer (1982) acknowledge, from different points of view, that while individuals and groups strive to construct their worlds to reflect chosen values and interests they are nevertheless also constrained by the structures of power and domination. Theorising the interconnection of action and structure presupposes a number of interrelated forms of analysis (Ranson *et al.*, 1980): *phenomenological,* to understand the meanings which actors create to make sense of their worlds; *comparative,* to explore the underlying regularities which actors may be unaware; and *temporal,* to explore how actors choose to construct and change social forms over time in the face of the constraints which confront them. These analyses enable explanations to be developed which are adequate at the level of meaning and cause across different contextual conditions and with the capacity to explain change over time. Such a framework suggests the need to examine the creation over time of education policy in the context of broader structural processes of social, cultural and economic reproduction (Power, 1992; Whitty, 1985, 1992).

(iii) Theory, practice and value: Perceived as mutually reinforcing by revealing the underlying relationships, theory can guide action, while the monitoring of practice informs theory. Because the task of theory is not only to explain why public policy is as it is within the polity, but also to theorise the conditions for a different form of polity and public policy, it is inescapably normative, driven by 'strong evaluation' of the moral and political order. Public policy analysis must describe, explain and propose public values. The personal values and political commitment of the critical policy analyst, argues Prunty (1985, p. 136), would be 'anchored in the vision of a moral order in which justice, equality and individual freedom are uncompromised by the avarice of a few'.

Thus policy analysis must be committed to the critical analysis of values within current policies as part of the process of clarifying the values which the analyst believes should inform educational and public policy (Troyna, 1994a/b). The literature on policy analysis, however, has lost a sense of the 'strong values' which provide the meaning and purpose for public policy. These values, it is argued are the need to regenerate a democratic public domain for the learning society.

3. A Philosophy of Public Purpose

The task of theory is to explain why public policy is as it is within the polity, but also to theorise the conditions for a different form of polity and public policy. Theorising the conditions for an alternative public domain requires a philosophy of its values and purposes (Ranson, 1992). Policy analysis is inescapably a normative as well as a conceptual and theoretical activity. Policy analysis, which is about changing practice in the public domain, needs to follow clear public values.

The education policy literature lacks a framework of values about the public domain which it brings to its analysis. The appropriate values for public policy and its analysis are those of democracy and citizenship for the learning society. The transformations of the time require a renewed valuing of and commitment to learning: as the boundaries between languages and cultures begin to dissolve, as new skills and knowledge are expected within the world of work and, most significantly, a new generation rejecting passivity in favour of more active participation, requires to be encouraged to exercise such qualities of discourse in the public domain. A learning society, therefore, needs to celebrate the qualities of being open to new ideas, listening to as well as expressing perspectives, reflecting on and inquiring into solutions to new dilemmas, co-operating in the practice of change and critically reviewing it. There is a need for the creation of a learning society as the constitutive condition of a new moral and political order. It is only when the values and processes of learning are placed at the centre of the polity that the conditions can be established for all individuals to develop their capacities, and that insititutions can respond openly and imaginatively to a period of change.

The theory which can provide the common language of agency to enrich a new moral and political order is that of citizenship within the learning society. The notion of a citizen captures our necessary duality as an individual and as a member of the public. The deliberative agency of the citizen is exercised in judgement, in choice and in action so that his or her powers and capacities are actively and reflectively expressed through the creative development of the self, through civic virtue within the community, and through discourse within the polity.

CONCLUSION

In conclusion, *a practical theory* is needed to develop understanding of the values, purposes, conditions and practice of public policy for a democratic learning society. Three interdependent processes are proposed – practices, institutional capacity, and cultural formation:

(i) Practice: What forms does the practice of citizenship take in the emergent learning society? What values, capacities and experiences are informing public service managers as well as the citizens they serve in the creation of a more active public domain which supports more active participation and responsibility?

(ii) Institutional capacity: The motivation and capabilities of citizens and public managers will depend much upon the capacity of new systems of public policy making to support and mediate the diversity of interests. There is a need to explore the implications for structures of decision making, power and legitimacy of the developing institutional capacity that supports the growth of democratic practice (cf. Stewart, *et al.,* 1994; Fishkin, 1991; Gyford, 1991; Burns *et al.,* 1994).

(iii) Cultural formation: While the form of public service management is always subject to institutional structuration, this process, in turn, is deeply shaped and inscribed by the cultural and national formations of any society. To understand public management we must grasp the deeper cultural values which define the very notions of citizenship and democratic practice.

REFERENCES

Aiken, M. and Hage, J. (1963). 'Organisational interdependence and intra-organisational structure', *American Sociological Review,* 33, pp. 912–30.
Aldrich, H. (1976). 'Resource dependency and inter-organisational relations', *Adminstration and Society,* 7, pp. 419–54.
— (1979). *Organisations and Environment.* Englewood Cliffs, NJ: Prentice Hall.
Alford, R. and Friedland, R. (1985). *Powers of Theory.* Cambridge: Cambridge University Press.
Althusser, L. (1971). 'Ideology and ideological state apparatuses', in Cosin, B. (ed.), *Education Structure and Society.* London: Penguin, pp. 242–80.
Archer, M. (1979) *Social Origins of Educational Systems.* London: Sage.
— (1981). 'Educational politics: a model for their analysis', in Broadfoot, P., Brock, C. and Tulasiewicz, W. (eds), *Politics and Educational Change.* London: Croom Helm.
— (1982). 'Morphogenisis versus structuration: on combining structure and action', *The*

British Journal of Sociology, 33, 4, pp. 455–83.

— (1992). 'Theoretical debates in education policy analysis: managing editor's note', *Journal of Education Policy,* 7, 5, p. 493.

— (1993a). 'Education policy, power relations and teachers' work', *British Journal of Educational Studies,* 41, 2, pp. 106–21.

— (1993b) 'What is policy? Texts, trajectories and toolboxes', *Discourse,* 13, 2, pp. 10–17.

— (1994). 'Some reflections on policy theory: a brief response to Hatcher and Troyna', *Journal of Education Policy,* 9, 2, pp. 171–82.

— (1994). 'Some Reflections on Policy Theory: A Brief Response to Hatcher and Troyna', *Journal of Education Policy,* 9, 2, pp. 171–82.

Ball, S. and Shilling, C. (1994) 'At the cross-roads: education policy studies', *British Journal of Educational Studies,* 42, 1, pp. 1–5.

Baron, G. and Howell, D. A. (1974). *The Government and Management of Schools.* London: Athlone Press.

Barraclough, G. (1967). *An Introduction to Contemporary History.* Harmondsworth: Penguin.

Beetham, D. (1987). *Bureaucracy.* Milton Keynes: Open University.

Benson, J. (1975). 'The inter organisational network as political economy', *Administrative Science Quarterly,* 20, 1, pp. 229–49.

Bernstein, B. (1975), *Class, Codes and Control,* Vol 3. London: Routledge.

Blau, P. (1964), *Exchange and Power in Social Life.* New York: Wiley.

— and Schoenherr, R. (1971). *The Structure of Organisations.* New York: Basic Books.

Bogdanor, V. (1979). 'Power and participation', *Oxford Review of Education,* 5, 2, pp. 157–68.

Bourdieu, P. (1977). *Outline of a Theory of Practice.* Cambridge: Cambridge University Press.

— and Passeron, J. C. (1977). *Reproduction in Education Society and Culture.* London: Sage.

Bowe, R. and Ball, S. with Gold, A. (1992). *Reforming Education and Changing Schools: Case Studies in Policy Sociology.* London: Routledge.

Briault, E. (1976). 'A distributed system of educational administration: an international viewpoint', *International Review of Education,* 22, 4, pp. 429–39.

Burgess, R. (ed.) (1989). *The Ethics of Educational Research.* London: Falmer.

Burns, D., Hambleton, R. and Hoggett, P. (1994). *The Politics of Decentralisation: Revitalising Local Government.* London: Macmillan.

CCCS (1981). *Unpopular Education: Schooling and Social Democracy in England since 1944.* London: Hutchinson.

Coates, R. (1972). *Teacher Unions and Interest Group Politics.* Cambridge: Cambridge University Press.

Crozier, M. and Thoenig, J-C. (1976). 'The regulation of complex organised systems', *Administrative Science Quarterly,* 21, 1, pp. 547–70.

Dale, R. (1982). 'Education and the capitalist state: contributions and contradictions', in M. Apple (ed.), *Cultural and Economic Reproduction in Education,* London: Routledge.

(1983). 'Review essay: the political sociology of education', *British Journal of Sociology of Education,* 4, 2, pp. 185–202.

— (1986). Perspectives on policy making, Part 2 of Module 1 of Open University Course E333, *Policy Making in Education.* Milton Keynes: Open University Press.

— (1989). *The State and Education Policy.* Milton Keynes: Open University Press.

— (1992a). 'Whither the state and education policy? Recent work in Australia and New Zealand', *British Journal of Sociology of Education,* 13, 3, pp. 387–95.

— (1992b). 'What do they know of England who don't know they've been speaking prose', Paper to ESRC Seminar on Methodological and Ethical Issues Associated with research into the 1988 Education Reform Act, University of Warwick, 29 April.

— (1994). 'Applied education politics or political sociology of education? Contrasting approaches to the study of recent education reeform in England and Wales', in Halpin and Troyna. op. cit.

— and Ozga, J. (1991). *Understanding Education Policy: Principles and Perspectives* (E333 Module 1). Milton Keynes: Open University Press.

Dunleavy, P. (1982). 'Is there a radical approach to public administration?' *Public Adminstration,* 60, 2, pp. 215–33.

— and O'Leary, B. (1987). *The Theories of the State.* London: Macmillan.

Evetts, J. (1973). *The Sociology of Educational Ideas.* London: Routledge.

Fenwick, I. (1976), *The Comprehensive School 1944–1970: The Politics of Secondary School Reorganisation.* London: Methuen.

Fenwick, I. and McBride, P. (1981), *The Government of Education in Britain.* Oxford: Martin Robertson.

Finch, J. (1986). *Research and Policy: The Uses of Qualitative Methods in Social and Educational Research.* London: Falmer.

Fishkin, J. (1991). *Democracy and Deliberation: New Directions for Democratic Reform.* New Haven: Yale.

Fowler, G., Morris, V. and Ozga, J. (1973). *Decision Making in British Education.* London: Heinemann.

Gellner, E. (1964). *Thought and Change.* London: Weidenfeld & Nicolson.

— (1988). *Plough, Sword and Book.* London: Collins Harvill.

Geras, N. (1972). 'Louis Althusser – an assessment', *New Left Review,* 71 (January–February), pp. 57–8.

— (1990). *Discourses of Extremity.* London: Verso.

Gewirtz, S. and Ozga, J. (1990), 'Partnership, pluralism and education policy: a reassessment', *Journal of Education Policy,* 5, 1, pp. 37–48.

Giddens, A. (1976). *New Rules of Sociological Method.*London, Hutchinson.

— (1984). *The Constitution of Society.* Cambridge, Polity.

Griffith, J. (1966). *Central Departments and Local Authorities.* London: Allen & Unwin.

Gyford, J. (1991). *Citizens, Consumers and Councils.* London: Macmillan.

Habermas , J. (1976). *Legitimation Crisis.* London: Heinemann.

Halpin, D. (1994). 'Practice and prospects in education policy research', in Halpin, D. and Troyna, B. (eds), op. cit.

Halpin, D. and Troyna, B. (eds), (1994), *Researching Education Policy: Ethical and Methodological Issues.* London: Falmer.

Ham, C. and Hill M. (1993). *The Policy Process in the Modern Capitalist State.* Hemel Hempstead: Harvester Wheatsheaf.

Hanf, K. and Scharpf, F. (1978), *Inter-organisational Policy Making.* London: Sage.

Hargreaves, A. (1983), 'The politics of adminstrative convenience', in Ahier, J. and Flude, M. (eds), *Contemporary Education Policy.* London: Croom Helm.

Hatcher, R. and Troyna, B. (1994). 'The "policy cycle": A Ball by Ball account', *Journal of Education Policy,* 9, 2, pp. 155–70.

Hawkes, T. (1977). *Structuralism and Semiotics.* London: Methuen.

Hobsbawm, E. (1994). *Age of Extremes: The Short Twentieth Century 1914–1991.* London: Michael Joseph.

Hogwood, B. and Gunn,? (1984). *Policy Analysis for the Real World.* Oxford: Oxford University Press.
Holloway, J. (1987). 'A note on Fordism and neo-Fordism', *Common Sense* No. 1, Edinburgh.
James, P. (1980). *The Reorganisation of Secondary Education.* Windsor: NFER.
Jones, G. (1980). *New Approaches to the Study of Central Local Relations.* Farnborough: Gower.
Kogan, M. (1971) *The Government of Education.* London: Macmillan.
— (1975). *Education Policy making: A Study of Interest Groups and Parliament.* London: Allen & Unwin.
— (1978). *The Politics of Educational Change.* London: Fontana.
— (1979). 'Different frameworks for educational policy-making and analysis', *Educational Analysis,* 1, 2.
— (1985)' Education policy and values', in Mcnay, I. and Ozga, J. (eds), *Policy Making in Education: The Breakdown of Consensus.* Oxford: Open University/Pergamon.
— and Becher, T. (1980). 'Patterns of change', *Times Higher Educational Supplement,* 2, May.
Lawn, M. (1987). 'The spur and the bridle: changing the mode of curriculum control', *Journal of Curriculum Studies,* 19, 3, pp. 227–36.
— and Ozga, J. (1986). 'Unequal partners: teachers under indirect rule', *British Journal of Sociology of Education,* 7, 2, pp. 225–38.
Leach, S. and Stewart, J. (eds) (1982). *Approaches in Public Policy.* London: Allen & Unwin.
Loughlin, M. (1986) *Local Government in the Modern State.* London: Sweet & Maxwell.
McLennan, G. (1984), 'Capitalist state or democratic policy', in McLennan, G., Held, D., and Hall, S. (eds), *The Idea of the Modern State.* Milton Keynes: Open University.
McNay, I. and Ozga, J. (eds) (1985). *Policy Making in Education: The Breakdown of Consensus.* Oxford: Pergamon/Open University.
McPherson, A. and Raab, C. (1988). *Governing Education: A Sociology of Policy since 1945.* Edinburgh: Edinburgh University Press.
Miliband, R. (1983). 'State power and class interests', *New Left Review,* 138 (March–April), pp. 57–68.
Offe, C. (1975). 'The theory of the capitalist state and the problem of policy formation', in L. N. Lindberg *et al., Stress and Contradiction in Modern Capitalism.* Lexington, MA: Lexington Books.
Ozga, J. (1986) 'A social danger: the contested history of teacher-state relations', in Corr, H. and Jamieson, L. (eds), *The State, Private Life and Political Change* .London: Macmillan.
— (1987). 'Studying education policy through the lives of policy makers: an attempt to close the micro-macro gap', in Barton, L. and Walker, S. (eds), *Changing Policies, Changing Teachers.* Lewes: Falmer.
— (1990). 'Policy research and policy theory: a comment on Fitz and Halpin', *Journal of Education Policy,* 5, 4, pp. 359–62.
Ozga, J. and Gewirtz, S. (1994). 'Sex, lies and audiotape: Interviewing the Education Policy Elite', in Halpin and Troyna, op. cit.
Pattison, M. (1980). 'Intergovernmental relations and the limitations of central government control: reconstructing the politics of comprehensive reorganisation', *Oxford Review of Education,* 6, 1.
Pfeffer, J. and Salancik G. (1978). *The External Control of Organisations.* London: Harper & Row.

Power, S. (1992), 'Researching the impact of education policy: difficulties and discontinuities', *Journal of Educational Policy,* 7, 5, pp. 493–500.

Prunty, J. (1985). 'Signposts for a critical educational policy analysis', *Australian Journal of Education,* 29, 2, pp. 133–40.

Raab, C. (1990). 'Review symposium: the state and education policy', *British Journal of Sociology of Education,* 11, 1, pp. 87–91.

— (1992a). 'Where are we now: some reflections on the sociology of education policy', in Halpin and Troyna, op. cit.

— (1992b) 'Taking networks seriously: education policy in Britain', *European Journal of Political Research* 21, 1–2, pp. 69–90.

— (1994) 'Theorising the governance of education', *British Journal of Educational Studies,* 42, 1, pp. 6–21.

Ranson, S. (1980). 'Changing relations between centre and locality in education', *Local Government Studies,* 6, 6, pp. 3–23.

— (1990). *The Politics of Reorganising Schools.* London: Allen & Unwin.

— (1992). 'Towards the Learning Society', *Educational Management and Adminstration,* 20, 2, pp. 68–79.

Ranson, S., Hinings, C. and Greenwood, R. (1980). 'The structuring of orgnaisational structures', *Administrative Science Quarterly,* 25, 1.

Regan, D. (1974), *Local Government and Education.* London: Allen & Unwin.

Rhodes, R. (1981). *Control and Power in Central Local Government Relations.* Farnborough: Gower.

Rhodes, R. (1988). *Beyond Westminster and Whitehall: The Sub-Central Governments of Britain.* London: Unwin & Hyman.

Ribbins, P. and Brown, R. (1979). 'Policy making in English local government: the case of secondary school reorganisation', *Public Adminstration,* 57, 2, pp. 187–202.

Salter, B. and Tapper, T. (1981). *Education Politics and the State: The Theory and Practice of Education Change.* London: Grant McIntyre.

Saran, R. (1973). *Policy Making in Secondary Education.* Oxford: Clarendon Press.

Simon, B. (1965). *Education and the Labour Movement.* London: Lawrence & Wishart.

— (1974). *The Radical Tradition in Education in Britain.* London: Lawrence & Wishart.

Skelcher, C. (1980). 'From programme budgeting to policy analysis', *Public Administration,* 59, pp. 155–72.

Stewart, J. (1980a). 'Guidelines to policy derivation', Birmingham University, Institute of Local Government Studies.

— (1980b). 'Dimensions of policy making systems', Birmingham University, Institute of Local Government Studies.

— (1984). 'A new concern for policy planning', Luton: Local Government Training Board.

— (1986). 'Do you sincerely want a policy discussion?' Luton: Local Government Training Board.

Stewart, J., Kendall, J. and Coote, A. (1994). *Citizens' Juries.* London: IPPR.

Taylor, W. (1978). 'Values and accountability', in Becher, T. and Maclure, S. (eds), *Accountability in Education.* Windsor: NFER.

Troyna, B. (1994a). 'Critical social research and education policy', *British Journal of Education Studies,* 41, 1, pp. 26–60.

— (1994b). 'Reforms, research and being reflexive about being reflective', in Halpin and Troyna, op. cit.

Turner, B. S. (1981). *For Weber: Essays on the Sociology of Fate.* London: Routledge.

Walford, G. (1991). *Doing Educational Research.* London: Routledge.

— (1994). *Researching the Powerful in Education*. London: University College London.

Weaver, T. (1976) *Tenth Report from the Expenditure Committee 1975–76*. HC 621, p. 379.

— (1979). *Department of Education and Science: Central Control of Education*. Milton Keynes: Open University.

Weber, M. (1949). *The Methodology of the Social Sciences* (eds E. Shils and H. Finch). New York: The Free Press.

Whitty, G. (1985). *Sociology and Social Knowledge: Curriculum,Theory, Research and Politics*. London: Methuen.

— (1992). 'Education, economy and national culture' in Boocok, R. and Thompson, K. (eds), *Social and Cutural Forms of Modernity*. Cambridge: Polity Press in association with the Open University.

Williams, R. (1978). *Marxism and Literature*. Oxford: Oxford University Press.

Wright, E. (1979). *Class, Crisis and the State*. London: New Left Books.

11

CURRICULUM STUDY

John Elliott

INTRODUCTION: THE THREE TRADITIONS OF CURRICULUM RESEARCH.

In this chapter I will identify and describe three traditions of curriculum research which have emerged in the UK over the past 30 years. They are:

1. Technical-rational research;
2. Critical social research;
3. Experimental innovation.

My account will be somewhat biased because my own work can be squarely located in the third of these traditions. I shall probably display this bias by defending the latter tradition against criticism coming from the perspectives of the other two, but doing less to defend these against criticism from the experimental innovation perspective. I do not feel particularly apologetic about this. Given my commitment to the experimental innovation tradition, which is founded on the conviction that it represents a more intellectually defensible tradition than the other two, any attempt on my part to portray the diversity of curriculum research traditions in neutral terms would in my view be an intellectually distorted portrayal. I would be less than intellectually honest in doing so because I do not believe that they are equally defensible, and I am sure that this bias would show through anyway.

I shall not discuss in any great detail the substantive findings of particular research studies that exemplify these traditions. Rather I shall refer to the central beliefs and assumptions which shape and condition the search for understanding and the form in which specific insights are represented.

Each of the three traditions differ with respect to their underpinning beliefs about:

i) the nature of curriculum and what is involved in curriculum change;

ii)   the kinds of values which ought to inform curriculum change strategies;

iii) the relationship between curriculum development and research;

iv)   the role of the intellectual disciplines in curriculum research.

I will try to clarify what is at stake between them in terms of these belief dimensions.

1. TECHNICAL-RATIONAL CURRICULUM RESEARCH

This tradition views the curriculum as a programme of learning activities or experiences which are 'rationally' planned in the light of pre-specified learning objectives. According to Stenhouse (1975, Ch. 5), an 'objective' is a technical term in Curriculum Studies, which refers to an intention to bring about observable changes in student behaviour. An objective is something that can be behaviourally defined. Stenhouse argued that the classic definition of a behavioural objective was provided by Ralph Tyler (1949) in his seminal book *Basic Principles of Curriculum and Instruction*. Tyler claimed that 'One can define an objective with sufficient clarity if he can describe or illustrate the kind of behaviour the student is expected to acquire so that one could recognise such behaviour if he saw it' (pp. 59–60).

Interestingly, Lawton (1989, Ch. 2) has argued that the concept of behavioural objectives was not part of Tyler's model of rational curriculum planning or of its further elaboration by Taba (1962). Their models of planning by objectives must be distinguished, according to Lawton, from the advocacy of behavioural objectives models proposed by Mager (1962) and Popham (1969). Lawton claims that Tyler never adopted the position of the latter in their opposition to 'non-behavioural objectives'; both he and Taba using the term 'objectives' in a much wider sense. The evidence Lawton cites to support this claim is Tyler complaining in 1973 about extremist versions of his planning rationale which fail 'to distinguish between the learning of highly specific skills for limited job performance and the more generalised understanding, problem-solving skills and other kinds of behavioural patterns that thoughtful teachers and educators seek to help students develop' (quoted by Lawton 1989, Ch. 2). I would suggest that Tyler is not so much complaining here about behavioural definitions of objectives as about narrow interpretations of observable behaviour. He is complaining about the reduction of behaviour to simple as opposed to complex skills.

Tyler's definition of an objective, as cited by Stenhouse, is indeed a definition in terms of observable changes in behaviour and Stenhouse is quite right to locate his and Taba's curriculum planning rationales (1962) in a behaviourist perspective. Lawton's attempt to uncouple planning by objectives from the concept of behavioural objectives is based on an erroneous assumption he appears to share with theorists like Mager and Popham; namely, that measures of observable behaviour must refer to simple rather than complex entities. Lawton associates behavioural objectives with an attempt to reduce education to training in specific job-related technical skills. His attempt to interpret the planning rationales of Tyler and Taba in terms of non-behavioural objectives represents an aspiration to distinguish training in specific vocational knowledge and skills from an education concerned with the development of more complex abilities. Lawton wants to divorce the planning by objectives model from its original context of use in the field of vocational training and to marry it to the concept of education.

However, the idea of planning by non-behavioural objectives constitutes a contradiction in terms. The use of the term 'objective' to describe an educational aim implies a fixed, concrete and visible target which can be defined in advance of selecting the means of 'hitting' it. Some curriculum theorists, like Stenhouse (1975, Ch. 6), claimed that educational aims cannot be defined in terms of objectives without distorting the nature of education. We shall return later to explore this claim more fully.

For the present we might simply argue that what Lawton is really objecting to is not so much the concept of behavioural objectives, although he thinks he is – but the commitment to a 'closed model of training' which many advocates of the concept appear to have made. In other words he confuses the concept with a particular interpretation of it. His argument, that objectives in curriculum planning can be more 'open' and 'concerned with understanding key concepts and ideas', can be understood as simply a broadening of the range of application of the behavioural objectives model. Such a broadening of the objectives model – exemplified by both Tyler and Taba – becomes necessary to accommodate Lawton's own specific contribution to Curriculum Studies: namely, cultural analysis.

From a technical-rational perspective curriculum change might be understood in any of the following terms:

– *as a 'rational' process of planned change whose effects can be measured against prespecified targets.*

This kind of change has implications for how teaching is understood. In the UK during the post-Second World War period the teaching profession had, until the 1988 Act, a great deal of discretion over the content and form of pupils learning experiences. Decisions and judgements about learning content and methods were grounded in intuitive understandings of what their pupils' were capable of or needed to learn. Such understandings were acquired through lots of 'hands-on' classroom experience in schools. Even though examination syllabuses restricted the exercise of discretion by individual teachers as pupils advanced in years, such syllabuses nevertheless represented the 'collective wisdom' of significant groupings within the profession, for example, of academic subject specialists.

A technical-rational perspective on the curriculum represents a threat to an occupational culture which defines teaching as an intuitive craft learned through immersion in experience. From this perspective teaching is grounded in a knowledge of explicit techniques or rules for achieving certain desired outcomes. Technical knowledge replaces craft knowledge as a basis for teaching. Changing the curriculum to make it more 'rational' implies changing teaching from a craft activity into a technical activity.

–   *as a process of developing the technology prescribed in the curriculum with respect to its instrumental effectiveness and efficiency in producing the desired learning outcomes.*

From the perspective of technical-rationality curriculum development is a process of planning, implementing, evaluating, and revising the plan. Design the programme of learning experiences and activities to achieve pre-specified learning outcomes, implement the programme, then evaluate its instrumental efficiency and effectiveness and revise the programme accordingly. Such is the process of curriculum development. It embodies a static conception of knowledge as informational content to be learned, a passive conception of the process of learning, and an instrumental conception of teaching as techniques of production. These conceptions are 'taken for granted' assumptions which underpin the technical-rational logic of the development process, a logic that has proved incapable of accommodating any critique which problematises them.

From a technical-rational perspective the process of curriculum development can be dissociated from that of teaching. Responsibility for developing the technology can be detached from responsibility for implementing it. The teacher can be both technologist and technician but it 'ain' t necessarily so'.

–   *as a form of social engineering.*

From the standpoint of technical rationality the development of a curriculum technology can be uncoupled from pedagogy. The teacher essentially becomes a technical operative while the role of the technologist or engineer can be allocated elsewhere, for example, within the state apparatus. Curriculum conceived as technology is attractive to policy makers who aspire to control the process of education and the role of the teacher in it. Socially engineered curriculum change, if it succeeds, implies an enhancement of state control over pupils learning experiences in schools.

Goodson, in his paper, 'A Genesis and Genealogy of British Curriculum Studies' (1995), argues that in many respects the early forms of Curriculum Studies in the UK in the 1960s inherited the technical-rational view of curriculum that was prominent in the US curriculum field at the time. He characterises this version of Curriculum Studies in terms of 'A belief in the science of education, a technological view of school knowledge, and an overwhelming concern with prescription and guidelines...'

Kerr (1968), one of the early advocates of the objectives model of curriculum planning in the UK, believed that it was a better basis for decisions about 'the selection and organisation of the content of courses, and about the relative merits of different teaching methods'. He and others inherited the aspiration of many US scholars to use the model as a basis for a new applied educational science which generated useful knowledge for curriculum decision-makers. One of the most detailed and influential articulations of the process of planning by objectives was by Hilda Taba (1962):

Step 1: Diagnose learning needs

Step 2: Formulate objectives

Step 3: Select content

Step 4: Organise content

Step 5: Select learning experiences

Step 6: Organise learning experiences

Step 7: Determine what to evaluate and the means of doing it.

Stenhouse (1975, Ch.5) argued that Taba offered the best account of how the principles of planning by objectives can be used to organise the study of education. He writes:

> The process of diagnosis of needs and statement of aims provides a focus for the consideration of high-level values, for an analysis of society's demands upon the schools, and for a consideration of the nature of knowledge and culture. The debate at this stage invites the participation of those interested and qualified in ethics, epistemology, sociology of knowledge and social philosophy.
>
> As the implications of these aims are worked across into practical form with constant reference back to principles by means of the formulation of objectives, the selection and organisation of content, and the selection and organisation of learning experiences, other relevant studies can be orchestrated

into the work. Epistemology and psychology are brought into relationship, particularly in the Piagetian tradition of empirical study of the development of concepts, logics, knowledge and affective responses, the child's reconstruction of the world in the mind. Learning theory, systematic pedagogy and social psychology inform the selection and organisation of learning experiences. And when the curriculum which is the product of this synthesising process emerges as a product, it can be tested, evaluated and improved by the application of the relatively refined techniques of psychometrics and educational measurement.

Lawton's account of the role of 'cultural analysis' in curriculum planning (1983, 1989) is entirely consistent with Taba's view of the role of different theoretical disciplines in curriculum planning and fits neatly into her 'step 1' of the process. However, he appears to be unaware of this. Lawton argues (1989, Ch. 2) that proponents of the objectives model, on both the narrow and broader interpretations, gave insufficient attention to the problem of justifying the selection of objectives. Ignoring Taba, he focuses on Tyler's planning principles. The latter described three ideological sources for such selection – child-centred, society-centred and knowledge-centred – but, argues Lawton, made no attempt to either evaluate their relative importance or judge 'specific inputs from any one source'.

Knowledge maps produced by such people as Hirst (1975) and Phenix (1964) also come in for criticism (see Lawton, 1989, Ch. 3) because little attention was paid to the analysis of society as a basis for judging what knowledge the young need to acquire 'at various stages in their development'. The mapping and selection of objectives for Lawton should not be the first step in curriculum planning. The initial focus should be on the development of a rationale for justifying the selection of objectives. He is attracted by Skilbeck's refinement of Tyler's model to incorporate 'situational analysis' as a first step in planning by objectives, and uses it as a basis for describing the process of cultural analysis. However, I would claim that it was Taba rather than Skilbeck who first modified Tyler's principles of curriculum planning to create room for a situational analysis of learning needs.

Lawton defines the curriculum as a selection from the culture of a particular society. And in order to justify that selection the curriculum planner needs to ground it in an analysis of a society's culture in terms of what he calls 'cultural sub-systems' that are universal and invariant in form if not content across all societies. Lawton claims that every society's culture can be mapped out in terms of nine sub-systems (see 1983, Ch. 3, 1989, Ch. 3). These are:

1. Socio-political system

2. Economic system

3. Communication system

4. Rationality system

5. Technology system

6. Morality system

7. Belief system

8. Aesthetic system

9. Maturational system

Mapping a culture in these terms provides a rational foundation for the selection of curriculum content and the specification of educational objectives. One might also add that it provides a foundation for social engineering by the state to construct a national curriculum.

Lawton's commitment to planning by objectives arises, I would suggest, from this implication: that state control over the curriculum experiences of children requires these experiences to be planned and monitored in the light of clearly specified learning outcomes. In legitimating state intervention in curriculum construction, cultural analysis tacitly endorses the use of the objectives model. This form of curriculum research serves the technical-rational interests of the state in its efforts to socially engineer curriculum reform in schools.

The objectives model clearly shaped the construction of the National Curriculum in England and Wales following a series of steps not dissimilar to those outlined by Taba. It is no coincidence that 20 years before the National Curriculum, this model emerged in the UK in a more hesitant and indirect attempt by the state to influence the school curriculum through the Schools Council for Curriculum and Examinations, during the 1960s and 1970s, a body representing the interests of central and local government as well as those of the teaching profession.

In his critique of the English and Welsh National Curriculum, based on a cultural analysis of British society, Lawton questions not the planning model but the criteria which underpin the selection of content.

Goodson (1995) cites his old mentor Bernstein's view that the rise of Curriculum Studies constituted 'a region inserted between education and professional studies, the beginning of the technologizing of teacher training'. One must place this view in a context where the kind of professional studies Bernstein had been actively advocating and developing at the London Institute of Education during the late 1960s and early 1970s was under threat. Bernstein and his associates at the Institute sought a foundation for professional studies in the theoretical disciplines: philosophy, psychology, sociology, and history. Goodson argues that Bernstein found himself undertaking sociological work in a field where the dominant paradigm of Curriculum Studies was 'decidedly antithetical to the scholarly traditions he was promoting'. But why is the technical-rational paradigm antithetical to scholarship when, as we have seen, it was construed by many as a way of organising the scholarly study of education in a practically useful form? From Bernstein's particular sociological perspective the paradigm implies an uncritical stance because it assumes that the disciplines are instruments of technical control over human behaviour. It therefore leaves no room for a sociological critique of the operation of technical rationality in social planning.

One form of curriculum research which emerged within the parameters of rational curriculum planning was that of programme evaluation. This type of research attempted to assess the instrumental effectiveness of 'curricula treatments' in producing the desired learning outcomes as these are measured by either standardised or criterion referenced tests. Some of the early critiques of the methodology employed pointed out that evaluators frequently presumed that the curriculum programmes were being faithfully implemented by teachers. Suppose the presumption was false, and the effects measured were not those of the curriculum that had been prescribed. House (1974) argued that 'a doctrine of transferability' across contexts was taken for granted by many evaluators. Curricula were viewed like washing machines. They operate in the same way regardless of the social and cultural context in which they are used. All that is required to ensure that they work is to give teachers a simple set of operating instructions. The doctrine was later well illustrated by the relatively small amount of time set aside for disseminating the National Curriculum to teachers *en masse* via a process of cascading. It soon became clear that the National Curriculum was being variably interpreted and shaping up rather differently in different classrooms and schools. Since 1989 curriculum research in the UK has largely taken the form of implementation studies which focus on the National Curriculum.

2. CRITICAL SOCIAL RESEARCH

In a recent review of policy implementation studies Fitz, Halpin and Power (1994) make a distinction between top-down and bottom-up studies, and argue that the former tended to precede the latter. Top-down studies focus on the implementation of policies developed at the centre in specific localised contexts. Their aim is to identify the conditions which would maximise the translation of policy objectives into practice. Bottom-up studies focus on the role of local agencies, organisations, and bureaucrats in mediating policies to the target groups, because they 'are most closely involved in the lives of target groups and individuals and, it is they, ...who determine the extent to which policies are rendered effective'. Fitz, Halpin and Power claim that while earlier implementation studies in education within the UK aimed to 'discover the conditions under which policy objectives could be most perfectly realised', more recent policy analyses are 'broadly academic in orientation'. This kind of policy sociology appears to be a descendant of the critical sociological tradition established by Bernstein and represents its reworking in the context of increasing state control over policy-making processes. The point is reinforced by Fitz, Halpin and Power, who claim that:

> These studies, organised around the narration and historical analysis of a single policy, are, in the case of education, further analysed in terms of its differential impact on social classes, groups and individuals.

These reviewers give the impression that the first wave of top-down implementation studies surrounding the Educational Reform Act of 1988 have subsided, and have been replaced by more academic and critical bottom-up studies. They suggest that one of the major theoretical contributions such studies are making is the reconceptualisation of the policy process. Ball and Bowe (1992) are particularly credited with a movement beyond the assumption that policy formulation and implementation are quite discrete processes. They argue that:

> ... the policy process ... is a dialectical process in which the 'moments' of legislation (the Act), documentation (from the NCC, the DES, etc) and 'implementation' (the work of teachers) may be more or less loosely coupled (Quoted in Fitz, Halpin and Power).

In other words policy is continuously renegotiated and reformulated in the process of its implementation. Ball and Bowie continue:

> It is our contention that it is in the micro-political processes of the schools that we begin to see not only the limitations and possibilities state policy places on schools but, equally, the limits and possibilities practitioners place on the capacity of the state to reach into the daily lives of schools (Quoted in Fitz, Halpin and Power).

However, I would argue that such 'insights' are by no means novel. They were articulated nearly twenty years ago by MacDonald and Walker (1976) on the basis of their case-studies of curricula innovations in England.

Fitz, Halpin and Power's review of implementation studies is heavily biased in favour of a group of sociologists of education whose work stems from the seminal influence of Bernstein. The journals and books they select their studies from are largely sociological in character. Only one article published in a prominent curriculum journal is cited: Ball and Bowe's paper (1992) in the *Journal of Curriculum Studies*. No reference is made to numerous National Curriculum implementation studies and critiques published in the *Curriculum Journal* which has more subscribers than most educational journals in the UK.

The 1993 Summer edition of the *Curriculum Journal*, edited by Jennifer Nias, especially focused on the National Curriculum in primary schools. Between its pages six implementation studies are published, four of which appear to fit the top-down category (see the contributions of Campbell, Richards, Webb, and Bage). Although these studies use implementation data to question aspects of national curriculum policy – Campbell's critique of the notion of a broad and balanced curriculum embodied in National Curriculum policy is particularly virulent – they are clearly concerned with helping to recast National Curriculum policy in more workable form. At no point could I find the authors calling the basic technical-rational logic which underpins the National Curriculum framework seriously into question.

Implementation studies in the curriculum field, which aspire to assist the translation of national policy objectives into practice, continue, it seems, to be carried out, and may even continue to provide useful information to those operating in the policy arena, in spite of lacking a solid foundation in an academic/theoretical discipline. The fact that academic sociologists of the curriculum choose to ignore them should not delude us into believing that the 'technical-rational' tradition in Curriculum Studies is on the wane, and therefore that curriculum research has finally emancipated itself as an instrument of centralising power. Certainly, sociologists of the curriculum would claim that their discipline does disconnect them from any instrumentality for the state. The general tenor of the Fitz, Halpin and Power review is that good implementation studies – scholarly works which measure up to academic standards – 'have been conducted in the knowledge that the state is unlikely to be persuaded by, or to act on any of their findings, however relevant'.

This view appears to underpin the second tradition of Curriculum Studies that has emerged: one that Fitz, Halpin and Power align themselves with, and whose sociological strand is represented in the articles they cite. It is a 'pessimistic sociological tradition' for reasons which will soon become clear.

The pessimistic sociological strand of critical social research emphasises the importance of first understanding how the curriculum is socially constructed before one tries to change it. It is sceptical about the capacity of individual agents to effect change since their thinking, feeling, and actions are shaped and constrained by power structures of which they may be largely unaware. 'Power' is the central concept here. Understanding the curriculum as a social construct involves understanding it as a power container for affecting the interests of some sector of society rather than others. It is always a critical process of unmasking relations of domination whose outcome is necessarily a critical theory of the curriculum.

It is now over two decades since Bernstein and Young edited *Knowledge and Control* (1971) which effectively established the sociology of the curriculum as a major force in the UK. Bernstein's theory about the social classification and framing of educational knowledge (published in the book) has recently found a new application in the study of cross-curricular themes within the National Curriculum. (see Whitty, Rowe, and Aggleton, 1994). Currently, the sociology of the curriculum is a sub-branch of what has become known as policy-sociology (see Troyna, 1994). Fitz, Halpin and Power's review of implementation studies is largely confined to researchers who label themselves in these terms.

The implementation studies of Ball and his associates might be regarded as representing the 'soft end' of policy sociology, inasmuch as they qualify a basically pessimistic stance towards the effects of policy-making processes by seeing a space for individuals to exercise a measure of freedom and agency within such processes. The following passage from *Education Reform: A Critical and Post-structuralist Approach* (Ball, 1994) illustrates this standpoint of a qualified pessimism. Citing Clegg (1989), Ball argues that:

> ... policy is no simple asymmetry of power: 'Control (or dominance) can never be totally secured, in part because of agency. It will be open to erosion and undercutting by the action, embodied agency of those people who are its object.'... Thus we need to go beyond the dominance/resistance binary. There is just more to school and classroom life than this, a third space – other concerns, demands, pressures, purposes and desires.
>
> In putting this argument I do not intend to minimise or underestimate the effects or impact of policy; rather I hope to problematize them. (Ch. 1).

Ball sees his research into the processes and outcomes of educational policy making as a Foucauldian unmasking of power for the use of those who suffer it. For example, his research into the impact of the policy of self-management for schools shows how the policy impacts by enhancing rather than diminishing social control over the teaching profession. Thus enlightened, teachers are placed in a better position to fight against the loss of professional agency. In unmasking the operations of power in the processes of curriculum construction and implementation, the policy sociologist can help grassroots practitioners to expand their sphere of agency, that third space which transcends those of domination and passive resistance.

In spite of acknowledging some space for individual agency within policy-making and implementation processes, Ball *et al.* presume that its enlargement is dependent upon the development of a critical sociological theory, which unmasks power relations that are hidden from the practical consciousness that shapes everyday human experience. Practical consciousness is dependent upon theoretical consciousness for enlightenment. Such is the implication of a curriculum sociology which rests on a qualified pessimism.

Goodson and Hargreaves want to strengthen the academic foundations of curriculum studies by including a historical studies strand within a broader critical social research paradigm. The possibility of achieving an adequate account of the social construction of the curriculum it seems requires history as a complement to sociology. In *Studying Curriculum* (1994) Goodson asserts:

> What we require is a combined approach: a focus on the construction of prescriptive curricula and policy coupled with an analysis of the negotiations and realisation of that prescribed curriculum, focusing on the essential dialectical relationship of the two (Ch. 8).

If the analysis of 'negotiations' and 'realisations' (the kinds of implementation studies cited by Fitz, Halpin and Power) is the task of policy sociology then understanding the social construction of prescriptive curricula, like the English National Curriculum, is the task of the curriculum historian. The context for the emergence of history as a major discipline in the curriculum field is, according to Goodson, the emergence of 'prescriptive curricula' from sources outside the schools themselves. He writes:

> At this point in time the most significant lacuna for such a reconceptualised programme of study is historical study of the social construction of school curricula (ibid., p. 113).

Goodson's recent attempts to redefine Curriculum Studies by coupling history with sociology are perhaps a reaction to the way the 1988 Education Act with its prescription of a national curriculum has shaped curriculum research since 1989. In his critical introduction to *Studying Curriculum*, Hargreaves (1994) refers to the variations in curriculum practices cited in the numerous implementation studies of the National Curriculum. In doing so he appears to be sniping at soft policy sociologists like Ball, who attempt to depict the power of individual agents to resist and subvert the prescriptions of the state. While he acknowledges that curriculum practice does not have a one-to-one correspondence with curriculum policy, he expresses a shared concern with Goodson that:

scholarly and policy debate gets deflected from the fundamentals of curriculum definition and who controls it, to the complicated details of curriculum implementation (p. 3).

Goodson's work on the history of school subjects offer explanations for the persistence of subject-based curricula in spite of numerous attempts by individuals and groups of teachers to organise the curriculum along different lines. Historical studies reveal the operations of power on curriculum construction in ways which leave little room for human agency. In doing so they provide a check on the tendency of policy sociology continually to qualify its pessimistic outlook. The details Hargreaves refers to are 'surface' features of curriculum practices masking the 'deep structures' which can only be apprehended with the help of the critical disciplines of sociology and history. Hargreaves finds it ironic that the implementation studies of recent years, claiming to demonstrate the state's incapacity to impose its prescriptions on teachers and schools, echo the concerns of a more optimistic, practical and deliberative tradition of Curriculum Studies at a time when 'the practice of curriculum reform has rarely been more profoundly social, systemic and political in nature ...'. From his perspective, this more optimistic tradition stemmed from 'the particular preoccupations of a specific and arguably aberrant historical moment: one characterised by optimism and expansion in the political sphere, and relative autonomy and discretion in the professional one' (p. 3). It is to this optimistic tradition of Curriculum Studies that I shall shortly turn.

* * * * *

Within the critical social research tradition we can therefore discern a tension between those who emphasise power-structures in Curriculum Studies, as determinants of the form and content of national curriculum policies and design, and those like Ball who believe there is space for the operation of human agency exercised at the grass-roots by teachers and others. Ball's position is continuous with that of the American sociologist of the curriculum, Michael Apple, who argued over a decade ago (1982) that the complexity and contradictions of the cultural, political, and economic spheres are lived experiences and can only be understood by grounding reflection in them. For both Apple and Ball the task of sociological studies of the curriculum is an emancipatory one. Such studies rest on a claim to enlighten practitioners about the way in which 'structures of domination' operating in policy-making and implementation processes shape and constrain their judgements, decisions and actions. (But see Elliott, 1993, for a critique of this way of understanding the relationship between 'structure' and 'agency'.)

Lawton's 'cultural analysis' perspective and Ball's 'political analysis' perspective on Curriculum Studies are highly conflictual. Ball, like most critical social researchers in the curriculum field, assumes a neo-Marxist position on the role of the state in capitalist societies: namely, that it exercises power to distribute social goods and benefits unequally and unfairly to favour some sectors of society rather than others. From this perspective Lawton's assumption that the technocratic state can be rationally influenced to distribute educational goods equitably and fairly on the basis of a theoretical analysis of a 'common culture' (an idea critical social researchers would be sceptical of) is not only erroneous but naive.

However, the question as to how the 'grass-roots enlightenment,' which at least some critical social researchers (like Ball) aspire to accomplish, can be translated into transformative social action is rarely, if at all, articulated. The researcher's stance towards the sphere of social action is a detached one. Critical social research, with its emphasis on the political analysis of curriculum processes and content is as rationalist in its orientation as Lawton's cultural analysis, in spite of its critical stance to the kind of social engineering Lawton endorses in his commitment to planning by objectives.

If Lawton's cultural analysis is underpinned by technical-rational interests then the political analysis of 'emancipatory' critical social researchers is underpinned by critical-rational interests. What both appear to have in common are shared rationalist assumptions about the relationship between theory and practice. Both are rationalist perspectives because they assume that theory constitutes a pre-condition of good practice; a foundation of knowledge which can be subsequently applied by policy-makers, in the case of Lawton, and by practitioners, in the case of Ball, and used to justify judgements and decisions and the form, content, and processes of the curriculum.

Within the British tradition of critical social research, Troyna (1994) has recently begun to criticise these rationalist assumptions. He argues that:

> ... education policy sociology, as it is presently constituted, is limited and limiting in its theoretical, disciplinary and strategic concerns. This is because it continues to turn a blind eye to issues arising from dialogue from cognate theoretical and disciplinary sources which have the potential to illuminate the policy process.

Particularly ignored, he claims, are the 'conceptualisations and empirical research which feature in feminist and anti-racist discourses'.

Initially his argument appears to be similar to that of Goodson and to Hargreaves' plea for greater inter-disciplinarity under the general rubric of critical social research. Both parties attack the hegemony of policy sociology, although the disciplines they want to bring together differ somewhat. However, Troyna challenges the claim of some policy sociologists to represent a specific discipline called sociology. He argues that education policy analysis as practised is less deserving of the title 'sociology' than it is of the more generic title 'social science' :

> ... even the most cursory glance at the projects said to exemplify this genre would reveal influences from an array of disciplinary traditions. It would also point to an equally wide range of methodologies and a concern with the 'collection' of data from a range of different research sites.

According to Troyna, education policy analysis, as conducted by the group who describe themselves as sociologists, is both theoretically and methodologically eclectic. Such an argument appears to contradict his earlier call for greater inter-disciplinarity. But as his argument develops it becomes clear that the inter-disciplinarity he has in mind not only broadens the framework of inquiry, 'in pursuit of the most appropriate analytical and conceptual tools', but orientates it more closely to 'critical social research'so that it becomes clearly distinguishable from other forms of social inquiry. The kind of inter-disciplinarity Troyna has in mind not only describes and explains events but 'aims to identify those elements which have the potential to change things'. He cites Lee Harvey's view (1990) that critical social research not only wants to show 'what is really going on at the societal level' but is also concerned 'with doing something about it'. It involves strategic political action against 'oppressive social structures'.

Unlike the policy sociologists, Troyna is not content with mere enlightenment as an aim of critical research but is concerned to articulate how analysis can be harnessed to transformative social action by education policy researchers themselves. Their research he argues must be continued by a commitment to change things through the research. He described how his own research into multi-cultural and anti-racist education policies involved going beyond 'explication towards the formulation ... of a political strategy which might effectively tackle inequalities in education'. This political strategy was then tested by his involvement in concrete campaigning activity in the course of which evidence was collected about its effectiveness.

The reason why Troyna advocates greater links with feminist and anti-racist research is that they have tended to evolve as forms of research which are conditioned by a commitment to change things in the light of certain values. Within these forms of research theory and practice are brought into an interactive relationship, where theoretical analysis informs practice and practice informs theory, and where the division of labour between researchers and practitioners is broken.

In effect what Troyna has done is to reconstruct critical social research in education as a form of action-research. It is interesting that his paper makes no mention of the fact that educational action research has been well established within what I shall call the experimental innovation tradition of curriculum research within the UK (see Elliott, 1991). How does his account of critical social research compare with that provided by those who operate from within this third tradition of Curriculum Studies? Before addressing this question I shall now explore the characteristics of this 'optimistic' tradition, about, which Hargreaves (1994) expressed such scepticism.

3. EXPERIMENTAL INNOVATION

The first major critique of the behavioural objectives model of curriculum planning and development in the UK context was that of Stenhouse (1970). This critique was further developed in his book *An Introduction to Curriculum Research and Development* (1975). Like Lawton, Stenhouse argued that a behavioural objectives design is appropriate for a curriculum concerned with instruction in specific practical skills and that it should not be extended as a model for planning all the curriculum experiences of students. Unlike Lawton, however, he did not find the idea of 'non-behavioural' objectives an intelligible one and saw all 'rational planning' by objectives as essentially grounded in behaviourist assumptions and inconsistent with the nature of education.

The basis of Stenhouse's critique of the objectives model was an educational theory. He claimed that a curriculum planned by objectives distorted the educational process because it was inconsistent with the aims of education and the nature of knowledge. His argument was influenced by the work of the philosopher of education, Richard Peters (1966). Peters argued that discourse about aims in education was an ethical discourse about the intrinsic qualities of educational processes and not a technical discourse about the extrinsic results of such processes. Conceptions of *educational* aims embody values to be realised in a worthwhile process of teaching and learning and implied principles of procedure to orientate the work of teachers in classrooms. The relationship between methods of teaching and learning and aims of education is one of logical consistency/inconsistency rather than technical effectiveness. A particular method is educationally appropriate if it constitutes a realisation in practice of principles of procedure that can logically be derived from an analysis of educational aims. Such aims refer to what counts as a worthwhile educational process and not to its extrinsic outcomes.

Stenhouse argued that it was inappropriate even to analyse aims which referred to a knowledge and understanding of concepts and ideas into behavioural objectives. The use of the objectives model in this way distorts the nature of human concepts and ideas, because their meanings are not closed, and unambiguous but open and ambiguous at the edges. Concepts provide a focus for discourses about problems and issues in human experience, structuring human thought but in the process being continuously redefined and reconstructed through it. For Stenhouse knowledge, conceived as structures of ideas, constitutes a medium in which thought could develop without predetermining its outcomes with precision. It was therefore quite inappropriate to treat concepts/ideas as concrete and tangible entities with fixed and immutable meanings as an objectives model of planning required. What is appropriate is to specify the principles which ought to govern students thinking and inquiry into problems and issues of human experience, both within and across intellectual disciplines, in the light of those ideas. Such principles are a logical implication of any educational aim which views knowledge as a process rather than a product; as a developing of the understanding rather than simply a mastering of concrete and tangible 'facts'.

Stenhouse practically exemplified his alternative 'process model' in the design and execution of the Humanities Curriculum Project which he directed from 1967–72 (see 1975, Ch. 7). From a specification of the kinds of human problems and issues it was worth young adolescents exploring in schools (controversial value issues) he proceeded to define a general aim to orientate the teacher's handling of the learning process ('understanding human acts, social situations, and the controversial issues they raised'). From this aim he analysed a form of procedure in the classroom which he claimed to be logically implicit in it. The cluster of procedural principles he specified included the 'infamous' principle of procedural neutrality which required teachers to refrain from using their authority in classrooms to promote their own views.

Stenhouse's principles of procedure were not viewed by him as rules which specified concrete teaching and learning methods. Rather they orientated the teacher to the process values they needed to realise in the methods they selected. Which methods were consistent/inconsistent with the principles of procedure was left open for the teacher to judge in the light of experimentation in a particular classroom context.

It was in this context of a process model of curriculum design and development that the idea of 'teachers as researchers' of their own practice emerged in the UK during the early 1970s. Stenhouse (1975, Ch. 10) defined a curriculum:

> as a particular form of specification about the practice of teaching and not as a package of materials or a syllabus of ground to be covered. It is a way of translating any educational idea into a hypothesis testable in practice. It invites

critical testing rather than acceptance...the uniqueness of each classroom setting implies that any proposal...needs to be tested and verified and adapted by each teacher in his own classroom. The ideal is that the curricular specification should feed a teacher's personal research and development programme through which he is progressively increasing his understanding of his own work and hence bettering his teacher...it is not enough that teachers' work should be studied: they need to study it themselves.

In advocating that teachers study their own teaching Stenhouse (1980) draws on Mao Tse Tung's analysis of the theory-practice relationship: Only through personal participation in the struggle to change reality can you uncover the essence of that thing or class of things and comprehend them.

From the perspective of a process model of curriculum development, the study of the curriculum or curriculum research is grounded in innovative experiments carried out by teachers in classrooms conceived as laboratories. Teaching as an activity is recast as the testing of action-hypotheses, and thereby fused with curriculum research recast as practical experimentation with the educational ideas or theories embedded in curricular specifications (see Elliott, 1994).

Stenhouse argued that his idea of curriculum research as grounded in the study of classrooms by teacher-researchers carries no implication about the authorship of curriculum proposals. The originator he argues 'maybe a classroom teacher, a policy-maker, or an educational research worker'.

Academic support for experimental innovation by classroom teachers, who are viewed as members of the educational science community, may consist of:

a)   translating educational ideas into experimental designs;

b)   recasting the curriculum change proposals of policy-makers at school, local and national levels in experimental form;

c)   providing consultancy on methodological issues in the areas of data gathering, analysis, and case study writing;

d)   utilising teachers' research as a basis for modifying experimental designs on an ongoing basis;

e)   disseminating teachers' research.

Curriculum development shaped by a process model can be conceived in terms of separate but complementary roles for academics and teachers. The former are responsible for experimental designs while the latter test them. In the dialogue which goes on between them curriculum designs are continually restructured.

Jean Rudduck's *Innovation and Change* (1991) constitutes a body of writing which can be located in the experimental innovation tradition in Curriculum Studies. Much of the material in Rudduck's book was written during the period of the Thatcher government in Britain and therefore depicts a leading figure in the development of the optimistic tradition coming to terms with a political climate that apparently renders the prospect of innovative experimentation increasingly a remote one. As MacDonald (1991) points out in his introduction to Rudduck's book:

> ... the word 'innovation' already has a dated feel. It seems to belong to a chapter of our post-war history that has closed. Reform is now the banner headline of the politicians who have seized upon the alleged failure of the innovators so as to take control of the process of change and, in the UK at least, to make the central issue one of relations rather than relationships (p. 1).

The change strategies that the innovators experimented with, MacDonald notes, have now been consigned by many innovation pathologists, some of whom were themselves part of the optimistic tradition, to the dustbin of history (see, for example, Fullen, 1989). He refers to the understandable pervasive gloom and sense of impotence which has emerged as politically initiated reform replaces professionally initiated innovation. Nevertheless, he contends that Jean Rudduck's book, in spite of 'her nostalgia for the false dawn of the 1960s' and a 'downbeat conclusion' which gives an impression 'of a terminal decline' in the tradition she espouses , can be given a different reading. It is a reading which demonstrates that, while it is difficult to be optimistic about the future prospects of the 'professional, communal, and fraternal culture' that lies at 'the core of her advocacy', it is not impossible. Such a reading implies a different account of the future direction of Curriculum Studies to that provided by social constructionists like Goodson and Hargreaves. It will be an account in which the study of the curriculum, the search for understanding, is not dissociated from attempts to change it: in which innovations constitute hypothetical probes into unknown and uncharted territory that cannot be mapped to assist future travellers simply by viewing it from a number of disciplinary helicopters. Such an account will continue to emphasise the significance of the practical for the study of the curriculum (see, for example, Carr, 1993).

From the perspective of social constructionists like Hargreaves and Goodson, the current political climate appears to legitimate their approach and to undermine that of innovators like Rudduck. But the antagonism is not new and first manifested itself in the years immediately following the publication of *Knowledge and Control*. MacDonald correctly recalls 'the sniping from the sidelines' by the new sociologists towards 'those liberal humanists who sought to engage the system and mend its ways'. The roots of the antagonism, MacDonald argues, the mocking of the very idea of engagement with the system, lay in theoretical certainties which denied any legitimacy for agency and involvement in concrete experience as opposed to theoretical discourse. He claims that they subsequently came to acknowledge the importance of human agency in processes of social transformation, citing Apple's (1982) argument that the complexity and contradictions of the cultural, political, and economic spheres are lived experiences and can only be understood by grounding reflection in them.

However, it appears that this movement towards a more qualified pessimism on the part of some social constructivists has been checked by the perceived impact of the 1988 Education Act on schooling in the UK. It is a pity because the movement of experimental innovators like Rudduck towards a position of qualified optimism could have led to an integration of the two traditions. However, Troyna's critique of 'education policy sociology' in which he attempts to reconstruct critical social research in a form which secures more leverage on the change process provides a possible contemporary meeting point between them. His account of the direction in which critical social research ought to be developing makes it look very much like a form of action research, as I argued earlier. The only difference appears to be with respect to aims. Whereas the innovative experiment is largely concerned with improving the educational quality of children's learning experiences, the critical social research is concerned about the social distribution of educational opportunities for children. If the former is conditioned by certain educational values, then the latter is conditioned by certain social values.

The practice of action research in the future may well be improved in present circumstances by integrating the 'experimental innovation' tradition with something like Troyna's version of critical social research. However, I would argue that such synthesis has already been achieved at a conceptual level, following the debates (see Elliott, 1987) stimulated by Carr and Kemmis's seminal book, *Becoming Critical: Knowing Through Action Research* (1983), over a decade ago. Troyna appears to be totally unaware of these debates.

LEARNING ABOUT CURRICULUM CHANGE THROUGH INNOVATIVE EXPERIMENTATION

In conclusion, I want to examine whether there are any grounds for optimism about the future of the experimental innovation tradition in Britain. MacDonald sees the papers in Rudduck's book to reflect changes in the social context of curriculum development, from one which sanctioned innovative curriculum experiments in schools to one characterised by government attempts to engineer curriculum reform through its policy-making apparatus. This transition from Innovation to Reform was justified politically, argues MacDonald (1991), on the 'alleged failure of the innovators'. He identifies an ambiguity in the rhetoric of reformers which he suggests explains 'why the most unlikely bedfellows', both élitists and egalitarians, 'can be found in their ranks'. For example, I would argue that egalitarian researchers like Lawton, and perhaps Campbell, Halpin and Whitty appear, as education policy researchers, to be concerned with influencing state reform policies as much as élitists on the new educational right.

The ambiguity, according to MacDonald, consists of a lack of clarity about whether the reformers are trying to achieve the same objectives as the innovators by more effective means, such as through the exercise of state power, or whether they are tacitly acknowledging the success of school and teachers-based innovations in the past by having the regressive aim of restoring the 'former virtues that are threatened by the abuses introduced and fostered by meddling and muddle headed professionals'. I would place the education policy researchers I have cited in the former category and distinguish them from the new right brigade of academics who are concerned to 'put the clock back' through the mechanism of policy-driven reform.

The papers in Rudduck's book on *Innovation and Change* were all written during the 1980s but contain reflections on her experience of innovative experiments in the 1970s, and MacDonald detects in these reflections a growing pessimism about the possibility of realising her core beliefs as the rhetoric of 'innovation'shifts into that of 'reform'. These core beliefs relate to the provision of equal opportunities for all children and its dependence on the development of a communal and fraternal professional culture which supports innovative experiments in schooling initiated by teachers.

While acknowledging the difficulty of remaining optimistic about realising these convictions in the contemporary political climate, MacDonald states that there are grounds for optimism, and that these can be found in the experience of people, like Rudduck, who engaged teachers and schools in innovative experimentation. He argues that Rudduck's book depicts a learning curve which would not be untypical of such people. He then proceeds to unpack this 'getting of wisdom'. His analysis can be summarised in terms of the following insights:

–   *it is very difficult to change schools from the outside and 'therefore teachers must play a generative role in the development of better curricula' by acquiring a sense of ownership over ideas and control over the means of realising them.*

– *teacher development is a necessary condition of curriculum development. Package-driven approaches to curriculum change don' t work because they by-pass teachers who subsequently subvert the realisation of their aims and objectives.*

– *if teachers are to play a generative role in developing innovatory curricula then teacher development needs to be coupled with the development of the organisational culture of the school. Teacher and school development are not separate processes. In developing their generative powers teachers need to work fraternally and communally on whole-school issues and in doing so both develop themselves and transform the organisational culture.*

MacDonald writes:

> It became clear as we entered the '80s that the unit of teacher development should be the school ... new notions of school based self-review, self-evaluation and self-development became more prominent in curriculum planning and innovation theory.

Rudduck's book, argues MacDonald, exemplifies one strand of thinking about curriculum development which has evolved over the past 25 years: from a belief in the power of externally designed curriculum packages to effect change, to a belief in the development of teachers' generative capacities, to the integration of this belief with the idea of whole school development.

In addition to these insights about curriculum change, MacDonald adds the beliefs that:

– *local enterprise is more likely to improve quality rather than national enterprise;*

– *national agencies should set policy in broad terms but leave them open to interpretation at the local level in the light of local needs. Teachers and schools should then be invited to make appropriate curricula responses;*

– *the exercise of professional autonomy in teacher initiated curriculum change can only be justified by the professional commitment of teachers to a form of accountability in which they submit their activities to public critique and demonstrate their responsiveness to it.*

These 'insights' about the nature of curriculum change are the legacy of curriculum projects which supported innovative experiments in schools. They provide grounds for optimism because they imply a) that the scenario of state engineered reforms will not work, whether they be engineered to realise 'élitist' or 'egalitarian' policies, and b) that rationalist attempts by critical social researchers to generate a theory of change which can then be applied by teachers, who played little part in generating it, is unlikely in itself to effect significant change either.

MacDonald points out that many like-minded curriculum researchers to Rudduck had been teachers or teacher trainers involved in the project initiated innovations of the 1960s and 1970s. In spite of their apparent failure to transform classrooms, they established careers in universities and polytechnics and local education authority advisory and inspection services. This invisible network of innovators constructed a new beachhead for attacking change issues in schools. The 'project' was replaced by a new branch of educational studies in higher education institutions, Curriculum Studies, which, with the support of 'friends' in the local education authorities, became the location of a new form of award-bearing in-service education for teachers (INSET). Within the higher education institutions, the innovators had to articulate and defend the kind of research they had learned to do with teachers and found the opportunity to practise it through the INSET courses provided. MacDonald claims that:

> ... the curriculum innovators found themselves free, not only to continue their mission, and not only to apply their wisdom through an avenue (teacher development) that corresponded with their perception of need, but also to construct a new authority for the extension of formal knowledge construction to those who had formerly been confined to the role of research consumption.

Within higher education institutions, MacDonald stated, the experimental innovators had more success than they anticipated in challenging an objectivist logic of research modelled on the natural sciences. What he describes as the unholy methodological improvisation which characterises their pursuit of useful knowledge in the circumstances of innovative action has, he believes, taken root and sustained by teacher demand, will not go away. He concludes that:

> The innovators who began in the classrooms have now penetrated the institutional order and are beginning to reshape the infra-structure of schooling.

This may appear to be a wildly exaggerated claim from the perspective of those who have already issued their verdict on the experimental innovation movement as a failure. But from MacDonald's perspective as a seasoned commentator on innovation pathologies it is not so wild. 'It takes 50 years', he argues, echoing Miles (1964), 'for a new social practice to become widely established.' The reshaping of the infrastructure of schooling that MacDonald refers to has not been characterised by a great deal of public visibility. But undoubtedly the relationship between knowledge-generating activities in higher education institutions and practice in schools has been in a process of transformation over the last 25 years. Many INSET courses carrying academic awards across the UK are now conceived as helping teachers to improve practice in schools through insider research. It is not only the teachers on courses who are seen as the recipients of such support but all those that have a close working relationship within their schools and are implicated in the research process. Through this form of research-based INSET, the boundaries between higher education institutions and the school system are rendered permeable so that the latter takes greater responsibility for knowledge generation and the former secures more purchase on the processes of development and change.

MacDonald cites House's (1974) assertion that the school is an institution 'frozen' in the order of the social institutions it is interlocked with, and suggests that this thawing of higher education institutions with respect to its knowledge generating activities 'could reasonably be seen as a necessary if not sufficient condition of school improvement'.

House's idea of schools as 'frozen institutions' has become central to an emerging theory of networking within the experimental innovation tradition.This theory marks the most recent stage of learning about curriculum change in schools. It underpins the emergence of action research networks linking teachers and teacher educators across established organisational boundaries. Twenty years ago the Ford Teaching Project (see Elliott, 1976–77) evolved into the Classroom Action Research Network (CARN) aimed at providing teacher researchers with supporting links to higher education facilitators on a continuing basis that transcended the short-term support provided by funded projects. Now called the Collaborative Action Research Network, CARN, under the leadership of Bridget Somekh has become a network of action-research networks clustered around higher education institutions both in the UK and overseas (see Altrichter, Posch and Somekh, 1993, Introduction, p. 4). Its growth and development over the years is indicative of the power of networking between teachers and between teachers and teacher educators in higher education to support innovative experimentation in schools. A growing awareness of the power of networking across formal organisational boundaries to effect significant change within them represents a new high point in the learning curve of the experimental innovators.

The emergence of networking as a curriculum change strategy is evidenced in a new wave of quite visible innovative experimentation which fuses the development of the curriculum, teachers and schools, with research. It is happening outside the UK in other European and, indeed, Far Eastern countries. There is, for example, a recently established Malaysian Action Research Network (MARN) linking schoolteachers with teacher educators working collaboratively on curriculum issues. An Austrian network centred on the University of Klagenfurt has been in existence for a decade under the leadership of Peter Posch. Both networks are linked through CARN.

The context of this international interest in developing teachers' capacities to play a generative role in curriculum development is one in which governments are beginning to devolve more responsibility for curriculum decision-making to the grass roots and local levels. Unfortunately, with the possible exception of Scotland, the UK is out of step, having centralised at a time when its economic competitors are busy going in the opposite direction.

The ideas of Stenhouse and his associates – 'the process model of curriculum development' and 'teachers as researchers' – are now attracting international recognition. In terms of concrete illustrations the most significant one I am aware of is the OECD's School Initiatives and the Environment Project (ENSI), which has been operating as an international curriculum development network for the past decade supported by the governments of OECD member states in anything between 12–19 countries. The design of ENSI was originally proposed by the Austrian government, using Peter Posch at the University of Klagenfurt as a consultant. Posch, in turn, had been heavily influenced by the ideas of Stenhouse and was linked to CARN.

The design of ENSI (see Posch, 1991), which was proposed and accepted by the OECD (CERI) Governing Board, gives schools and teachers an initiating role in developing a new kind of Environmental Education Curriculum with a common framework of aims and procedural principles. These emphasise the development of dynamic qualities in students and the growth of environmental awareness through an action learning process which engage students in a direct experience of environmental issues within their local communities. ENSI also emphasises the importance of teachers undertaking action research into the problems of realising the project's aims and principles in practice, and required them to produce case-studies as a basis for sharing experience and insights both within and across the participating countries (see OECD, 1991, Part 2). It also recommended the establishment of pedagogical support persons from teacher education institutions to facilitate teachers' action research.

The project has been hailed as a great success by participating countries and schools. The teachers' case-studies of their 'innovative experiments' and the National Evaluation Reports illustrate the continuing potential of a paradigm of curriculum development which fuses the processes of research, development and implementation into a unified process, located in schools but supported by both policy-makers and collaborating researchers in higher education. Central to this success was the establishment through the mediating influence of the OECD of 'dynamic networks' of teachers and teacher educators/researchers operating in each country and linked together through an international network for the purpose of sharing experience and ideas across national cultures. The strength and power of this international network of networks is that the programme refuses to die and now has a life of its own, continuing with only a minimum of support from the OECD.

The 'learning curve' of participants in ENSI echoes many of the insights cited by MacDonald. In his recent study of the effects of a 'dynamic networking' of innovative experimentation in ENSI schools, Posch (1994a) shows why they generate the power to change curricula in ways which social engineering on a technical-rational model cannot. Drawing also on the work of House (1974), he argues that efforts to direct change from outside schools largely fail because they adopt the research, development and diffusion paradigm of change. This paradigm implies a vertical/hierarchical division of labour which denies teachers a generative role in inventing, constructing and disseminating innovations. Dynamic networks on the other hand effect change by creating a learning culture in which the roles of external change agents are redefined in terms of horizontal relationships with teachers. Posch claims that such a redefinition implies a logic of supportive growth for the development of reflective rationality (see also Posch, 1994b). Researchers become facilitators of innovative experimentation in schools, and policy makers – using a metaphor provided by House (1974) – become 'atomic stock pile regulators'. Posch quotes House's use of this metaphor to describe the role of government in the innovation process:

> Government activity should be stimulating and regulating like withdrawing or inserting a lead rod in an atomic stock pile…Directions and energies must be mobilised within the system itself.

Posch states that although House's metaphor should not be overstrained it does acknowledge that innovative potential is already present in schools and amongst teachers. It need not be imported and imposed.

Dynamic networks, according to Posch, do not assume any technical rational doctrine about the transferability of innovations across the educational system. Rather they mediate understandings generated by teachers in one context to inform judgement in others. He writes:

> …one can grasp an idea that materialised in one context and can use its power to construct one's own concretisation, adapted to one's own situational context

and personal strengths and weaknesses. The result then is not a copy nor an application of a general principle but is a new solution for which ownership can be claimed. In this sense, dynamic networks provide cross-situational links which allow a 'reflective transformation of ideas' (D. Schon) and thereby a spread of innovative activities without 'disseminating' anything.

The power of a dynamic network such as the one which evolved through the ENSI project lies in its capacity as a learning system to sustain and spread innovative experimentation by teachers. In other words, dynamic networks empower teachers to play a generative role in the curriculum change process within their schools.

However, the experience of the ENSI project suggests that the dynamic networking of teachers and teacher educators/educational researchers across schools and higher education institutions is not a sufficient condition of curriculum change in schools. The thawing of schools as 'frozen' institutions requires also a thawing of the boundaries between them and the social environments in which they are located. The ENSI project not only created, via the concept of dynamic networking, a learning system for teachers which transcends the traditional organisational boundaries between schooling and higher education institutions, but it also created a learning system for students which transcends the traditional boundaries between school and community.

Within their localities many ENSI schools have become nodes in a learning network which links their students to people and agencies in the community. Rather than simply controlling the transmission of abstract knowledge to passive learners, the schools have begun to support a dynamic learning process in which students collaborate with local citizens and agencies to construct and test, through action research, solutions to environmental problems in their locality. The local environment becomes the location of learning experiences for students, and the school becomes a facilitator in a learning system which transcends its traditional organisational boundaries. Posch (1994a) argues that:

> Dynamic networks contradict one of the traditional assumptions of schooling, the assumption of a separation of school and society. If dynamic networks develop it is difficult to say where the educational organisation ends and where society and its abundance of personal and institutional relationships begin.

In his paper he provides a number of examples of the thawing of the boundaries between schooling and society within the ENSI project. As an innovative experiment the project has pushed the learning curve of the experimental innovation tradition to further heights, with the insight that school development as a condition of curriculum change involves dissolving the boundaries of schooling and society through the construction of dynamic learning systems (networks) which transcend these boundaries. In relation to learning within such systems schools re-position themselves as facilitating rather than controlling agencies.

This insight into what is involved in school development as a condition of curriculum change shows the limitations of the currently fashionable 'school effectiveness' movement (Mortimore, 1995). This movement has tended to focus on surface features of schools as organisations and not questioned the assumptions about the role of schools in society which underpin their research. Recently more attention is being given to the relationship between the organisational cultures of schools and the ways student learning is shaped by the structures of belief and value they consist of. However, the school effectiveness movement has yet to learn that any fundamental transformation in the organisational culture of schools will depend on innovative curriculum experiments with learning systems that transcend the traditional boundaries between schooling and society.

SELECT BIBLIOGRAPHY

Ball, S. J. (1994). *Education Reform – a critical and post-structural approach.* Buckingham: Open University Press.

Carr, W. and Kemmis, S. (1983). *Becoming Critical: Knowing Through Action Research.* Victoria: Deakin University Press (republished by London: Falmer Press).

Elliott, J. (1991). 'What have we learned from Action Research in School-based Evaluation?' *Educational Action Research*, Vol.1.

— (1991). *Action Research for Educational Change.* Milton Keynes: Open University Press.

Goodson, I. F. (1994). *Studying Curriculum.* Buckingham: Open University Press.

House, E. (1974). *The Politics of Educational Innovation.* Berkeley: McCutchan.

Lawton, D. (1989). *Education, Culture and the National Curriculum.* London: Hodder & Stoughton.

MacDonald, B. and Walker, R. (1976). *Changing the Curriculum.* London: Open Books

Pettigrew, M. and Somekh, B. (eds) (1994). *Evaluating Innovation in Environmental Education.* Paris: OECD.

Stenhouse, L. (1975). *An Introduction to Curriculum Research and Development.* London: Heinemann.

Taba, H. (1962). *Curriculum Development.* New York: Harcourt, Brace & World.

Tyler, R. W. (1949) *Basic Principles of Curriculum and Instruction.* Chicago: University of Chicago Press.

REFERENCES

Altrichter, H., Posch, P. and Somekh, B. (1993). *Teachers Investigate their Work.* London: Routledge.

Apple, M. W. (1982). *Education and Power.* Boston: Routledge & Kegan Paul.

Ball, S. and Bowe, R. (1992) 'Subject Departments and the Implementation of National

Curriculum Policy: an overview of the issues', *Journal of Curriculum Studies*, 24, 2, pp. 97–115.

Ball, S. J. (1994). *Education Reform – a critical and post-structural approach*. Buckingham: Open University Press.

Carr, W. (1993). Editorial in *Curriculum Studies*, 1, 1.

Carr, W. and Kemmis, S. (1983). *Becoming Critical: Knowing Through Action Research*. Victoria: Deakin University Press (republished by London: Falmer Press).

Clegg, S. (1989). *Framework of Power*. London: Sage.

Elliott, J. (1976–77). 'Developing hypotheses from teachers' practical constructs: an account of the work of the Ford Teaching Project', *Interchange*, 7, 2. Ontario Institute for Studies in Education.

— (1991). 'What have we learned from Action Research in School-based Evaluation?' *Educational Action Research*, Vol. 1.

— (1991). *Action Research for Educational Change*. Milton Keynes: Open University Press.

— (1994). 'The teachers' role in curriculum development: an unresolved issue in English attempts at curriculum reform'. *Curriculum Studies*, 2, 1.

— (1987). 'Educational Theory, Practical Philosophy and Action Research', *British Journal of Educational Studies*, 25, 2, pp. 149–69.

Fitz, J., Halpin, D. and Power, S. (1994). 'Implementation Research and Education Policy', *British Journal of Educational Studies*, 42, 1.

Goodson, I. F. (1994). *Studying Curriculum*. Buckingham: Open University Press.

— (1995). 'A Genesis and Genealogy of British Curriculum Studies', mimeo, University of Western Ontario.

Hargreaves, A. (1994). Critical Introduction to Goodson, I. F., *Studying Curriculum*. Buckingham: Open University Press.

Harvey, L. (1990). *Critical Social Research*. London: Allen & Unwin.

House, E. (1974). *The Politics of Educational Innovation*. Berkeley: McCutchan.

Kerr, J. F. (1968) 'The Problem of Curriculum Reform' in Kerr, J. F. (ed.), *Changing the Curriculum*. London: University of London Press.

Lawton, D. (1983). *Curriculum Studies and Educational Planning*. London: Hodder & Stoughton.

— (1989). *Education, Culture and the National Curriculum*. London: Hodder & Stoughton.

MacDonald, B. (1991). Critical Introduction to Rudduck, J., *Innovation and Change*. Milton Keynes: Open University Press.

MacDonald, B. and Walker, R.(1976) *Changing the Curriculum*. London: Open Books.

Mager, R. F. (1962). *Preparing Objectives for Programmed Instruction*. San Francisco: Fearon.

Miles, M. B. (ed.) (1964). *Innovation in Education*. New York: Columbia Teachers' College.

Mortimore, P. (1995). *Effective Schools: current impact and future potential*. Inaugural lecture as new Director of the Institute of Education, London, 7 February 1995.

Nias, J. (ed.) (1993). 'The National Curriculum in Primary Schools: current concerns', *The Curriculum Journal*, 4, 2.

OECD (CERI) (1991). *Environment, Schools, and Active Learning*. Paris: CERI/OECD.

Peters, R. S. (1966). *Ethics and Education*. London: Allen & Unwin.

Popham, W. J. (1969). 'Objectives and Instruction',in Popham, W. J., Eisner, E. W., Sullivan, H. J., and Tyler, I. I. (eds), *Instructional Objectives*. Washington DC: AERA Monograph/Rand McNally.

306 A GUIDE TO EDUCATIONAL RESEARCH

Posch, P. (1991). 'Environment and School Initiatives: Background and Basic Premises of the Project', in *Environment, Schools and Active Learning*. Paris: CERI/OECD.
— (1994a). 'Professional Development in Environmental Education, Networking and Infrastructures', paper for International Conference on Environmental Education Policy and Practice, Braunschweig (Lower Saxony), Germany, 6–11 March 1994. Paris: OECD.
— (1994b). 'Networking in Environmental Education', in Pettigrew, M. and Somekh, B. (eds), in *Evaluating Innovation in Environmental Education*. Paris: OECD.
Stenhouse, L. (1970). 'Some Limitations on the Use of Objectives in Curriculum Research and Planning', *Paedagogica Europaea*, 6, pp. 73–83.
— (1975) *An Introduction to Curriculum Research and Development*. London: Heinemann.
— (1980). 'Curriculum research and the art of the teacher', *Curriculum*, 1, 1 Spring.
Taba, H.(1962). *Curriculum Development*. New York: Harcourt, Brace & World.
Troyna, B. (1994). 'Critical Social Research and Education Policy', *British Journal of Educational Studies*, 42, 1.
Tyler, R. W. (1949). *Basic Principles of Curriculum and Instruction*. Chicago: University of Chicago Press.
Tyler, R. W. (1973). 'The Father of Behavioural Objectives Criticises them', *Phi Delta Kappan*, 55, 57.
Whitty, G., Rowe, G. and Aggleton, P. (1994). 'Subjects and Themes in the Secondary School Curriculum', *Research Papers in Education: Policy and Practice*, 9, 2.
Young, M. F. D. (1971). *Knowledge and Control*. London: Collier-Macmillan.

12

CHILDREN'S LEARNING

Kathy Sylva

During the last decade we have learned much about the psychological processes involved in learning, and this chapter will focus on two lines of research. Classroom teaching has direct effects on children's educational achievement, their acquisition of literacy, numeracy and scientific knowledge. However, schools also influence children's social cognitions and motivations and these psychological processes are as powerful in predicting later attainments as intelligence or curriculum. The indirect effects of schooling are more elusive because they concern children's motivation to learn or avoid learning, their conception of themselves as learners, and the models they create for social life in classrooms. Cognitions and motivations acquired during school continue to shape individual development outside and beyond school. This chapter focuses on the ways pre-school and primary education shape psychological development, which in turn will influence educational outcomes.

Classroom and schools have been on a roller-coaster of change since the late 1980s. At the descriptive level this has been well documented; the job of teachers has changed dramatically, the curriculum has undergone a revolution, assessment has burgeoned into a large-scale industry and schools are managed in new ways. In this chapter the changes in education are the back-drop against which we consider recent research in the psychology of education.

First, a brief summary of the main changes in British primary schools since 1988:

1. From child-centred to subject-centred learning

2. From informal to formal teaching methods

3. From classroom-based to standard assessment

4. From teachers as tutors, guides and resource to teachers as managers

This chapter will not argue the immediate gains and losses attributed to educational reform because that has been done elsewhere in this volume. Rather, it will describe some psychological underpinnings of children's learning so that we can evaluate the recent changes in primary education in the light of new insights into psychological development.

THE EFFECTS OF PRE-SCHOOL EDUCATION ON CHILDREN'S ASPIRATIONS AND INDEPENDENCE

Where do educational attitudes and aspirations begin? Many believe they emerge before formal schooling. Research on the effects of pre-school programmes shows how they affect children's orientation to learning. Lazar and Darlington (1982) carried out a meta-analysis of the effects of pre-school programmes in the US. They ignored the low quality, often community-based programmes (which included Head Start), to focus on projects of excellent curriculum and rigorous research design, mostly aimed at disadvantaged groups. Results from the eleven studies in Lazar's meta-analysis showed that attendance at excellent, educationally orientated pre-school programmes was associated with later competence in school and adult life. Pre-school graduates were less likely to be assigned to 'special' education or to be held back in grade while their peers moved up. Where information was available, pre-school graduates were more likely to be employed when young adults.

How had pre-school education changed these children's lives? Interviewers found that pre-school graduates were more likely than those in the control group to give achievement-related answers to the invitation, 'Tell me something you've done that made you feel proud of yourself'. When parents were interviewed about their own attitudes towards their child's school performance, mothers of pre-school graduates expressed more satisfaction with their children's school achievements. The greater satisfaction with schoolwork appears related to the mother's aspiration for her child's future employment. In answer to the question, 'What kind of job would you like (your child) to have later in life?', mothers of children who had attended pre-school replied with skilled or managerial jobs, while mothers in the control group had much lower aspirations for their offspring. Taken together with the test outcomes, the attitudinal findings suggest that pre-school education changed the social environment of children. This then affected the way children settled into school, beginning a 'virtuous cycle' of positive expectations, followed by achievements.

The most carefully controlled of the eleven programmes reviewed by Lazar was the Perry Pre-school Project, later known as High/Scope

(Schweinhart and Weikart, 1993). Research on it employed random assignment to experimental and control groups and longitudinal follow-up for almost 30 years. Although an initial IQ advantage for pre-school graduates disappeared by entry to secondary school, there were startling differences in other outcomes between the 65 children who attended the half-day educational programme between the ages of three and five and the control group of 58 children who had remained at home. By the age of 27, the High/Scope 'graduates' had:

- significantly higher monthly earnings at age 27 (29 per cent vs 7 per cent earning $2,000 or more per month);

- significantly higher percentage of home ownership (36 per cent vs 13 per cent) and second car ownership (30 per cent vs 13 per cent);

- a significantly higher level of schooling completed (71 per cent vs 54 per cent completing 12th grade or higher);

- a significantly lower percentage receiving social services at some time in the past ten years (59 per cent vs 80 per cent);

- significantly fewer arrests by age 27 (7 per cent vs 35 per cent with 5 or more), including significantly fewer arrested for crimes of drug taking or dealing (7 per cent vs 25 per cent).

Why is pre-school education effective?

The researchers speculated on the reasons for such lasting change in disadvantaged children:

> The essential process connecting early childhood experience to patterns of improved success in school and the community seemed to be the development of habits, traits, and dispositions that allowed the child to interact positively with other people and with tasks. This process was based neither on permanently improved intellectual performance nor on academic knowledge (Schweinhart and Weikart, 1993, p. 4).

Schweinhart and Weikart carried out a cost-benefit analysis which showed that for every $1000 that was invested in the pre-school programme, at least $7160 (after adjustment for inflation) had been saved or returned to society. Pre-school education turned out to be a wise investment.

This causal model, supported by statistical analysis, suggests that pre-school education changes the children's views of themselves as learners and their goals. In turn, these cognitions lead to greater school readiness and a smoother transition to school (Berrueta-Clement, Schweinhart, Barnett, Epstein and

Weikart, 1984). Children leave the nursery 'ready to learn' and are easily recognised by teachers, who develop positive expectations of their success. This, in turn, fosters improved student attitudes towards school and better school behaviour (called 'school commitment' by Weikart and colleagues).

Research in the UK confirms the causal model. Jowett and Sylva (1986) studied two groups of children in the reception class. Half came from educationally-orientated nurseries and had attended playgroups. During the reception year children who had 'graduated' from nursery education were observed to be more independent and learning-orientated than those who attended playgroups. They had higher aspirations for learning and significantly higher test scores in language.

The positive conclusions to be drawn from these pre-school studies are not new. In 1985 Michael Rutter reviewed the literature on the effects of pre-school education on children's development and concluded that: 'The long term educational benefits stem not from what children are specifically taught but from effects on children's attitudes to learning, on their self esteem, and on their task orientation'. Further 'learning how to learn may be as important as the specifics of what is learned' (Rutter, 1985, p.700). The most lasting impact of early education appears to be children's aspirations for education and subsequent employment, their motivations and independence (Sylva, 1992). These are not moulded directly through classroom learning of facts or skills but appear to be acquired in a curriculum based on guided play, such as High/Scope.

THE EFFECTS OF EARLY SCHOOLING ON CHILDREN'S EXPLANATIONS OF THEIR OWN SUCCESS AND FAILURE

Mastery v. helpless behaviour

For the past fifteen years Carol Dweck and other American psychologists have been exploring academic motivation and attribution via a series of ingenious experiments involving problem-solving. The bedrock of this work is an experimental procedure whereby children in the later primary years are given a series of problem-solving tasks in which success is assured, followed by tasks designed to promote failure (Dweck and Leggett, 1988 and Dweck, 1986). Researchers found that children responded with two different patterns of behaviour when given tasks to which there was no solution.

'Mastery'-oriented children maintained a positive orientation to the task and continued to employ problem-solving strategies. They were observed to monitor their strategies and to maintain positive effect throughout. From interviews it was clear that they viewed the difficult problems as challenges to be mastered through effort rather than indictments of their low ability. In contrast, children characterised as 'helpless' in orientation began to chat about irrelevant topics, show a marked decline in problem-solving effort, and to show negative effect. These children appeared to view their difficulties as signs of their low ability; they rarely engaged in self-monitoring or self-instruction. Apparently, one group of children saw the harder problems as challenges to be overcome by effort and self instruction while the others viewed the new problems as 'tests' of their innate ability, convinced that they would fail. To summarise:

a.   Helpless children avoid challenge and give up easily, whereas mastery-orientated children persist in the fact of obstacles and seek new, challenging experiences.

b.   Helpless children report negative feelings and views of themselves when they meet obstacles while 'mastery' children have positive views of their competence, when meeting difficulties. This makes them task-orientated and resilient in the face of difficulties because they are confident and enjoy challenge.

c.   The style of 'helpless'or 'mastery'-orientated behaviour is not related to intelligence, rather it is a personality characteristic, a way of viewing oneself and one's capacity to be effective in the world of things and people.

Mastery v. performance goals

Further experiments (Dweck and Leggett, 1988) revealed wholly different goal structures in the two kinds of children. Helpless children were pursuing performance goals through which they sought to establish their ability and avoid showing of inadequacy. Interviews showed that they view achievement situations as tests of their competence. In contrast, mastery-orientated children were pursuing learning goals in which the problem-solving tasks were just one more opportunity to acquire new skill.

To test this theory Elliott and Dweck (1988)) manipulated children's goals of 'performance' or 'learning' in classrooms, then gave them the opportunity to choose either challenging tasks or easy ones. Those in classrooms orientated to mastery goals chose challenging tasks when given the choice whereas children in classrooms with performance goals chose easy ones. The researchers summarised: 'What was most striking was the degree to which the manipulations created the entire constellation of performance, cognition, and affect characteristic we had described earlier. For example, low ability children exposed to performance orientation and critical feedback showed the same attributions, negative affect and strategy deterioration that characterised the helpless children in their earlier studies.'

Following the success of the experimental manipulation, Dweck and her colleagues (Bandura and Dweck, 1985; Leggett, 1985) explored students' existing goal preferences and their link to classroom behaviour. In another, larger study they found that children with performance goals in class are vulnerable to distraction and show a tendency to avoid challenge similar to children in whom these goals were experimentally manipulated.

Dweck and her colleagues have demonstrated that the goals an individual pursues create a framework for interpreting and responding to events as they occur. Thus the same event may have an entirely different meaning and impact if it occurs within the context of a learning or a performance goal. Within a performance goal the student is concerned with answering the question 'Is my ability adequate?' In contrast, learning goals create a concern with increasing one's ability and lead individuals to pose the question, 'What is the best way to increase my skill?'

Outcomes provide information which answers the two different questions. Failure is merely task-information when a child operates under learning goals but it is a crushing blow when a child is acting according to performance goals. Other research described by Leggett and Dweck (1986) showed that goal preferences were related to beliefs about the role of effort in problem-solving. Children with performance goals viewed effort as an index of high or low ability; they viewed effort and ability as inversely related and interpreted high effort as a tell-tale sign of low talent. Children with learning goals were quite different because they regarded effort as a useful strategy in achieving mastery. For them, high effort did not mean low talent. Events that produced negative or depressed affect in one individual appeared to produce positive affect and heightened problem-solving in another.

Thus, performance goals lead the student to judge ability and trigger cognitive and affective processes that make the child vulnerable to maladaptive behaviour patterns. Learning goals lead to students putting into action cognitive and affective processes that promote adaptive seeking of challenge, persistence in the face of difficulty and sustained task performance.

Beliefs concerning intelligence and effort

The last piece in Dweck's far-reaching theory comes from research by Bandura and Dweck (1985), Cain and Dweck (1987) and Leggett (1985) which points to a link between mastery orientation and the belief that intelligence is malleable. Specifically, these studies suggest that when children view intelligence as a malleable quality, learning goals come to the fore. These children believe that effort will lead to increased intelligence and tend to maintain persistence in the face of difficulty. They may view problem-solving or achievement outcomes as reflecting only effort or current strategy – not immutable talent. In contrast, children who view intelligence as immutable, eschew effort and worry about the judgements of others, that is, performance becomes paramount (Bempechat, London and Dweck, 1991).

Ames and Archer (1988) reported a series of studies in classrooms to test whether students' perceptions of the 'goals' embodied in real-life classrooms were related to the ways they approached, engaged in, and responded to learning tasks. Results were in the predicted direction: when students perceived an emphasis on learning goals in the classroom, they used more learning strategies, preferred tasks that offered the possibility of challenge and had a more positive attitude towards the class. This pattern was reversed for students who perceived the class as performance oriented. These pupils used fewer strategies, preferred easy tasks and had a negative attitude towards the class.

'Effort' v. 'innate talent' in different cultures

Views about the mutability of intelligence are related to attributions. Stevenson and Lee (1990) and Stevenson, Lee, Chen and Lummis (1990) studied large samples of primary students in similar environments in China, Japan and the USA. They found that mathematics achievement was considerably lower in the USA than in the Asian countries despite smaller classes. Although classroom experiences varied considerably across the countries, central to this review is the finding that parents in the two Asian countries appeared to believe that children's effort was crucial in school success, and *even more important than innate ability*.

Interviews showed that parents and teachers in Asian countries placed great weight on the possibility of children's advancement through effort. American adults, on the other hand, seemed quite satisfied with the mathematical achievement of their children, expected less of them in terms of skill, and passed on to their children the belief that 'natural talent' was more important in determining school grades than sheer hard work. Such cross-cultural studies are important because they show how children's cognitions about schoolwork and their own success/failure are easily shaped by the social environment.

Teaching strategies can influence pupil self- evaluation

Marshall and Weinstein (1984) reviewed a host of studies on school factors affecting students' self evaluation and concluded that different teaching strategies shaped the ways pupils evaluated their own work. These included: high visibility and comparativeness of teacher evaluations, variety and divergence of tasks and competitive tasks assigned to students. Marshall and Weinstein showed experimentally that social comparison on its own need not lead to students' low self-assessments. For example, teachers who believed that intelligence was multidimensional (Gardner, 1983) and who used strategies that supported achievement in a variety of areas had students who engaged regularly in self-evaluation but did not condemn themselves as worthless.

SOCIAL RESPONSIBILITY, ATTAINMENT AND GROUP LEARNING

Social responsibility

A second area of psychological research explores the contribution of social responsibility of children's educational attainment. Wentzel (1991b) defines social responsibility as 'adherence to social rules and role expectations'. She demonstrates that it is instrumental in the acquisition of academic knowledge and skills. Social responsibility contributes to learning in two ways: 1) Behaving responsibly can aid learning by promoting positive interactions with teacher and peers, for example, peer sharing of materials or exchanging help with assignments; 2) Students' goals to be compliant and responsible can constrain and enhance the learning process, for example, pupils' striving to complete assignments on time to comply with requirements. Most relevant in the classroom are the rules and norms that define the student role. In them students are required to adhere to rules for interpersonal conduct as well as those related to curricular tasks.

Evidence comes from research studies such as that of Wentzel (1991a) which demonstrated that socially responsible behaviour (measured in the classroom) contributed directly to academic performance after adjusting statistically for IQ, social background and school absence. Moreover, the effect of sociometric status on academic attainment was mediated through children's social responsibility scores. This means that children's popularity in the classroom was only indirectly related to their school attainment; the 'linking factor' was social responsibility.

There is a tension here, however, in that an over-emphasis on co-operation and compliance with rules may be at odds with the 'learning' or 'mastery' orientation to schoolwork advocated by Dweck and by Ames. How can we reconcile the two theories, the one advocating intrinsic goals and the other advocating socially responsible pupils who aim at rule compliance and look towards others for support? Wentzel neatly resolves the issue by suggesting that pupils may pursue two sets of goals simultaneously: the intrinsic one of curiosity and the extrinsic one of responsibility. Nakamura and Finck (1980) provide some evidence from their research showing that the combination of social and task-related goal orientations was associated with better pupil performance in evaluative situations than children's working towards task goals on their own. Similarly, Reuman, Atkinson and Gallop (1986) found that attempts to master tasks and gain social approval can combine additively to increase the likelihood of achievement behaviour.

Lastly, a recent study (Wentzel, 1989) suggests that the pursuit of goals compatible with the social requirements of the classroom is related to academic achievement in secondary as well as primary education. In their research, pupils' distinct social goals differentiated the high, medium and low achieving students (measured by classroom grades). High achieving students reported trying to achieve several goals, including being 'dependable' and 'responsible' as well as 'learning new things'. In contrast, the goals frequently pursued by the average or low achievers were to 'make friends' and 'have fun'. Thus, the simultaneous pursuit of social responsibility and learning goals appears to enhance academic performance rather than inhibit it. Presumably this is because both types of goals are compatible with the performance requirements of the classroom.

Learning tasks, class grouping, class management

How can schools nurture social responsibility? Whereas much of the research in the 'effective education' literature (Brophy and Good, 1988) supports a traditional 'no nonsense' style of teaching, research on classroom management suggests that group processes, especially amongst peers, are vital and support of learning. This is at odds with more traditional teaching. Brophy and Good remind us that the teacher behaviours associated with higher test scores are not the same ones associated with positive student attitudes towards teachers, subjects or the class. Positive student attitudes are linked to teacher warmth, praise and socialising with students, in addition to instructing them. How can effective teaching be reconciled with the need to encourage positive attitudes and behaviour towards peers?

Collaborative groupwork: is it centred on exchange of ideas or social commitment to the group?

Slavin's (1980) perceptive reconciliation of cognitive and motivational theories of groupwork shows them to be complementary. The cognitive theory of groupwork stresses the benefits of students articulating their ideas

(Doise and Mugny, 1984); the motivational theory of groupwork focuses on the motivation engendered by the group to sustain effort and positive interaction (including help for slower learners). Slavin suggests that active peer discussion and peer explanation during groupwork is more frequent under group rewards for learning than under conditions in which collaborative work is encouraged but there are no rewards based on group members' learning. Thus, he stresses the necessity of the motivational basis for co-operative learning at the expense of the 'concept clarification' found in intellectual disagreement during group discussions.

Research shows that when children learn interactively in class they like school more, and believe more than control subjects that their success depends on their own efforts (Slavin, 1987a,b). Does co-operative learning work? In other words, is it linked to higher attainment? The majority of co-operative learning studies have been concerned with achievement outcomes such as basic computational skills and recall of simple facts. However, problem-solving skills acquired through this method have been shown to remain up to six months post instruction (Ross and Maynes, 1985). Despite these successful evaluations, there is some controversy as to whether co-operative learning is successful when pursuing higher order learning like the Tower of Hanoi task (Bargh and Schul, 1980) or learning science concepts (Rogan, 1988). There is no doubt, however, that groupwork leads to students' positive feelings toward school and their belief that success depends on their own efforts (Slavin, 1987a,b).

CONCLUSION

American studies have demonstrated clearly that high-quality, child-centred pre-school programmes can have lasting effects which are measurable and cost-effective. Researchers involved in the strongest of the studies pointed to changed aspiration and independence as the main outcome of good pre-school programmes. Mastery orientation seems to link early intellectual gains with later educational and community outcomes. British research (Jowett and Sylva, 1986) has been cited to show that 'learning orientation' was nurtured in pre-school settings which were 'educational'. In fact, systematic observation during the first year of school measured increased aspiration, persistence and independence in children who had attended the higher quality pre-school settings.

The studies reviewed here suggest that pupil cognitions and motivations will have an effect on attainment that will far surpass that of individual IQ or school curriculum. 'Mastery orientation' and 'learning goals' have been shown in experimental studies to shape the ways pupils approach, carry out and evaluate their work on tasks. Moreover, social responsibility is also related to achievement and co-operative group work promotes it.

There is some evidence that schooling affects children differently at different ages. Sammons, Mortimore and Thomas (1996) found that the overall effects of primary school on educational attainment were greater than secondary. One reason for this might be that the psychological processes described in this review are taking shape during the primary years. We know that early teacher feedback influences the formation of pupil self-concept. We know a little now about the roots of social responsibility and it is suggested that groupwork may facilitate it. It is tempting to say that the legacy of effective pre-school education is the 'will and goal to do'; the legacy of the effective primary school is preference for learning goals, belief in the power of effort and development of social responsibility in the classroom.

Two powerful themes have emerged in the review. First, the impact of early schooling on cognitions and motivations is large. Second, social responsibility is learned in school and like cognitions about the self, it also underpins classroom learning. This chapter has drawn on psychological research to explore some indirect pathways by which children follow successful or unsuccessful educational careers. When schools change pupils' self-concepts, goals, beliefs about success and social responsibility, they will exert powerful influence not only on subsequent education but also on adult employment and community participation. Our current conception of primary schooling – at least that embedded in the educational policy of the mid-1990s – ignores much of the psychological research reviewed in this paper. This is not a call to turn back the clock but it is a plea to shift the agenda away from the curriculum to the social processes of learning.

REFERENCES

Ames, C. and Archer, J. (1988). 'Achievement goals in the classroom: students' learning strategies and motivation processes', *Journal of Educational Psychology*, 80, pp. 260–67.

Bandura, A. and Dweck, C. (1985). 'The relationship of conceptions of intelligence and achievement goals to achievement-related cognition, affect and behaviour'. Cited in Dweck, C. and Leggett, E. (1988).

Bargh, J. and Schul, Y. (1980). 'On the cognitive benefits of teaching', *Journal of Educational Psychology*, 72, pp. 593–604.

Bempechat, J., London, P. and Dweck, C. (1991). 'Children's conceptions of ability in major domains: an interview and experimental study', *Child Study Journal*, 21, pp. 11–35.

Berrueta-Clement, J.R., Schweinhart, L., Barnett, W., Epstein, A. and Weikart, D. (1984). *Changed lives: the effects of the Perry pre-school programme on youths through age*

19. Ypsilanti, Michigan: The High/Scope Press.

Brophy, J. and Good, T. (1988). 'Teacher behaviour and student achievement', in Wittrock, M. (ed.), *Handbook of Research on Teaching*. 3rd edition. New York: Macmillan, pp. 328–75.

Cain, K. and Dweck, C. (1987). 'The development of children's theories of intelligence'. Cited in Dweck and Leggett (1988).

Doise, W. and Mugny, G. (1984) *The Social Development of the Intellect*. Oxford: Pergamon.

Dweck, C. (1986). 'Motivational processes affecting learning', *American Psychologist*, 41, pp. 1040–8.

— and Leggett, E. (1988). 'A social-cognitive approach to motivation and personality', *Psychological Review*, 95, pp. 256–73.

Elliott, E. and Dweck, C. (1988). 'Goals: An approach to motivation and achievement', *Journal of Personality and Social Psychology*, 54, pp. 5–12.

Gardner, H. (1983) *Frames of Mind: The Theory of Multiple Intelligence*. London: Heinemann.

Jowett, S. and Sylva, K. (1986). 'Does kind of pre-school matter?' *Educational Research*, 28, pp.21–31.

Lazar, I. and Darlington, R. (1982). 'Lasting effects of early education: a report from the consortium for longitudinal studies', *Journal of the Society for Research in Child Development*, 47, pp. 2–3.

Leggett, E. L. (1985). *Children's entity and incremental theories of intelligence: relationships to achievement behaviour*. Cited in Dweck and Leggett (1988).

— and Dweck, C. (1986). *Goals and inference rules: sources of causal judgements*. Cited in Dweck and Leggett (1988).

Marshall, H. and Weinstein, R. (1984). 'Classroom factors affecting students'self-evaluations: an interactional model', *Review of Educational Research*, 54, pp. 301–25.

Mortimore, P., Sammons, P., Stoll, L., Lewis, D. and Ecob, R. (1988a). *School Matters: The Junior Years*. Wells, Somerset: Open Books Publishing Ltd.

Nakamura, C. Y. and Finck, N. D. (1980). 'Relative effectiveness of socially oriented and task oriented children and predictability of their behaviours', *Monographs of the Society of Research in Child Development*, 45, pp. 3–4.

Reuman, D., Atkinson, J. W. and Gallop, G. (1986). 'Computer simulation of behavioural expressions of four personality traits', in Kuhl, J. and Atkinson, J. W. (eds), *Motivation, Thought and Action*. New York: Praeger, pp. 203–34.

Rogan, J. (1988). 'Development of a conceptual framework of heat', *Science Education*, 72, pp. 103–13.

Ross, J. A. and Maynes, F. (1985). 'Retention of problem solving performance in school contexts'. *Canadian Journal of Education*, 10, pp. 383–401.

Rutter, M. (1985). 'Family and school influences on cognitive development', *Journal of Child Psychology*, 26, pp. 683–704.

Sammons, P., Nuttall, D., Cuttace, P. and Thomas, S. (1995). 'Continuity of school effects: A longitudinal analysis of primary and secondary school effects on GCSE performances', *School Effectiveness and School Improvement,* 6, 14, pp. 1–21.

Sammons, P., Mortimore, P. and Thomas, S. (1996). 'Do schools perform consistently across outcomes and areas?' in Gray, J. (ed.), *Merging Traditions: The Future of Research on School Effectiveness and School Improvement*. London: Cassell.

Schweinhart, L. J. and Weikart, D. P. (1993). 'A summary of significant benefits: the High Scope Perry pre-school study through age 27', Ypsilanti, M: High/Scope UK.

Slavin, R. (1980). 'Cooperative learning'. *Review of Educational Research*, 50, pp. 315–42.

— (1987a). 'Small group methods', in Dunkin, M. J. (ed.), *International Encyclopedia of Teaching and Teacher Education*. Oxford: Pergamon Press, pp. 237–43.

— (1987b). 'Developmental and motivational perspectives on co-operative learning: a reconciliation', *Child Development*, 58, pp. 1161–7.

Stevenson, H. and Lee, S. (1990). 'Contexts of achievement', *Monographs of the Society for Research in Child Development*, 1–2, pp. 1–119.

Stevenson, H., Lee, S., Chen, C. and Lummis, M. (1990). 'Mathematics achievement of children in China and the United States', *Child Development*, 61, pp. 1063–6.

Sylva, K. (1992). 'Conversations in the nursery: how they contribute to aspirations and plans'. *Language and Education*, 6, pp. 141–8.

Wentzel, K. R. (1989). 'Adolescent classroom goal, standards for performance, and academic achievement: an interactionist perspective on primary prevention', *Journal of Consulting and Clinical Psychology*, 59, pp. 830–41.

— (1991a). 'Relations between social competence and academic achievement in early adolescence', *Child Development*, 62, pp. 1066–79.

— (1991b). 'Social competence at school: relations between social responsibility and academic achievement', *Review of Educational Research*, 61, pp. 1–24.

13

SPECIAL EDUCATION

Seamus Hegarty

The past 20 years have seen a great deal of activity in special education research, both in the United Kingdom and abroad. This chapter presents an overview of this research, focusing principally though not exclusively on British research. Given the volume and range of research activity, it is not possible to be exhaustive. What is offered is an account of research reviews of the field, followed by a discussion of the changing conceptual, legislative and policy contexts within which special education research has been conducted. To illustrate the diversity of the field, three research topics within it – integration, specific learning difficulties and further education – are outlined. Finally, some challenges for future research agendas are considered.

RESEARCH REVIEWS

Research in special education has grown in volume, substance and sophistication since the 1960s. This can be attributed to a number of factors: increasing levels of special educational provision; better understanding of the complexity of the issues involved; more investment in teacher training and staff development generally, and a consequent increase in academic activity; some government initiatives to promote research in the field; the emergence of a recognised body of researchers; and easier opportunities to publish research findings.

A particular stimulus came from the Warnock Report (DES, 1978). Not only did this report revitalise special education through the debates it stimulated, the practical recommendations it made and the legislation which followed it, but it also commissioned a survey of research in special education (Cave and Maddison, 1978). Completed in 1976, this survey concentrated on research published in the first part of the 1970s, and provides a convenient point of departure.

Cave and Maddison began by referring to the growth in research in special education: what had begun to accelerate in the 1960s had now become an avalanche. Most of this research was taking place in the United States, however, and the relative paucity of British studies meant that schools in this country were less likely to be buried in the snow of research findings!

The key issues for Cave and Maddison's review were defined by the Warnock Committee of Enquiry: diagnosis and assessment; the incidence of handicapping conditions; categories and labelling; early education and the role of parents; the organisation of special education; and the training of teachers. The research review is structured around these issues plus an additional set of issues concerned with the learning process itself.

The review drew on a large number of studies, principally American and British but including some Scandinavian, Canadian and other sources. Studies are briskly summarised, with considerable attention to methodological and contextual factors which affect the generalisability of findings. The authors did not hesitate to draw conclusions where they could, for example, in relation to assessment practice, incidence estimates, the inutility of categories and the efficacy of early education. They also pointed out the inconclusiveness of research findings in relation to topics such as educating handicapped children in ordinary schools. One of the strengths of the review is its clear sense of what can, and cannot, be inferred from the available data; some questions indeed are not amenable to research, and research into them will necessarily be inconclusive. The authors identified a number of key policy themes and may be presumed to have had some impact on the subsequent Warnock Report. Some of their conclusions were very forward-looking if not ahead of their time, such as the emphasis on the importance of curricular and pedagogical differentiation in ordinary schools and the insistence on the limited educational relevance of handicap categories.

Since Cave and Maddison's review there has been a great deal of research activity and a number of other reviews have appeared. These have generally focused on particular topics, however, rather than attempting to cover the whole field. This presumably reflects the growing volume of research on any given topic but also perhaps the difficulty of securing resources – and publishing outlets – for comprehensive literature reviews.

Two general reviews may be noted: Wedell and Roberts (1981, 1982) and Wang, Reynolds and Walberg (1987, 1988, 1989). Wedell and Roberts sought to collect information on completed and current research in special education in the United Kingdom and to set out priorities for future research. Wang et al. aimed to give a comprehensive review of the state of the art and the state of practice in the field in special education in the United States. In three volumes, they cover learner characteristics and adaptive education, mildly handicapping conditions (mild mental retardation, behavioural disorders and learning disabilities) and low-incidence conditions (deafness, visual handicap and handicapped infants). This is a scholarly and – within the United States context – comprehensive work that pulls together the voluminous research and programme development that took place following the enactment of The Education for All Handicapped Children Act (PL 94-142) in 1975. Despite the US focus and a conceptualisation of learning difficulty that occasionally jars, it is an authoritative and most valuable sourcebook on research in special education.

There have been two registers of research in special education in the United Kingdom published by the National Foundation for Educational Research (NFER): Hegarty (1986) and Hegarty, May-Bowles and Taylor (1991). These registers sought to offer a comprehensive listing of all special education research taking place within the United Kingdom. Abstracts, researcher details and so on are given but no attempt is made to evaluate the studies or provide an overview. Further details on research activity are provided by the biennial Register of Educational Research in the United Kingdom also produced by the NFER, and the Directory of non-medical research relating to Handicapped People produced by the Special Needs Research Unit at the University of Northumbria in Newcastle.

Reviews of particular topics in the field have been published as documents in their own right or as part of more extended documents. There have been numerous reviews of studies of integration, for example, ranging from a chapter in Hegarty and Pocklington (1981) to an entire issue of the *European Journal of Special Needs Education* (8,3, October 1993). Special needs in further education were reviewed by Bradley and Hegarty (1981) and subsequently by Bradley, Dee and Wilenius (1994). Dyslexia and specific learning difficulties have been the subject of several reviews: Tansley and Panckhurst (1981), Miles and Miles (1990) and Pumfrey and Reason (1991). Other examples of reviews include special needs and early years education (Clark, 1988), parental roles in the education of children with severe learning difficulties (Wells, 1989) and children with disabilities and their families (Philp and Duckworth, 1982).

Mention may also be made of two series of books that embody a considerable amount of reviewing of the research literature. The first is the *Special Educational Needs Review* published in three volumes by Jones (1989a), (1989b) and (1990). Second, there is the 18-volume series on meeting special needs in ordinary schools published by Cassell. Beginning in 1987, this series consists of overview volumes – Hegarty (1993), Wolfendale (1992) and Sayer (1993) – as well as books covering specific topics such as speech and language difficulties, assessment, teaching science in the secondary school and improving classroom behaviour.

Finally, it may be noted that opportunities for publishing research findings have increased considerably. Apart from the many publishers who have detected a buoyant market in special needs books – and have thereby facilitated a wider dissemination of research – there are new journals which provide outlets for research reports. Examples include the *European Journal of Special Needs Education* (Routledge), *British Journal of Special Education* (National Association for Special Educational Needs) and *Disability and Society* (Carfax). These greater publishing opportunities have certainly led to wider knowledge of research findings; it is possible too that they have stimulated research inquiry by fostering a research culture and helping to introduce research evidence into special education debates.

CONCEPTUAL BACKGROUND

The conceptual world inhabited by special education today is different in significant ways from that of 20 years ago. This is reflected in the research enterprise. Indeed, there is a complex relationship between the research questions pursued at a given point in time and the prevailing understanding of key concepts: research questions are posed in a particular theoretical context and are articulated for practical investigation in the light of it but, equally, some research findings call into question prevailing ways of thinking and stimulate new theoretical developments. The picture is complicated further by the fact that, in a time of change such as we have seen, different, even competing theories and ideologies coexist. For these reasons a precise delineation of the conceptual changes is not presented here. What is being offered is an outline of the key developments in special needs thinking in recent years, particularly in so far as these bear on the research enterprise.

In earlier times special education was concerned with handicapped children who had to be educated in certain ways and in certain settings. Educational aspirations for them had to be limited and indeed some were not deemed capable of benefiting from education. In line with practice in other countries handicapped children were grouped into categories – blind, partially sighted, deaf, partially hearing, physically handicapped, educationally subnormal, epileptic and so on. Dating from 1945, these categories reflected medical or pseudo-medical ways of regarding children who differed from the norm. For many years they were central to the administration and the practice of special education and were reflected in assessment and diagnosis, the organisation of special schools and special classes, and educational programming. As an aside, these categories implied a clear division between handicapped and non-handicapped children; there may have been borderline cases where ascertainment was difficult but the whole system was based on a clear, qualitative distinction between those who were handicapped and those who were not handicapped.

The contemporary way of regarding children and young people who have difficulties at school is based on the concept of 'special educational need'. Used by various writers in the 1970s (for example, Gulliford, 1971) in deliberate opposition to the prevailing language of handicap, it was taken up by the Warnock Report in 1978 and adopted for the Education Act 1981. The concept moves away from the fixed, child-based ideas of handicap where children had characteristic defects which required particular educational measures to be taken and implies instead a relative, provision-orientated way of regarding children's difficulties. The legislative definition spells out the relativity: a child is deemed to have special educational needs if s/he has 'a learning difficulty which calls for special educational provision to be made'. This necessitates two further definitions, namely, 'learning difficulties' and 'special educational provision'. Children have a learning difficulty if they have a significantly greater difficulty in learning than the majority of children of their age or if they have a disability that either prevents or hinders them from making use of the educational facilities generally available to age peers. Special educational provision is defined as 'educational provision which is additional to, or otherwise different from, the educational provision made generally for children in schools maintained by the local education authority concerned'.

Alongside the relativity, other features of the concept that bear on the research enterprise may be noted. First, the thrust of the concept is toward provision. It is concerned with the schooling a child receives and how s/he responds to it rather than innate characteristics or constructs derived from psychological measurement. Second, special educational needs cannot be categorised easily. Unlike the traditional categories of handicap, with their often irrelevant and sometimes spurious precision, they do not give a ready means of categorising children's need of special provision. Third, they can only be operationalised at the level of the school: it is only within schools that the individual's special needs emerge in specific form and corresponding special educational provision can be defined.

The language of special needs, and the conceptual shift associated with it, gradually established itself over the 1980s and early 1990s, though the process was uneven and both forms of discourse coexisted in various ways. Typically, academic and policy discourse tended to eschew the language of handicap, whereas informal and some practitioner discourse tended to use the more familiar language of handicap. It should be remembered, too, that in most other countries special education has continued to be conceived and organised in terms of handicap categories.

A further challenge to the conceptual cartographer comes from the emerging critique of special needs discourse. This is voiced by authors such as Norwich (1990), Dyson and Gains (1993) and Ainscow (1993). All of these share a view of special educational needs as problematic and, depending on their perspective, needing to be modified or abandoned. Dyson and Gains, for instance, locate their critique in an analysis of current changes in educational provision and their argument that there is a fundamental shift taking place in thinking about it. This is characterised as a move from focusing on structures to focusing on processes. The traditional response to pupil diversity has been to create special schools, special classes, support services and other structural solutions to supposedly predictable patterns of need, but this is giving way to a concern with the underlying, and less predictable, processes and the consequent need to develop flexible, unique solutions.

In their view, special educational needs thinking is associated with the traditional approach; it is based upon identifying characteristic patterns of difficulties experienced by students and allocating them to the appropriate structural solution. Dyson and Gains argue instead for a conceptualisation in terms of effective learning and the factors bear on it, particularly when it breaks down. This leads to a different model of practice where the focus is on problem solving and collaboration. The authors set out some of the implications of adopting such a model for schools, teacher trainers, local authorities and government. Not spelt out but implicit is a new research agenda – determining the skills and resources required by schools, clarifying the nature of collaborative arrangements between schools, training teachers in areas such as organisational development and problem solving, defining and implementing new relationships between schools and local authorities, and so on.

LEGISLATIVE AND POLICY CONTEXT

Special education has been subject to a great deal of legislative and policy change over the past 25 years. This has been true of education in general for some 10 years now, but special education has been going through reforms for far longer. There have been three major pieces of legislation in addition to the quaintly styled Education Reform Act of 1988 – other legislation presumably is not concerned with reform! – plus further policy changes emanating from new ways of regarding disability and learning difficulty, administrative and resourcing considerations, professional concerns and parental pressure. All of this has had considerable impact on the research agenda, whether through specific government initiatives to commission research to further particular reforms or through shaping research priorities in a more general way.

The Education (Handicapped Children) Act 1970 effectively broadened the scope of special education by transferring responsibility for those with the most severe difficulties from Health to Education. In April 1971 some 30,000 children and young people, generally deemed severely educationally subnormal, had to be offered education. This stimulated research and curriculum development as the education sector had to respond to the challenges posed by these students. The Hester Adrian Research Centre at the University of Manchester, with its remit to investigate learning processes in the mentally handicapped, was a major centre for these studies. With funding from the Department of Education and Science, the Schools Council and the Social Science Research Council, it carried out a large-scale survey of over 3,000 pupils with severe learning difficulties in special schools (Mittler and Preddy, 1981), developed the curriculum in language and communication (Leeming et al., 1979), examined methods of studying language and approaches to teaching language (Berry, 1976) as well as numerous other studies.

Special education debates in the 1970s were dominated by Section 10 of the Education Act 1976 and the Warnock Enquiry. Section 10 repealed Section 33(2) of the Education Act 1944 with a view to furthering integration. Though it was never in fact implemented (and was eventually superseded by the Education Act 1981), it had a significant impact. It helped to focus the growing interest in the practice of integration and provided the context for major funded research such as the NFER study of integration (Hegarty and Pocklington, 1981 and 1982). The Warnock Enquiry, eventually reporting in 1978, contributed to the research agenda in a number of ways. As mentioned above, the Committee commissioned a research review (Cave and Maddison, 1978) and its adoption of the term 'special educational needs' facilitated significant conceptual developments. At a broader level, the stimulus it gave to thinking about special education led to numerous investigations, student dissertations and so on.

A further research context was provided by the Schools Council. From 1980 to 1983 its curriculum development work included a programme entitled Individual Pupils. This comprised a number of projects 'united by a concern for individuals who, for some reason, make exceptional demands on their teachers' skills'. The programme encompassed gifted pupils and pupils from ethnic minority backgrounds but the major focus was on pupils with special educational needs where the particular concern was to develop the curriculum and assist teachers in facilitating their learning, whether in special schools or in ordinary schools. Publications from the programme include Wilson (1980), Hegarty, Pocklington and Bradley (1982), and Hodgson, Clunies-Ross and Hegarty (1984).

The Education Act 1981, implemented in 1983, enshrined a good deal of the new thinking articulated in the Warnock Report and elsewhere. It also led to many changes in the administration and practice of special education, and in that way affected the research agenda. There was a more direct effect, however. The Department of Education and Science commissioned a programme of research to investigate the situation of special education in the wake of the Act, and to assist in furthering the reforms it introduced. The programme comprised three major studies conducted, respectively, at the NFER, the University of London Institute of Education, and the University of Manchester in association with Huddersfield Polytechnic.

The NFER study, 'Meeting special educational needs – support for the ordinary school', pursued three distinct but interrelated areas in which ordinary schools could be helped in their task of providing appropriate education for all their pupils: the provision made by local education authorities, especially in form of support services (Moses, Hegarty and Jowett, 1988); links between ordinary schools and special schools (Jowett, Hegarty and Moses,1988); and in-service education for teachers of pupils with special educational needs (Hegarty and Moses, 1988). The London study was concerned explicitly with the implementation of the Act, looking in detail at the links between legislation and outcome in local education authorities, social services departments and district health authorities (Goacher et al., 1988). (A parallel study was conducted at the University of Edinburgh to examine the impact of the corresponding Scottish legislation (Thomson, Riddell and Dyer,1989).) The Manchester study was concerned with teacher training and, in particular, sought to evaluate a modular approach to training provision (Robson et al., 1987).

The 1988 Education Act and subsequent developments led to major changes in the context for special educational provision. The introduction of a national curriculum and the associated national assessment, the delegation of many financial and management responsibilities from local education authorities to individual schools, the reduction in local authority support services and the emergence of grant-maintained schools, all posed a variety of challenges to special education and influenced the research agenda. A good deal of research within this new context is still going on but some important pieces of work have been concluded. Thus, the National Curriculum Council commissioned research and development work on implementing the national curriculum in respect of pupils with severe learning difficulties (NCC, 1992). Writers such as Ashdown, Carpenter and Bovair (1991) and Lewis (1991) have assembled examples and analysed the issues entailed in addressing the curriculum challenge. The effects of local management of schools on special educational provision have attracted considerable research attention. Relevant reports include Lee (1991), Lunt and Evans (1991), Evans and Lunt (1992) and Fletcher-Campbell (1993).

The new funding arrangements examined in these studies have major implications for local authority support services. Garner, Petrie and Pointon (1991) and Bowers (1991) have examined this area directly. It is also the subject of current research at the National Foundation for Educational Research.

The contemporary legislative framework for special educational provision is governed by the Education Acts of 1992 and 1993 along with the Code of Practice on identification and assessment introduced in 1994. These will determine a new research agenda or at least change the shape of existing agendas. Topics coming to the fore will include the impact of the new inspection arrangements on special educational provision, developments in assessment practice and the implementation of the Code of Practice.

EXAMPLES OF RESEARCH

While it is impossible to do justice to the great scope of the research in the area, a flavour of it can be given by selecting a few topics and outlining some of the issues within each. Three topics have been selected here: integration, specific learning difficulties/dyslexia and further education. Integration has been a central concern of debate and inquiry for many years, and it is appropriate to start with it since it impinges on so many issues on special education and draws on a very wide research base. Research into specific learning difficulties/dyslexia is wide-ranging in a different sense. Targeted on children who have difficulty in reading, writing or spelling, it draws extensively on disciplines outside education and psychology. Further education is the Cinderella of special education research: despite a growing literature on special needs in further education, the research clothing remains scant and not always of the highest quality.

1. Integration

Integration has been the dominant topic in special education research for many years. Numerous studies into various aspects of integration have been carried out and, as noted above, several reviews of these studies have been conducted. This dominance reflects both the centrality of the topic itself and the political and public interest in it. Special education is defined essentially in terms of ordinary school provision (and particularly its limitations) and, as a consequence, most topics in special education have an integration angle. Moreover, integration and segregation are bound up with value positions; sometimes these are strongly held and lead to campaigning and consumer pressure.

There has been a considerable methodological shift in studies of integration. Initially, the effort – particularly in the United States – was to determine the efficacy of integrated programmes, in relation to segregated ones, by conducting comparative studies. A particular handicapped population was selected and matched samples studied in integrated and segregated settings to determine progress in academic attainment or social development. These studies had a good deal of prima facie appeal, since they promised to settle important questions about the best choices for children and the provision that should be made for them, and hundreds of them were conducted. Despite this volume of research activity, relatively little useful information was gained: findings tended to be inconclusive or contradictory. Combined with the limitations of control group studies and the heterogeneity of the population and of the educational settings they experienced, this led to a shift in methodological approach to qualitative measures.

An early, pioneering study was conducted by Jamieson, Parlett and Pocklington (1977) into the integration of pupils with visual impairments. This was a deliberate attempt to apply the methods of so-called illuminative evaluation to special education and marked a radical departure from the prevailing research approaches. In the event, it generated a wealth of useful information, documenting the experience of integration and analysing the factors that bear on pupils' schooling.

A major study of integration conducted at the National Foundation for Educational Research from 1977 to 1980 (Hegarty and Pocklington, 1981 and 1982) also drew heavily on qualitative methods and set a pattern which has been widely copied. This study and others in similar vein are not concerned to arbitrate between integration and segregation but rather seek to document the practice of integration and identify the factors that bear on its successful implementation. Recognising the weakness of research methods in respect of the comparative question and the fact that it is generally settled by reference to principle or ideology rather than empirical data, they seek to clarify the implications for ordinary schools of including pupils with special needs in their educational programmes and thus focus on curriculum, academic organisation, support structures, in-service training and so on.

The characteristics of effective integration programmes have been a recurring theme of research. Two broad approaches to this can be discerned, though as time goes by they tend to converge. One approach consists of identifying a potentially relevant characteristic, such as a particular way of teaching or the availability of a certain kind of support, and investigating what impact it has on practice, particularly how it bears on individual pupils' learning. The second approach is a holistic one, starting with the school and investigating how it must change if it is to include pupils with special educational needs in its general learning activities. This builds on the study of single characteristics that are deemed relevant but seeks to relate them to each other and produce a coherent account of the requisite school reform.

There is broad agreement from research as to the key characteristics of effective integration programmes. These are articulated in various ways but include the curriculum and how it is differentiated, academic organisation within the school and how pupils are grouped for teaching purposes, pedagogical and other support provided from within the school and from outside, staffing levels and deployment, staff attitudes and expertise, in-service training, school ethos, parental involvement and physical environment of the school. These different factors are interwoven in various ways and affected by size of school, nature of the catchment area, pattern of special educational needs, pupil age and so on. The contribution of research is to build up an understanding of how these factors operate. A great deal has been learned from research to date but the task is an on-going one as schools and the environment in which they operate continue to change.

2. Specific learning difficulties

Specific learning difficulties constitute an area of research quite unlike any other in special education. It is highly complex and far from fully understood. Efforts to understand it go well beyond educational research into psychology and medicine. A great deal of research has been carried out but the area remains riven with controversy. Disagreement stretches from the basic terminology to be used through the interpretation of incidence data to the most appropriate educational programmes.

Discussion on the topic goes back to the last century with the identification of so-called 'word blindness', quickly named dyslexia. Since that time there has been a constant stream of debate and enquiry into the learning situation of children who exhibit an unexpected discrepancy between their (low) ability to cope with written material and their (high) abilities in other areas. Miles and Miles (1990) set out the historical picture, albeit from a particular perspective – that dyslexia exists as a definite syndrome and can be attributed to phonological weakness.

A major review of the research was conducted by the NFER (Tansley and Panckhurst, 1981). This was sponsored by the Department of Education and Science and had a degree of influence on thinking and further research in the area. The review has four main sections – terminology, aetiology, incidence and remediation – and highlights the complexity of the findings in each. It insists on a broad definition of specific learning difficulties which includes dyslexia in the narrow sense but extends well beyond it. Causation and treatment are as a consequence regarded as multi-faceted; in particular, single-factor approaches are eschewed.

A further investigation of the area and research conducted in it was carried out in 1989–90 by a team of psychologists on behalf of the Division of Educational and Child Psychology of the British Psychological Society. This was a national inquiry and led to a comprehensive report (Pumfrey and Reason, 1991). The research is grouped under three broad disciplinary headings: psychological, psycho-educational and psychomedical (covering neuropsychology, psycho-ophthalmology and psycho-pharmaceutics). The report also presents four sets of survey findings compiled by the team, covering respectively the policies and practices of local education authorities, the views of educational psychologists concerning professional practice and development, the views of a selection of organisations involved in or holding a position regarding specific learning difficulties/dyslexia, and the policies and practices of examination bodies concerning concessions for pupils with specific learning difficulties/dyslexia. This is a sound and broadly based enquiry, displaying both the complexity of the field and what has been achieved to date.

The debate on specific learning difficulties/dyslexia in this country is paralleled by a corresponding debate on 'learning disabilities' in the United States and some other countries. This term was introduced into widespread use by Kirk in 1962. In the years since it has been defined in numerous ways and has led to an enormous body of research and educational programming. Hammill (1990) conducted an exhaustive study of definitions in use during the 1980s; he presents 11 competing definitions from them but suggests that a consensus is emerging. Keogh (1988) takes a contrary view: her review of the field confirms that controversy is alive and well, and leads her to make the conclusion that 'it seems unlikely that a single theoretically sound and empirically verifiable definition is possible, at least at this time in our history' (p. 242).

3. Further education

The further education sector is of particular interest here because it encompasses a great deal of special needs provision, much of it in challenging environments. However, provision tends to be ad hoc and occasionally unco-ordinated, and the sector as a whole has a limited research tradition. Fortuitously, research in the area has been the subject of detailed review, most recently by Bradley, Dee and Wilenius (1994).

Some substantive conclusions can be drawn but the most striking fact to emerge from reviewing the field is how little research is contained in the plethora of writing about it. The Bradley et al. review located 1,130 potentially useful references on the further education of students with disabilities and/or learning difficulties, but closer investigation revealed that most of them either contained no research element whatsoever or duplicated work appearing elsewhere. This leads the authors to conclude that 'the field is dominated by discourse rather than research, by conjecture rather than evidence, by intuition rather than evaluation' (p. 53). This is a stark statement of a reality that obtains elsewhere in special education, and indeed in educational research more generally. In certain topics there is an undoubted evidence base but in many others the absence of decisive evidence is no barrier to fulsome writing and strongly held views.

The Bradley *et al.* review is structured in terms of a number of discrete areas: conceptual models, patterns of provision, assessment process, funding arrangements, support for learning, quality and achievement, transition process and inter-agency working. The one area that had generated a substantial body of research was the transition process. A number of studies have followed cohorts of young people through the end of schooling into further education and other post-school experiences, sometimes even on a modestly longitudinal basis. These have produced a good deal of useful information on the preparation and other support necessary at school level and on the factors in post-school provision that make for a successful transition to adult and working life.

Apart from transition, the main contribution of research has been to highlight the piecemeal way in which students are recruited into the sector and the provision made for them. There has been much development in assessment practice, for instance, but this has led to unexamined – and probably unjustified – diversity. What also emerges from this review of research is that differing concepts of learning difficulty and disability coexist in the field, to a far greater extent than is the case in the school sector. Otherwise, the review draws attention to significant areas where there is little research evidence to draw on: support for student learning, professional development, inter-agency collaboration, the impact of funding mechanisms and the monitoring of quality.

CHALLENGES

An agenda for research in special education was proposed by Hegarty (1991). This flowed from two broad aims: to come to a better understanding of special educational provision; and to identify efficient ways of bringing about necessary changes. First, certain conceptual clarification was held to be necessary. Then proposals in respect of understanding and facilitating change at classroom, school and system level were put forward. Finally, a number of broad issues were considered.

Much of this agenda is still relevant, though certain topics need to be conceptualised differently in the light of developments since 1991 and other topics have become more significant. Four areas in particular stand out as still requiring a major research thrust: teaching and learning; school effectiveness and school improvement as applied to special educational provision; the evolution of special schooling; and resource allocation.

The central business of the school is learning, and this is no less true of pupils with special educational needs than of others. Though much work has been done in relation to this, much more remains to be done. Three areas of inquiry are noted: existing theories of learning need to be extended and refined to make them applicable to individuals at different stages of development and with different handicapping conditions; instructional theories must be developed which take full account of classroom variables; and the practical classroom setting must be studied in detail.

The great bodies of research on school effectiveness and school improvement have generally ignored pupils with special educational needs and the provision they require. While the whole-school reforms emanating from within special education have led to some useful research, what is required now is that the issues concerning pupils with special educational needs become an integral part of the school reform movement and that research seeking to understand and promote the latter subsume special needs issues within it.

Special schools are likely to continue to be a significant feature of the map of special educational provision for some time to come, but their roles are likely to change in response to conceptual, legislative and policy developments. This is likely to mean new relationships with ordinary schools, support services and local authorities. Research is needed not only to monitor these changes and evaluate their impact but also to develop new models of specialist support which are not necessarily based on existing institutions.

Resource allocation continues to pose major challenges in special educational provision. There are two broad considerations: establishing the level and type of extra resource required by individual pupils; and channelling such extra resources to schools in an effective way. How much should be spent on an individual is a complex – and shifting – calculation, depending as it does on the pattern of learning difficulties, available provision, global budgetary constraints and so on. Given agreement on the quantum of additional expenditure, there remains the question of how it is distributed. The way in which resources are allocated to ordinary schools in respect of pupils with special educational needs is a major determinant of how these resources are applied. It affects the amount of individual support pupils receive, whether individuals participate in mainstream curriculum activities and the extent to which ordinary schools promote effective learning for all their pupils. There is a great deal of experimentation going on in this area, fuelled in part by the changes in educational funding arrangements and in part by legitimate professional uncertainties. Research will have an important role in clarifying the salient features of the different approaches in use and identifying their impact on practice.

Doubtless, others would produce a different list and advance other priorities. What seems clear, however, is that special education for the remainder of this decade and beyond will be located in and constructed by a mainstream education system dominated by concerns to raise achievement levels, secure value for money and generally create a market in education. These concerns will shape the research agenda – and it is right that they should – but it must be hoped that the educational experiences offered to individuals and the quality of learning they achieve remain central.

A final challenge relates to the theoretical framework underlying research in special education. Research to date has drawn on a number of theoretical approaches embedded within different disciplinary backgrounds – medicine, psychology, sociology – and using methods ranging from positivistic experiments to ethnographic case studies. These different approaches occupy distinctive, albeit occasionally unexpected, positions within the research field. Thus, the much-criticised medical paradigm has an influence still, as evidenced by the voluminous literature on attention deficit disorders and psychomedical research on specific learning difficulties. By contrast, sociological approaches for all their popularity continue to produce a meagre trawl of data, to a point indeed where one writer is provoked to question whether there *is* a sociology of special education (Copeland, 1993).

Given these different approaches, the challenge is to put them together in a coherent way. An integrated theoretical framework is a long way off, if indeed it is possible, but some rapprochement between the different theoretical approaches is desirable. If each research strand adds to the understanding of individuals' difficulties and facilitates their learning in some way, it behoves us to weave the strands together and ensure that the whole of the research enterprise is more than the sum of its parts. Given the multiplicity of approaches and the occasionally conflicting nature of the assumptions underpinning them, this is not going to be an easy task but it is one that must be addressed if those who are the subject of special educational research are to gain maximum benefit from it.

REFERENCES

Ainscow, M. (1993). *Towards Effective Schools for All*. Stafford: National Association for Special Educational Needs.
Ashdown, R., Carpenter, B. and Bovair, K. (eds) (1991). *The Curriculum Challenge:*

Access to the National Curriculum for Pupils with Learning Difficulties. London: Falmer Press.

Berry, P. (ed.) (1976). *Language and Communication in the Mentally Handicapped.* London: Arnold.

Bowers, T. (ed.) (1991). *Schools, Services and Special Educational Needs: Management Issues in the Wake of LMS.* Cambridge: Perspective Press.

Bradley, J., Dee, L. and Wilenius, F. (1994). *Students with Disabilities and/or Learning Difficulties in Further Education: A Review of Research.* Slough: NFER.

Bradley, J. and Hegarty, S. (1981). *Students with Special Needs in FE.* London: Further Education Unit.

Cave, C. and Maddison, P. (1978). *A Survey of Recent Research in Special Education.* Windsor: NFER.

Clark, M. (1988). *Children under Five: Educational Research and Evidence.* London: Gordon & Breach.

Copeland, I. (1993). 'Is there a sociology of special education and integration?', *European Journal of Special Needs Education*, 8, 1, pp. 1–13.

Department of Education and Science (DES) (1978). *Special Educational Needs.* (Warnock Report). London: HMSO.

Dyson, A. and Gains, C. (1993). *Rethinking Special Needs in Mainstream Schools: Towards the Year 2000.* London: David Fulton.

Evans, J. and Lunt, I. (1992). *Developments in Special Education under LMS.* London: University of London Institute of Education.

Fletcher-Campbell, F. with Hall, C. (1993). *LEA Support for Special Educational Needs.* Slough: NFER.

Garner, M., Petrie, I. and Pointon, D. (1991). *LEA Support Services for Meeting Special Educational Needs: A Survey.* Liverpool: Special Educational Needs National Advisory Council (SENNAC).

Goacher, B., Evans, J., Welton, J. and Wedell, K. (1988). *Policy and Provision for Special Educational Needs: implementing the 1981 Education Act.* London: Cassell.

Gulliford, R. (1971). *Special Educational Needs.* London: Routledge & Kegan Paul.

Hamill, D. D. (1990). 'On defining learning disabilities: an emerging consensus', *Journal of Learning Disabilities*, 23, 2, pp. 74–84.

Hegarty, S. (1986). *Register of Research in Special Education in the United Kingdom: Vol. 1.* Windsor: NFER-Nelson.

— (1991). 'Toward an agenda for research in special education', *European Journal of Special Needs Education*, 6, 2, pp. 87–99.

— (1993). *Meeting Special Needs in Ordinary Schools.* London: Cassell.

— May-Bowles, J. and Taylor, C. (1991) *Register of Research in Special Education: Vol. 2.* Slough: NFER.

— and Moses, D. (1988). *Developing Expertise: INSET for Special Educational Needs.* Windsor: NFER-Nelson.

—, Pocklington, K. and Bradley, J. (1982). *Recent Curriculum Developments in Special Education.* York: Longman for Schools Council.

— and Pocklington, K. with Lucas, D. (1981). *Educating Pupils with Special Needs in the Ordinary School.* Windsor: NFER-Nelson.

— and Pocklington, K. with Lucas, D. (1982). *Integration in Action.* Windsor: NFER-Nelson.

Hodgson, A., Clunies-Ross, L. and Hegarty, S. (1984). *Learning Together: Teaching Pupils with Special Educational Needs in the Ordinary School.* Windsor: NFER-Nelson.

Jamieson, M., Parlett, M. and Pocklington, K. (1977). *Towards Integration: A Study of Blind and Partially-Sighted Children in Ordinary Schools*. Windsor: NFER.

Jones, N. (ed.) (1989a). *Special Educational Needs Review, Vol. 1*. London: Falmer Press.

— (ed.) (1989b). *Special Educational Needs Review, Vol. 2*. London: Falmer Press.

— (ed.) (1990). *Special Educational Needs Review, Vol. 3*. London: Falmer Press.

Jowett, S., Hegarty, S. and Moses, D. (1988). *Joining Forces: A Study of Links Between Special and Ordinary Schools*. Windsor: NFER-Nelson.

Keogh, B. (1988). 'Learning Disability: diversity in search of order', in Wang, M., Reynolds, M. and Walberg, H. (op.cit.).

Kirk, S. A. (1962). *Educating Exceptional Children*. Boston: Houghton Mifflin.

Lee, T. (1991). *Additional Education Needs and LMS: Methods and Money 1991–2*. Bath: University of Bath.

Leeming, K., Swann, W., Coupe, J. and Mittler, P. (1979). *Teaching Language and Communication to the Mentally Handicapped*. London: Evans and Methuen Educational.

Lewis, A. (1991). *Primary Special Needs and the National Curriculum*. London: Routledge.

Lunt, I. and Evans, J. (1991). *Special Educational Needs under Local Management of Schools*. London: University of London Institute of Education.

Miles, T. and Miles, E. (1990). *Dyslexia: A Hundred Years On*. Milton Keynes: Open University Press.

Mittler, P. and Preddy, D. (1981). 'Mentally handicapped pupils and school leavers: a survey in North West England', in Cooper, B. (ed.), *Abilities and Needs of Mentally Retarded Children*. New York: Academic Press.

Moses, D., Hegarty, S. and Jowett, S. (1988). *Supporting Ordinary Schools: LEA initiatives*. Windsor: NFER-Nelson.

National Curriculum Council (1992). *The National Curriculum and Pupils with Severe Learning Difficulties*. York: National Curriculum Council.

Norwich, B. (1990). *Special Needs in Ordinary Schools: Reappraising Special Needs Education*. London: Cassell.

Philp, M. and Duckworth, D. (1982). *Children with Disabilities and their Families: A Review of Research*. Windsor: NFER-Nelson.

Pumfrey, P. D. and Reason, R. (1991). *Specific Learning Difficulties (Dyslexia): Challenges and Responses*. Windsor: NFER-Nelson.

Robson, C., Sebba, J., Mittler, P. and Davies, L. (1987). *In-service Training and Special Educational Needs:Running Short School-focused Courses*. Manchester: Manchester University Press.

Sayer, J. (1993). *Secondary Schools for All? Strategies for Special Needs*. London: Cassell.

Tansley, P. and Panckhurst, J. (1981). *Children with Specific Learning Difficulties*. Windsor: NFER-Nelson.

Thomson, G., Riddell, S. and Dyer, S. (1989). *Policy, Professionals and Parents: Legislating for Change in the Field of Special Educational Needs*. Edinburgh: University of Edinburgh.

Wang, M., Reynolds, M. and Walberg, H. (1987). *Handbook of Special Education: Research and Practice, Vol. 1*. Oxford: Pergamon Press.

—, Reynolds, M. and Walberg, H. (1988). *Handbook of Special Education: Research and Practice, Vol. 2*. Oxford: Pergamon Press.

—, Reynolds, M. and Walberg, H. (1989). *Handbook of Special Education: Research and Practice, Vol. 3*. Oxford: Pergamon Press.

Wedell, K. and Roberts, J. (1981). 'Survey of Current Research in the UK on Children with Special Educational Needs' (unpublished report). London: SSRC.
— and Roberts, J. (1982). 'Special education and research: a recent survey', *Special Education: Forward Trends*, 9, 3, pp. 19–25.
Wells, I. (1989). *Evidence on Parental Roles in the Education of Children with Severe Learning Difficulties*. Belfast: Northern Ireland Council for Educational Research.
Wilson, M. (1980). *The Curriculum in Special Schools*. York: Longman for Schools Council.
Wolfendale, S. (1992). *Primary Schools and Special Needs: Policy, Planning and Provision*. London: Cassell.

14

GENDER

Sara Delamont

INTRODUCTION

This chapter is in four main sections, which summarise the current state of British research on sex roles and the education system, outline the changes in UK education policy that have had particular impact on gender in education, evaluate the main methods available to gather data, and propose some promising areas for future research. Material from countries other than Britain is not covered systematically, although some key scholars from English-speaking countries are mentioned where appropriate. The school system is the central focus, although some coverage is given to further and higher education.

Before these four major sections there is a brief introduction to the subject matter of the paper in a vivid form. On 1 November 1991 *The Times Educational Supplement* published a letter from a school governor in a regular advice column. The letter queried the activities of a primary school headmistress. Among the problems listed by the governor was:

> Finally, we had put in our behaviour guidelines that no punishment should be embarrassing to the child. Now we've heard that she's made girls wear boys' caps if they're caught fighting.

The governor clearly felt that the headmistress's behaviour was unacceptable in itself *and* contrary to agreed school policy. Crystallised in this reported disciplinary strategy is a striking example of sex-stereotyping in a British school.

If this disciplinary strategy has been accurately reported, the gender stereotyping is marked. First the school has a uniform, with different headgear for boys and girls, and therefore probably outfits which separate male and female pupils (see Delamont, 1990, pp.15–16). Second, it appears that aggressive behaviour, especially fighting, is seen as a 'male' pastime, thus stereotyping both sexes (see Askew and Ross, 1988 for a discussion of this problem in schools). Third, it appears that social control and discipline is partially based on shaming one sex by comparing them unfavourably with the other. Managing boys by comparing them unfavourably with girls, or vice versa, was a common control strategy in English comprehensive schools in the late 1970s (see Delamont, 1990, p. 29 and p. 59) and in classes for slow learners in some Welsh comprehensives in the mid-1980s (Delamont, 1990 p. 60). However, to hear of a headteacher using it so cold-bloodedly in 1991 is a dramatic and forceful reminder that thinking about anti-sexism has not penetrated very far into the British educational system (see Sikes, 1991; Lloyd and Duveen, 1993; Hilton, 1991).

It is also salutary to realise that gender stereotyping is a two-way problem: both boys and girls are damaged by such behaviour and attitudes. Many readers will be shocked to discover a headmistress operating such an antiquated and sexist disciplinary strategy. Such shocks have stimulated much of the research on gender and education, which has grown in bulk and sophistication over the past 25 years.

THE CURRENT STATE OF RESEARCH

When Acker (1981) reviewed educational research in Britain from the 1950s to the 1970s, she found that gender issues were frequently ignored, and that female experiences and the outcomes of education for women were regularly left unresearched. Many highly respected studies were based on male-only samples. The 1972 social mobility study of England and Wales (Halsey, Heath and Ridge, 1980), for example, was based on a sample of 10,000 men. During the 1980s research on all-male samples became less and less acceptable, so that researchers and funding bodies came to an agreement that both sexes were equally worthy of investigation. When Marshall, Rose, Newby and Vogler (1988) came to do a partial replication of the Halsey, Heath and Ridge study they used a sample of males and females. They had decided that both the British education system and the British labour market were too fully integrated to make a single-sex sample meaningful. That is, if men and women are competing for educational places and credentials, and then for jobs, life chances cannot sensibly be treated as an all-male contest in an all-male arena.

The rise of the contemporary feminist movement in the 1970s produced educational researchers who wanted to examine sex differences in the outcomes of school and higher education (such as exam results), to explore how females experienced learning, and to conduct action research to try and change both the experiences and the outcomes (see Britton, 1991, for a 317 page bibliography of this research). Subsequently, it has become clear that although the bulk of the research had focused on boys and men, there were many aspects of maleness, masculinity and education that we knew nothing about (see Mac an Ghaill, 1994). There are still many gaps in our knowledge; many aspects of the schooling of girls and boys we know little or nothing about. Before this chapter goes on to review what is known, these gaps in the research need documenting. This is done for each constituent 'nation' of the UK in turn, mentioning first any large-scale data on schooling outcomes, then any research on the processes of schooling, and finally the major pieces of action research. It is important to start from a recognition that there are four distinct educational systems up to the age of 18 in Britain, each with its own 'gender agenda'.

The British research is, first, lacking in coverage of Northern Ireland. There is no monograph on the school experiences of young women in Northern Ireland either in Catholic or Protestant institutions. As Northern Ireland has many single-sex schools *and* maintains academic selection at 11, comparisons could be drawn between Northern Ireland and other regions of the UK if research on gender were carried out. The lack of data on gender and schooling in Northern Ireland is not the only gap in British regional coverage. Wales has not yet had much research carried out on gender and education. There is a brief overview of the statistics in Jones (1988), while Sanders (1992) has unpicked the data on gender and maths in Wales but no process studies have been published. In particular, the lack of research on girls' and boys' experiences in the fast-growing Welsh-medium sector is unfortunate. It is possible that gender relations are quite different in schools where Welsh is the medium of instruction. There is an evaluation of one action-research programme aimed at broadening young women's experiences: the Women's Training Roadshow programme (Pilcher *et al.*, 1989), but little else.

Scotland has had its educational outcomes thoroughly documented, but there have been few innovations to evaluate and Scotland has yet to produce the range of school process studies focused on women that its unique education system deserves. The impact on girls of moving to secondary education at 12 rather than 11 and the comparative success of Scottish comprehensives at reaching working-class teenage girls and harnessing their educational potential (McPherson and Willms, 1987) both deserve Scottish-based process studies. Fewell and Patterson (1990) is a starting-point for researchers interested in gender in Scottish education. The young women I studied at 'St. Luke's' are now 36, and mine is still the only published research on the processes of schooling in the high prestige, high cost and explicitly *feminist* independent sector (Delamont, 1989).

Most of the British research on gender and schooling has actually been done in England, especially urban England. The bulk of all the investigations, and certainly all the best known studies, such as that of Willis (1977) on masculinity and Stanworth (1983) on classroom processes in an 'A' level group, are English not British. The statistical pattern of male and female achievement has been mapped by Arnot (1996). The 1980s saw female achievement at 16 overtake that of males, and female success at 'A' level increase markedly, but the reluctance of women to do any science after 16 is still evident and causing concern to policy-makers. There is a body of material on the school experiences of male and female pupils in England. Indeed, most of the research on the experiences of schooling done in Britain has actually been English rather than Scottish, Welsh or Irish. Like most of the British ethnographic research it has concentrated on pupils in state schools (see Delamont and Atkinson, 1994). There is a shortage of work on girls' and boys' experiences in denominational schools (especially fee-paying ones), and in élite 'public' schools (but see Walford, 1993). The majority of the action-research aimed at reducing sex inequality in education has taken place in England, most famously the Girls into Science and Technology (GIST) project which ran in Manchester in the 1980s (see Whyte, 1985).

Because of the sexist biases in the sociology of education in the 1960s and 1970s (see Acker, 1981), there are gaps in the historical record of girls' schooling in Britain. The only experiential data on young women in single-sex grammar schools were collected by Lambert (1977, 1982) and Llewellyn (1980) and are mostly unpublished. There are no ethnographic data on young girls' experiences of the 11+ or 12+ exams, or of streamed primary schooling; none on young women in the few Technical High Schools established after the 1944 Act, and none on life in secondary modern schools before CSE and the raising of the school leaving age to 16. All these experiences are now past and therefore lost, and sociologists failed to collect data on them when they existed.

There has also been a pattern of research on male adolescents being published in monographs, while equivalent data on young women have been only available in journal articles or research reports, which have lesser impact (see Delamont, 1989, Appendix 1). Hargreaves (1967), and Lacey (1970) are frequently described as pioneers of school ethnography, while Lambert (1977, 1982), their contemporary, is ignored, because her study of the girls in 'Lumley' and 'Hightown' was never a monograph.

There is also a shortage of research that compares the lives of pupils in mixed schools and in single-sex schools of otherwise similar types, which means we are often unable to determine whether findings are due to the dynamics of schooling or the presence of males and females in the same rooms. Researchers have been interested in the study of patterns of talk in co-educational classrooms: to see whether boys and girls contribute differently and whether teachers treat male and female pupils alike (for example, Shuy, 1986). However, we lack studies on all-male or all-female classrooms to compare with those on the co-educational ones, which are themselves not numerous.

Some of the best-known and most frequently cited studies have been based on very small numbers of teachers and tiny amounts of classroom interaction (see Delamont, 1989, pp. 270–72). At primary, secondary and tertiary level there are polemical claims that (1) males dominate the discourse in mixed classes, and that (2) if a teacher attempts to increase female participation males perceive this as grossly unfair and resist vociferously. In the most colourful version of this position Spender (1982) argued that males regard two-thirds of the classroom talk in mixed lessons as a 'fair' share, and will not accept any reduction.

The available data on primary classrooms in Britain have been reviewed by Croll and Moses (1990), who conclude that 'there is a consistent tendency for girls, on average, to receive slightly less individual teacher attention than boys' (p.197). This is largely, but not entirely, because boys are reprimanded more than girls. Croll and Moses are able to come to this conclusion in part because there has been a series of large-scale observational studies of primary classrooms in Britain. The data on secondary classrooms are sparser and simply do not allow for such generalisations to be made except as polemical outbursts.

Hammersley (1990) has challenged the conclusions of two previous sets of researchers both philosophically and in terms of the small size of the data bases used to draw conclusions that there are unjustified gender imbalances in talk in primary classrooms. The arguments advanced by Hammersley (1990) could only be addressed by a comprehensive research programme in a large number of classrooms with a carefully designed coding schedule.

Much of the research on gender has failed to address the multi-racial nature of contemporary Britain. There is a distinct shortage of investigations of gender issues within ethnic and linguistic minority communities, especially beyond London. There are a few studies of British West Indian and South Asian women in education, but not enough, and some other ethnic groups (for example, Greek and Turkish Cypriots) have not yet been the focus of published research. The school experiences of a female pupil of Chinese origin are unlikely to be 'the same' as those of the British West Indians studied by Furlong (1976), Fuller (1980) and Mac an Ghaill (1988). No one could suggest that our data on the latter were an adequate number of studies of British West Indian women and men in school, but we have nothing, for example, on the Chinese, Vietnamese, Somali or Maltese communities. Just as there is a shortage of research on gender and ethnic minority schooling focused on communities which have grown up in Britain since 1945 such as the Punjabis, so too there has been a failure to explore the topic among Gypsies, and among the indigenous linguistic minorities of Gaelic and Welsh speakers.

Higher education in the UK is less differentiated than schooling across the four nations, and the position of women has recently been documented by Sutherland (1994). There are published data on the outcomes of higher education, but few process studies and action research has been rare.

This overview of the gaps in our knowledge of gender in British education, though brief, shows how little is known about the topic. The next section deals with policy changes that effect gender issues.

MAIN POLICY CHANGES

The past 50 years have brought many policy changes in education at school, further education and higher education levels. Some have been embodied in legislation, some have been more organic, growing up from within educational institutions. Some apply only in England or England and Wales, while others are common to the whole UK. Some emanate from Westminster, others from the European Parliament. This significance of European Union Law for women in the UK is discussed in McIntosh (1990) and Rendel (1992) but is under-researched. Two pieces of British legislation, the 1975 Sex Discrimination Act and the 1974 Equal Pay Act, which did apply throughout the UK, led to the Equal Opportunities Commission and a series of investigations into alleged discriminations in education. Detailed research on their educational consequences is still awaited.

There are six main post-war policy changes in the school system of England and Wales which have had, or may have had, consequences for gender. These include the 1944 (Butler) Act which introduced compulsory free secondary schools for the majority of the population who previously had only received an elementary schooling. As this applied to both sexes, it opened secondary schooling to girls whatever their families felt about the education of females. It is mainly remembered for the introduction of the 11+ exam, and the fact that this was 'rigged' to prevent more girls than boys going into the higher prestige grammar school. The main focus of research on the 1944 Act today is, of course, historical, especially oral histories of girls who experienced the grammar school (see Evans, 1991). The gradual arrival of comprehensive schooling for the majority of secondary pupils following a circular issued by the Labour government of the 1960s, which occurred throughout the 1970s, led to the abolition of the 11+ and had implications for gender divisions that were largely unconsidered and unresearched at the time. However, the accompanying shift from single-sex secondary grammar and secondary modern schools to co-education in comprehensive schools, which was, as Sutherland (1985a) pointed out, a largely unconsidered consequence of comprehensivisation, had a major impact on the school lives of girls *and* the career prospects of women teachers. The raising of the school leaving age (ROSLA) from 15 to 16, which came into force in 1971, meant that most females were forced to be still at school when the public exams were taken, cutting into the previously substantial pool of female 'unqualified' school leavers. Youth unemployment and the rise of 'vocationalism', and youth training schemes, which effectively raised the school leaving age to 18 (as no welfare benefits are payable till 18) were the main policy changes of the late 1970s and the early 1980s (see Wolpe, 1978). All those policy changes have been absorbed into experience, and are no longer discussed.

In the early 1990s *the* school level policy change believed to affect gender is the Education Reform Act (1988, ERA) with its provisions for schools to opt out of Local Education Authority control, for the local management of schools, national testing, City Technology Colleges, and the imposition of the 'National' Curriculum (see Ball, 1990): this last not being 'National' at all, for it does not exist in Northern Ireland or Scotland, and is not mandatory in private schools.

It is noticeable that only four of these school level reforms were implemented in Scotland, and none in Northern Ireland. Scotland's national curriculum runs only to 14 (not 16 as in England and Wales), national testing has been abandoned in the face of popular protest, and both City Technology Colleges and opting out have been complete flops in Scotland. These are further reminders that Britain does not have a national education system, and research needs to be done in all parts of the country, not just England.

We do not yet know what effects the 1988 Act has had on gender issues in schools, because the research has not yet been done and because the changes have yet to work through the school system. For instance, the generation of young women prevented from 'giving up' science by the introduction of the National Curriculum has yet to enter the labour market. Ball (1990) is a vital source of background data on the reforms and Arnot (1992) has written of their potential impact on gender equality.

The higher education system has experienced a series of changes since 1945, especially the expansion of degree courses after the Robbins Report of 1963, documented by Sutherland (1994). Among the most significant for gender equality were the closure of many teacher training colleges, the end of the binary line between Universities and Polytechnics, expansion of student numbers alongside financial cuts in the late 1980s and early 1990s, the development of 'access' courses and the increased entry of mature students, and the blossoming of Women's Studies.

The closure of many small, single-sex teacher training colleges, either absolutely or by merger with multi-disciplinary higher education institutions closed a career path for women (as lecturers and principals in such colleges) and ended a feminist experiment of the nineteenth century (see Delamont, 1989, pp.174–6). In 1991–92 the abolition of the 'binary line' in higher education between the 52 universities and the 'public' sector institutions created 37 new universities at a stroke. This changed the landscape of higher education. The closure of the teacher training colleges seems to have diverted many bright women into degree courses, the impact of the end of the binary line on gender is not yet known. At the time of the reform women formed 49 per cent of undergraduates in the 'public' sector, but only 45 per cent of those in the 'old' universities.

The total number of students and the proportion of the age group going into higher education has risen since 1944, with two boosts: in 1963 the Robbins Report led to a substantial increase, and the 1980s saw another 'great leap forward'. In the 1980s there was also a growth in 'access' courses, designed to give a second chance to unqualified adults who wish to enter higher education. Women make up nearly half of the mature students in UK higher education.

Finally, in the last 20 years a new 'subject' has entered the higher education curriculum: women's studies (Aaron and Walby, 1992). There has also been a growth of 'options' and 'modules' on women in many arts and social sciences courses, with an accompanying boom in books on 'women and' and 'women in'. These developments have not yet received much research attention: we know little about the motivation which leads a history or classics undergraduate to choose an option on 'Women in Ancient Greece' rather than 'The Political Thought of Pericles' or 'The Spartan Army'.

Many of the policy changes implemented since 1944 were not intended to change the education of women relative to men: they were designed to improve male education or that of both sexes together. A scholarly historical investigation of changing policy since 1944 as it impacted on gender would be an extremely valuable addition to the literature on the history, social policy and sociology of British education.

Bearing these policy changes – and their unintended and frequently uncharted consequences – in mind, this chapter moves on to a discussion of the main methods available to the researcher.

THE MAIN METHODS AVAILABLE TO GATHER DATA

This section outlines the main methods of gathering data on gender and education. These are individual interviews designed to gather data of three kinds (life and oral history, narratives, current experience and opinion), focus groups and group interviews, diaries, open-ended writing, direct observation with or without pre-specified coding schedules, surveys and the experiment and the quasi-experiment. A thumb-nail sketch is given with the citations of a sensible methods text, an apposite research project on gender and, if available, an autobiographical account of conducting research on gender using that method. There is also brief reference to the debates surrounding action-research and feminist methods.

Cutting across all the methods is an ethical issue about gathering data from children (see Fine and Sandstrom, 1990 and Denscombe and Aubrook, 1992) and a major problem about doing research on sex, gender, sexuality and sexual identity which are private, hidden areas of many people's lives. The 'hidden curriculum' of beliefs about sex, gender, sexuality and sexual identity is sympathetically described by Raphaela Best (1983). She followed a cohort of pupils through childhood and into adolescence, learning about their culture and simultaneously confronting them with the illogicalities in their sex role stereotypes. Her central argument is that schools teach children three curricula – one overt, two hidden. The academic curriculum and the official school rules are manifest, but behind them, and largely invisible to adults were the rules of appropriate male and female behaviour learnt from peers and enforced by them. Concealed behind that first 'hidden' curriculum was a third, even more secret children's culture, where sexuality and obscenity were crucial. The third area was the most carefully hidden from adults, because as Bauman (1982, p.178) explains:

> The free peer group activity of children is by its very nature a privileged realm in which adults are alien intruders, especially so insofar as much of the children's folklore repertoire violates what children understand to be adult standards of decorum.

Pupils' feelings about gender are frequently in this 'privileged realm'. It is both practically difficult and ethically problematic to gather data on the two hidden curricula. Fine (1987, pp. 238–40) reports the complex process of getting pre-adolescent boys to trust him with the vulgar-obscene aspects of their culture, as do Canaan (1986), and Measor (1989). This deeply concealed pupil culture is revealed in the scary stories told about school transfer (Measor and Woods, 1984; Delamont, 1991), and researchers can gradually gain access to it, if, like Best, they reveal themselves to be unshockable and trustworthy. Such things as sexual harassment (Mahoney, 1985; Herbert, 1989), attacks on 'sissies' as 'poofters', and accusations about young women being sexually immoral flourish in this privileged realm.

INTERVIEWS WITH INDIVIDUALS

There are three main types of data that researchers gather from single respondent interviews: life and oral histories; narratives; and current experiences and opinions.

Life History and Oral History: Interviews, usually multiple interviews each lasting several hours, are the normal way of collecting oral history (that is unwritten, eyewitness accounts of the past) and life history data. The classic text on oral history is Thompson (1988). Gluck and Patai (1991) is a collection containing pieces of oral history gathered by feminists. There is an oral history of the Burnham system of adjudicating teachers' pay in Saran (1982) and Goodson (1983) includes oral histories of curriculum change.

A good introduction to life history is Denzin (1991). Peterson (1964) is a classic piece of life history, done on women teachers in the USA, and more recently Sikes, Measor and Woods (1985) and Connell (1985) carried out life history work on men and women teachers in England and Australia respectively. Heyl (1979) is the life history of a thoroughly unorthodox teacher: a woman who ran a brothel and taught trainee prostitutes how to be safe, successful hookers. We lack life histories of teachers of education or oral histories in Wales, Scotland and Northern Ireland.

Narratives: In the 1990s the collection and analysis of stories, especially teachers' stories, has become a major research activity. Cortazzi (1993) is an excellent methods book on narrative, and his earlier book (Cortazzi, 1991) is a useful example of the type of data produced. Feminist researchers have been particularly enthusiastic about the collection of narratives from women and girls: Michelle Fine (1988) and the collection edited by Witherall and Noddings (1991).

Experiences and opinions: Most interviewers are trying to collect data on their respondents' current experiences and opinions. Some use a schedule, with pre-specified questions, while others have a few 'headings' and aim to elicit the respondents' world views in an open-ended conversation. The latter type is sometimes called an ethnographic interview, and Spradley (1979) is a useful methods text.

FOCUS GROUPS AND GROUP INTERVIEWS

A focus group is basically a group interview:

although not in the sense of an alternation between the researcher's questions and the research participants' responses. Instead, the reliance is on interaction within the group, based on topics supplied by the researcher, who typically takes the role of moderator (Morgan, 1991, pp. 9–10).

The conversation is taped and transcribed, and the data are the transcripts. Sometimes researchers assemble a group; sometimes they use one that already exists (like the mothers at mother and toddler club). Sometimes the researcher works with a group over time, regularly collecting their talk, sometimes the study is a one-off. Morgan (1991) is a useful introduction to the focus group method.

The focus group method is frequently used when the researcher wants to discover how opinions are formed, or views about something complex or not part of everyday immediate experience. So, for example, how young women weigh up the pros and cons of contraception, or of studying 'A' level sciences could be topics for focus groups. The processes by which views are shared, contrasted, and develop are a central concern of the research.

A group interview is exactly what it sounds like: getting a group of people to respond to a series of questions. Educational researchers use group interviews more often than focus groups, especially with pupils because it saves time, pupils often feel 'braver' in a group, and will egg each other on to tell stories of deviance or humour. For example, Woods (1986, p. 73) justifying his decision to interview pupils in small groups, says:

> Other advantages were that they acted as checks, balances and prompts to each other, inaccuracies were corrected, incidents and reactions recalled and analysed.

The main difference from focus groups is that in a group interview, the researcher works through an agenda of questions and solicits answers to them. Group interviews with teachers are rarer than group interviews with pupils. Pilcher *et al.* (1989) did an evaluation of the Women's Training Roadshow in Cardiff using group interviews with pupils.

WRITTEN EVIDENCE

There are three main types of written evidence: documents, diaries and open-ended writing.

Documentary Sources

Scott (1990) is an introduction to social research using documentary sources. Scholars interested in gender have used historical material to recreate the lives of women and girls in education which had been 'lost' from the mainstream accounts. Fletcher's (1980) analysis of the material held in the Public Record Office relating to the Endowed Schools Act of 1869, which enabled her to discover the evidence collected on girls' schools, is an exemplary study of this kind.

Diaries

Researchers have used diaries of two kinds. They have analysed diaries kept in the past for private consumption as a source of historical data (Plummer, 1983), and they have asked people to keep diaries and submit them to the researcher. Coxon (1988), for example, asked gay men to keep diaries of their sexual encounters as part of a project on risk behaviour and HIV/AIDS. An educational example is Lacey (1970) who got the teenage boys at Hightown Grammar to keep diaries for him. Many feminist scholars see diaries as a useful way of gathering data on women in the past and in the present.

Open-ended Writing

There are projects which ask respondents to write something – letters, essays, autobiographies – for them. The ORACLE project (Delamont and Galton, 1986) used essays written for the team by young secondary school pupils to get data on their early days in their new school, as had Bryan (1980). These essays revealed deep-seated ideas about masculinity and femininity held by nine to 12-year-olds. Delamont (1991) draws on scary stories specially written for her by sixth formers.

DIRECT OBSERVATION: ETHNOGRAPHIC AND SCHEDULE-BASED

Delamont (1983) is a general introduction to the direct observation of classrooms and schools. Croll (1986) deals with observation using a pre-specified coding schedule, Delamont (1992) with the more open-ended ethnographic approach, and Edwards and Westgate (1987) with collecting data on language use in educational settings. Large-scale projects using pre-specified coding schedules would be ideal for discovering if there are systematic differences between male and female patterns of classroom talk. Ethnography has been widely used to study the experiences of males and females in education. In Britain the pioneers were Hargreaves (1967), Lacey (1970) and Lambert (1977 and 1982). In the USA, educational anthropologists were first to study classroom processes, both inside the USA, and Canada (for example, Wolcott, 1967) and abroad (Spindler, 1974). Gender was not a focus of the early work. In the USA anthropologists were interested in describing minority cultures that came into conflict with dominant values inside schools, while in the UK researchers focused on social class and school achievement (see Atkinson and Delamont, 1980, 1990, 1994, for details).

The work on educational experiences has produced British and American studies of gender in nursery (Lloyd and Duveen, 1992; Paley, 1984), infant (King, 1978; Serbin, 1978), primary (Clarricoates, 1987; Best 1983), secondary (Measor, 1989; Grant and Sleeter, 1986), and further education classes (Cockburn, 1987; Valli, 1986), and among teachers (for example, Beynon,1987, Wolcott, 1973), and in the USA there are projects on gender in higher education (for example, Holland and Eisenhart, 1990; Moffat, 1989) as well as a much greater sensitivity to gender issues in educational process studies generally.

The papers collected in Woods and Hammersley (1993) address the contentious issue of how ethnographers can collect reliable and valid data on sex inequalities (or racial inequalities) in everyday school life. There are many autobiographical or confessional accounts of ethnographic work. Delamont (1984) and Galton and Delamont (1985) describe trying to use both types of observational methods.

SURVEYS

The survey, either by a questionnaire that is completed by respondents in writing, or worked through by an interviewer, is probably the commonest social research method. Oppenheim (1992) is the classic text on questionnaire design and Marsh (1982) is a more recent work on the survey. Cohen and Manion (1989) provide clear guide-lines on the conduct of surveys in educational research. Examples of gender-related surveys are Kelly (1985) who did a national survey of teachers' attitudes to gender issues, and Smithers and Zientek (1991) who surveyed 218 infant teachers about gender and the 1988 ERA.

EXPERIMENTS AND QUASI-EXPERIMENTS

Cohen and Manion (1980) define the experiment and the quasi-experiment as follows:

> the essential feature of experimental research is that the investigator deliberately controls and manipulates the conditions which determine the

events in which he (*sic*) is interested (1980, p. 188).

The quasi-experiment is more common in educational research, because as Cohen and Manion point out: 'often in educational research, it is simply not possible for investigators to undertake true experiments' (1980, p. 163).

Tann's (1981) investigation of mixed and single-sex small groups performing educational tasks and Galton and Delafield's (1981) work on self-fulfilling prophecies are both quasi-experiments carried out in real schools, where gender is one key variable.

ACTION RESEARCH

Cohen and Manion define action research as a small-scale intervention in the functioning of the real world and close examination of the effects of such intervention (1980, p. 74). In other words, action research means setting some change in progress and carefully monitoring its effects.

Whyte (1985) is the full report on the most famous piece of action research on gender done in Britain: the Girls into Science and Technology (GIST) project. This ran in ten Manchester schools, and involved a set of innovations designed to encourage young women to persevere with the 'male' craft and science subjects after the choice point of 14. The team brought adult women working as scientists and technicians into the schools to act as role models, raised the consciousness of the teachers about the gender dynamics of classrooms, and experimented with teaching maths and science to single-sex classes in co-educational schools.

An outstanding piece of action research on gender done in the USA and too little known in the UK is Guttentag and Bray (1976).

FEMINIST METHODS

Cutting across the literature on research methods is a set of arguments about how gender issues should be researched. Since the 1970s there has been a philosophical debate about the nature of 'scientific' enquiry in Western capitalist societies (see Harding, 1986) and whether its whole basis was actually contaminated by *unexamined* assumptions about masculinity versus femininity, male versus female, objectivity versus subjectivity, mind versus body and reason versus emotions. For many researchers in the social sciences these debates were acutely relevant to studies of gender, because there is no neutral ground from which a scholar can investigate males and females (see Haste, 1993). Such concerns led to the calls for developing feminist methods to do research on both women and men.

Maynard and Purvis (1994) is a recent collection which explores feminist methods. Maynard's (1994) chapter is an excellent discussion of the interrelated arguments over qualitative *versus* quantitative methods and whether feminist research must use the former to be true to the experiences of women. Any researcher investigating gender issues in the 1990s needs to read some of the debates on feminist methods and epistemologies, but these are not explained further here.

THE 'BEST' METHOD FOR RESEARCH ON GENDER

Good research on gender and education can be done using any methods or combination of methods. The important thing is *not* to treat gender as something known and familiar, but as an issue for the research. So a well-designed survey that investigates whether both girls and boys can be good at maths or play leadership roles is 'better' than a qualitative study that assumes that only boys can do maths or be leaders.

Good researchers need to do several things. First, it is vital to collect and report data on gender in the field setting; second, it is vital to pay equal attention to all the informants in the setting, whether they are male or female (see Smith, 1978 for an excellent example of the benefits); third, it is important to collect data on how the actors in a field setting understand and view gender; fourth, it is necessary to gather data on how those beliefs are enacted (for example, in speech, or in non-verbal behaviour); fifth, it is necessary to examine the relation between gender and power in the field setting; *and* all the time the researcher needs to make his or her *own* beliefs about gender (in all these ways) problematic.

PROMISING AREAS FOR FUTURE RESEARCH

Throughout this chapter gaps in our knowledge about gender and education have been mentioned. In this final section some potential research projects are highlighted. However, almost any topic on gender can usefully be investigated, if only because the economic climate and the policy context keep changing, and because each successive cohort of young people may differ significantly from its predecessors.

One of the biggest gaps in our knowledge is why British and, indeed, Anglo-Saxon, culture is so scared of 'sissies' (see Connell, 1987). Take this letter, originally from the tabloid *Daily Star*, reprinted in *New Statesman and Society* (16 Oct. 1992):

My eight-year-old boy is a strange lad. He's bothered about the planet and interested in butterflies and insects as well as other animals. He never watches football. Do you think he's going to be gay? (*Daily Star*, reprinted in *New Statesman and Society*)

When pupils hold stereotyped views about male and female behaviour, then the school teachers' reinforcement of them makes classrooms uncomfortable places for the pupil who diverges from the stereotype. Wolpe (1977) and Abraham (1989a and 1989b) have both reported secondary teachers' repulsion when faced with boys they saw as 'effeminate' (see also Mac an Ghaill, 1991 and 1994), and Clarricoates (1987) reports similar distaste for a primary age sissy. One of the three schools she studied had a boy – Michael – who really worried Miss Mackeson, his teacher, and his classmates:

When Miss Mackeson asked him what he wanted to be when he grew up he said he wanted to be a butterfly. He's just a great big sissy (p. 91).

This gap is part of a general shortage of research on masculinity in educational settings. Mac an Ghaill (1994) is the first monograph to treat the area seriously, and there is scope for a great deal more research in all sectors of education. Moffatt (1989) is an American study which touches on masculinity in student culture, a topic totally neglected in the UK or Australia. See also Adler and Adler (1992) on college athletes.

It must also be noted that there is a chronic shortage of research on men as teachers in schools, further or higher education. Connell (1985) stands alone in his attempt to show how masculine identity and working as a schoolteacher interact. The experiences of straight and gay men in all spheres of teaching need documenting along the lines of Skelton (1993) and Sparkes (1994).

RESEARCH PRIORITIES ON WOMEN AND GIRLS

Despite the research done in the last 20 years there are many areas of female pupils' school experience which are not yet properly investigated and the further education and higher education sectors have been relatively neglected too. Apart from the lack of studies in Northern Ireland, Scotland and in Wales, more research on young women in rural areas of England is needed (see Mason, 1990). The school experiences of females in fee-paying schools, both single-sex and co-educational, need studying. The percentage of 16-year-old girls opting to enter the sixth form has risen over the last decade without any research on why these 16-year-olds are staying on rather than leaving as their predecessors did. Many of the initiatives designed to change women's experience of education, such as the Women Into Science and Engineering buses have not been evaluated by researchers (see Delamont, 1990, pp.114–115).

There is a grave shortage of research on women in higher education (Thomas, 1990). The gender balance of universities has changed markedly over the past twenty years, and the proportion of women reading medicine, law, accountancy and other 'professional' subjects has increased rapidly. Greed (1991) has written about surveying, but the other areas urgently need investigation. The UK lacks anything equivalent to Holland and Eisenhart (1990) on women students.

There is a body of research on women in schoolteaching, but less on women lecturing in further or higher education. The factual position of the latter can be gleaned from Lie, Malik and Harris (1994), but the experiential side is only represented by a few journal articles (for example, Bagilhole, 1993) and occasional books such as Sutherland (1985b) and (1994). There is nothing in the UK to match Aisenberg and Harrington's (1988) study of women with and without tenure in the US.

THE MOST URGENT TASKS

Most serious, however, is the lack of a large, reliable database on classroom interaction patterns from four to 18 in all subjects, which compares males' and females' experiences of classroom interaction in mixed and single-sex classes. It is a matter of urgency to discover whether girls are routinely receiving less teacher attention, and/or teacher attention of different kinds from boys, and how their learning experiences are different when only girls are in the room. Only when we have this large body of data can we really claim to know what the male and female pupils' experiences of schooling are.

There is also an urgent need to design effective ways to incorporate feminist insights into teachers' occupational culture, so that schools change as a result of existing research.

Lloyd's (1989) observations in the south east of England in reception classes at two schools and Hilton's (1991) data on playgroup workers show teachers of young children in the UK reinforcing the behaviour in girls that they dislike. Serbin's (1978) research showed nursery schoolteachers objecting to girls 'clinging' and keeping close to them. Yet, observation made it clear that girls could only get teachers' attention and response when they were physically close. Girls beyond touching distance were ignored unlike boys who received teacher attention wherever they were in the nursery.

Other studies of teachers (see Delamont, 1990), and of recruits to the occupation (for example, Sikes, 1991) reveal an occupational group unaware of feminist perspectives, ideas of gender as socially constructed, and unconscious of the school's role in reinforcing conservative messages about sex roles.

These data on feminism's lack of impact on schoolteachers show the urgency of the action-research task on occupational culture. They can also sensitise researchers to investigate how far other intellectual currents and bodies of scholarly findings (such as post-modernism or the findings on the positive impact of parents reading aloud to children) have penetrated teachers' occupational culture. Despite the currency of feminist ideas in recent years, the apparent resistance to them in many educational settings, highlights the resilience of occupational and institutional cultures.

CONCLUSION

Research on gender and education is an exciting area, where there are many unexplored topics and untouched problems. Thoughtful scholars should have no difficulty finding themselves a piece of the action.

ACKNOWLEDGEMENTS

I am grateful to Pat Harris for typing this paper, and Lesley Pugsley for checking the sources and chasing up recalcitrant references for me.

REFERENCES

Aaron, J. and Walby, S. (eds) (1992). *Out of the Margins*. London: Falmer.
Abraham, J. (1989a). 'Teacher ideology and sex roles in curriculum texts', *British Journal of Sociology of Education*, 10, 1, pp. 33–52.
— (1989b) 'Gender differences and anti-school boys', *Sociological Review*, 37, 1, pp. 65–88.
Acker, S. (1981). 'No woman's land', *Sociological Review*, 29, 1, pp. 65–88.
Adler, P. and Adler, P. (1992). *Backboards and Blackboards*. New York: Columbia University Press.
Aisenberg, N. and Harrington, M. (1988). *Women of Academe*. Amherst, MA: University of Massachusetts Press.
Arnot, Madelaine (1992). 'Feminism, education and the New Right', in Arnot, M. and Barton, L. (eds), *Voicing Concern*. Wallingford: Triangle Books.
— (1996). *The 1988 CRA and Gender Equality Part I Exam Results*. Manchester: The Equal Opportunities Commission.
Askew, S. and Ross, C. (1988). *Boys Don't Cry*. Milton Keynes: Open University Press.
Atkinson, P. and Delamont, S. (1980). 'The two traditions in educational ethnography', *British Journal of Sociology of Education*, 1, 2, pp. 139–52.

— (1990). 'Writing about teachers', *Teaching and Teacher Education*, 6, 2, pp. 111–25.

Bagilhole, B. (1993). 'How to keep a good woman down', *British Journal of Sociology of Education*, 14, 3, pp. 261–74.

Ball, S. (1990). *Politics and Policymaking in Education*, London: Routledge.

Bauman, R. (1982). 'Ethnography of children's folklore', in Gilmore, P. and Glatthorn, A. (eds), *Children in and out of school*. Washington DC: Centre for Applied Linguistics.

Best, Raphaela (1983). *We've all got scars*. Bloomington: Indiana University Press.

Beynon, J. (1987) 'Miss Floral mends her ways', in Tickle, L. (ed.), *The Arts in Education*. London: Croom Helm.

Britton, M. C.(1991). *Improved Visibility*. Leeds: The University for LISE (The Librarians in Schools and Institutes of Education).

Bryan, K. A. (1980). 'Pupil perceptions of transfer', in Hargreaves, A. and Tickle, L. (eds), *Middle Schools*. London: Harper & Row.

Canaan, J. (1986). 'Why a "slut" is a slut', in Varenne, H. (ed.), *Symbolizing America*. Lincoln, NB: University of Nebraska Press.

Clarricoates, K. (1987). 'Child culture at school', in Pollard, A. (ed.), *Children and their Primary Schools*. London: Falmer.

Cockburn, C. (1987). *Two Track Training*. London: Macmillan.

Cohen, L. and Manion, L. (1980). *Research Methods in Education*. London: Croom Helm.

— (1989). *Research Methods in Education* (3rd edn). London: Routledge.

Connell, R. W. (1985). *Teachers' Work*. Sydney: Allen & Unwin.

— (1987). *Gender and Power*. Oxford: Polity Press.

Cortazzi, M. (1991). *Primary Teaching: How it is*. London: David Fulton.

— (1993). *Narrative Analysis*. London: Falmer.

Coxon, A. P. M. (1988). 'Something Sensational', *Sociological Review*, 36, 2, pp. 353–67.

Croll, P. (1986). *Systematic Classroom Observation*. London: Falmer.

Croll, P. and Moses, D. (1990). 'Sex roles in the primary classroom', in Rogers, C. and Kutnick, P. (eds), *The Social Psychology of the Primary School*. London: Routledge.

Delamont, S. (1983). *Interaction in the Classroom* (2nd edn). London: Methuen.

— (1984). 'The Old Girl Network', in Burgess, R. G. (ed.), *The Research Process in Educational Settings*. London: Falmer.

— (1989). *Knowledgeable Women*. London: Routledge.

— (1990). *Sex Roles and the School* (2nd edn). London: Routledge.

— (1991). 'The Hit List and other horror stories', *Sociological Review*, 39, 2, pp. 238–59.

— (1992). *Fieldwork in Educational Settings*. London: Falmer.

— and Atkinson, P. A. (1994). *Fighting Familiarity*. Cresskill, NJ: Hampton Press.

— and Galton, M. (1986). *Inside the Secondary Classroom*. London: Routledge and Kegan Paul.

Denham, C. and Leiberman, A. (eds) (1980). *Time to Learn*. Washington DC: NIE/ DHEW.

Denscombe, M. and Aubrook, L. (1992). '"It's just another piece of schoolwork": the ethics of questionnaire research on pupils in schools', *British Educational Research Journal*. 18, 2, pp. 113–32.

Denzin, N. (1991). *Interpretive Biography*. Newbury Park, CA: Sage.

Edwards, A. and Westgate, D. (1987). *Investigating Classroom Talk*. London: Falmer.

Evans, M. (1991). *A Good School*. Reading: Box & Wayman.

Fewell, J. and Patterson, F. M. S. (eds) (1990). *Girls in their Prime*. Edinburgh: Scottish Academic Press.

Fine, G. A. (1987). *With the Boys*. Chicago: The University Press.

— and Sandstrom, K. (1990). *Knowing Children*. Newbury Park, CA: Sage.

Fine, Michelle (1988). 'Sexuality, Schooling, and Adolescent Females', *Harvard Educational Review*, 58, 1, pp. 29–53.

Fletcher, S. (1980). *Feminists and Bureaucrats*. Cambridge: Cambridge University Press.

Fuller, M. (1980). 'Black girls in school', in Deem, R. (ed.), *Schooling for Women's Work*. London: Routledge.

Furlong, V. J. (1976). 'Interaction sets in the classroom', in Stubbs, M. and Delamont, S. (eds), *Explorations in Classroom Observation*. Chichester: Wiley.

Galton, M. and Delafield, A. (1981). 'Expectancy effects in primary classrooms', in Simon, B. and Willcocks, J. (eds), *Research and Practice in the Primary Classroom*. London: Routledge.

— and Delamont, S. (1985). 'Speaking with forked tongue', in Burgess, R.G. (ed.), *Field Methods in the Study of Education* London: Falmer.

— Simon, B. and Croll, P. (1980). *Progress and Performance in the Primary School*. London: Routledge.

Gluck, S. B. and Patai, D. (eds) (1991). *Women's Words: The Feminist Practice of Oral History*. London: Routledge.

Goodson, I. (1983) *School Subjects and Curriculum Change*. London: Croom Helm.

Grant, C. and Sleeter, C. (1986) *After the School Bell Rings*. London: Falmer.

Graves, Robert (1966) *Collected Poems*. Harmondsworth: Penguin Books.

Greed, Clara (1991). *Surveying Sisters*. London: Routledge.

Guttentag, M. and Bray, H. (eds) (1976). *Undoing Sex Stereotypes*. New York: McGraw-Hill.

Halsey, A. H., Heath, A. and Ridge, J. M. (1980). *Origins and Destinations*. Oxford: Clarendon.

Hammersley, M. (1990). 'An evaluation of two studies of gender imbalances in primary classrooms', *British Educational Research Journal*. 16, 2, pp. 125–44.

Hargreaves, D. (1967). *Social Relations in a Secondary School*. London: Routledge & Kegan Paul.

Harding, S. (1986). *The Science Question in Feminism*. Milton Keynes: The Open University Press.

Haste, Helen (1993). *The Sexual Metaphor*. London: Harvester Wheatsheaf.

Herbert, C. (1989). *Talking of Silence*. London: Falmer.

Heyl, B. (1979). *The Madam as Entrepreneur*. New Brunswick, NJ: Transaction Books.

Hilton, G. L. S. (1991). 'Boys will be boys – won't they?' *Gender and Education*, 3, 3, pp. 311–14.

Holland, D. C. and Eisenhart, M. A. (1990). *Educated in Romance*. Chicago: Chicago University Press.

Jones, P. E. (1988). 'Some trends in Welsh secondary education 1967–1987', *Contemporary Wales*, 2, pp. 99–17.

Kelly, A. (1985). 'Traditionalists and Trendies', *British Educational Research Journal*, 11, 2, pp. 91–104.

King, R. (1978). *All Things Bright and Beautiful*. Chichester: Wiley.

Lacey, C. (1970). *Hightown Grammar*. Manchester: The University Press.

Lambert, A. (1977). 'The Sisterhood', in Hammersley, M. and Woods, P. (eds), *The Process of Schooling*. London: Routledge & Kegan Paul.

— (1982). 'Expulsion in Context', in Frankenberg, R. (ed.), *Custom and Conflict in British Society*. Manchester: The University Press.

Lie, S. S., Malik, L. and Harris, D. (eds) (1994). *The Gender Gap in Higher Education*. London: Kogan Page.

Llewellyn, M. (1980). 'Studying girls at school', in Deem, R. (ed.), *Schooling for Women's Work*. London: Routledge.

Lloyd, B. (1989). 'Rules of the gender game'. *New Scientist*, 2 December, pp. 66–70.

Lloyd, B. and Duveen, G. (1992). *Gender Identities and Education*. London: Harvester Wheatsheaf.

Mac an Ghaill, M. (1988). *Young, Gifted and Black*. Milton Keynes: The Open University Press.

— (1991). 'Schooling, sexuality and male power' *Gender and Education*, 3, 3, pp. 291–310.

— (1994). *The Making of Men*. Buckingham: The Open University Press.

MacPherson, A. F. and Willms, D. (1987). 'Equalisation and Improvement', *Sociology*. 21.

Mahoney, P. (1985). *Schools for the Boys*. London: Hutchinson.

McIntosh, S. (1990). 'Human rights and "free and fair competition": the significance of European education legislation for girls in the UK', *Gender and Education*, 2, 1, pp. 63–79.

Marshall, G., Rose, D., Newby, H. and Vogler, C. (1988). *Social Class in Modern Britain*. London: Unwin Hyman.

Marsh, C. (1982). *The Survey Method: The Contribution of Surveys to Sociological Explanation*. London: Allen & Unwin.

Mason, K. (1990). 'Not waving but bidding: Reflections on research in a rural setting', in Burgess, R. G. (ed.), *Studies in Qualitative Methodology*. London: JAI Press.

Maynard, M. (1994). 'Methods, Practice and Epistemology', in Maynard, M. and Purvis, J. (eds), *Researching Women's Lives from a Feminist Perspective*. London: Taylor & Francis.

— and Purvis, J. (eds) (1994). *Researching Women's Lives from a Feminist Perspective*. London: Taylor & Francis.

Measor, L. (1989). 'Are you coming to see some dirty films today?', in Holly, L. (ed.), *Girls and Sexuality*. Milton Keynes: Open University Press.

— and Woods, P. (1984) *Changing Schools*. Milton Keynes: Open University Press.

Moffat, M. (1989). *Coming of Age in New Jersey*. New York: Rutgers University Press.

Morgan, D. L. (1991). *Focus Groups as Qualitative Research*. Newbury Park, CA: Sage.

Noddings, N. (1991). 'Stories Lives Tell', in Witherall, K. and Noddings, N. (eds), *Narrative and Dialogue in Education*. New York: Teachers College Press.

Oppenheim, A. N. (1992). *Questionnaire Design Interviewing and Attitude Measurement*. London: Pinter.

Paley, V. G. (1984). *Boys and Girls: Superheroes in the Doll Corner*. Chicago: The University Press.

Pilcher, J. *et al.*, (1989). 'Evaluating a women's careers convention', *Research Papers in Education*, 4, 1, pp. 57–76.

Peterson, W. (1964). 'Age, Teachers Role and the institutional setting', in Biddle, B. J. and Elena, W. (eds), *Contemporary Research on Teacher Effectiveness*. New York: Holt, Rinehart & Winston.

Plummer, K. (1983). *Documents of Life*. London: Allen & Unwin.

Rendel, M. (1992). 'European Law: ending discrimination against girls in education'. *Gender and Education*, 4, 1 and 2, pp. 163–74.

Sanders, S. (1992). 'Girls and Mathematical performance in Wales'. *The Welsh Journal of Education*, 3, 2, pp. 23–38.

Saran, R. (1982). 'The politics of bargaining relationships during Burnham negotiations', *Educational Management and Administration*, 10, 2, pp. 39–43.

Scott, John (1990). *A Matter of Record*. Cambridge: Polity Press.

Serbin, L. (1978). 'Teachers, peers and play preferences', in Sprung, B. (ed.) *Perspectives on Non-Sexist Early Childhood Education*. New York: Teachers College Press.

Shuy, R. (1986) 'Secretary Bennett's teaching', *Teaching and Teacher Education*, 2,4, pp. 315–24.

Sikes, P. J. (1991). 'Nature took its course?' *Gender and Education*, 3, 2, pp. 145–62.

Sikes, P., Measor, L. and Woods, P. (1985). *Teachers' Lives and Careers*. Milton Keynes: The Open University Press.

Skelton, A. (1993). 'On becoming a male physical education teacher: the informal culture of students and the construction of hegemonic masculinity', *Gender and Education*. 5, 3, pp. 289–304.

Smith, L. S. (1978). 'Sexist assumptions and female delinquency', in Smart, C. and Smart, B. (eds), *Women, Sexuality and Social Control*. London: Routledge.

Smithers, A. and Zientek, P. (1991). *Gender, Primary Schools and the National Curriculum*. Manchester: The University, School of Education.

Sparkes, A. C. (1994). 'Self, silence and invisibility as a beginning teacher'. *British Journal of Sociology of Education*, 15,1, pp. 93–118.

Solomon, J. (1991). 'School laboratory life', in Woolnough, B. E. (ed.), *Practical Science*. Milton Keynes: Open University Press.

Spender, Dale (1982). *Invisible Woman*. London: Writers and Readers Publishing Cooperative.

Spindler, G. (1974). 'Schooling in Schonhausen', in Spindler,G. (ed.) *Education and Cultural Process*. New York: Holt, Rinehart & Winston.

Spradley, J. (1979). *The Ethnographic Interview*. New York: Holt, Rinehart & Winston.

Stanworth, M. (1983). *Gender and Schooling*. London: Hutchinson.

Sutherland, M. (1985a). 'Whatever happened about co-education?' *British Journal of Educational Studies*, 33, 2, pp. 155–63.

Sutherland, M. (1985b). *Women who teach in Universities*. Stoke on Trent: Trentham Books.

— (1994). 'Two steps forward and one step back', in Lie, S. S., Malik, L. and Harris, D. (eds), *The Gender Gap in Higher Education*. London: Kogan Page.

Tann, S. (1981). 'Grouping and Group Work', in Simon, B. and Willcocks, J. (eds), *Research and Practice in the Primary Classroom*. London: Routledge.

Thomas, K. (1990). *Gender and Subject in Higher Education*. Milton Keynes: Open University Press.

Thompson, P. (1988). *The Voice of the Past* (2nd edn). London: Oxford University Press.

Valli, L. (1986). *Becoming Clerical Workers*. London: Routledge.

Walford, G. (ed.) (1993). *The Private Schooling of Girls: Past and Present*. London: The Woburn Press.

Whyte, J. B. (1985). *Girls into Science and Technology*. London: Routledge.

Willis, P. (1977). *Learning to Labour*. Farnborough: Gower.

Wolcott, H. F. (1967). *A Kwakiutl Village and School*. New York: Holt, Rinehart & Winston.

Wolcott, H. (1973). *The Man in the Principal's Office*. New York: Holt, Rinehart & Winston.

Wolpe, A. M. (1977). *Some Processes in Sexist Education*. London: WRRC.

— (1978). 'Girls and Economic Survival', *British Journal of Educational Studies*, 26, 2, pp. 150–62.

Woods, P. (1986). *Inside Schools*. London: Routledge.

— and Hammersley, M. (eds) (1993). *Gender and Ethnicity in Schools*. London: Routledge.

15

COMPARATIVE EDUCATION

Keith Watson

INTRODUCTION

Comparative education has a long history, and many people have written about its early developments (for example, Bereday, 1964; Gezi, 1971; Holmes, 1965; Jones, 1971; Kazamias and Massialas, 1965, *et al.*; and more recently Brock, 1986; Cowen, 1980; McDade, 1982) and even its 'prehistory' (Brickman (1960). It is a complex and fascinating story. However, as an academic discipline in its own right, or as a sub-discipline of education, the debates really only go back to the aftermath of the Second World War and the late 1950s/early 1960s, when in both the UK and the USA it struggled for recognition as a subject that should be taught at higher education. For the past 30 years it has been riven with debates and disagreements as to whether or not it is a discipline in its own right or whether it is merely a mechanism for using different social science research paradigms but within the context of 'comparison', whether or not there is one comparative method for educational research (for example, Holmes, 1965); or whether, indeed, it is a method, a content, a subject, or a framework for conducting research. As a result it is probably fair to say that it is an area of academic research which has suffered from an identity crisis and from a degree of confusion.

Yet, ironically, in spite of the above caveats, and in spite of its decline as an academic discipline taught in university departments of education or other teacher training institutions in the United Kingdom (Watson, 1982; Watson and Williams, 1984; Watson and King, 1991) and in the United States (Altbach *et al.*, 1982), largely as a result of institutional mergers and staff cutbacks, though also in the context of England and Wales because of criteria laid down by the Council for the Accreditation of Teacher Education (CATE) in the early 1980s and, more recently, as a result of changes in initial teacher training), comparative education is more popular, more important and more widely used than ever before. There are at least 28 national comparative education societies around the world, there are more individual academics and scholars, students and travellers who have an interest in education in different societies, and greater use is made of comparative statistical data by international organisations such as the Organisation for Economic Cooperation and Development (OECD), the United Nations Development Programme (UNDP), United Nations Educational, Scientific and Cultural Organisation (UNESCO) and the World Bank, for policy-making decisions than at any previous time. Indeed UNESCO ended its analysis of educational trends, in its most recent World Education Report, with these words:

> At a time such as the present, when profound changes are occurring in the whole structure of global, economic, social and cultural relations, and the role of education in these changes is coming to be recognised as fundamental, all countries can only benefit from knowing about more of the cultural premises of each other's education (UNESCO, 1993, p. 89).

This view has always been at the heart of comparative studies in education and always will be, despite academic wrangles and disagreements.

The purpose of this chapter, therefore, is to clarify what is meant by comparative education and to show how it is closely interwoven with international education and other related fields; to trace its development as a subject, highlighting the debates about research methodology and purpose; to explore the main social science paradigms that have shaped thinking in the field and the parameters of the research undertaken; to discuss some of the main difficulties arising out of undertaking comparative education research; and to comment on some of the trends and issues that have dominated the field in the 1980s and 1990s.

COMPARATIVE EDUCATION: SOME ISSUES AND DEFINITIONS

At the outset it is important to be clear about what is understood by the terms 'comparative education' or 'comparative studies in education', which are often used interchangeably, since anyone coming new to the subject has to face a confusion of terminology and difficulties over definition. As Kelly, Altbach and Arnove (1982) commented at the beginning of the 1980s:

> Comparative education remains a field characterised by methodological debates and diversity of opinion as to what constitutes its subject matter and orientation (p. 505).

Ten years later, they still described it as 'a field in search of a distinct identity' (Arnove, Altbach and Kelly, 1992, p. 3):

> a loosely bounded field held together, largely by a belief that education can serve and bring about improvements in society and that lessons can be learnt from developments in other societies (ibid., p. 1).

Kelly concludes her discussion about comparative education debates and trends with these sentiments:

> Comparative education remains an ill-defined field whose parameters are fuzzy. No simple theory or method guides scholars and the importance of culture and historical specificity continue to be debated...The field has no center, rather it is an amalgam of multidisciplinary studies, informed by a number of different theoretical frameworks (Kelly, 1992, in Arnove *et al.*, op. cit., p. 21).

Although for most of the century there have been attempts to develop comparative education conceptually and systematically so that is seen as an integral part of educational research it has not, according to Mitter (1992, p. 1788),

> yet gained the status of a fully recognised academic discipline; there are legitimate doubts whether this status will ever be achieved at all, given its subject matter and methodological component.

The only points that most people do agree on is that there is no clearly agreed definition, there are no clearly agreed rules about the parameters of comparative study and research, and there are no agreed purposes for undertaking comparative studies, though, usually, the reform or improvement of education systems, identifying educational trends and trying to understand and explain the differences and similarities between educational systems are recognised as among the main purposes.

A second difficulty is that certain issues and problems arising out of comparative studies in education have dogged it as a discipline from the outset. What is comparison? Is there such a thing as comparative method? Should scholars be concerned with one country only or with many countries? Should they be concerned with school systems, and their interaction with society, politics, the labour market and other aspects of socio-economic development, or should they be concerned only with sub-systems, for example, primary schooling, teacher training, higher education, technical and vocational education and training? In either case should researchers confine themselves to the *processes* of education (for example, what happens *within* schools, the teacher/learner interaction, school ethos, the curriculum, formal or informal, etc.) in different societies or only with the measurable *outcomes* of education and what happens to school or college graduates (for example, numbers graduating, examination results, routes to employment, etc)? Should the nation state be the focus of concern or should comparativists be more concerned with larger groupings such as regions – for example, the European Union, Sub-Saharan Africa, the Association of South East Asian Nations – or with identifying international trends in education? Should research focus on testable hypotheses or should hypotheses and general propositions be drawn from the study of education in different contexts? Should educational policy, systems, reform or problems be considered only over similar historical timescales or over different periods of time? (See, for example, Phillips, 1994.) As will be shown, it is in grappling with these and other issues that scholars have sought to shape and refine both the nature and the purposes of comparative education.

It is, therefore, important at the outset to examine a few definitions, but it needs to be recognised that it is sometimes difficult to separate these from arguments put forward in favour of comparative studies in education – a better understanding of other countries' and of one's own country's problems (Sadler, 1900; Bereday, 1964; Hans, 1964; Mallinson, 1975); curiosity and academic interest (Bereday, 1964); to help in solving problems in education (Holmes, 1965); to help in policy formulation and decision-making (King, 1968); to help reform or improve an education system (Kay and Watson, 1982; Thomas, 1990) and so on.

Michael Sadler, one of the English pioneers of comparative education, argued in one of his most famous addresses that:

> The practical value of studying in a right spirit and with scholarly accuracy, the working of foreign systems of education is that it will result in our being better fitted to study and to understand our own (Sadler, 1900).

Among the early pioneers of the subject explanation and analysis were key features of comparative studies. Kandel (1933), for example, said that:

> The chief value of a comparative approach to educational problems lies in an analysis of the causes which have produced them, in a comparison of the differences between the various systems and the reasons underlying them, and finally in a study of the solutions attempted.

Mallinson (1975) maintained that 'the highest goal of comparative education must be to describe, explain and compare educational systems in terms of their cultural totality', a theme to which he referred frequently. Bereday (1976) likewise argued that 'comparative education seeks to make sense out of the similarities and differences among educational systems' within particular cultural and social contexts. On the other hand, Hans (1959) picked up the theme of reform as a key aspect of comparative studies:

> Comparative education is not only to compare existing systems but to envisage reform best suited to new social and economic conditions. ...comparative education quite resolutely looks into the future with a firm intent of reform.

More recently, Farrell (1979, p. 1) has suggested that 'there can be no generalising scientific study of education which is not the comparative study of education'. Without the use and analysis of data related to important educational issues, firmly rooted in the inter-relationship of specific education systems with their own particular societies, there can be no realistic attempt to build up any theories about education and its role in society, let alone can one be able to understand or test these theories within different contexts. Furthermore, Farrell (1979, p. 5) argues that:

> Comparative education is one of several fields of enquiry which attempts to study a class of phenomena usually called education which seeks to explain the complex web of inter-relationships which can be observed within education systems and between education systems and other kinds of systems.

Le Thanh Khoi (1986) would go even further. He proposes that:

> Comparative education is more than a discipline: it is *a field of study* [my italics] that covers all the disciplines that serve to understand and explain education.... Comparison permits us to classify and develop typologies and, under given conditions, to make 'indirect experiments'.

Raivola (1985) would share this view, since he feels very strongly that because no general conclusion can be drawn from the analysis of any single situation, 'all research that seeks to offer general explanations must be comparative'.

Finally, perhaps one of the most all embracing definitions comes from a young African scholar who was seeking to justify the need to introduce a course in comparative education into the University of Botswana:

> Comparative education is a *study of education behaviour* and its *causal effects*. It is a study of the *factors* which lead to certain educational behaviours in an attempt to help in *the improvement of education systems*. *It attempts to make predictions* of what is most likely to happen under given circumstances as far as the education process is concerned. Comparative education *examines the educational outcomes* in the light of different *philosophies* and different *national characteristics* described in terms of social, economic and political systems as well as different times (Tsayang, 1992, p. 3, my italics).

It is quite apparent from these varied and diffuse definitions about comparative studies in education and about the purposes of comparisons, however, that certain themes recur. One can only really understand the purposes of education within the framework of a particular socio-economic, historical and cultural context. It is only possible to develop a 'theory of education' by examining the same, or similar, phenomena in different settings. It is not very sensible to undertake a programme of educational reform without first seeking information about whether similar reforms have been introduced elsewhere, and with what results. It might be possible to predict certain outcomes if a particular policy is pursued in the light of evidence gleaned from particular situations elsewhere.

Harold Noah (1984) once observed that there are both uses and abuses in studying and applying comparative education to particular problems and situations. He argued that unless, or until, some cross-cultural studies of education are undertaken it will never be possible to identify the potentials and limitations of international borrowing and adaptation:

> The authentic use of comparative study resides not in wholesale appropriation and propagation of foreign practices but in careful analysis of conditions under which certain foreign practices deliver desirable results, followed by consideration of ways to adopt those practices to conditions found at home (ibid., pp. 558–9).

Apart from the range of definitions and purposes of comparative education outlined above, any newcomer to the field also has to contend with a third difficulty that, in trying to define 'pure' or 'realistic' methodological approaches (for example, Cowen and Stokes, 1982; Holmes, 1965, 1981; Kelly, Altbach and Arnove, 1982; Noah and Eckstein, 1969; Schriewer and Holmes, 1988), the subject has been brought into disrepute and has faced ridicule from many quarters. In the UK public disagreements in the 1960s and 1970s between Holmes and King led to the loss of credibility in the subject's value among many academics, while in the USA two decades of debate over methodology finally so exasperated one of the World Bank's leading economic planners and education researchers that he wrote a scathing critique in the Comparative Education Review of 1990 (Psacharopoulos, 1990). In it he highlighted the futility of many of the theoretical arguments, analysed the value of many of the papers that had appeared over a number of years, both in Comparative Education Review and Comparative Education, and ended in the following manner:

> My conclusion is that the articles in the sample volumes of these journals are overly descriptive, in the sense that they provide long, non-quantitative accounts of the educational system of a single country. Seldom are the papers analytical, in the sense of statistically testing the hypothesized relationships.

As a result few comparative lessons can be drawn to assist decision makers in educational planning (ibid., p. 369).

According to Psacharopoulos, instead of being obsessed with theoretical perspectives, comparative education ought to have a practical application, a view shared by this author (Kay and Watson, 1982; Watson, 1991a). Comparative education has a value for policy-makers and planners, especially in such areas as educational finance and private education, only if lessons can be learnt from the practical experience of different solutions devised by different governments. To illustrate this argument Psacharopoulos puts forward a number of propositions or 'lessons', for example:

Comparative Lesson No.10 – (re fees) the public state budget is insufficient to provide for educational expansion, therefore, novel ways of financing are needed, including cost recovery...

Comparative Lesson No.11 – Private schools should be an integral part of a country's educational expansion effort...' (ibid., pp. 377–8).

COMPARATIVE OR INTERNATIONAL EDUCATION?

It is this concern for a practical application for comparative education (Brock, 1986; Heyneman, 1984) that has dogged the subject throughout the twentieth century, especially since the Second World War, and has led to subdivisions within the field. Kay and Watson (1982) show that in the UK by the 1950s there were two distinct fields of study being pursued, *comparative education*, largely concerned with the description and analysis of education systems and related fields in the industrial societies of the world, whether capitalist or socialist command economies, and *education in developing countries*, largely concerned, initially at least, with those countries that had gained their independence in the 1940s and 1950s. As more countries became independent from colonial rule and as the international agencies such as UNESCO became concerned with Less Developed Countries (LDCs), it is understandable that this area gained in importance.

Unfortunately, much of the early writing in comparative education was largely historical or culturally informative but it was 'of little use to or little used by policy-makers' (Farrell, 1979), and, as will be shown subsequently, it was riddled with disagreements about methodology. Such a problem did not affect the study of education in developing countries, at least in the early days, so much as that field's relationships with two subdisciplines in the 'comparative' field – development education and multicultural education. While the latter straddles the developed/developing country divide, given the ethnic, cultural and linguistic divisions of most countries of the world, the former straddles the comparative education/education in developing country divide. In the end the British approach was to embrace all those fields that had an 'international' flavour to them under the epithet 'Comparative and International', as, for example, when the British Comparative Education Society was redesignated the British Comparative *and* International Education Society (BCIES) in 1979.

However, it is quite clear that there are fundamental disagreements about the place of comparative education as opposed to international education from a North American perspective, as can be seen from recent papers by Epstein (1992, 1994) and Wilson (1994).

Epstein clearly sees a degree of confusion between the terms used and believes that this confusion has been sustained through the literature. Fernig (1959), for example, wrote that 'the major purpose of 'international' action in education is to aid the improvement of the school systems of one or more countries', which was always one of the major purposes of comparative education, while Arnove (1980) confuses the debate even further when he says that:

> World-systems analysis restores the 'international' dimension to the field of comparative and international education...by providing ...a framework that is essential to an understanding of educational developments and reforms...that are simultaneously sweeping many countries of the world.

Thomas (1990) goes even further in confusion by suggesting that the work of bilateral and multilateral aid agencies and many NGOs is applied 'international comparative education' (p. 1).

Epstein (1994, p. 918) believes that comparative education is 'a field of study that applies historical, philosophical and social science theories and methods to international problems in education'. It is 'primarily an academic and interdisciplinary pursuit'. On the other hand, he believes that 'international education fosters an international orientation in knowledge and attitudes' and brings together teachers and scholars from different backgrounds and nationalities on academic exchange or interchange. He goes on to say that 'comparativists...are primarily scholars interested in explaining *why* educational systems and processes vary and how education relates to wider social factors and forces...' whereas 'International educators *use* the *findings* derived from comparative education to understand better the educational processes they examine and thus to enhance their ability to make policy relating to programmes such as those associated with international exchange and understanding'. Paulston (1994, p. 925) offers yet another view. He argues that by the late 1960s international agencies and comparative educators turned to international education, 'a new branch of comparative education', which addressed the problems of educational planning, development and theory construction in macrostudies of educational and social change, 'especially in Newly Industrialising Countries' (NICs).

Perhaps the real problem is that Epstein traces the development of two parallel fields which he believes grew separately because they had different purposes, though they came together with the work of Michael Sadler at the turn of the century, whereas most writers in the field would not split hairs over these origins or over differences of function. Nevertheless he believes that international education can trace its roots back to César Auguste Basset (1808) through Victor Cousin and John Dewey. Basset called for a scholar 'free from national pedagogical principles', who would observe education outside France with the intention of making recommendations for reform. Comparative education, on the other hand, began when Marc-Antoine Jullien (1817) called for statistical data on different aspects of education in different societies in order 'to deduce true principles and determined routes so that education would be transformed into an almost positive science'. He had little impact until the founding of the International Bureau of Education (IBE) in Geneva in the early 1930s. Interesting though this debate may be – and it has attracted many pages of typescript in North America – it is probably fair to say that *comparative* education is *research* based whereas *international* education is *practical* and makes use of comparative data.

COMPARATIVE EDUCATION AS A SUB-DISCIPLINE OF EDUCATION

1900–45

Mention has already been made of the early history of the subject. Until the end of the Second World War much of the concern of comparative education was a preoccupation with conflict and ideological competition. Part of Kandel's work in the 1930s and 1940s was to highlight the superiority of democratic systems over totalitarian ones. His *Studies in Comparative Education* (1933) is still seen as a classic in the field in which he argued that a comparative approach should use common concepts or problems to *contrast* the forces that lead to differences between national education systems. The basic parameters of study, explanation and analysis were those of the nation state.

It was during this period also that saw the development of a number of institutions concerned with teaching about comparative education. Among these were Teachers College at Columbia University, New York, Syracuse and Michigan Universities, and the University of London Institute of Education. Other developments were associated with the creation of a number of yearbooks and journals, most notably the *Education Yearbook* (1924–44), the *World Yearbook of Education* (1932), the *International Yearbook of Education* (1933) and the *International Review of Education* (1931); the latter fell under Nazi control in 1940 but is still one of the leading journals in the field.

1945–60

The Second World War marked a watershed, not only in national governments' attitudes to education but also in the development of comparative education. There was a need to introduce educational reforms in the post-war period, a belief that we needed to understand how education is shaped by, or helps to shape, social and political structures. Governments were spending ever-increasing sums of money on educational provision. International organisations, such as UNESCO, the Organisation for Economic Cooperation and Development, the World Bank and the Council of Europe, were established and began to seek, interpret and disseminate data, including educational data, from a wide range of countries. Planning, including educational planning, began to grow in importance, especially with the growth of newly independent countries which wished to expand their formal education systems but which only had limited resources. The creation of the UNESCO/International Institute of Educational Planning (IIEP), in Paris in 1963, was designed to help them. Additional impetus was given by the founding of the Comparative Education Society (CES) (1956) in the USA, redesignated the Comparative and International Education Society (CIES) in 1969; and the Comparative Education Society in Europe in 1961, with national sections developing in a range of European countries, most of which have subsequently become national societies. In 1964 Japan founded its own Comparative Education Society. In 1968 an International Committee of Comparative Education Societies was convened in Vancouver, and in 1970 a World Council of Comparative Education Societies was established to bring together national representatives at an international congress to be held every four years. Three leading comparative/international education journals were launched – *Comparative Education Review*, the Comparative and International Education Society journal, in 1957; *Comparative Education* (1974); and *Compare* (1970), the journal of the British Comparative and International Education Society. In 1979 the *International Journal of Educational Development* was founded to fill a niche of relating comparative and international education to the specific needs and issues facing LDCs (Watson, 1990), while in 1990 a new journal, *Oxford Studies in Comparative Education*, was launched.

By the 1960s, therefore, comparative education had become established as an educational discipline in higher education in the USA and Canada, Europe and Japan. Since then it has grown as a field of study involving ever more people, institutions and organisations.

Currently there are 28 national societies and comparative and international education programmes are being taught in 71 locations in every continent (Altbach and Tan, 1995). Those who read the journals, attend the courses and conferences and use the information and data produced range from students, academics involved in education, international agencies, consultants, educational planners, politicians and business and industrial firms. Nevertheless, it is probably fair to say that it has been a field of study not so much in search of a role as one beset with methodological disagreements. It is to these that we now turn.

METHODOLOGICAL DEBATES

Early writers in the field like Kandel (1933), Hans (1964), Mallinson (1975, 4th edn), laid great stress on historical antecedents to explain and understand the existing pattern of education within countries and why these were similar or different. All of them, but especially Mallinson, laid great stress on 'national character' as a crucial aspect of educational development. Their accounts were largely descriptive, historical and cultural. Their main purpose was to compare and contrast educational systems with the intention of helping international understanding and bringing about education reform or improvements. *Comparison* was the unifying aspect of their method, irrespective of what was being compared. Thus Kandel was concerned with the 'forces', while Hans stressed the 'factors' that helped to shape education systems. They all believed that they could not hope to understand education systems and practices without a historical understanding of how they had arrived at their present development. They were largely concerned with *explanation* rather than with *prediction* or the use of education for social engineering purposes. As a result their work was 'of little use to or little used by policy-makers' (Farrell, 1979).

Critics of this approach came to the fore in the late 1950s/early 1960s. They were more concerned with the *methodology* of conducting research than with the description and analysis of education systems. The early critics – Anderson (1961), Bereday (1964), Kazamias and Massialas (1965) and Noah and Eckstein (1969) – all came from the USA. They argued that the historical approach was too 'unscientific' because it failed to draw causative linkages between schools and society, because it provided no basis for school improvement and because it had no clear methodological framework. Thus began attempts to develop a 'respectable' methodology which would place comparative education among the social sciences, and which would have a distinctive approach.

Bereday was the first to seek to develop a 'scientific method' in which he developed a highly complex methodology to compare school systems and other educational phenomena across societies and regions but within 'areas' (for example, South East Asia, Europe). His approach was very ambitious, not only because he broke new ground by looking at developing countries comparatively, but because one needed to be linguistically competent, historically and culturally aware and capable of analysing complex data. It is doubtful if any individual could successfully implement Bereday's methodology. Nevertheless he did believe that by using comparison with quantitative and qualitative methods it would be possible to develop a rigorous and scientific approach to explaining school/society relationships.

Noah and Eckstein, students of Bereday, likewise sought to develop a 'scientific method' of hypothesis formation, testing and validation through the use of quantitative data about education system and their outcomes. They tended to equate 'scientific' with statistics, and believed that by looking cross nationally at a number of countries they could identify 'laws' governing the relationship between schools and society. Unfortunately, while their approach might reveal trends it ignored contextual specifics. Nevertheless they became the forerunners of approaches adopted by UNESCO and the World Bank. Their approach also coincided with an ongoing debate in the social sciences in the USA especially, which stressed the need to be concerned with the *outcomes* of schools, social, economic and political, rather than with the internal workings of schools.

In the UK Holmes (1965) sought to develop 'a problem approach' to the study of education by using a scientific approach. The flaws of the 'problem approach' were highlighted subsequently (for example, Kay, 1981). Holmes was greatly influenced by Karl Popper's 'critical dualism' and believed that it could be possible to develop laws governing school and society relationships. He sought to identify solutions to clearly identified 'problems', and he believed that it was possible to predict outcomes by pursuing policy A as opposed to policy B, given the cultural, political and economic constraints in a particular country. On the basis of this he argued that it was possible to transfer solutions and educational practices from one country to another.

King (1968) also defined comparative education as practical and school based and as an essential tool for decision-making and policy formulation. However, while he wished to develop a scientific approach he disagreed with Holmes and Noah and Eckstein that comparative education could be developed as a science of prediction of the future. Moreover, while King shared some of the concerns about developing a scientific methodology, which he used to good effect in his study of post-secondary education in Western Europe (King, *et al.*, 1974, 1975), he was also concerned with the interaction and relationships between school and society. This led to a series of books on *Society Schools and Progress* in a wide variety of countries. The second editions were subsequently generically renamed *Education, Culture and Politics* in France, the USA, and so on highlighting the shift in emphasis to the political aspects of educational reform.

Other scholars with an interest in comparative and international education did not necessarily believe that developing a comparative methodology was either desirable or necessary, because comparative education is essentially a multi-disciplinary field concerned with both in-school and out-of-school phenomena, looking at complex inter-relationships and employing different perspectives and research methods depending upon the research questions being asked. C. Arnold Anderson (1961) was one of these. He wanted to see if it was possible to develop theories of school–society relationships that could be tested in different contexts and that might generate general rules that would be of use to policy-makers and planners, but he also believed that it was important to undertake in-depth studies in one country. Perhaps his real contribution to the debate was his belief that neither the nation state nor national school systems needed to be the focus of research. It was just as legitimate to explore social stratification or educational achievement in the light of political regimes or according to economic growth. In so doing it would be possible to isolate certain variables for closer analysis. According to Kelly, Altbach and Arnove (1982), Anderson's impact was profound since while few books or articles openly accepted this view, in practice most published research articles tacitly accepted it.

The result of these debates was that a field which hitherto had largely described education systems within specific national contexts now moved to becoming a 'discipline' that focused on educational *phenomena* – for example, numbers of students, teachers, finance and on specific educational outcomes, for example, the number of graduates or the growth of the economy. By seeking to isolate statistical data across societies and decontextualising education from within specific nation states it was hoped that 'scientific laws ' governing schools and society could be developed by using examples from a variety of situations. However, this new focus raised important issues. Should comparative education confine itself to in-school issues (for example, finance, administration, teaching and the curriculum) or to the school and society? If it did the latter how did it differ from sociology and political science? If it concentrated on schools how did it differ from the sociology of education, curriculum studies, history of education or educational administration? The only unifying aspect was comparison.

Moreover, should it be taught at undergraduate or post-graduate levels, or both? During the 1960s and 1970s it was generally taught at both but by the late 1970s its relevance for teaching purposes was being increasingly questioned. According to Kelly *et al.* (op. cit., p. 514) what held the field together were the study of schooling, the outcomes of schooling and their relationships to society. The nation state as the defining parameter had gone and, in terms of much of the American writing, so had schools and schooling. Most US writers regarded the school as a 'black box', that is, what happened in schools was largely irrelevant for comparative education purposes. Fortunately, in terms of LDCs, World Bank researchers in the 1980s became increasingly concerned with what happens in schools to see if they could identify the most important contributors to educational improvement and quality, especially important for focusing aid support.

One upshot of these debates and a search for an ideal methodology was a growing cynicism among academics and the demise of comparative education as an academic discipline in university departments of education and colleges of education. As the subject matter became divorced from the concerns of teacher trainers and education faculties its relevance to mainstream education was also seen by hard-nosed administrators and finance officers as esoteric and expendable. Thus, by the time Watson (1982a) undertook research into the state of comparative education in UK teacher training establishments in the early 1980s, the picture was somewhat depressing.

PREDOMINANT SOCIAL SCIENCE PARADIGMS

Being a social science it is inevitable that comparative education should be influenced by the prevailing debates in the social sciences. Whereas the nineteenth-century writers had been concerned with encyclopaedic description and macro comparisons for generalisation, by the 1950s/60s the dominant paradigm was one of *structural-functionalism* based on modernisation theory. The belief was that because education systems were part of the socio-economic and political structures of a nation investment in education would bring about economic development. This view was held initially because of post-war expectations and beliefs in the efficacy of education to prevent further conflict and to produce the necessary manpower needs of societies in the process of reconstruction. However, as LDCs gained political independence and as aid efforts concentrated on developing their educational infrastructure, much comparative education also focused on the developing countries. A number of writers argued that educational investment would bring about development and modernisation (for example, Adams and

Bjork, 1971; Beeby, 1966; Black, 1966; Hanson and Brembeck, 1966; Inkeles and Smith, 1971. See also Watson, 1988, for a detailed list of others).

However, this position began to be challenged by the late 1960s/early 1970s for a variety of reasons. First, many Western societies, not least the USA, were becoming increasingly plural, ethnically, linguistically and religiously. It was felt that the traditional interpretation of, and responses to, schooling were now outmoded. Second, the defeat of the USA at the hands of the Vietcong in 1973 shattered the illusions that the Western democratic systems were necessarily the best, or the only, way forward. Third, the growing gulf between HICs and LDCs, as shown through a wide range of indicators, revealed that structural-functionalist promises for educational investment were not being fulfilled. In spite of educational expansion, often helped by foreign aid, economic growth was very uneven and democracy and equality of opportunity had not taken root. If anything, there was political and social unrest and there was a growing feeling that by emphasising structural-functionalism, education systems favoured the political and economic status quo. Far from being a liberating force, therefore, schooling was perceived as an instrument for reproducing inequalities within societies as well as between them.

Another set of critiques also argued that by emphasising structural-functionalism and by concentrating on the social, political and economic outcomes of schooling rather than on the cognitive and educational outcomes comparative education had somehow failed in its primary task of writing about, and encouraging, *educational* reforms (Apple, 1978; Tibbs, 1973; Paulston, 1976).

By far the most damning and influential writers, however, came from schools which perceived the structural-functionalist modernisation role of education as perpetuating Western domination and leading to dependency, and that comparative studies had been distorted because they concentrated on certain European countries and a few English speaking countries in Africa and Asia while largely neglecting many others. This was perhaps inevitable in the light of the Cold War and foreign policy and aid considerations. As a result several strands of comparative analysis emerged from a Marxist or neo-Marxist perspective. Among the 'radical functionalists', as Paulston (1994) calls them, who perceived education as repressive, maintaining the social status quo, upholding the political élites and condemning the rest to failure and/or menial tasks, were Althusser (1990), Bowles and Gintis (1976) and Carnoy (1974). They maintained that reforms in school systems were meaningless without corresponding reforms in society and the political economy.

It was the growing disparities between the rich and the poor countries, however, that led a number of writers to seek explanations for this. From this came discussions about dependency and education as a form of neo-colonialism (Altbach, 1971, 1977; Altbach and Kelly, 1978; Apple, op. cit.; Arnove, 1980; Carnoy, op. cit.). These theories will be explored later in the chapter. Suffice it to say that by the 1980s a number of critiques of dependency theory as over-simplistic began to emerge, especially from the UK (for example, McLean, 1983; Noah and Eckstein, 1985; Watson, 1984a, 1984b).

Further subdivisions of these critiques came from those seeking a less economic and more human analysis of the situation on grounds of gender, class and ethnic discrimination. Kelly and Nihlan (1982) for example, criticised all previous comparative education texts for ignoring education's role in reproducing gender inequalities and how male domination suppresses females. Subsequently there have been a range of studies on gender issues across national boundaries, (for example, Brock and Cammish, 1993; King and Hill, 1993).

The growing pluralism of societies and recognition of the ethnic and linguistic rights of minorities have also spawned a whole genre of comparative education writing in areas hitherto perceived as multi-cultural education. As a number of studies have shown, however (Banks and Lynch, 1986; Brock and Tulaciewicz, 1985; Grant, 1979; Megarry et al., 1981; Watson, 1991b, 1992), international studies of multicultural education, which might embrace language issues, ethnic minorities, gender issues and religious minorities, cross over the comparative education/education in developing countries divide simply because the majority of the world's nations are multi-ethnic and multicultural.

Many of these latter studies have also fitted into another debate in comparative education during the 1970s and 1980s as to whether or not comparative education should be concerned with micro-analytical study (for example, the nation state and the school system within it) or with macro-analysis or world-systems analysis (Arnove, 1980; Ramirez et al., 1982). In many ways the growing convergence of educational systems, the commonality of problems and the similarity of trends in solving these problems, together with the role of international agencies in shaping the educational debate, have lent themselves to world systems, macro-studies (Ilon, 1994; Jones, 1992; McGinn, 1994; Samoff, 1993; Watson, 1995). With the growing importance of UNESCO's World Education Reports and the World Bank's *World Development Reports*[1] this is perhaps an area of future direction in comparative education – seeking to identify trends in education – though as Rust (1991) has shown, comparative education has not yet really come to terms with post-modernist and chaos theories which make future prediction even more difficult.

On the other hand, there are always voices that go against the tide.

Heyman (1979), for example, argued that comparative educators should cease to be obsessed with grand theories and generalisations at the macro level and should concentrate instead on microstudies to see if theories could be developed and replicated in other situations. There are also those, like Epstein (1983) who, in his presidential address to the Comparative and International Education Society, put forward the proposition that there is little to be gained from theoretical disputes because they are divisive. Instead it is far more important to gather data and to use it for practical purposes, a view shared by Psacharopoulos (1990, op. cit.). Some have even begun to question whether or not education policies and practices can be transferred across cultural divides, a view put forward by comparative writers in the early twentieth century! Based on her work in China, for example, Hayhoe (1989) contended vigorously that Western social science theories, techniques and educational policies could not be applied in a society and context so totally different, politically, historically and culturally.

FOCUS OF COMPARATIVE RESEARCH IN THE 1980s AND 1990s

By the 1980s, economists and planners were demanding that a practical use should be made of comparative data, a view echoed by the present author (Kay and Watson, op. cit.) but one shared by Sadler at the turn of the century in his famous address: 'How can we learn anything of practical value from the study of foreign systems of education?' (Sadler, 1900, reprinted, 1964). Thus the purpose and focus of much comparative education research has come round full circle, partly because organisations like the World Bank are far more concerned with the practical aspects of educational improvement than they are with theories (Lockheed and Verspoor, 1990; World Bank, 1988; 1994). By the mid-1980s, therefore, efforts were being concentrated on educational institutions, how far improvements in areas like school finance, teacher education, textbooks, curriculum, the training of heads, decentralised administration and planning could improve quality and the outcomes of schooling.

There were two reasons for this change of direction. First, was the belief that too much education theory had been influenced by human capital theory and modernisation theory, which might have applied to Western industrial democracies but did not seem to apply in the same way to most LDCs, where inequalities, inefficiency and dropout seemed endemic. On the other hand, that pessimistic view, highlighted by Coombs, failed to take into account the enormous progress achieved in most LDCs, especially the Newly Industrialising Countries (NICs). Only the poorest LDCs seem to be caught in a spiral of debt, inflation, increasing population and falling economic output.

The second reason for the change of emphasis was the growing concern among the aid agencies, especially the World Bank, with how to improve the efficiency and effectiveness of education systems. Following the World Bank Berg Report (1981), the Bank increased its research in the 1980s. The key arguments put forward were that on the basis of human capital theory state support for public education was dysfunctional for development. Psacharopoulos (1977) and Mingat and Tan (1986) maintained that public education favoured the rich and privileged in society over the poor who were those most in need of education. In Sub-Saharan Africa, Hinchcliffe (1988) showed this to be the case especially in higher education. As a result, the Bank began to emphasise the introduction of 'user fees' and the expansion of private education, the raising of non-government funding for education by shifting resources away from tertiary to primary education and of privatising large portions of higher education (Buchert and King, 1995; Colclough and Lewin, 1993; World Bank, 1988; 1994).

During the latter part of the 1980s and the 1990s there have been intense debates about the use of privatisation as a means of increasing the effectiveness and efficiency of school systems. Whereas the deschoolers of the 1970s, Holt, Illich and Reimer, had argued that schooling was a form of social and political oppression and began to advocate a voucher system, 'The World Bank sought to reduce the state's role in education by urging that not only should individuals finance their own education but that schools, opened for profit and run by private entrepreneurs, would be superior to the public schools simply because they were subject to the demands of the free market' (Kelly, 1992, p. 19). Most educators rejected these arguments on the grounds of equity and justice but Bank officials vigorously defended their position on the grounds that the poor would benefit because the introduction of 'user fees' would increase efficiency and quality, would hit those who stood to gain most and would raise additional revenue'. Given the influence and power of the Bank it is very hard to gainsay the pressures now being exerted on individual governments to change their ways (Jones, 1992; King, 1993; McGinn, op. cit.; Samoff, op. cit.; Watson, 1995).

Closely linked with finance and privatisation has been the whole area of planning and the belief that it is far better to devolve power to regional, local or even institutional levels, on the grounds that those closest to the grass roots can ascertain the most accurate data, can plan strategically accordingly and can raise revenue locally (Bray, 1984a, 1992; Chapman and Mahlck, 1993; Hallak, 1990; Lewin, 1987; Rondinelli et al., 1990). The debate about decentralisation and the failures of central planning are by no means confined to LDCs but are being implemented in the UK, Australia, and New Zealand and in many parts of Europe. The success or failure of these, or even the different models adopted, have interested comparative educators for several years (Bray, 1985, 1992, Lauglo and McClean, 1985; Lauglo 1995) but simplistic views expressed by the World Bank have been challenged by a number of critics (Lauglo, 1995; McGinn, 1996). This is an issue that is likely to persist throughout the 1990s.

Because of the growing crisis in education (Coombs, op. cit.) and because of the belated recognition that, given that demographic growth patterns will shape the future of the world's education in favour of LDCs – by the end of the century over 75 per cent of students enrolled will be in the LDCs – much comparative education research has concentrated on developing countries (Watson, 1988). During the past few years the Overseas Development Administration (ODA) has begun to publish a number of booklets commissioned especially to bring together the research findings in a range of areas and countries (for example, Brock and Cammish, 1991; Hough, 1994; Pennycuik, 1994; Rogers, 1992; Williams, 1993). They provide a useful overview of recent research, especially from a British perspective as opposed to a predominantly American or World Bank one. The impact of educational reform and innovation in LDCs (Lewin and Stuart, 1991) and the best methods of undertaking research in LDCs (Vulliamy, Lewin and Stephens, 1990) have also exercised a number of UK scholars.

Related issues that have been at the centre of much comparative education research during the past 15–20 years have focused on community education in all its manifestations – community schooling, community financing, schools as community centres for adult and non-formal education (Bray and Lillis, 1988; Dove, 1980; La Belle and Verhine, 1980; Watson, 1982b). Other studies have focused on the impact of aid on educational development and the changing role of aid agencies in shaping the educational agenda of many sovereign nation states, especially because of the impact of structural adjustment programmes on the ability of the poorest countries to plan, organise and administer their educational system (Buchert, 1994; Ilon, op. cit.; King, 1993; Lewin, 1992; 1994; Verspoor, 1993). Concern about the viability of universal primary education has also been a rich vein for research (Bray, 1981, 1986; Smith 1979) and even more so following the Jomtien Conference and the pledge of Education for All by 2000, given that 198 million children are not enrolled in schools (Colclough and Lewin op. cit.; WCEFA, 1991).

Of special interest to a number of British scholars have been the particular problems facing small states, either in terms of geography or population or because they are small island communities. Consequently there have been studies on particular problems facing small states (Bacchus and Brock, 1987), administration and planning in small states (Bray, 1991a, 1992) and curriculum development in small states, especially in the Pacific (Crossley, 1990). Curriculum studies have also attracted comparative analysis (Homes and McLean, 1989; Mangan, 1993, Marsh and Morris 1991) as have the implications of the European Community (Neave, 1992; Ryba, 1992). A new branch of comparative curriculum studies, also associated with teacher education, has been in the field of music education, which has appealed to writers from both sides of the Atlantic (Kemp, 1992). Ways in which US educational thinking has helped to shape educational reforms in the UK, a form of cross-cultural borrowing, have also attracted considerable interest (see, for example, Finegold *et al.*, 1992) as has teacher education (Heafford, 1996; Judge *et al.*, 1994; Pritchard, 1983, 1996), comparative adult education (Rogers, 1992) and reforms in examinations and assessment (Noah and Eckstein, 1993). Facets of educational planning, including the difficulties and changes facing planners, continue to exercise the minds of educational economists and planners from a comparative perspective (Hallak, 1990; Lewin, 1987; Verspoor, 1993) and the IIEP continues to produce excellent little booklets on many facets of educational improvement, quality, finance and planning. Finally, an entirely new genre of comparative education has emerged in the past decade, that of comparative higher education (Altbach, 1979, 1982, 1988; Mitter, 1992). The publication of an *International Encyclopedia of Higher Education* implies that this is an important field of study, which is here to stay (Clark and Neave, 1992).

One of the most striking contrasts between American, European and British comparativists is that the former have been far more concerned with theories, research paradigms and methodological debates, whereas most British researchers have been far more practically focused. CER frequently carries papers on research debates – and the Annual Presidential Address of the CIES is always an opportunity for this – while the UK scene has been far more pragmatic. There have been a few exceptions (for example, Cowen, 1990; Schriewer and Holmes, 1988). This may be because of critical mass, such that in the USA the size of the CIES and the number of departments across the country have encouraged intellectual debate, whereas most departments in the UK, if there are any as such, are relatively small and individual academics often feel quite isolated. To break down this sense of isolation and to stimulate intellectual debate were reasons for the formation of the UK Forum on International Education and Training and the development of a bi-annual Oxford Conference on International Education (Watson and King, op. cit.).

For the past 30 years, however, running parallel to, and to some extent influenced by, the comparative debates have been the International Evaluation of Achievement (IEA) studies. In spite of methodological difficulties the IEA studies are considered to be the most valuable and influential comparative work undertaken at international level by international academics. The first of the studies was launched in 1959 by the

UNESCO Institute for Education in Hamburg. Initially the idea was to measure mathematic achievements of 13- and 18-year-olds across a dozen countries. Gradually more than 20 countries joined the programme, and other subjects – science, reading, literature, a foreign language and civics – were added. The basic argument underlying the early IEA studies was that if educational achievements and outcomes across a variety of countries could be measured, it should be possible to identify common factors of importance in explaining the differences in academic achievement.

Despite the initial difficulties of comparability, isolating key variables, identifying as similar groups of schools and pupils as possible, and producing 'culture free' assessment tests, the IEA surveys have produced an enormous amount of data that help to explain the processes by which schooling is more or less effective and have led to significant breakthroughs in valid cross cultural measurement of student achievement. There are still problems of unreliable data, variations in curriculum content, different administrative and organisational structure and there need to be at least two classrooms per school involved for validity to be meaningful, but at least the IEA findings have alerted politicians and educational planners to the large and growing differences across nations in basic achievement tests. Some governments, not least the USA government, have used this information to reformulate policies; for example, in the late 1980s the USA was shown to be fourteenth out of 15 nations in mathematics scores at secondary level and 9th graders (15+) were thirteenth out of 17 in science achievement tests (IEA, 1988).

The IEA studies are not without their critics, however. Inkeles (1979), for example, argued that gathering such data leads to a kind of 'Olympic gamesmanship' between nations. Others (for example, Thiessen et al.,1983) have maintained that the expense and effort involved in developing cross-cultural comparisons ignores the national contexts, whereas if we had a better understanding of the latter this might better inform national education policies. Keeves and Adams (1994) believe that lack of theory has resulted in the collection of masses of data which are ineffectively examined and used because the right questions have not been asked or tested. We have acquired more data than ever before and we have analytical techniques, but the absence of theory limits the use to which the data can be put. Nevertheless, Thiessan and Adams (op. cit.) would argue that whatever the failings, the IEA studies have helped to develop methodological tools for cross-national comparisons and have revealed that there are key differences in academic achievement between countries, and within countries, though they have not yet adequately explained why. This brings us back to the need to understand the workings of the school system within the broader socio-economic, cultural and historical context in order to be able to formulate the correct research questions and to interpret and apply the research findings. It is to the research techniques used in comparative education together with the problems faced in undertaking comparative studies that we must now turn.

RESEARCH TECHNIQUES AND PARADIGMS USED IN COMPARATIVE STUDIES

Because comparative education is the product of many disciplines it cannot lay claim to any single conceptual or methodological tool that sets it apart from other areas of education or from the applied social sciences. It must be stressed, therefore, that there is *no* single scientific comparative research method in spite of the efforts of some scholars to argue that there is. The research methods used by those involved in comparative/international education are as varied as those in all educational research – for example, historical, descriptive, evaluative and ethnographic. The methods used will depend upon the area being studied, the information being sought and the questions being asked. The only important point is that the adjective *comparative* helps to narrow the focus, but even here there are problems. First, because many so called 'comparative' studies are essentially studies of education in *one* national context, that may be different from one's own, but nevertheless do not involve comparison. Second, because the term 'comparison' lacks precision. We are always comparing – books, cars, jobs, schools – but often the criteria used for such comparisons are subjective and intuitive and lack any scientific basis. On the other hand, in terms of social sciences some authors argue that comparison is a universal method and there can therefore be no understanding of education or other social science phenomena unless there is an element of comparison (Levy, 1970; Raivola, 1985; Swanson, 1971).

Educational research usually employs two different investigative strategies: (1) a *holistic* or *systematic* approach where parts or the sum of parts are seen in relation to each other, and (2) a *comparative* or *contrastive* approach where similarities and differences are sought and explained and or contrasted. Comparative methodology can use both approaches but to be truly comparative it must use (2). Research can also be essentially humanistic, that is, largely ethnographic and/or descriptive, or it can be scientific, relying on measurement and analysis of statistical data. It can be rather vague and general at one level or extremely detailed and precise at another. Indeed the whole area of comparative research is complex and controversial, not so much because of methodological problems but because of the nature of the task and the difficulties of focusing down in a potentially enormous field. One of the problems of Bereday's methodology was its vastness of scope and the complexity of data gathering and analysis. How do we decide what to compare? Where? Over what timescale? What are the issues to be studied? Are there hypotheses to be tested or is data being sought from which hypotheses can be deduced? Where there is depth of analysis it is usually at one country level; where the concern is for large-scale cross-national surveys, as for example the IEA surveys, considerable data will be generated but the depth of analysis and the interpretation of data may be superficial.

Keeves and Adams (1993, p. 949) identify four fallacies relating to comparative education research:

(1) There is no single scientific comparative method;

(2) It is impossible to distinguish between qualities and quantities – both are needed;

(3) The distinction between policy-orientated and discipline-orientated studies is artificial;

(4) Comparative education should not simply be concerned with either educational processes or outcomes: it should be concerned with both.

If these fallacies are clearly acknowledged researchers can then focus on one area of research and can select the most appropriate methodology for the research in hand.

Because those undertaking comparative research are generally influenced by their original academic training and discipline they will generally seek those models, theories, world views and strategies with which they feel most comfortable. Thus an historian, such as the present author, will seek to explain the causes and historical antecedents of a particular policy or situation and would argue that these were essential prerequisites for any comparative study. A political scientist, on the other hand, would use policy documents, together with officially published data, and, like the economist, would rely on cross-national data. Both might use questionnaires, survey techniques and interviews. On the other hand, a researcher with a sociological or social anthropological background would probably use participant observation and ethnographic research techniques.

TYPES OF COMPARATIVE EDUCATION RESEARCH

1. At the basic level is a *descriptive* account of the components of an education system within a national setting. Most International Bureau of Education country profiles would fit this type of approach, with some

attempt to explain how the situation has arisen but with little level of analysis. According to Thiessen and Adams (op. cit., pp. 280–3), based on a study of all the articles appearing in CER from 1957 to 1989, 86 per cent of the work undertaken in the 1950s and 1960s was descriptive. On the other hand, this had declined to 45 per cent during the 1980s.

2. *Analytical studies* would begin with description but would seek to explain and interpret how and why certain developments have come about. Studies in this mould would seek to understand how different variables relate to one another and why one system behaves in one particular way, as opposed to another, and why certain developments have taken a particular route in different countries (for example, comprehensive secondary schooling). Most of the early comparative writers, Kandel, Hans and Mallinson, would have largely fitted this type of analysis with their stress on forces, factors and national character. However, their analysis had limitations because it never sought to develop universals that apply across boundaries. Subsequently, for example, their approach could never explain why Universal Primary Education or Marxist polytechnic education developed across such a diverse range of countries. To some extent Archer (1979) did seek to identify common aspects of educational development by focusing on the social and philosophical origins of a country.

3. *Evaluative* research seeks to show how far education functions in terms of a particular set of goals, and to test particular hypotheses or principles in one or more context. In other words it seeks to explore the strengths and weaknesses of education systems by looking at outcomes. This has been the basis of the IEA and other evaluation studies.

4. *Exploratory research* is designed to generate hypotheses or research questions rather than to test propositions or to find answers. It tries to identify areas or associations not yet fully recognised or understood among educationists.

5. *Predictive* research is closely associated with planning and moves on from description, analysis and evaluation to suggest that future outcomes are likely to emerge from the pursuance of certain policies based on past experience from across a range of national examples. This view was taken by Holmes (1981) and certainly by Thomas (1992b) and Hallak (1990).

Superimposed upon these research approaches have been a number of social science 'theories', some of which have already been alluded to in a previous section. Historical analysis, for example, has been mentioned. Supporters of an historical approach would argue that the present can only be understood in the light of the past but critics would suggest that historical studies fail to produce any significant principles which can be applied across cultures. In other words historical analyses are too particularistic. Advocates of a historical approach would refute this, arguing that hypotheses can be developed and then tested in other societies for their general applicability.

Structural functionalist theory has sought to show that the task of education in whatever society is designed to perpetuate the social, political and economic structures of that society. The crucial aspect of the theory for comparative studies has been that the latter have sought to clarify the way education functions in different societies to support the structures. The theory spawned various models in support of investment in education – for human capital (Bowman and Anderson, 1973; Harbison and Myers, 1964; Schultz, 1961); for modernisation (Inkeles and Holsinger, 1974; Inkeles and Smith, 1974); for production and economic improvement (Heyneman and Loxley, 1983).

Marxist and neo-Marxist critiques in the late 1960s and 1970s spawned a range of theories to explain education's role in society that strongly influenced comparative analyses. Among these are the correspondence theory, conflict theory, dependency theory, liberation theory and world systems theory.

Correspondence theory is an extension of structural-functionalist theory but from a radical perspective insofar as it argues that education and work/employment opportunities are interrelated and that the curriculum content and school structures are designed to maintain the social structures in a society. The work of Bowles and Gintis (op. cit.) fits this mould. Closely associated with correspondence theory, and in the eye of some writers a subsection of it, is *legitimation theory* – for example, that educational policies, school structures and the curriculum are used by those in power and authority to reinforce the existing political and power structures. The works of Carnoy (1974) and Price (1977) would strongly take this line.

Conflict theory is in stark contrast to the above insofar as it concentrates on the *divisions within society* rather than on the supportive elements that help society to function. In other words, the argument is that conflict is inevitable between those with power and those without it and that the need is to analyse the causes of conflict, the dissident groups in society (for example, students, minorities, women), their motives and possible solutions to conflict. A classic study in this genre is Horowitz, *Ethnic Groups: A Study in Conflict* (1985).

Liberation theory, as enunciated by Freire, is based on his studies of Latin

America in which he stressed that the oppressed and powerless in LDCs should use education, in its broadest sense, to become aware of their situation so that they can do something about it.

Latin America also spawned *dependency theory* in the early 1950s which sought to explain the continuing gap between HICs and LDCs. It was adopted by comparativists in the 1970s. The world is seen as interdependent but because of the economic power of the rich industrialised countries at the centre of the world's economic relationships and the majority of poor countries at the periphery, this has led to the growth of dependency both in terms of economics but also in education. Altbach (1977) even argues that the world knowledge system that links scholars, academics and professionals across the world is part of this pattern and favours the rich countries. Others have taken a similar view (for example, Bray, 1984; Mazrui, 1978).

A *world systems approach* develops this theory though it does not have to be based on a Marxist critique. The argument is that global social, economic, and political relationships should be considered in any attempt to account for the overall condition prevailing in any modern society, including its education system and institutions, since many developments can only be understood in the light of these relationships (Arnove, 1980; Ramirez and Boli-Bennett, 1982, Watson, 1995).

At the other extreme are *interpretist* and *problem centred theories*. In the former, the point of interest is not some grand macro-analysis but an attempt to understand what education means to those who are participants in the education process – students, teachers, administrators etc. In the latter the point of focus is the *identification* of specific problems, either in education or in society that education might be able to solve, by looking at similar problems or situations cross-culturally.

Finally, the *human capital theory* must be regarded as central to much educational analysis, especially in the developing countries over the past 40 years. This seeks to show how education, or lack of it, enhances or hinders an individual's economic productivity. The theory was at the heart of the debate for investment in education in the 1960s and has returned as central to World Bank thinking in the 1980s and 1990s. According to Woodhall (1985), 'the basic assumption of the notion that education is a form of investment in human capital is that education raises the productivity of workers and that the higher earnings of the educated reflect the value of their product.'

Whatever theory informs the comparative education researcher, however, or whatever type of research is undertaken, it needs to be reiterated that there is no such thing as a comparative research method. Like all social science or education researchers the comparativist will use historical research methods – analysis of data, archives, records, legal documents and interviews; or survey research techniques, which might include questionnaires, opinionaires, interviews, and attitude scales; experimental research using pre-test and post-test situations in different contexts; or *observation* techniques as participant observer or simply as an observer. The strengths and weaknesses of each research method apply just as much to the comparative researcher as to any social science researcher, except that they can be compounded by a number of fundamental problems arising from the nature of comparative research. It is worth highlighting these.

THE PROBLEMS OF UNDERTAKING COMPARATIVE RESEARCH

Apart from the already stated problem of a lack of any theory a number of undoubted difficulties face any researcher in comparative education. The first is that of getting official permission. This may be easier said than done, especially if the researcher wishes to probe an area perceived to be highly sensitive in certain countries. A second difficulty is that of *ethnocentric* bias. This arises where a researcher fails to appreciate that education systems are context-specific or that the underlying philosophy and assumptions prevailing in one context may be very different from those elsewhere, especially the researcher's home context. As Raivola (1985, pp. 268–9) puts it, 'The essence of cultural bias is this: the way individuals represent the world to themselves and their concept of knowledge and truth are such an organic part of their culture-bound thinking that they cannot recognise a different world or a different truth'.

The danger is that the information sought, or the observations made, will be conditioned by a particular set of presuppositions or assumptions which subconsciously assume a degree of cultural superiority. The result is that the data acquired may be wrongly interpreted.

Another problem arises if *general conclusions* are drawn from specific examples or particular situations. Parkyn's (1976) warning of this difficulty is all too frequently forgotten. It is important to examine a number of particular situations in as wide a range of countries as possible before any general conclusions can be drawn. There is also a problem of *terminology*. Are we comparing like with like? The same word may be used in different contexts but it may have quite different meanings. This is particularly true in the area of technical and vocational education as Cantor (1989) rightly reminds us.

The largest difficulty facing the comparativist, however, must be that of the *reliability* of *official databases* and *international statistics*. Increasingly most international databases are provided by individual governments to the international agencies such as the IBE (Geneva), UNESCO and the OECD

(Paris) or the World Bank (Washington), or they are gathered by the agencies themselves. The problems of how these statistics are collected and aggregated has become the focus of several recent studies (for example, Porres-Zuniga, 1994; Puryear, 1995). However, that apart, the data still have limitations. Not only do they ignore the human and cultural dimensions of societies, which for many scholars are the heart of comparative education, not only do they fail to reveal the political or educational philosophy which undergirds the system, but, because the figures are averaged out, or aggregated, they overlook regional variations, urban/rural dichotomies, ethnic and gender disparities. Attempts have been made in recent years to isolate these variables, but as Chapman and Boothroyd (1988) have shown in the context of many LDCs, not only are the statistical data only as good as the information fed into the system, but if that information is unreliable, attempts at planning, forecasting and comparing are severely hampered. Given these caveats, however, as Grant (1986, p. 49) has pointed out:

> Effective use of international data require a basic understanding of comparative education, the study of educational systems as functioning wholes in their contexts and the drawing of generalisable principles from it.

CONCLUSIONS AND FUTURE DIRECTIONS

In spite of the ambiguity over definitions, in spite of the lack of theory, in spite of a large number of subsets of comparative education and in spite of the weaknesses of research methodology and areas of research, there is little doubt that comparative education research has led to a substantial increase in our understanding of, and awareness of, educational systems and processes in different parts of the world; of the infinite variety of aims, purposes, philosophies and structures; and of the growing similarities of the issues facing educational policy-makers across the world. We now have a wealth of statistical and other data, information and knowledge from around the world, though it is not always easily understood or analysed. Perhaps more significant than anything else, however, is the realisation that education and development, education and social change and the impact of educational reform on society are far more complex than was originally thought. Moreover, it is becoming recognised that major difficulties arise from the transfer of educational ideas from one culture to another, let alone from the transfer of structures and curriculum content.

Whereas Kelly (op. cit.) sees the present state of comparative education as one of confusion and ferment, which she regards as a strength, Thiessen and Adams (op. cit., p. 298) believe that the current state of the field can be summed up in two words – balance and integration. Balance requires the interplay of different disciplines and methodologies. Integration means pooling different research and experience from different parts of the world to help solve problems. Some years ago Kay and Watson (op. cit., p. 138) wrote:

> While we should not wish to make inflated claims for comparative education...its contribution to research in education as a whole is still under utilized and it is in an almost unique position to throw light on some of the common and pressing problems which confront world education today.

That was in 1982. It is as true now as it was then.

Potential areas for ongoing or new research must be in educational administration – the strengths and weaknesses of centralised and decentralised provision and autonomous institutional management; in educational reform, not only of structures but of experiments in planning and management, in parental choice, in higher education, in the raising of educational quality; in the role of women and minorities, and their particular needs; in assessments and examination reform; in school finance; and in the role of international agencies. The list is almost endless. What is certain is that by a right study of different education systems across the world, something of value can be learnt that can assist policy-makers and planners as we move towards the twenty-first century.

NOTE

1. For many years the World Bank's Annual *World Development Reports* were the major source of indicators of development. More recently the UNDP has produced its *Human Development Reports* and the OECD has produced Annual Country Statistics on member states. UNESCO's *Educational Statistics* Yearbooks and its *World Education Report* have focused on educational indicators.

REFERENCES

Adams, D. and Bjork, R. M. (1971). *Education in Developing Areas*. New York: McKay.
Altbach, P. G. (1971). 'Education and neo-colonialism', *Teachers College Record*, 72, pp. 543–58.
— (1977). 'Servitude of the mind? Education, dependency and neocolonialism', *Teachers College Record*, 792, pp. 187–204.
— (1979). *Comparative Higher Education: Research Trends and Bibliography*. London: Mansell.
— (1982). *Higher Education in the Third World: Themes and Variations*, Singapore: Maruzen Asia.
— (1988). 'Comparative Studies in Higher Education', in Postlethwaite, T. N. (ed.), *The Encyclopedia of Comparative Education and National Systems of Education*. Oxford: Pergamon, pp. 66–8.

Altbach, P. G., Arnove, R. F. and Kelly, G. P. (eds) (1982). *Comparative Education*. New York: Macmillan.

Altbach, P. G., and Kelly, G. P. (1978). *Education and the Colonial Experience*. New York: Transaction Books.

Altbach, P. G., and Tan, Eng Thye Jason (1995). *Programs and Centers in Comparative and International Education: a Global Inventory*. Buffalo: State University of New York Press.

Althusser, L. (1990). 'Theory, theoretical practice and theoretical formation', in Althusser, L. (ed.), *Philosophy and the Spontaneous Philosophy of the Scientists and Other Essays*. London: Verso.

Anderson, C. A .(1961). 'Methodology of Comparative Education', *International Review of Education*, 7, 1, pp. 1–23.

Apple, M. W. (1978). 'Ideology, Reproduction and Educational Reform', *Comparative Education Review*, 22 (Oct.), pp. 367–87.

Archer, M. (1979). *Social Origins of Education Systems*. London: Sage.

Arnove, R. F. (1980). 'Comparative Education and World Systems Analysis', *Comparative Education Review*, 24 (Feb.), pp. 48–62.

—, Altbach, P. G. and Kelly, G. P. (eds) (1992). *Emergent Issues in Education: Comparative Perspectives*. Buffalo: State University of New York Press.

Bacchus, K. and Brock, C. (eds) (1987). *The Challenge of Scale*. London: Commonwealth Secretariat.

Banks, J. and Lynch, J. (eds) (1986). *Multicultural Education in Western Societies*. London: Holt, Rinehart & Winston.

Beeby, C. E. (1966). *The Quality of Education in Developing Countries*. Cambridge, MA: Harvard University Press.

Bereday, G. Z . F. (1964). *Comparative Method in Education*. New York: Rinehart & Winston.

Black, C. (1966). *The Dynamics of Modernization*. New York: Harper & Row.

Bowles, S. and Gintis, H. (1976). *Schooling in Capitalist Society: Educational Reform and the Contradictions of Economic Life*. London: Routledge & Kegan Paul.

Bowman, M. J. and Anderson, C. A. (1973). 'Concerning the role of education in development', in Goertz, C.(ed.), *Old Societies and New States*. New York: Free Press.

Bray, M. (1981). *Universal Primary Education in Nigeria: A Study of Kano State*. London: Routledge & Kegan Paul.

— (1984a). *Educational Planning in a Decentralized System: The Papua New Guinean Experience*. Sydney: Sydney University Press.

— (1984b).'International Influences on African Educational Development', *International Journal of Educational Development*, 4, 2, pp. 129–36.

— (1985). 'Education and Decentralization in Less Developed Countries: A comment on Trends, Issues and Problems, with particular reference to Papua New Guinea', *Comparative Education*, 21, 3, pp. 183–96.

— (1986). 'If UPE is the answer, what is the Question? A Comment on the weaknesses in the rationale for universal primary education in less developed countries', *International Journal of Educational Development*, 6, 3, pp. 147–58.

— (1991a) (ed.). *Ministries of Education in Small States: Case Studies of Organisation and Management*. London: Commonwealth Secretariat.

— (1991b). 'Centralization v Decentralization in Educational Administration: Regional Issues', *Educational Policy*, 5, 4, pp. 371–85.

— (1992). *Educational Planning in Small Countries*. Paris: UNESCO.

Implications in Less Developed Countries. Oxford: Pergamon Press.

Brickman, W. W. (1960). 'An historical introduction to comparative education', *Comparative Education Review*, 3, 3, pp. 1–24.

— (1966). 'Prehistory of Comparative Education to the end of the eighteenth century', *Comparative Education Review*, 10, 1, pp. 30–47.

Brock, C. (1986). 'Comparative Education: What do we think of it so far?' in Corner, T. (ed.), *Learning Opportunities for Adults*. Glasgow: University Department of Education.

— and Cammish, N. (1991). 'Factors Affecting Female Participation in Education in Six Developing Countries', ODA Research Project 4532, Serial 9. London: Overseas Development Administration.

— and Tulaciewicz, W. (eds) (1985). *Cultural Identity and Educational Policy*. London: Croom Helm.

Buchert, L. (1994). 'Education and development: a study of donor agency policies on education in Sweden, Holland and Denmark', *International Journal of Educational Development*, 14, 2, pp. 143–57.

— and King, K. (eds) (1995). *Learning from Experience: Policy and Practice in and to Higher Education*. The Hague: Centre for the Study of Education in Developing Countries (CESO Paperback No.24).

Carnoy, M. (1974). *Education as Cultural Imperialism*. New York: McKay & Sons.

Cantor, L .(1989). *Vocational Education and Training in the Developed World*. London: Routledge.

Chapman, D. and Boothroyd, R. A. (1988). 'Threats to data quality in developing country settings', *Comparative Education Review*, 33, 1, pp. 2–39.

Chapman, D. W. and Mahlck, L. O. (eds) (1993). *From Data to Action: Information Systems in Educational Planning*. Oxford: Pergamon Press/UNESCO IIEP.

Clark, B. R. and Neave, G.(eds) (1992). *The Encyclopedia of Higher Education*, 4 vols. Oxford: Pergamon.

Cowen, R. (1980). 'Comparative Education in Europe: A Note', *Comparative Education Review*, 24, 1, pp. 98–108.

— (1990). 'The national and international impact of comparative education infrastructure' in Halls, W. D. (ed.), *Comparative Education: Contemporary Issues and Trends*. Paris: UNESCO.

— and Stokes P. (1982). *Methodological Issues in Comparative Education*. London: London Association of Comparative Educationists.

Colclough, C. and Lewin, K. (1993). *Educating All the Children: Strategies for Primary Schooling in the South*. Oxford: Clarendon Press.

Coombs P. (1985). *The World Crisis in Education: A View from the Eighties*. Oxford: Oxford University Press.

Corner, T. (ed.) (1981). *Education in Multicultural Socieites*. London: Croom Helm.

Crossley, M. (1990). 'Curriculum, Policy and Practice in Papua New Guinea', *Compare*, 20, 2, pp. 141–54.

Dove, L. (1980). 'The teacher and the rural community in developing countries', *Compare*, 10, 1, pp. 7–29.

Epstein, E. H. (1983). 'Currents left and right: Ideology in comparative education', *Comparative Education Review*, 27, 1, pp. 3–29.

— (1992). Editorial, *Comparative Education Review*, 36, 4.

— (1994). 'Comparative and International Education: Overview and Historical Development', in Husen, T. and Postlethwaite T. N. (eds), *The International Encyclopedia of Education* (2nd edn.),Vol. 2, pp. 918–23. Oxford: Pergamon Press.

Encyclopedia of Education (2nd edn.),Vol. 2, pp. 918–23. Oxford: Pergamon Press.

Farrell, T. P. (1979).'The necessity of comparisons in the study of education: the salience of science and the problems of comparability', *Comparative Education Review*, 23, 1, pp. 3–16.

Fernig, L. (1959). 'The global approach to comparative education', *International Review of Education*, 5, 3, pp. 341–7.

Finegold, D, McFarland, L, and Richardson, W. (eds) (1992). *Something Borrowed, Something Blue? A Study of the Thatcher Government's Appropriation of American Education and Training Policy*. Wallingford: Triangle Books.

Gezi, K. E. (ed.) (1971). *Education in Comparative and International Perspectives*. New York: Holt, Rinehart & Winston.

Grant, N. (1979). 'Educational Policy and Cultural Pluralism: A task for comparative education', *Comparative Education*, 13, 2, pp. 139–50.

— (1986). 'Future roles for comparative education', in Corner, T. (ed.), *Learning Opportunities for Adults*. Glasgow: University of Glasgow Department of Education.

Hallak, J. (1990). *Investing in the Future: Setting Educational Priorities in the Developing World*. Paris: UNESCO/IIEP.

Halls,, W. D. (ed.) (1989). *Comparative Education: Contemporary Issues and Trends*. London: Jessica Kingsley.

Hans, N. (1959)..'The historical approach to comparative education', *International Review of Education*, 5, 3, pp. 299–309.

Hans, M. (1964) (3rd edn) *Comparative Education*. London: Routledge & Kegan Paul.

Hanson, J. W. and Brembeck, C. S. (1966). *Education and the Development of Nations*. New York: Holt, Rinehart & Winston.

Harbison, F. and Myers, C. A .(1964). *Education, Manpower and Economic Growth*. New York: McGraw Hill.

Hayhoe, R. (1989). 'A Chinese Puzzle', *Comparative Education Review*, 33, 2, pp. 153–75.

Heafford, M. 1(996). 'Teacher Training – Some Lessons from France', in Watson, K., Modgil, S. and Modgil, C. (eds), *Educational Dilemmas Debates and Diversity*. London: Cassell, forthcoming.

Heyman, R. (1979). 'Comparative education from an ethno-methodological perspective', *Comparative Education*, 15, 3, pp. 241–9.

Heyneman, S. P. (1984). 'Research on education in the developing countries', *International Journal of Educational Development*, 4, 3, pp. 293–304.

— and Loxley, W. (1983). 'The effect of primary school quality on academic achievement across 29 high and low income countries', *American Journal of Sociology*, 88, 6, pp. 1162–94.

Hinchcliffe, K. (1988). *Education in Sub Saharan Africa*. Washington: World Bank.

Holmes, B. (1965). *Problems in Education*. London: Routledge & Kegan Paul.

— (1981). *Comparative Education: Some Consideration of Method*. London: George Allen & Unwin.

— and Mclean, M. (1989). *The Curriculum: A Comparative Perspective*. London: Allen & Hyman.

Horowitz, D. (1985). *Ethnic Groups: A Study in Conflict*. Berkeley: University of California Press.

Hough, J. R. (1994). *Educational Cost Benefit Analysis*. London: Overseas Development Administration.

IEA (International Association for the Evaluation of Educational Achievement) (1988). *Science Achievements in 17 Countries*. Oxford: Pergamon.

Ilon, L. (1994). 'Structural Adjustment and Education: Adopting to a growing global market', *International Journal of Educational Development*, 14, 2, pp. 95–108.

Inkeles, A. (1973). 'National differences in scholastic performance', *Comparative Education Review*, 23, 3, pp. 386–407.

— and Holsinger, D. B. (1974). *Education and Individual Modernity in Developing Countries.* Leiden: Brill.

Inkeles, A. and Smith, D. H. (1974). *Becoming Modern.* Cambridge, MA: Harvard University Press.

Jones, P. E.(1971). *Comparative Education: Purpose and Method.* Australia: University of Queensland Press.

Jones, P. W. (1992). *World Bank Financing of Education: Learning, Teaching and Development.* London: Routledge.

Judge, H., Lemosse, M., Paine, L. and Sedlak, M. (1994). *The University and the Teachers: France, the United States, England.* Oxford: Studies in Comparative Education, 4, 1/2.

Kandel, I. L. (1933). *Studies in Comparative Education.* London: Harrap & Co.

Kay, W. K. (1981). 'Problems with the problem approach', *Canadian and International Education*, 10, 1.

— and Watson, J. K. P. (1982). 'Comparative Education: the need for dangerous ambition', *Educational Research*, 24, 2, pp. 129–39.

Kazamias, A. M. and Massialas, B. G. (1965). *Tradition and Change in Education.* Englewood-Cliffs, NJ: Prentice–Hall.

Keeves, J. P. and Adams, D. (1994) 'Comparative Methodology in Education', in Husen, T. and Postlethwaite, T. N. (eds), *The International Encyclopedia of Education*, 2nd edn., Vol. 2. Oxford: Pergamon, pp. 948–58.

Kelly, G .P. (1992). 'Debates and Trends in Comparative Education', in Arnove, R .F., Altbach, P. G. and Kelly, G. P. (eds), *Emergent Issues in Education: Comparative Perspectives.* Buffalo: State University of New York Press, pp. 13–22.

—, Altbach, P. G. and Arnove, R. F. (1992). 'Trends in Comparative Education: A Critical Analysis', in Altbach *et al.,* op. cit., *Comparative Education*, pp. 505–33.

— and Nihlen, A. S. (1982). 'Schooling and the reproduction of patriarchy', in Apple, M. (ed.), *Cultural and Economic Reproduction in Education.* London: Routledge & Kegan Paul.

Kemp, A. E. (ed.) (1992). *Some Approaches to Research in Music Education*, ISME Research Commission. Reading: University of Reading.

King, E. J. (1968). *Comparative Studies in Educational Decision Making.* London: Methuen.

— (1979) (5th edn). *Other Schools and Ours.* London: Holt, Rinehart & Winston.

—, Moor, C. H. and Mundy, J. A. (1974). *Post Compulsory Education: A new Analysis in Western Europe*, Vol. 1. London: Sage.

—, Moor, C. H. and Mundy, J.A. (1975). *Post Compulsory Education: The Way Ahead.* London: Sage.

King, E. M. and Hill, M.A. (1993). *Women's Education in Developing Countries.* Baltimore: Johns Hopkins University Press for the World Bank.

King, K. (1975). *Education and Community in Africa.* Edinburgh: University of Edinburgh.

— (1993). *Aid and Education in the Developing World: The Role of the Donor Agencies in Educational Analysis.* London: Longman.

Labelle, T. J. and Verhine, R. E. (1980). *Community Schools: A Comparative and International Perspective.* New York: McGraw Hill.

Lauglo, J. (1995). 'Forms of Decentralization and their Implications for Education', *Comparative Education*, Vol. 31, 1, pp. 5–29.
— and Mclean, M. (ed.) (1986). *The Control of Education*. London: Heinemann.
Le Thanh Khoi (1986). 'Towards a general theory of education', *Comparative Education Review*, 30, 1, pp. 12–39.
Levy, M. J. (1970). 'Scientific analysis is a subset of comparative analysis', in McKinney, J. C. and Tiryakkin, E. A. (eds), *Theoretical Sociology*. New York: Appleton-Century-Crofts.
Lewin, K. M. (1987). *Education in Austerity: Options for Planners*. Paris: UNESCO/IIEP.
Lewin, K. M. (1992). *Dialogue for Development: A Policy Review of British Education Aid towards 2000*. Research Report on Policy for the Overseas Development Administration, London.
— (1994). 'British bilateral assistance to education: how much, to whom and why?' *International Journal of Educational Development*, 14, 2, pp. 159–176.
— and Stuart, J. (1991), *Educational Innovation in Developing Countries: Case Studies of Changemakers*. London: Macmillan.
Lockheed, M. and Verspoor, A. (1990). *Improving the Quality of Primary Education in Developing Countries*. Washington, DC: World Bank.
Mallinson, V. (1974). (4th edn) *An Introduction to the Study of Comparative Education*. London: Heinemann.
McDade, D. F. (1982). 'The things that interest mankind: a commentary on thirty years of comparative education', *British Journal of Educational Studies*, 30, pp. 72–84.
McGinn, N. (1994). 'The Impact of Supranational Organisations on Public Education', *International Journal of Educational Development*, 14, 3, pp. 289–98.
— (1996). 'The failures of educational decentralization', in Watson, K., Modgil, S. and Modgil, C. (eds), *Educational Dilemmas: Debate and Diversity*. London: Cassell, forthcoming.
Mclean, M. (1983). 'Educational Dependency: A Critique', *Compare*, 13, 1, pp. 25–41.
Mangan, J. A. (1993). *The Imperial Curriculum: Racial Images and Education in the British Colonial Experience*. London: Routledge.
Marsh, C. and Morris, P. (1991). *Curriculum Development in East Asia*. London: Falmer Press.
Mazrui, A. A. (1978). 'The African university is a multinational corporation', in Mazrui, A. A. (ed.), *Political Values and the Educated Classes in Africa*. Berkeley, CA: University of California Press.
Megarry, J., Nisbet, S., and Hoyle, E. (eds) (1981). *The Education of Minorities*, World Yearbook of Education, 1981. London: Kogan Page.
Mingat, A. and Tan, J. P. (1986). 'Who Profits from the Public Funding of Education: A Comparison of World Regions', *Comparative Education Review*, 30, 2, pp. 260–70.
Mitter, W. (1992). 'Comparative Education', in Clark, R. B. and Neave, G. (eds), *The Encyclopedia of Higher Education*, Vol. 3, pp. 1788–97.
Neave, G. (1992). *The Teaching Nation: Prospects for Teachers in the European Community*. Oxford: Pergamon.
Noah, H. J. (1984). 'The use and abuse of comparative education', *Comparative Education Review*, 28, 4, pp. 550–62.
— and Eckstein, M. A. (1969). *Towards a Science of Comparative Education*. London: Macmillan.
— and Eckstein, M. A. (1985). 'Education and Dependency: The New Simplicitude', *Prospects*.
— and Eckstein, M. A. (1993). *Educational Assessment: International Perspectives*.

Oxford: Pergamon.

Parkyn, G. W. (1976). 'The particular and the general: towards a synthesis', *Compare*, 5, 3, pp. 20–6.

Paulston, R. G. (1976). *Conflicting Theories of Social and Educational Change*. Pittsburg, University of Pittsburg Center for International Studies.

Paulston, R. G. (1994). 'Comparative and International Education: Paradigms and Theories', in Husen, T. and Postlethwaite, T. N. (eds). *The International Encyclopedia of Education*, Vol.2, pp. 923–33.

Pennycuick, D. (1994). *School Effectiveness in Developing Countries: A Summary of the Evidence*. London: Overseas Development Administration.

Phillips, D. (1994). 'Periodisation in Historical Approaches to Comparative Education: some considerations from the Examples of Germany and England and Wales', *British Journal of Educational Studies*, 42, 3, pp. 261–72.

Porras–Zunigar, J. (1994). 'Comparative Statistics in Education', in Husen, T. and Postlethwaite, T. N. (eds), *The International Encyclopedia of Education*, 2nd edn., Vol. 2, pp. 958–64.

Price, R. F. (1977). *Marx and Education in Russia and China*. London: Croom Helm.

Pritchard, R. (1983). 'The Status of teachers in Germany and Ireland', *Comparative Education Review*, 27, 3.

— (1996). 'Some International Perspectives in British Teacher Training', in Watson, K., Modgil, S., and Modgil, C. (eds), *Educational Dilemmas: Debates and Diversity*. London: Cassell, forthcoming.

Psacharopoulos, G. (1990). 'Comparative education: from theory to practice or are A:/neo* or B:/disc? *Comparative Education Review*, 34, 3, pp. 369–80.

Puryear J. M. (1995). 'International Education Statistics and Research: Status and Problems', *International Journal of Educational Development*, 15, 1, pp. 79–91.

Raivola R. (1985). 'What is comparison? Methodological and philosophical considerations', *Comparative Education Review*, 29, 2, pp. 261–73.

Ramirez, F. O. and Boli–Bennett, J. (1982). 'Global patterns of educational institutionalization', in Altbach, Arnove and Kelly (eds), op. cit., pp. 15–36.

Rogers, A. R. (1992). *Adults Learning for Development*. London: Cassell.

Rondinelli, D. A., Middleton, J. and Verspoor, A. M. (1990). *Planning Education Reforms in Developing Countries: The Contingency Approach*. Durham, NC: Duke University Press.

Rust, V. (1991). 'Post modernism and Its Comparative Implications (Presidential Address)', *Comparative Education Review*, 35, 4, pp. 610–26.

Ryba, R. (1992). Towards a European Dimension in Education: *Comparative Education Review*, 36, 1, pp. 10–24.

Sadler, M. (1964). 'How can we learn anything of practical value from the Study of Foreign Systems of Education?' *Comparative Education Review*, 7, 2, pp. 307–14 (reprinted from speech of 1900).

Samoff, J. (1993). 'The Reconstruction of Schooling in Africa', *Comparative Education Review*, 37, 2, pp. 181–222.

Schriewer, J. and Holmes, B. (eds) (1988). *Theories and Methods in Comparative Education*. Frankfurt: Peter Lang.

Schultz, T. W. (1961). 'Investment in Human Capital', *American Economic Review*, 51, March, pp. 1–17.

Smith, R. L .(ed) (1979). *Universal Primary Education*. London: University of London.

Swanson, G. (1971). 'Framework for comparative research: Structural anthropology and the theory of action', in Valier, L. (ed.), *Comparative methods in Sociology: Essays on trends and applications*. Berkeley: University of California Press, pp. 141–202.

Thiessen, G., Achola, P. and Boakari, F. (1983). 'The under–achievement of cross national studies of achievement', *Comparative Education Review*, 27, 1, pp. 46–68.

— and Adams, S. D. (1990) 'Comparative Education Research, in Thomas, R. M. (ed.) *International Comparative Education: Practices, Issues and Prospects*. Oxford: Pergamon.

Thomas, R. M. (ed.) (1990). *International Comparative Education Practices, Issues and Prospects*. Oxford: Pergamon.

— (ed.) (1992). *Education's Role in National Development Plans: Ten Country Cases*. New York: Praeger.

Tibbs, D. C. (1973). 'Modernization Theory and the Study of National Societies: A Critical Perspective', *Comparative Studies in Society and History*, 15, pp. 199–226.

Tsayang, G. (1992). 'Comparative education, an overview', Proceedings of the Comparative Education Awareness Seminar, Botswana Educational Research Association, Gabarone, pp. 3–12.

UNESCO (1993). *World Education Report 1993*. Paris: UNESCO

Verspoor, A. (1993). 'More than business as usual: reflections on the new modalities of education aid', *International Journal of Educational Development*, 13, 2, pp. 103–12.

Vulliamy, G., Lewin, K. M. and Stephens, D. (1990). *Doing Educational Research in Development Countries: Qualitative Strategies*. London: Falmer Press.

Watson, K. (1982a). 'Comparative Education in British teacher training institutions', in Goodings, R., Byram, M. and McPartland, M. (eds), *Changing Priorities in Teacher Education*. London: Croom Helm, pp. 193–225.

—(1982b). *Teachers and Community Schools as Instrument of Rural Development: The Rhetoric and the Reality*. Victoria, Australia: International Community Education Association.

—(1984a). *Dependence and Interdependence in Education, International Perspectives*. London: Croom Helm.

—(1984b). 'Dependence or Independence in education? Two case studies from post colonial South East Asia', *International Journal of Educational Development*, 5, 1, pp. 83–94.

—(1988). 'Forty years of education and development: from optimism to uncertainty', *Education Review*, 40, 2, pp. 137–74.

—(1990). 'Information dissemination: the role of the International Journal of Educational Development', 1979–89, *International Journal of Educational Development*, 10, 2, pp. 95–114.

—(1991a). 'Teachers and Teaching in an Interdependent World', *Compare*, 21, 2, pp. 107–26.

—(1991b). 'Cultural diversity and education in an international context', in Lynch, J., Modgil, S. and Modgil, C. (eds), *Cultural Diversity and the School*. London: Falmer Press.

—(1991c). 'Alternative funding of education systems: Some lessons from Third World experiments', in Phillips, D. (ed.), *Lessons of Cross–National Comparison in Education*, pp. 113–46. Wallingford: Triangle Books.

—(1992) 'Language, Education and Political Power: Some Reflections on North–South Relationships', in Beveridge, M. C. .and Reddiford, G. (eds), *Language, Culture and Education*, pp. 19–41. Clevedon: Multilingual Matters.

—(1995). 'Educational Provision for the 21st Century: Who or What is Shaping the Agenda and Influencing Developments?' *Proceedings of the Southern African Comparative and History of Education Society*.

education: the need for reappraisal', *Journal of Education for Teaching*, 10, 3, pp. 249–55.

—and King, K. (1991). 'From Comparative to International Studies in Education: Towards the Coordination of a British Resource of Expertise', *International Journal of Educational Development*, 11, 3, pp. 245–53.

Williams, E. (1993). Report on *Reading in English in Primary Schools in Zambia*, ODA Research Project 4770, Serial No.5. London: Overseas Development Administration.

Wilson, D. (1994). 'Comparative and International Education: Fraternal or Siamese Twins? A preliminary genealogy of our twin fields', CIES Presidential Address, *Comparative Education Review*, 38, 4, pp. 449–86.

Woodhall, M. (1985). 'Earnings and education', in Husen, T. and Postlethwaite, T. N. (eds), *International Encyclopedia of Education* (1st edn.), Vol 3, pp. 1495–505. Oxford: Pergamon.

World Bank (1981). *Accelerated Development in Sub–Saharan African and an agenda for action* (Berg Report). Washington, DC.

— (1988). *The Educational Crisis in Sub–Saharan Africa*. Washington, DC.

— (1994). *Higher education: the lessons of experience*. Washington, DC.

World Conference on Education For All (1991). *Final Declaration*. New York: UNICEF/WCEFA.

KEY TEXTBOOKS AND PERIODICALS

a) The classical texts are still:

Bereday, G. Z. F. (1964). *Comparative Method in Education*. New York: Holt, Rinehart & Winston.

Hans, N. (1964). *Comparative Education*. London: Routledge & Kegan Paul.

Holmes B. (1965). *Problems in Education*. London: Routledge & Kegan Paul.

— (1981). *Comparative Education: Some Consideration of Method*. London: George Allen & Unwin.

Kandel, I. L. (1933). *Studies in Comparative Education*. London: Harrap & Co.

King, E. J. (1979). (5th edn) *Other Schools and Ours*. London: Holt, Rinehart & Winston.

Mallinson, V. (1975). *An Introduction to the Study of Comparative Education*. London: Heinemann.

Noah, H. J. and Eckstein, M. A. (1969). *Towards a Science of Comparative Education*. London: Macmillan.

b) More recent textbooks include:

Altbach, P. G., Arnove, R. F., and Kelly, G. P. (eds) (1982). *Comparative Education*. London and New York: Macmillan.

— and Kelly, G. P. (eds) (1986). *New Approaches to Comparative Education*. Chicago: University of Chicago Press.

Arnove, R. F., Altbach, P. G. and Kelly, G. P. (eds) (1992). *Emergent Issues in Education: Comparative Perspectives*. Albany, New York: State University of New York Press.

Halls, W. D. (ed.) (1989). *Comparative Education: Contemporary Issues and Trends*. London: Jessica Kingsley.

Thomas, R. M. (ed.) (1990). *International Comparative Education: Practices, Issues and Prospects*. Oxford: Pergamon Press.

c) *The main periodicals are:*

Compare
Comparative Education
Comparative Education Review
International Journal of Educational Development
International Review of Education
Oxford Studies in Comparative Education
Prospects

NOTES ON CONTRIBUTORS

Martin Booth has been a lecturer in history and education in the University of Cambridge Department of Education since 1981 and is Head of the Department of Education. Before that he taught at Goldsmiths' College, London and in secondary schools. His research has centred on the teaching and learning of history in schools and the development of professional skills and competence. He has recently been involved with the University of Yamanashi in a comparative study of history teaching in England and Japan; he is currently Executive Director of a two-year research and development project on the training of doctors in hospitals. He has published in learned journals, contributed to collections of essays and has co-edited a volume on school-based initial teacher training. He is co-editor of a journal for GCSE history students entitled *Hindsight*.

Tony Burgess is Reader in Education at the Institute of Education, University of London. He has been a research officer in projects on writing and language diversity, and is joint author of *The Development of Writing Abilities 11–18* and *The Languages and Dialects of London Schoolchildren*. He has also written widely on various topics in English teaching and on classroom discourse. His present interests include the history of the subject and the teaching of literature.

Sara Delamont is Reader in Sociology and Dean of the Faculty of Humanities and Social Sciences at University of Wales College of Cardiff. She graduated from Cambridge with a degree in Social Anthropology, and did a PhD at Edinburgh. She then lectured in the School of Education at Leicester, and worked on the ORACLE (Observational Research and Classroom Learning Environment) Project with Brian Simon, Maurice Galton and Paul Croll. Her main publication from ORACLE is *Inside the Secondary Classroom* (with M. Galton). She is the author of seven other books including *Sex Roles and the School* (1990), *Knowledgeable Women* (1989) and *Fieldwork in Educational Settings* (1992). She was the first Woman President of the British Educational Research Association in 1984.

John Elliott is Professor of Education and Director of the Centre for Applied Research in Education at the University of East Anglia. He was a founding member of the Centre for Applied Research in Education and has directed a number of action research projects involving local teachers and schools from the Centre. He has designed in-service courses for teachers which support reflective practices in schools and directed research projects on teachers' jobs and lives, pupil autonomy in learning with micros, the assessment of experiential learning, competency based professional education, and teachers as researchers in the context of award bearing higher education. He is a consultant for the OECD, helping to support international curriculum development in environmental education. In 1984 John Elliott was a member of a Home Office commissioned review of Police recruit training and has continued to undertake research and consultancy work in the field of Police Education.

Leslie J. Francis is the D. J. James Professor of Pastoral Theology and Mansel Jones Fellow at Trinity College Carmarthen and University of Wales, Lampeter. He holds higher degrees from the Universities of Oxford, Cambridge, London and Nottingham in theology, education and psychology and is an ordained priest in the Anglican church. His research interests concern theological and empirical studies in religious education, social attitudes and practical theology, leading to books like *Youth in Transit* (1982), *Experience of Adulthood* (1982), *Young and Unemployed* (1984), *Teenagers and the Church* (1984), *Rural Anglicanism* (1985), *Partnership in Rural Education* (1986), *Religion in the Primary School* (1987), *The Country Parson* (1989), *Christian Perspectives for Education* (1990), *Churches in Fellowship* (1991), *Christian Perspectives on Faith Development* (1992), *Christian Perspectives on Church Schools* (1993), *Critical Perspectives on Christian Education* (1994), *Teenage Religion and Values* (1995), *Research in Religious Education* (1995) and *Psychological Perspectives on Christian Ministry* (1995). He is also co-author of the *Teddy Horsley* series of religious books for 3–7-year-olds.

Peter Gordon is Emeritus Professor of Education and former Head of Department of Huistory and Humanities, Insitute of Education, University of London. He has taught history in primary and second schools and was a member of Her Majesty's Inspectorate, specialising in history and the social sciences. He has written and researched widely in the fields of history of the curriculum, history of education, family history and modern political history. He is General Editor of the Woburn Education Series.

Seamus Hegarty is Director of the National Foundation for Educational Research. He has conducted extensive research in special education, particularly in the field of integration, and has published widely. He acts as a consultant for UNESCO and OECD, and has advised several national ministries of education on matters related to special education and educational research. He is editor of *Educational Research* and *The European Journal of Special Needs Education.*

Richard Kimbell was the first Professor of Technology Education in the University of London. He has taught technology in schools and been course director for undergraduate and postgraduate courses of teacher education. Between 1985 and 1991 he directed the DES-funded Assessment of Performance Unit research project in Design and Technology. In 1990, he founded the Technology Education Research Unit (TERU) at Goldsmiths College, which is now running a wide range of funded research projects in design and technology and information technology. He has published widely in the field, including reports commissioned by the Congress of the United States, UNESCO and NATO; he has written and presented television programmes and regularly lectures internationally.

Bill Marsden is Emeritus Professor of Education in the University of Liverpool and was formerly Dean of its Faculty of Education and Extension Studies. He is the author of *Unequal Educational Provision in England and Wales: the Nineteenth-century Roots* (1987), *Educating the Respectable* (1991), *Geography 11–16: Rekindling Good Practice* (1995), and co-editor of *The City and Education in Four Nations* (1992) and *Primary School Geography* (1994), as well as many articles and contributions to books in geographical education, the urban history of education and the history of the curriculum.

Jon Ogborn is Professor of Science Education at the Institute of Education, University of London. He was – with Paul Black – joint organiser of the Nuffield Foundation Advanced Physics Project, and he was co-ordinator of the Higher Education Learning Project. More recent research and development work includes data analysis, computational modelling, and the teaching of energy. His research interests centre on understanding the nature of common-sense reasoning and its relation to scientific reasoning. He is currently collaborating with Professor Gunther Kress on research into the nature of explanations in science classrooms.

Stewart Ranson is Professor of Education in the School of Education at the University of Birmingham. Before his appointment in 1989 he spent 15 years at the Institute of Local Government Studies in the same University. The focus of his work has been on the changing government, politics and management of education. Early research interests included relations between central and local government and the politics of reorganising schools in response to demographic change. Recent studies have included parent participation and curriculum development on 'the birth of democracy'. Currently, he is directing a major UK-wide project on learning in contexts of disadvantage as part of ESRC's Local Governance Initiative. This research will develop his analysis of the Learning Society on which he has now produced a trilogy of works: *The Learning Society*; *Management for the Public Domain: Enabling the Learning Society* (with John Stewart); and *Encouraging Learning: Towards a Theory of the Learning School* (with Jon Nixon, Jane Martin and Penny McKeown). Other publications include *The Role of Local Government in Education*; *The Politics of Reorganizing Schools*; *The Changing Government of Education and School Cooperation: New Forms of Local Governance* (both with John Tomlinson); *Democracy Then and Now* (with John Lloyd and Jon Nixon).

Piers Spencer taught in schools in Essex and inner London and did research in music education at York University. He was a lecturer in music education at the University of Wales, Cardiff, 1980–90, and worked as an inspector in the London Borough of Wandsworth, 1990–91. He is currently a lecturer in music education at the University of Exeter. He has written a book on GCSE music coursework and has contributed to two others: *Pop Music in School* and *Pop, Rock and Ethnic Music in School*.

Kathy Sylva is Professor of Child Development and Primary Education at the Institute of Education, University of London. After earning a PhD at Harvard University she moved to Oxford where she taught psychology while serving on the Oxford Preschool Research Group. Her book *Childwatching at Playgroup and Nursery School* broke new ground by questioning an unbridled 'free play' ideology. With Teresa Smith and Elizabeth Moore she evaluated the High/Scope pre-school programme with its emphasis on 'plan, do, review' in each session. Now in London, her research has moved to assessment and curriculum in primary schools. In *Early Intervention in Children with Reading Difficulties* she and Jane Hurry showed that Reading Recovery is a successful intervention and cost-effective as well. A dominant theme throughout her work is the impact of curriculum not only on 'subject knowledge' but on children's problem-solving and commitment to learning.

Keith Watson is Professor of Comparative and International Education at the University of Reading where he has been on the staff since leaving the British Council in 1975. He is author of *Educational Development in Thailand, Education in the Third World* and numerous articles and chapters on aspects of comparative education. He is currently Editor in Chief of the *International Journal of Educational Development* and Director of the

Centre for International Studies in Education, Management and Training at the University of Reading.

David J. Whitehead is Senior Lecturer in Economics Education at the Institute of Education, University of London. He has had wide experience in the training of teachers of economics and business studies and his fields of interest include the dissemination of curriculum innovations, values and attitudes in economics education and tests of economic literacy. He was editor of the journals *Economics* and *Economia* and is currently editor of *Research Papers in Economics Education* and has edited and written many books, including *Handbook for Economics Teachers* (1979), *Trade Offs, Role Plays and Simulations for Teaching Economics* (1988), *Teaching about the EEC, 1992 and the Developing World* (1990) and *New Developments in Economics and Business Education* (1991) with D. H. Dyer. David Whitehead was elected member of the Social Science Education Consortium in 1986 and has lectured in many countries abroad.

Colin Wringe read Modern Languages at Oxford and gained his PhD at the Institute of Education, University of London. He has taught in secondary schools and further education and is currently Reader in Education at Keele. He has written widely on both the teaching of Modern Foreign Languages and wider aspects of education and has edited the *British Journal of Language Teaching* and the *Language Learning Journal*. He has produced two successful language laboratory courses and other language teaching materials, and, more recently, co-edited the series 'Introductory Studies in Philosophy of Education'. His other works include *Children's Rights: a Philosophical Study, Understanding Educational Aims* and *The Effective Teaching of Modern Languages*. At present he is engaged in editing two foreign language teaching INSET publications sponsored by the European Union.

INDEX